SOCIALIST
REGISTER
2 0 0 5

THE SOCIALIST REGISTER

Founded in 1964

Visit our website at:

http://www.yorku.ca/socreg/
for a detailed list of all our issues, order forms and an online selection of
past prefaces and essays,

...and join our listserv by contacting
sreg@yorku.ca

SOCIALIST REGISTER 2005

THE EMPIRE RELOADED

Edited by LEO PANITCH and COLIN LEYS

THE MERLIN PRESS, LONDON
MONTHLY REVIEW PRESS, NEW YORK
FERNWOOD PUBLISHING, HALIFAX

First published in 2004
by The Merlin Press Ltd.
PO Box 30705
London
WC2E 8QD
www.merlinpress.co.uk

British Library Cataloguing in Publication Data is available from the British
Library

Library and Archives Canada Cataloguing in Publication
Socialist register 2005 : the empire reloaded / edited by Leo Panitch and Colin
Leys.
Includes bibliographical references and index.
ISBN 1-55266-136-9
1. United States—Foreign relations—2001- 2. Balance of power.
3. Imperialism. 4. World politics—1995-2005. I. Leys, Colin, 1931- II. Panitch,
Leo, 1945-

E895.S62 2004   327.73   C2004-904676-4

ISSN. 0081-0606

Published in the UK by The Merlin Press
0850365473 Paperback
0850365465 Hardback

Published in the USA by Monthly Review Press
1583671188 Paperback

Published in Canada by Fernwood Publishing
1552661369 Paperback

Typeset by Jon Carpenter

Printed in the UK by Antony Rowe Ltd., Chippenham

CONTENTS

PREFACE

This, the 41st annual *Socialist Register*, is a companion volume to the hugely successful 2004 volume on *The New Imperial Challenge*. Originally planned as a single volume that soon proved to be too large, they now form a complementary pair. *The New Imperial Challenge* dealt with the overall nature of the new imperial order – how to understand and explain it, what its strengths and weaknesses are. *The Empire Reloaded* rounds this out with an analysis of finance, culture and the way the new imperialism is penetrating major regions of the world – Asia Minor, Southeast Asia, India, China, Africa, Latin America, Russia, Europe.

The two volumes are united by some distinctive themes. All the essays see globalized capitalism and US imperialism as two dimensions of a single phenomenon – a point made very explicit in Gill's overview essay in the present volume. All recognize that what most distinguishes US supremacy in the new imperial order is not its military and surveillance power, huge though that is, but the penetration of the states, economies and social orders of the other leading capitalist countries by the US state, US corporations, and US values. Contributors differ, however, on various questions. One is how far inter-imperial rivalry persists in the new global order. Another is the extent to which the US economy and the US-led global financial structure is stable. The essays by Cammack on Latin America and Kagarlitsky on Russia suggest that there is significant competition and rivalry between the US and Europe and that this implies serious constraints on US supremacy. The essays by Panitch and Gindin and Rude suggest that the US-dominated global economy and its financial structures are both inherently strong and efficiently locked into a global financial hierarchy in whose stability all the leading capitalist states and their ruling classes have a crucial collective stake.

The essays also reflect differences of opinion on the left about the nature of the responses to neoliberalism and US dominance. In the current volume the contributions by Greenfield, Chibber, Zhao and Friedmann all point to the need for a much more radical analysis of neoliberalism by anti-capitalist, anti-imperialist popular movements, and a much more self-critical analysis of some of their own strategies. And the essays by Grahl, Bohle and Deppe challenge the idea, popular in some left quarters, that the allegedly regulated capitalism and rights-based internationalism of 'social Europe' offer a worthwhile and realistic alternative to US-led globalization.

Another strong theme of the present volume is its focus on culture, broadly defined – from Burstyn's account of the extent to which even the most fantastic elements of Huxley's and Orwell's dystopic nightmares have already been realized, or soon will be, in the imperial heartland; to Forsyth's analysis of the nature and phenomenally pervasive impact of Hollywood's pre-eminent product, the 'action' blockbuster; to Zhao's account of the role played by US media power in the turn to capitalism in China.

We believe that taken together the two volumes offer a so far unmatched guide to the new imperialism – and its contradictions.

Among our contributors to this year's volume, Varda Burstyn is an independent Canadian writer and activist. Stephen Gill and Sam Gindin teach political science at York University, Toronto. Christopher Rude, who previously worked for the New York Federal Reserve Bank, has just completed his doctoral dissertation in economics at the New School University in New York. Scott Forsyth is in the Department of Film and Video at York University, and Harriet Friedmann teaches sociology at the University of Toronto. Vivek Chibber is in the Department of Sociology at New York University, and Gerard Greenfield is an independent labour and environmental researcher and organizer, living in Bangkok. Yuezhi Zhao is in the School of Communication at Simon Fraser University in Vancouver, and Patrick Bond is Director of the Centre for Civil Society at the University of Kwazulu-Natal in Durban. Doug Stokes teaches international politics at University of Wales, Aberystwyth, and Paul Cammack is Head of the Department of Politics and Philosophy at Manchester Metropolitan University. Boris Kagarlitsky is an independent writer and activist living in Moscow, and John Grahl is Professor of Global Business Management at London Metropolitan University. Dorothee Bohle is in the Department of Political Science at the Central European University in Budapest, and Frank Deppe teaches politics at Marburg University in Germany. Tony Benn, after five decades as an MP, Cabinet Minister and foremost voice of the left in the British Labour Party, is 'free at last'.

We thank all the contributors for the effort they put into this volume, while reminding readers that neither the contributors nor the editors necessarily agree with everything in it. We also want to thank our contributing editors, whose involvement in planning this and the previous volume has been especially important to their range and quality. We are sorry to have to report the resignation of Norman Geras, a brilliant contributor to many previous *Registers*, after a decade on our editorial collective. We are, however, very happy to report the acquisition of three new contributing editors: Barbara Harriss-White, Director of Oxford's development studies centre, Queen Elizabeth House; Terry Eagleton, Professor of Cultural Theory in the Department of English and American Studies at the University of Manchester; and Vivek Chibber, whom we have already mentioned as a contributor to this volume. We are also very pleased to announce that Atilio Boron, Executive Secretary of CLACSO (Consejo Latinoamericano de Ciencias Sociales) will be joining us as our corresponding editor in Buenos Aires.

Times are changing, and the Register has been registering them not only in its pages but in its sales. *The New Imperial Challenge* quickly sold out and has been reprinted, the first time this has happened since 1990, and new overseas editions have been initiated. There are now separate annual editions in English published in India and Greece; a Korean edition began with the 2003 volume, and a Turkish edition with the 2004 volume; and, also starting with the 2004 volume, a Spanish edition published in Latin America will be launched and widely distributed at the World Social Forum in Porto Alegre in January 2005. The Merlin Press has also recently brought out *The Globalisation Decade*, a collection of ten key essays from the *Register* from 1994 to 2003, edited by Martijn Konings, Alan Zuege and ourselves. Alan Zuege has also performed heroic work as our editorial assistant for the current volume; and Louis McKay has once again designed a brilliant cover. We thank them, and also Marsha Niemeijer who keeps our website going. To Tony Zurbrugg and Adrian Howe at Merlin Press are due very special thanks not only for their work on this volume but for all their efforts on behalf the Register.

We can't close this year's Preface without expressing our sadness at the passing of so many leading socialists in the past year, among them Hamza Alavi, Paul Foot, William Hinton, Maxim Rodinson, Edward Said, Paul Sweezy, and Neal Wood, members of a brilliant and courageous generation of left intellectuals and activists who inspired much of the work that has appeared in the Register over the years.

LP.
CL.
July 2004

THE NEW IMPERIAL ORDER FORETOLD

Varda Burstyn

In the world of *The Matrix* and its sequels intelligent machines have taken over a devastated planet and factory-farm human beings as their primary energy source. Packed like larvae in ghastly, slimy breeding quarters, guarded and oppressed by avatars of the machine, humans are induced to experience a life-long hallucination of ordinary existence, a hallucination geared to ensure that they will remain passive and unresisting fuel to the great, omnipotent computers. At the end of the three-film cycle the few resisters have won a temporary and – in light of what has gone before – completely unrealistic reprieve with an uncertain future.

In the past twenty-five years Hollywood has produced quite a crop of grimly dystopian films, from *Blade Runner* to *The Matrix* (reloaded and otherwise) – and not a single utopian one, to my knowledge. The same themes are constantly reiterated: apocalyptic disaster due to human folly (war, artificial intelligence run amok, environmental or nuclear disaster, plague, or all the above); the total power of elites and their weaponry; the dwindling to less-than-nothing of the value of ordinary people (as against rich, genetically and technologically enhanced people, and/or machines); the driving, irresistible force of greed; and heroic resistance by a few, which may win a momentary victory but does nothing to really overthrow 'the system'. This body of work is disturbing evidence that such horrors are seen as a great box-office draw because they resonate at the emotional level for many, many people, and – perhaps – that the film-makers are unable to envision more positive futures.

Are the futures depicted in these films really possible ones – projections of things that already exist? Or are they meant to be symbolic or metaphorical? In these early years of the twenty-first century – the 'New American Century', if the imperialists have their way – it is sobering and enlightening to re-read, with these questions in mind, two earlier futurist visions that have deeply influenced the makers of these and other modern dystopias – Aldous

Huxley's *Brave New World* and George Orwell's *Nineteen Eighty-Four*. These books have been extraordinarily influential, both on generations of readers whose political consciousness has been affected by them, and on generations of writers, in non-fiction as well as fiction. A re-reading today yields some very striking lessons in assessing our present, and in thinking about our future.

Huxley came from a comfortable family of distinguished intellectuals and scientists; Orwell (born Eric Blair), by contrast, came from a family of minor colonial officials long stationed in Burma, who, once back in England, clung precariously to their status in the lower middle class. Huxley attended Oxford and afterwards moved in a circle of writers, living easily in France, Italy, and England – with an American sojourn providing the model for *Brave New World*. Orwell was sent to Eton, but instead of going on to Oxford or Cambridge he spent five years in the colonial service in Burma. Hating the role of imperial enforcer, he returned to England to eke out a hard existence as a chronicler of the lives led by the poor and dispossessed, and went on to fight with the Anarchists in the Spanish Civil War.

Accordingly, *Brave New World* is full of hot showers and leisure activities and good clothes, while *Nineteen Eighty-Four* is full of cold, crumbling, smelly apartments and terrifying torture rooms. Yet the two authors' nightmare futures have some important similarities. For example, both feature steep social hierarchies with tiny elites and vast, powerless masses: Huxley suggested ten 'World Controllers', Orwell an 'Inner Party' approximating 2 per cent of the population. Both picture the disintegration of love, parenting, and family: in *Brave New World* parents are considered an obscenity, in *Nineteen Eighty-Four* they are betrayed by their children. And both visions emphasize the power of communications technologies, of multitudinous forms of propaganda and deliberately induced collective amnesia, which condition people into accepting a social order that has utterly abandoned them.

Still, there are fundamental differences between the worlds they portray. Huxley's *Brave New World* rests on the seduction of adults, not their terrorization. 'A really efficient totalitarian state', he wrote in his introduction to the 1945 reprint, 'would be one in which the all-powerful executive of political bosses and their army of managers control a population of slaves who do not have to be coerced, because they love their servitude.' His *Brave New World* has more groovy personal transportation vehicles than all the motor ads in an issue of *Vanity Fair*, with fabulous apartments and autoerotic gadgets, luscious, legal drugs, and glittering entertainments – the Feelies and Scent Organs, playing in huge entertainment complexes. And sex. Everyone gets sex – though only with their peers, to be sure. The most important quasi-religious rite in *Brave New World* is the 'Orgy-Porgy', performed in the name of the Supreme Being – 'Our Ford'.

'Everyone is happy now', goes the *Brave New World* slogan, because everyone's been conditioned to love what they do – from the moment of *in vitro* conception through manipulated gestation in bottles to 'hypnopaedia' and aversion-conditioning in childhood; then seductively and with the mind-numbing joys of the drug Soma in adulthood. Infantile comportment – that is to say, mindless obedience – is considered optimum, even for Alphas. *Brave New World* is global, with 'Savage Reservations' for the few atavistic holdouts, and some remote islands for incorrigible nonconformists. But there are no wars, and no demonstrations or riots, because delicious, pacifying Soma melts away all opposition.

Orwell's future is grimly different: 'How does one man assert his power over another?... By making him suffer .... Power is in inflicting pain and humiliation. Power is in tearing human minds to pieces and putting them together again in shapes of your own choosing .... If you want a picture of the future, imagine a boot stamping on a human face – forever.'

So *Nineteen Eighty-Four* is a claustrophobic study in grunge and grey, steeped in poverty and misery. The Proles – the majority – and the members of the Outer Party live in draughty, filthy housing, where the food is disgusting, friendship doesn't exist and the sun never shines. The tiny ruling elite – members of the Inner Party – have all the good stuff. Personified by Big Brother, they have achieved a suffocating, terrifying degree of control over everyone else, thanks to the surveillance potential of advanced communications technology – above all, two-way television. Love is impossible under these conditions; sex is merely for procreation. Children inform on their parents and cheer as they are taken to prisons and torture chambers. And there's no Soma to relieve the pain.

The elite rules through a monopoly of information, with vast bureaucratic apparatuses for rewriting history and institutionalizing lies, as well as for producing pornography, sports, and crime writing for the Proles; and through unrelenting, vicious brute force. Big Brother is watching everyone, and so is everyone else. Big Brother never hesitates to mete out imprisonment, torture, and death to all non-conformists. Co-workers disappear from work with terrifying regularity. Hence there's no dissent, no opposition, no alternative.

And war, entirely absent from *Brave New World*, is at the centre of *Nineteen Eighty-Four*'s politics, economy, and culture. War never ends. It's fought with enemies who used to be friends and friends who used to be enemies. The most important communal rite in Orwell's future world is an orgy not of sex but of hatred. 'Hate Sessions' create intense and infantile emotional bonding to Big Brother. In *Nineteen Eighty-Four* all is deprivation, pain, and madness.

Today, it's these differences between the novels that continue to attract most comment, and are the focus of a still-lively debate about which author was more 'right'. For Christopher Hitchens and John Rodden, among many others, Orwell was the real seer, especially because he projected an imperialist world – three huge supranational powers dominating the globe. For Neil Postman, by contrast, Huxley was the true prophet of the rise of the ultimate consumer society and the orchestration, through entertainment media and creature comforts and drugs, of passive consent to tyranny. And for Frances Fukuyama, Huxley was far ahead because of his prediction of eugenic genetic engineering and its potential to destroy what is valuable and rewarding in human experience.[1]

My view, by contrast, is that in fact both writers were 'right' – that we are living in a Janus-faced present that features the fundamental characteristics of both their visions. We are living in *Brave New Nineteen Eighty-Four*.

LIVING IS BUYING

'In the nurseries, the voices were adapting future demand to future industrial supply.... I love new clothes, I love new clothes, I love ...'

Aldous Huxley, Brave New World

Let's begin with life at the heart of the Empire. In the United States today, malls dot the landscape like an intractable skin disease. These are the outlets for the huge transnationals, consumer palaces for the masses and for the elites. From high-toned boutiques to Wal-Mart, the malls are groaning with goods produced by low-wage workers in the South. They have become the archetypal American meeting-places, and represent a whole social system exported by the United States to the rest of the world. US television and radio weather forecasts announce whether or not it's a good day 'to get out to the malls', because this has become the central American experience. The malls are straight out of *Brave New World*: mountains of household and personal goods, food in surfeit, and entertainments – films and video games – so realistic that, like Huxley's Feelies, they provide surrogate experience for a complacent and compliant population.

It's hardly news that consumerism is the *raison d'être* of the corporate order, or that this order will do almost anything to secure buyers. But it is still unnerving to learn how closely the manipulation of the consumer's mind has truly approached what Huxley imagined – that is, full, reason-destroying conditioning.

With the introduction of demographics in the 1950s corporations and their advertisers took a look at rough indices of consumption patterns, such as sex, age, region, community, socio-economic status and ethnicity, the better to target consumers for their products. Each succeeding decade brought refinements in this interrogation, with 'psycho-demographics' – a deeper study of emotional responses via focus groups and questionnaires – emerging in the 1980s and 1990s to yield even more profitable indicators.[2] But in the first decade of the twenty-first century, a new level of consumer 'management' has been reached. It's called neuromarketing, and it uses MRI (magnetic resonance imaging) machines, developed for medical diagnosis, to bypass all ego-mediated critical perception and go straight for the unconscious, uncontrollable, limbic response. Leading the way is an Atlanta-based business called BrightHouse.[3]

In 1994, after a successful career in advertising, a fellow called Joey Reiman closed his $100 million advertising agency and founded BrightHouse, a firm whose clients have included Coca-Cola, Pepperidge Farm, K-Mart, and Home Depot. Convinced that advertising firms were producing so much clutter they couldn't effectively communicate ideas any more, he set out to launch a marketing revolution. BrightHouse now refers to itself as 'the world's first Ideation Corporation™' and declares that it 'emerged from stealth mode' to launch the 'Thought Sciences Institute'.[4] The TSI 'bridges the gap between business and science and provides its clients with unprecedented insight into their consumers' minds.'

BrightHouse boasts of having the 'most-advanced neuroscientific research capabilities and understanding of how the brain thinks, feels, and motivates behavior', adding that this knowledge of the brain enables corporations to 'establish the foundation for loyal, long-lasting consumer relationships.' This new field seeks, in the words of *Forbes* magazine, to 'find a "buy button" inside the skull',[5] or, in the words of BrightHouse, 'to more effectively engage and drive the target audience's behavior.' Indeed.

Neuromarketing is not developing unchallenged. A coalition of progressive consumer groups and prominent educators and scholars of childhood is totally opposed to it, calling it a terrifying form of hucksterism with frightening implications of just the kind Huxley warned about.[6] These critics claim that repeated exposure to the strong magnets in MRI machines could harm the human subjects of the research in various ways, but the real threat, they claim, is to the people – especially children – who are the consumers targeted by the neuromarketeers.[7] American children, immersed like no others in commercially driven and saturated culture, are already in deep trouble. Epidemics of learning, attention and behavioural disorders have been documented; obesity, bulimia and anorexia are rampant; and so are a variety of psychological problems associated with immersion in violent screen culture

– all of which are interwoven with incessant advertising. For the critics of neuromarketing, the project of further extending the reach of advertising into childhood is socially suicidal.

BrightHouse's neuromarketing experiments are conducted under supposedly benign and scholarly auspices of the Emory University Hospital in Atlanta. BrightHouse's principals hold teaching positions at Emory and the neuroscience wing at Emory University is the epicentre of the neuromarketing world. Emory University was founded by the Methodist Church in 1836. The mission statement of its School of Medicine commits it to 'advance the detection, treatment and prevention of disease processes.' By what perverse criteria might neuromarketing be considered the prevention of a disease process? In Huxley's Brave New World, *not consuming* was considered a serious pathology, to be treated pharmacologically and with psychotherapy. Welcome to Brave New World. The future is now.

THE RESURRECTION OF BIG BROTHER

> To know and not to know, to be conscious of complete truthfulness while telling carefully-constructed lies, to hold simultaneously two opinions which cancelled out, knowing them to be contradictory and believing in both of them; to use logic against logic, to repudiate morality while laying claim to it … that is doublethink.
>
> George Orwell, *Nineteen Eighty-Four*

When the governments of Eastern Europe and the Soviet Union collapsed in the late 1980s and early 1990s, many commentators pronounced Big Brother and his special brand of ideological doublethink dead. In reality, Big Brother had relocated to the United States, where, grown huge on the fear generated by September 11, 2001, and the political initiatives taken since, he morphed into a hybrid creature, made up at once of the heads of the huge corporations – industrial, military, finance, communications, armaments, pharmaceutical, agricultural – and the politicians and the state institutions that serve them. Doublethink Dubya is only his perfectly-fitting figurehead.

Leaving aside the questions posed by many improbable or suspicious aspects of the official account of the events of 9/11, many of the ways in which the Bush Administration has used the events of that day to advance an agenda of doublethink and hypersurveillance would make Orwell's Inner Party drool with envy. The Patriot Act and the Department of Homeland Security have created a vast range of laws and actions that increasingly subvert the democracy the Bush administration pretends to defend. Today, as even a monopolized and subservient media are unable to ignore the overflowing supply of scandals, lies, and atrocities, Orwellian criticism of US actions since 9/11 has become quite common. Web sites on Orwell have sprung up like mushrooms. Maureen Dowd, an editorial writer for the *New York Times*, describes the Bush regime in Orwellian terms almost weekly. 'It's their reality', she wrote in April 2004. 'We just live and die in it.'

> In Bushworld, our troops go to war and get killed, but you never see the bodies coming home. In Bushworld, flag-draped remains of the fallen are important to revere and show the nation, but only in political ads hawking the president's leadership against terror. In Bushworld, we can create an exciting Iraqi democracy as long as it doesn't control its own military, pass any laws or have any power. In Bushworld, we can win over Falluja by bulldozing it.[8]

Inside the US, the de facto criminalization of dissent, hence the direct and undisguised undermining of democracy, has been enormously ramped up. To take one graphic instance, at the FTAA Summit in Miami in November 2003 – a meeting that did not go well for the US – 'the more control the US trade representatives lost at the negotiating table', as Naomi Klein observed,

> the more raw power the police exerted on the streets. Small, peaceful demonstrations were attacked with extreme force; organizations were infiltrated by undercover officers who used stun guns; buses of union members were prevented from joining permitted marches; people were beaten with batons; activists had guns pointed at their heads at checkpoints ...[9]

The latest techniques honed in Iraq – from a Hollywoodized military to a militarized media – were now being used on a grand scale in a major US city. Manny Diaz, the mayor of Miami, proclaimed that the police response should serve as 'a model for homeland defence'. And well he could boast. The response brought together over forty law-enforcement agencies, from the FBI to the Department of Fish and Wildlife. Miami police chief John Timoney classified FTAA opponents as 'outsiders coming in to terrorise and vandalise our city', thus equating domestic democratic protest with foreign terrorism – and making Miami eligible for the huge pool of public money available for the 'war on terror'.

Meanwhile, also in the fall of 2003, the attorney general of Florida, serving under Governor Jeb Bush, revived a hundred-year-old law prohibiting pimps from boarding ships in Florida harbours to solicit for prostitution, believe it or not, in order to prosecute Greenpeace USA. The ostensible excuse was an action taken a year earlier in which activists had attempted to place a banner on a ship, protesting against its cargo of contraband mahogany from the Amazon rainforest. Commentators, including editorial writers for the *New York Times* and the *Washington Post*, denounced the initiative as unprecedented in US history and extremely dangerous, the first step on the way to breaking Greenpeace, and, in its footsteps, other national and international NGOs critical of the transnational order. The word 'Orwellian' got a heavy workout in this coverage, and for good reason.

Fortunately, in May, 2004, a Miami judge threw the case out of court. But there are other manifestations – less subject to judicial and public oversight – of the use of the 'war on terror' as a pretext for tightly concentrating and deepening the power of the forces that make up the US's equivalent of Orwell's Inner Party. Two months after September 11 a super-elite of corporate CEOs, including the heads of International Group, Bechtel, Citigroup, Dow Chemical, Lockheed Martin, Exxon Mobil, GE, Ford, and Raytheon, were linked together in a structure entitled CEO (for 'Critical Emergency Operations') COM LINK. This is a hot-line that 'allows chief executives to speak directly with Secretary of Homeland Security Tom Ridge and other officials during a terrorist attack.'[10] It was created by the exclusive Business Roundtable, an association of Fortune 500 corporations, in cooperation with the Department of Homeland Security. It has already been utilized on several occasions when the 'terror threat level changed', and it meets from time to time to stage simulations of emergencies in which it might swing into action.

The Business Roundtable's web site approvingly notes that more than 85 per cent of America's infrastructure – the power grid, financial services, information services, railroads, airlines, water – is now controlled by the private sector, and this serves as the government's justification for the hotline. This unprecedented and unequalled communications apparatus creates the possibility, if not the likelihood, that in an emergency it would be the White House and the unelected CEOs of the top corporations that would make all key policy decisions, displacing and usurping the houses of Congress, state governors, and other governmental structures. Indeed, with the announcement, in April, 2004, that the Department of Homeland Security was awarding $350 million to Northrup Grumman to build a super-intelligence network that could coordinate intelligence services at all three levels of government, CEO COM LINK will have at its disposal a fully Orwellian surveillance system. 'It's a paradigm shift at the classified level', the DHS security chief told Information Week, in order to 'help the government fight terrorism ... and defend the U.S.'s borders and trade.'[11] Hiding in plain view, CEO COM LINK itself has never been publicized or even discussed by politicians or White House officials. It is, is in sober truth, the Orwellian Inner Party.

BYE-BYE LOVE, HELLO HATCHERIES

> It took eight minutes for the eggs to go through [the machine].... A few died; of the rest, ... all were returned to the incubators ... [each eventually] becoming anything from eight to ninety-six embryos .... Identical twins, but not in piddling twos and threes as in the old viviparous days, when an egg would sometimes accidentally divide; actually by the dozens, by scores at a time.
>
> Aldous Huxley, *Brave New World*

If *Nineteen-Eighty-Four*'s signature is Big Brother, *Brave New World*'s is its babies-in-bottles, its biotechnologically produced elite of superhuman Alphas and competent Betas, and its masses of stunted Deltas, Gammas, and Epsilon 'semi-morons'. Each class is reproduced, not by inherited status or wealth, or by merit and effort, or even by media manipulation and coercive power, as in *Nineteen-Eighty Four*, but by genetic engineering and artificial procreation, closely directed by a miniscule, omnipotent elite. This is a society composed of something entirely new, which I call 'bioclasses'. It's the 'application of industrial principles to human reproduction', in Huxley's words, that creates the kind of people who keep the consumer totalitarianism of *Brave New World* ticking over. For Huxley, this process was an extension of the eugenics movement – a movement based on the idea that some human life is worthy, other life is less worthy, or not worthy at all. *Brave New World* practiced 'negative eugenics' by discarding babies and gametes that were undesirable; and 'positive eugenics' by producing, to specification, those babies and gametes that were deemed to be valuable to fill the pyramidal layers of an acutely stratified society.[12]

But just as the eugenic mass production of bioclasses is the most sinister of Huxley's projections, involving a universal totalitarianism with dominion over cells and tissues, its potential components are also the least visible and least well understood in today's world. The necessary technologies are no longer science fiction, but their development is taking place behind the closed doors of labs and clinics, with little government oversight or public regulation. As a result, public knowledge of the extent and power of 'reprogenetics' (as one of its most ardent proponents has dubbed it), and the ambitions, aspirations, financial backing and goals of those engaged in it, remains very limited.[12] As well, there is a misperception that, thanks to President Bush's Christian fundamentalism, there is little motion toward these technologies in the US. Not so.

In vitro fertilization (IVF) – far from a perfect technology, with its low success rates, its massive doses of hormonal drugs for prospective mothers, and its uncertain record of health for children successfully carried to term – has become a major money-maker for a group of physicians who call themselves 'techno-docs'. It is very well established in the United States, and is the first step toward 'babies-in-bottles'.[13] In taking the embryo out of the maternal body and putting it in a petrie dish, IVF made possible something entirely new: the discarding of 'defective' embryos – or, through micromanipulation, their modification for therapeutic purposes. This also meant that for the first time, inheritable germ-line modification (IGM) – designer babies, made to order – became possible. *New Scientist* has recently reported that Japanese scientists have found a way to alter the genetic makeup of sperm, so that designer manipulation of a potential embryo can take place even before in-vitro conception.[14] And in April 2004 scientists reported that they managed to create two baby mice without any sperm at all, just through manipulation of the ovum, further liberating them from the old biological imperatives and making IGM even easier.

Of course, an artificial womb is also required for the creation of bioclasses. This entered the experimental field in 1999, when Dr. Yosinori Kuwabara and his colleagues at Juntendou University in Tokyo began the construction of an artificial uterus, successfully 'birthing' a goat foetus from a tank that contained mimicked amniotic fluid and a mechanical umbilical cord. Two years later a team of scientists from Cornell University's Weill Medical College announced that they had succeeded, for the first time, in creating an artificial (human) womb lining.[15]

Still, without some form of cloning – the process described with stunning prescience in the quotation from Huxley at the beginning of this section – mass eugenics and real bioclasses would not be possible, since every manipulated embryo would presuppose individual attention and the high risk of failure on each attempt. Cloning technology isn't there yet, either in animals or humans. Most attempts fail in the petrie dish or the first few weeks post-implantation. Moreover, as the editors of *Wired* noted in their March 2004 issue, of those carried successfully to term, so far 'all cloned mammalians live sick and die young.' But the work is being pushed ahead, and major breakthroughs in 'therapeutic' cloning were announced in February 2004.[16]

Most cloners, such as US scientists Dr. Robert Lanza and Dr. Young Chung of Advanced Cell Technology near Boston, who made the first stem-cell breakthroughs and are cloning human embryos for the therapeutic value of stem cells (totipotent cells that can be used to repair any differentiated body tissues), loudly disavow any intention of proceeding to 'reproductive cloning', declaring it unethical and out of the question. But the history of reprogenetics is nothing if not the story of technologies that travel from the margins to the centre. And so, by the late 1990s, mainstream American scientists and doctors such as Gregory Stock – no less a personage than the director of the Program on Medicine, Technology and Society at the University of California at Los Angeles (UCLA) – had begun to advance such intervention as not only 'inevitable' but also desirable.[17]

Princeton professor of molecular biology Lee Silver is among the most prestigious of cloning's advocates, but by no means its only one.[18] Silver argues that a truly Huxleyan future is inevitable, if not necessarily marvellous. As he sees it, the market will permit wealthy parents to select, enhance, and clone their most promising embryos – creating, eventually, a 'gen-rich' class; while the economically poor, bereft of enhancing reprogenetics, will become 'gen-poor' as well. Eventually, Silver believes this will create a process of speciation, in which the two classes of humans may no longer be able to procreate together. Although in Silver's scenario it is the market rather than World Controllers who bring this about, the result would be the same: *Brave New World* would be upon us.

A few years ago, Silver was one of very few voices in the wilderness. Today, you can go to the web site for the Human Cloning Foundation and see advertisements for many books with titles such as *Who's Afraid of Human Cloning?*, *When Science Meets Religion*, *Cloning: For and Against*, and *Flesh of My Flesh: The Ethics of Cloning Humans*.[19] You can visit GenLife.com and order a service that allows you to store not only your pet's DNA but also your own, in the expectation that one day in the not-too-distant future you will be able to bring both you and kitty back to life. Until that day comes, you can store your head or your whole body with Alcor Life Extension Foundation. Or GenScript Corporation offers a new technology that allows you to synthesize genes, which enables many applications in gene science, including allowing you to 'Design your own genes/cDNAs (deletion, mutation, and rearrangement etc.).'[20] The Center for Genetics and Society has grouped and listed the many different players in the highly variegated sector of those who think artificial is better than natural when it comes to procreation. The main clusters include neo-eugenicists, libertarians, pro-cloners, and a category called transhumanists, who are an eclectic group of people that includes influential scientists (such as Ray Kurzweil), physicians, and bioethicists, who seek to use informatic technologies as well as reprogenetics in taking us beyond our current morbid and mortal status.[21]

Whether these very technologies eventually become the means for the imposition of bioclasses is, of course, an open question. But if the transhumanists and the techno-docs and all the others who hubristically and instrumentally appropriate and deploy procreative and genetic properties have their way, the enabling technologies for bioclasses will develop, and power-hungry bureaucrats and politicians, always spouting the rhetoric of therapeutics and happiness, of course, will surely attempt to impose them to this end – in one way or another.

KILL, KILL, KILL FOR PEACE

> Oceania was at war with Eastasia: Oceania had always been at war with Eastasia. A large part of the political literature of five years was now completely obsolete. Reports and records of all kinds, newspapers, books, pamphlets, films, sound tracks, photographs–all had to be rectified at lightning speed....
>
> George Orwell, *Nineteen Eighty-Four*

The key features of war in Orwell's novel are this: it is central to society, it is prosecuted constantly, enemies and friends change places in a cynical dance of regimes and alliances that benefits the elites and screws the popular classes across the globe and this dance is concealed by propaganda, censorship, and lies. Are we there yet?

In *The Clash of Fundamentalisms*, Tariq Ali shows how, for more than fifty years in the Arab east, from Turkey to Afghanistan, the US state funded dictators, tyrants, feudal emperors, and dynasties against the secular, democratic forces whose victory might have spelled the end of the region's ruthless exploitation and underdevelopment – lying about it to its own people, of course.[22] It did this to protect US access to oil, and to maintain its edge in its geopolitical battle with the former USSR. Ali also chronicles how, countless times, once a regime had served its purpose for the US, it was abandoned. ('Pakistan was the condom the US wore when it entered Afghanistan', one furious Pakistani general told him.) In these ways, Oceania-like, the United States laid the foundations for the fundamentalist terrorism that has arisen in many countries, and now uses this to justify feeding the maw of a ravenous military–industrial complex and the devastating wars it unleashes. The process has been Orwellian in every aspect: war is more than ever at the centre of the US economy, as in *Nineteen Eighty-Four*. War is justified by doublethink ideas – 'fighting to defend and extend democracy' is as close as dammit to the Party slogan, 'war is peace'. Meanwhile, 'politics and mainstream media coverage', Ali observes, 'have invoked disinformation, exaggeration of enemy strength and capability, TV images are accompanied by brazen lies and censorship .... The aim of all this is to delude and disarm the citizenry. Everything is either oversimplified or reduced to an exhausting incomprensibility' – a scenario that seems to be taken directly from *Nineteen Eighty-Four*.[23]

Just as Oceania's enemies morph into its friends, and vice versa, the US's former friends (Iran, the Taliban, Saddam Hussein, large parts of the Saudi Royal family, to name only a few) have turned into its enemies, while a number former foes have become its friends. Again, consider one striking example: post–9/11, the Bush administration and several arms of government have come to embrace that odious group of Russian billionaires called the Oligarchs, even though in his early days in office Bush vowed to bring them down in order to advance the cause of democracy in Russia.[24] Deeply implicated in this extended move is the Carlyle Group, the Washington-based private equity fund with more than $17.5 billion in assets under its management, and investments in thirteen countries across three continents. The Carlyle Group is the power base of the Bush circle. With an overlap of cadres that has included James Baker, Bush Sr. and Jr., Dick Darman, Frank Calucci, Dick Cheney, and a host of other familiar faces, it can accurately be said to drive many critical administration policies and initiatives. The Carlyle group used to contain Shafiq bin Laden, one of Osama's brothers. Apparently no more. After 9/11 he was asked to withdraw his funds, along with a number of other Arab investors. This caused a drain on finances that Carlyle decided should be plugged by Russian money. Hence a stunning about-face in White House attitudes, and a set of initiatives to bring the most powerful Oligarchs into Carlyle, and to help them establish themselves in the US.

Goodbye Arabia, hello Eurasia. At least for now.

THE FEELIES GO TO WAR

'Take hold of those metal knobs on the arms of your chair', whispered Lenina. 'Otherwise you won't get any of the feely effects.'

Aldous Huxley, *Brave New World*

We are seeing many of the central features of both Huxley's and Orwell's dystopias come to life; more than this, they are actually fusing. With the technologies made possible by computers, the entertainment industry is not only producing a simulacrum culture of mass distraction very like Huxley's Feelies, but using the technologies and writing of Huxleyan mindless entertainment to wage Orwellian war.

For almost ten years now, a mind-blowing convergence of military, entertainment and informatics industries has been taking place, working to use simulation capabilities from all three sectors to enhance the ability of Hollywood and Silicon valley to make entertainment products (video games now outsell films and videos combined) on the one hand, and to enable the United States military to increase its capacity to wage deadly war on the other. Generously funded, extensively orchestrated, with goals that seem benign and matter-of-fact to its personnel but to others are sinister in the extreme, this new convergence has been dubbed 'militainment'.

Jonathan Burston, in his excellent introduction to the players and the products of this new hybrid, lists the participants: CADRE (the College of Aerospace, Doctrine, Research and Education) at Maxwell Air Force Base in Montgomery, Alabama; SIGGRAPH (Special Interest Group on Computer Graphics and Interactive Techniques); and SIGART (Special Interest Group on Artificial Intelligence). These groups come together to brainstorm at the North American Simulation and Gaming Association annual meeting. Moreover, Burston writes: 'The city of Orlando, Florida, is headquarters for the Department of Defence (DOD)'s Simulation Training and Instrumentation Command (STRICOM), whose mission is to create "a distributed computerized warfare simulation system" and to support "the twenty-first century warfighter's preparation for real world contingencies".'[25] Orlando is also home base to 'Team Disney' – 'the legendary cohort of R&D "imagineers" at Disney World.' And the regional offices of Silicon Graphics and defence giant Lockheed Martin are 'more or less across the street from STRICOM' in Orlando. Finally, there are the nearby Universities of South Florida and Central Florida – all comprising what STRICOM likes to call 'Team Orlando'.

Not to be outdone, California is the base of what Burston appropriately calls 'the most notable development inside this ominous new techno-industrial formation … the disingenuously-named Institute for Creative Technologies (ICT).' The ICT has resulted from a $45 million grant from the US military. It's housed in offices designed by *Star Trek* designer Hermann Zimmerman at the University of Southern California (USC) in Marina Del Ray. Its mandate is 'to enlist the resources and talents of the entertainment and game development industries and to work collaboratively with computer scientists to advance the state of immersive training simulation.' Senior executives from NBC, Paramount and Disney collaborate with the military and with designers from the digital effects houses of Silicon Valley and have a dazzling array of ongoing simulation projects.[26]

As James Der Derian writes in his book about 'militainment', the enemy soldier has become nothing more than an electronically signified 'target of opportunity'; one that is much easier to 'disappear' than a living soldier, in both the symbolic and material register.[27] New wars

> are fought in the same manner as they are represented by simulations and public dissimulations, by real-time surveillance and TV feeds ….
> In this high-tech rehearsal for war one learns how to kill but not to take responsibility for it, one experiences 'death' in a virtual manner only, but not the tragic consequences of it. It's a new kind of drama without tragedy where television wars and video war games blur together.

By its potential power to create totally immersive environments – where one can see, hear and perhaps even touch and emotionally interact with digitally created agents – militainment is leading the way into a brave new world that threatens to breach the last firewalls between reality and virtuality and break down inhibitions to violence and killing among 'warfighters'. This is particularly troubling if you consider the implications for young people, because militainment has your children in its sights. The ICT's web site states: 'In addition to specific military training tasks, the Experience Learning System (ELS) will have applications for a broad range of educational initiatives.' That's 'educational' in the doublethink sense. Cut to the video arcades, cut to millions of homes in which children, mostly boys, play video games such as 'American Soldier' and 'Quake' and 'SOCOM: Navy SEALs', designed by the US Army and Navy respectively to attract young people to the military, and to train up their beliefs and their reflexes so they will become good 'warfighters'.[28]

Significant numbers of parents, educators and scholars have organized into a variety of groups and coalitions to address the harms of such games within a regime of childhood impoverished by overworked parents, a surfeit of screen and computer culture, disappearing spaces for play, floundering public schools.[29] A leading spokesperson for this current, Gloria DeGaetano, a former teacher and now media consultant and lecturer and author of *Parenting Well in a Media Age*, has been joined by Lieutenant-Colonel Dave Grossman, a former West Point psychology professor, military historian and army ranger who now chairs the Department of Military Science at Arkansas State University. They argue that 'due to overexposure to gratuitous violent imagery, our children undergo a systematic conditioning process that alters their cognitive, emotional and social development in such ways as to embed in them a desire and/or conditioned reflex to act out violently without remorse.'

> A constant diet of violent portrayals can make people more distrusting and exaggerate the threats of violence that really do exist. Nightmares and long episodes of anxious behaviour are common for young children exposed to violence on TV or film. Research demonstrates that media violence distorts a person's concept of reality, changing his or her attitudes and values. It creates, for example, a perceived need for guns, which in turn creates violence, which reinforces the 'need' for guns, and so on, in an endless, tragic spiral.[30]

It's a scenario eerily reminiscent of Orson Scott Card's *Ender's Game*, in which children were unknowingly enlisted into waging war by involving them in 'games'.[31]

'IT'S LIFE, JIM, BUT NOT AS WE KNOW IT': BIG BROTHER AND NANOTECHNOLOGY

Yet if Orwell and Huxley were brilliantly prescient about so many things, neither of their famous novels foresaw the massive scale of today's environmental crisis (though Huxley did eventually become a dedicated environmentalist). It was a serious failure, because both the contours and the urgency of today's global crisis are profoundly shaped by the degree of biospherical catastrophe that humans have wrought. Still, the dangers they pointed to can help us in evaluating the dimensions of this crisis because these are very much the result of dangerous technologies deployed by powerful elites without regard for their impacts.[32]

Regarded from this perspective, no technologies are more potentially frightening than those that are, once again, quietly taking shape in richly-funded experimental labs under the name of nanotechnology.[33] Here biology, chemistry, informatics and the cognitive sciences converge at the molecular level below and beyond wood and metal, tissues and genes. Nano science is the science of manipulating atoms and molecules. Its potential for both social control and environmental disaster outstrips even that of genetic engineering. Pat Mooney, a long-time UN adviser on technology, predicts that nano – or what he terms 'atom' – technologies will surpass old biotechnologies worldwide within fifteen years, making this the 'Nanotech', not the 'Biotech Century'.[34] Yet today the average person couldn't tell you what nanotechnology was if her mortgage depended on it.

Proponents claim that nanotechnologies can eventually deliver virtual immortality, create limitless food supplies, achieve miraculous environmental remediation, in short, fix everything. As Mooney points out these are paradisical claims – which, he cautions, is a sure sign that, according to the law of unintended consequences, their potential dangers will be commensurately hellish. And this road to hell is being paved with corporate dollars. Whether endowing prestigious university labs and nano-niche start-ups, or funding research in their own R&D labs, the Gene Giants – Monsanto, Dow Chemical, DuPont, Aventis, Novartis – are becoming the Nano Nabobs. These are the folks who stealthily brought us genetically engineered soya, corn, canola (rape), and cotton, who introduced fish genes into strawberries, who are pushing 'terminator seed' technology through the international trade organizations, who are invading and destroying native flora and fauna, colonizing and privatizing the source points of life itself.[35] Already their investment in nanotechnology R&D worldwide exceeds $4 billion – not including their investments in the production of elementary nano-products and related technologies – without any public or scientific evaluation or scrutiny whatsoever. And, in December 2003, Washington authorized $3.7 billion to finance nanotechnology research.[36]

The potential of nanotechnology to effect the Huxleyan agenda of eugenics and tranquilizing pharmacology is unsurpassed, since its microtechniques would allow for extraordinarily refined manipulations of the components of pharmaceutical substances, genes and cells. Hence nanotechnology has the potential to accelerate radically the fabrication of designer animals, insects, plants and micro-organisms of all kinds. In humans it could give reprogenetics the tools it needs to attempt a fully Huxleyan system of reproduction – again, for those who could afford it, or for those who lack the power to resist its imposition.

But that's not all. While the manipulation of matter is very much a Huxleyan feature, a number of the potentials of nanotechnology express Orwellian prospects much more directly – for example, the potential for surveillance and war. The US Army's NanoSoldier Institute is working on creating an invincible warrior, fitted out with impermeable nano-armour, wielding nano-weapons (think Robocop multiplied a couple of hundred thousand times.) And of course, the potential of atom technologies for the monopolization and patenting of matter itself has a terrifying Big Brother dimension.

And worse: critics say that nano science and unregulated nano production are attempting to create atom technologies that could endanger the human race and the biosphere in ways even more deadly than biotechnology. This is hard to fathom. What, one asks, could really be worse than the genetic contamination of the world by herbicide-resistant weeds and pesticide-resistant cockroaches that have been able to survive in oxygen-depleted environments?

The answer, in a phrase, is 'Grey Goo' – the reduction of all matter to a primal molecular mush, created by self-replicating nanomachines that use all matter as basic fuel – this is the great fear and the ultimate caution about nanotechnology, as expressed even by one of its first, most famous and most visionary architects, Eric Dexler.[37] Pat Mooney suggests the danger may lie in 'Green Goo': 'Molecular self-assembly is what living materials do best. You don't need tiny tin robots. Science is merging biotechnology and nanotechnology into nanobiotechnology in order to fashion unique amino acids, proteins, molecules and cells. These will be organized in new manufacturing processes that could replace conventional machines and workers.'[38] The Goo does not yet exist, but, apparently, it could. Grey or Green, the Goo gives new and unwelcome meaning to the *Star Trek* refrain, 'It's life, Jim, but not as we know it.' And with this we come full circle back to the world of *The Matrix*.

FUTURE TENSE

Sir Martin Rees, astrophysicist and British Astronomer Royal, has declared that the human race has only a 50/50 chance of surviving another century. He predicts that natural disasters, asteroid impacts, man-made viruses, and nuclear terrorism could wipe us out before the year 2100.[39] The chances of the species coming to a dead end are, indeed, high. This is because at this moment humanity has not yet found a way to exercise intelligent control over harmful technologies, old or new, that could make it impossible for the web of life to reknit and renew itself. Nor have we yet found effective ways to take the necessary socio-political measures to ensure the conditions that would create a healthy population and contain new or renewed epidemics that have the potential to bring us to our collective knees, or worse.

If we do succeed in hanging on, however, we might well ask ourselves: what are the trajectories inherent in the rule of the transnationals and the new American empire, should resistance fail to turn these scenarios around? If, in the past, the most compelling visions of the future belonged to two British socialist men, perhaps the most compelling visions of the future seen through contemporary lenses belong to two North American left-leaning and feminist women, Marge Piercy and Margaret Atwood. Neither's novels make for happy reading, for the loss of democracy on which both are predicated is embedded in environmental catastrophe and total corporate control. In Piercy's 1991 novel *He, She, and It* the world partakes of *Nineteen Eighty-Four*, in the sense that the vast majority of humanity have the status of Proles and live diseased lives of appalling poverty and complete ignorance in eco-ravaged metropoles; a tiny, ruthless elite of corporate personnel live in material luxury and spiritual servitude in artificially sustained domes of luxury and good health from which they rule the world. Small islands of scientists live apart from both, able to survive, at least for the most part, because they invent technologies that are useful to the elite. At the same time, Piercy's Planet Earth is *Brave New World* as well, in that the elites use genetic engineering to enhance themselves, in order to maintain power (and the very few rebels steal it to enhance their ability to fight).[40] In Piercy's first futurist novel *Woman on the Edge of Time*, written in 1972, utopia (cooperative and egalitarian communities, in gender and racial as well as economic terms) and dystopia (a horrible, consumerist, eco-blighted corporate world) co-existed and did battle in a contained war-zone where the outcome was left uncertain.[41] In *He, She, and It*, the corporate order has spread like a fungus and the rebels have shrunk back to the far margins.

In Margaret Atwood's *Oryx and Crake*,[42] corporate greed drives a long, horrible social and environmental degradation, until, as in Piercey's vision, the Proles live in endless urban slums ('the pleeblands') and the corporate elite in protected domes, lulled by drugs and video everything, blithely producing monstrous transgenic plants and animals to fill every perceived need. But all this institutional madness gets rolled up into one character – a geek genius at the 'Watson and Crick Institute' – who plays God with no compunctions and attempts to destroy humanity, the better to make room for his new, improved humanoid species. He seeds an apocalyptic plague, and at the end, it's an open question whether humanity or the humanoids, or either species, can make a comeback in a totally ravaged world. In both these women's novels, and in Orwell's and Huxley's books, resistance is almost nil – and, except for its own sake, for a handful of existentially troubled individuals, utterly futile.

Since I became an environmental activist more than thirty years ago, I have dreaded the potential of hierarchical societies – whether capitalist or bureaucratic – to bring humans and our planet to levels of irreversible destruction, simply in the course of doing business. (As the book and documentary film entitled *The Corporation* point out, if corporations were individuals they would be classified as psychopaths – incapable of regard or concern for their environment or for others, capable only of self-seeking greed and violence.)[43] But every day I remind myself that unlike Orwell's, Huxley's or even Piercy's and Atwood's future worlds, resistance to the corporate order today is neither small, nor contained, nor futile. It is both local and global and inherently anti-imperialist. It fights against every ill I have written about, through direct action, through legal and political work, through art and theatre and video and comics, and it has a sharp, life-affirming sense of humour. Unlike the monoculture of the dystopias it is fabulously diverse, and it constitutes the hope of this world. My wish for the future is that, despite the brilliance of all these progressive futurists, the pessimism of their visions will be challenged by the victories of this resistance and that before this century is out, some far-sighted writer will write a novel of life and hope, and not just a requiem for all that is valuable and good.

NOTES

1   Christopher Hitchens, *Why Orwell Matters*, New York: Basic Books, 2002. Neil Postman, *Amusing Ourselves To Death: Public Discourse In The Age Of Show Business,* New York: Penguin Books, 1986, c1985. Francis Fukuyama, *Our Post-Human Future: Consequences Of The Biotechnology Revolution*, London: Profile, 2002.

2   See Joyce Nelson, *The Perfect Machine: TV in the Nuclear Age*, Toronto: Between the Lines, 1987; Naomi Klein, *No Logo: Taking Aim at the Brand Bullies*, New York: Picador, 2000; and the regular coverage of many years of

AdBusters, a magazine devoted to deconstructing consumerism and advertising. See also my discussion of the evolution of advertising in *The Rites of Men: Manhood, Politics and the Culture of Sport*, Toronto: University of Toronto Press, 1999.

3   BrightHouse: The IDeation Corporation, www.brighthouse.com.

4   Press release, 3 June 2002, www.brighthouse.com.

5   Melanie Wells, 'In Search of the Buy Button', *Forbes.com*, 1 September 2003.

6   See 'Commercial Alert Asks Feds to Investigate Neuromarketing Research at Emory University', 17 December 2003, http://www.commercialalert.org/index.php/category_id/1/subcategory.

7   See Sharna Olfman, ed., *All Work and No Play: How Educational Reforms Are Harming Our Preschoolers*, Westport: Praeger, 2003.

8   Maureen Dowd, 'The Orwellian Olsens', *New York Times,* 25 April 2004.

9   Naomi Klein, 'America's Enemy Within', *Guardian*, 26 November 2003.

10   Tim Shorrock, 'Executive Privilege: Inside Corporate America's Homeland Security Hotline', *Harper's Magazine*, April, 2004, pp. 81-83. Curt Weldon, a Republican congressman from Pennsylvania, a former firefighter, and head of a House Committee on emergency preparedness, claims that, by contrast, the public sector has been struggling to link and coordinate its efforts over the last two years, without either the economic or intelligence resources available to CEO COM LINK.

11   See Larry Greenmeier and Eric Chabrow, 'A Network of Networks', *Information Week*, 19 April 2004.

12   For critiques of the New Eugenics, see Bill McKibben, *Enough: Staying Human in an Engineered Age,* New York: Times Books, 2003; and Michael J. Sandel, 'The Case against Perfection', *The Atlantic*, April, 2004.

13   See Alastair G. Sutcliff, 'Health Risks in Babies Born After Assisted Reproduction', *British Medical Journal*, 325(20 July), 2002, pp. 117-18; and Janis Kelly, 'Increased Risk of Cerebral Palsy in Babies Born After In Vitro Fertilization', *Neurology Reviews.com*, 10(5), May, 2002.

14   In Brief, 'Sperm goes GM', *New Scientist*, 181(31 January), 2004, p. 16.

15   See Natalie Angier, 'Baby in a Box', *New York Times Magazine*, 16 May 1999 and Fr. Joseph Howard, 'The Construction of an Artificial Human Uterus', *American Bioethics Advisory Council Quarterly*, Spring, 2002, http://www.all.org/abac/aq0202.htm.

16   Jonathan Amos, 'Scientists Clone 30 Human Embryos', BBC News Online, 12 February 2004.

17   See Gregory Stock's homepage, http://research.arc2.ucla.edu/pmts/. See also Gregory Stock, *Redesigning Humans: Our Inevitable Genetic Future*, New York: Houghton-Mifflin, 2002, for a fluent argument for germ-line intervention.

18   Lee Silver, *Remaking Eden: How Genetic Engineering and Cloning Will Transform the American Family*, New York: Avon, 1998. See also Allen Buchanan et al., *From Chance to Choice: Genetics and Justice*, Cambridge: Cambridge University Press, 2002, where four American bioethicists argue that public policies should be adopted to make IGM freely available to all. Cf. Martha C. Nussbaum, 'Brave Good World', *New Republic*, 4 December 4 2001.

19   To get a sense of what's what and who's who in the pro-cloning world, see: Human Cloning Foundation at http://www.humancloning.org and http://home.cfl.rr.com/chaosdriven. This last site is aimed at scientists and contains a published scientific protocol for cloning.

20   You can visit GenScript at http://www.genscript.com/gene_synthesis.html.

21   Web sites with large lists of transhumanist links are available from the Center for Genetics and Society. Some seem pretty mundane. Others, such as Transtopia at http://www.transtopia.org/transhumanism.html give a good indication of the full program.

22   Tariq Ali, *The Clash of Fundamentalisms*, London: Verso, 2002.

23   The stories of censorship of US war-related policy are legion, and censorship by omission rather than commission is the most powerful form of censorship today. To take just one example, in February 2004 a suppressed report by a group of Pentagon analysts was leaked to the press. This report, *An Abrupt Climate Change Scenario and Its Implications for United States National Security*, claimed that looming environmental catastrophes present an infinitely greater threat to the national security of the US than terrorism, and urged the White House to urgently turn its attention to this. While the *Guardian* picked the story up in the UK, and progressive web sites around the world trumpeted the news – after all, this was hardly the Greenpeace or the Sierra Club speaking – there was a virtual blanket of silence in the mainstream media and among national politicians in the United States. A few days after the leak, the sensational story slipped quietly into oblivion.

24   Andrew Meier, 'The Oligarch's Ball', *Harpers*, April, 2004, pp. 79-81.

25   Jonathan Burston, 'War and the Entertainment Industries: New Research Priorities in an Era of Cyber-Patriotism', in Daya Kishan Thussu and Des Freedman, eds., *War and the Media: Reporting Conflict 24/7*, London: Sage, 2003. For further analysis, see his 'Synthespians Among Us: Re-thinking the Actor in Media Work and Media Theory', in James Curran and David Morley, eds., *Media and Cultural Theory: Interdisciplinary Perspectives*, London: Routledge, forthcoming. Also see www.stricom.army.mil.

26   Burston writes: 'The ICT's Flat World project "updates flats, a staple of Hollywood set design, into a system called Digital Walls" (Hart 2001), transforming an empty room into a convincing 3-D simulation of some far-away battle terrain (into which a trainee is "immersed"). It is only one of the ICT's several state-of-the art virtual reality projects, all of them instantly evocative of *The Matrix*. In November 2002, for example, the ICT premiered its long-awaited Mission Rehearsal Exercise (MRE), a curved-screen simulation in front of which officers-in-training are presented with a number of different options for emergency action, each of which results in a different outcome, in a virtual Bosnian village. Trainees interact with digital actors, who themselves "listen" and "respond" with instantly variable "emotions".'

27   James Der Derian, *Virtuous War: Mapping the Military-Industrial-Media-Entertainment Network*, Boulder, CO: Westview Press, 2001.

28   See 'Army is looking for a few good gamers', CNN.com/Sci-Tech, May 22, 2002 http://www.cnn.com/2002/TECH/ptech/05/22/e3.army.game.

29   Gloria DeGaetano, *Parenting Well in a Median Age: Keeping Our Kids Human*, Fawnskin, CA: Personhood Press, 2004.

30   Gloria DeGaetano and Dave Grossman, *Stop Teaching Our Kids to Kill: A Call to Action Against TV, Movie and Video Game Violence*, New York: Crown Publishing, 1999. See also, Dave Grossman, *On Killing: The Psychology of Learning to Kill in War and Society*, Boston: Little Brown & Co., 1995.

31   Orson Scott Card, *Ender's Game*, New York: Tor Books, 1985.

32   See Varda Burstyn, 'The Dystopia of Our Times: Genetic Engineering and Other Afflictions', in *Socialist Register 2000*, London: Merlin Press, 2000. Also see Laurie Garrett, *Betrayal Of Trust: The Collapse Of Global Health*, New York: Oxford University Press, 2001; and Ronald J. Glasser, M.D., 'We are not immune: Influenza, SARS, and the collapse of public health', *Harper's*, July, 2004.

33   For information on the players, the extent, and the scale of development of nano/atom technologies, as well as for an excellent critique of their dangers, see 'The Big Down: From Genomes to Atoms', ETC Group, 2003, available at http://www.etcgroup.org. The ETC Group monitors scientific and industrial publications and makes the information available on its web site.

34   See Mooney's comment in 'The Big Down'. See also Jeremy Rifkin, *The Biotech Century: Harnessing the Gene and Remaking the World*, New York: Jeremy P. Tarcher/Putnam, 1998.

35   See Kathleen Hart, *Eating in the Dark: America's Experiment with Genetically Engineered Food*, New York: Pantheon, 2002, and also 'Gone to Seed: Transgenic Contaminants in the Traditional Seed Supply', Union of Concerned Scientists/Citizens and Scientists for Environmental Solutions, 23 February 2004.

36   See Ted C. Fishman, 'The Chinese Century', *The New York Times Magazine*, 4 July 2004, p. 31.

37   K. Eric Drexler, *Engines of Creation*, Garden City, NY: Anchor Press/Doubleday, 1986; and K. Eric Drexler and Chris Peterson with Gayle Pergamit, *Unbounding the Future: The Nanotechnology Revolution*, New York: Quill/William Morrow, 1991. Grey Goo now has a convention of its own in science fiction. See Greg Bear, *Blood Music*, New York: Arbor House, 1985; and Kathleen Ann Goonan, *Queen City Jazz*, New York: Tor Books, 1994, and *Crescent City Rhapsody*, New York: Avon Eos, 2000.

38   *Green Goo: Nanotechnology Comes Alive!*, ETC Group Communiqué, 77, January/February, 2003, www.etcgroup.org.

39   Interview with Martin Rees, http://www.bbc.co.uk/pressoffice/pressreleases/stories/2003/08_august/08/hardtalk_reesmartin.shtml.

40   Marge Piercy, *He, She, and It: A Novel*, New York: Alfred A. Knopf, 1991.

41   Marge Piercy, *Woman on the Edge of Time*, New York: Alfred A. Knopf, 1976.

42   Margaret Atwood, *Oryx and Crake*, Toronto: Seal Books/Random House, 2003.

43   Joel Bakan, *The Corporation: The Pathological Pursuit of Profit and Power*, Toronto: Penguin, 2004; Mark Ackbar, Jennifer Abbott and Joel Bakan, *The Corporation*, Big Pictures Media Corporation, Canada, 2003.

THE CONTRADICTIONS OF US SUPREMACY

STEPHEN GILL

This essay seeks to conceptualize and analyze some of the central principles, practices and contradictions of US efforts to unify global political,
social and economic space under a particular form of Western supremacy.
The use of the term 'supremacy' is deliberate, intended to connote a form
of rule based on economic coercion and the use – potential or actual – of
organized violence as a means of intimidating and fragmenting opposition.[1]

A central, long-term goal of US strategy is to secure what Marx called the
world market, ultimately subordinating the role of the state to the private
forces of civil society – so that social development is determined by capital,
whose property rights are militarily and constitutionally guaranteed and
upheld. However, this US strategy is neither consistent nor far-sighted, nor
free from crises, contradictions and resistance. Supremacy is characterized on
the one hand by the effort to establish a US-led, disciplinary neo-liberal form
of globalization, and on the other by patterns of resistance. With this dialectic
in mind the two main aims of this essay are, first, to identify how, over the
past twenty-five to thirty years, and especially since the collapse of the Soviet
Union, US strategy has sought to secure the supremacy of militant neoliberal forces, with the goal of strengthening the power of capital; and second,
to identify the limits and contradictions of this strategy – a strategy that entails
increasingly obscene and intolerable levels of inequality, the extraction of
surplus through intensified exploitation, renewed primitive accumulation and
mechanisms of debt bondage, and increased surveillance and coercion on a
world scale.

As we shall see, there are two main faces of US power in the contemporary world order. On the one hand, US strategy involves the globalization
of Anglo-American constitutional principles and neo-liberal mechanisms of
accumulation and economic discipline. These are analogous to John Locke's
conception of property rights and limited government, i.e. one that asserts

the primacy of private property over political jurisdiction. Thus from the Marshall Plan onwards the US took initiatives to make foreign territories more permeable for mobile capital. These measures included: dismantling old sphere-of-influence imperialisms associated with European colonization; defeating economic nationalism; transforming the relatively autarkic Soviet Bloc; and, most recently, liberalizing China and India.[2]

On the other hand, whilst US leaders represent 'the empire of civil society'[3] they are also heirs of Karl Schmitt: they claim the power to decree national and international rules, laws, and norms, whilst reserving 'exceptional powers' for themselves.[4] The assumption is that the US has not only the might but also the right to act as a global state – one that decrees rules of world order, whilst selectively deciding, with impunity, which rules apply to US actions and which do not. This central political contradiction of the US role in world order – one that involves both a justification of limited government and its direct repudiation by arbitrary state power – is crucial to an understanding of the nature and limits of US power, and resistance to that power.

In this sense, US efforts to secure the 'empire of civil society' in the early 21st century do not necessarily involve colonies or indeed permanent occupation of territories (although extended occupation may well occur). They do, however, entail a far-flung capacity for intervention, discipline and punishment, including US military bases, surrogate forces, covert and intelligence operations and surveillance facilities in over 130 countries – deployed in line with the Pentagon's strategy of 'full spectrum dominance'. In sum, securing the world market relies mainly on state power, including constitutional, regulatory, military and 'exceptional' police powers – exercised in a global hierarchy of states with the US superpower at its apex, claiming the right to be the arbiter of world politics.

Thus, over the past twenty-five years political forces and institutions of the right have been considerably strengthened, opening the way to an increasingly disciplinary and punitive neo-liberalism, especially after the collapse of the USSR – while, of course, representing it as the only viable development option for humankind. Mainstream political rhetoric represents this either negatively, as a set of abstract forces beyond human control, as in Margaret Thatcher's dictum that 'there is no alternative' to neo-liberal globalization; or more positively, as in US rhetoric, which tends to be more triumphal, equating globalization with 'progress' and 'freedom'. In this discourse it is the providential mission of the US, acting as God's agent, to deliver freedom on a world scale; His calling is thus currently being followed in Iraq. It appears that George W. Bush, as a born-again Christian, does actually think of his mission as divinely ordained.

In reality, both of these positive and negative dimensions of the neo-liberal ideology of globalization are colossal obfuscations that seek to conceal not only the real costs of disciplinary neo-liberalism, but also its principal bene-ficiaries, i.e. the global plutocracy of the mega-rich. This explains why James K. Galbraith has characterized neo-liberalism as 'a perfect crime', since in these official discourses there appear to be neither perpetrators nor any direct victims. This, despite incontrovertible evidence of a systematic redistribution of wealth from the bottom to the top echelons of society, resulting in a glob-alization of the extreme patterns of inequality hitherto associated with a country like Brazil. Disciplinary neo-liberalism fundamentally involves the increasing use of market-based structures to secure social discipline and orga-nize distribution and welfare, for example in capital and labour markets, with the costs of adjustment forced upon the weakest by the strong, backed by the coercive apparatus of the state.

In light of the growth of police and emergency powers after September 11, 2001, when mainly Saudi-born terrorists flew commercial airliners into the World Trade Center and the Pentagon, Galbraith significantly noted that: 'It is not by accident that the effects of neo-liberalism at a global level resemble those of a *coup d'état* at a national level.'[5] Perhaps what Galbraith had in mind was an earlier September 11th – the 1973 *coup d'état* led by General Pinochet against the democratically elected government of Salvadore Allende in Chile.[6] That coup, promoted secretly by the Nixon Administration, produced the first instance of disciplinary neo-liberalism. The dictatorship imposed order through firing squads to facilitate an economic 'shock therapy' programme designed by the so-called 'Chicago boys' under the right wing formula: 'a free economy in a strong state'.

AMERICAN SUPREMACY AND THE SOCIAL REPRODUCTION OF AFFLUENCE

Despite intense competition within the ranks of capital, disciplinary neo-liberal governance is associated with ruling elites from the historical or power blocs that dominate global accumulation, i.e. corporate capital (in manufac-turing, finance and services) and who are pre-eminent in the political and civil societies of the OECD, much of Latin America, the Former East Bloc, Asia and China. These globalizing elites are also drawn from the ranks of international financial institutions, parts of the UN, and plutocratic organs such as the World Economic Forum in Davos. Whilst organized labour is largely excluded from its inner circles, these power blocs incorporate some privileged and affluent workers, e.g. drawn from professional firms (accoun-tants, consultants, architects, urban planners, designers, advertising and public relations firms), small businesses (i.e. subcontractors of large transnational corporations, import-export businesses), as well as top sports stars and celebrities who market corporate images and identities. The principal beneficiaries of disciplinary neo-liberalism are integrated into elaborate networks of global production and consumption and their affluent lifestyles are increasingly protected by social and spatial segregation, coercive surveillance and punitive systems of incarceration, ultimately enforced by police and military power.

Here we might note that whilst the US has less than 5 per cent of world population it accounts for almost a third of global GDP; while China, with almost 20 per cent of the world's population, accounts for less than 4 per cent of global GDP – although this is rising rapidly, to the point where China is now the second largest consumer of oil after the USA. To consider the implications of this we start with the well-known statement of President Bush Sr. before the UN Conference on the Environment in Rio 1992, that 'Our lifestyle is not negotiable'. President Bush Jr. has also adopted this political stance, which depends for its satisfaction on very large amounts of foreign finance, as well as a huge proportion of the world's natural resources and energy supplies.

By analyzing what this lifestyle entails we can get a sense of some of what is being secured culturally and politically by the exercise of American supremacy. What Bush Sr. was referring to was the unwillingness of the most politically significant and affluent segments of the US population – and their counterparts elsewhere – to give up their attachment to energy-intensive patterns of production and consumption – large houses, cars and appliances. This attachment drives a broader societal dependence upon the automobile and an apparently insatiable appetite for cheap consumer goods and food (and a growing problem of obesity).[7] As Mike Davis has shown, the social reproduction of this type of affluence is linked to the militarization, privatization and redrawing of social space.[8] Indeed this phenomenon may well be part of a worldwide development: a proliferation of gated communities that resemble medieval fortresses with panic rooms, surrounded by fortifications and patrolled by armed security guards who police these privatized spaces against envy, crime and terror.

In a social and spatial sense there is a new global politics of inequality, a process that has been attributed mainly to race, thus obscuring its class dimensions. Increasingly, the affluent are socially, spatially and politically segregated from the poor of the world's population (except of course their domestic servants). This pattern of global 'Brazilianization' – of extreme inequality, racialization and stigmatization – rests on a distinct pattern of economic linkages between capital and labour throughout the world.

Everyday low prices, everyday low wages

A good example of the mechanisms that link everyday, mainstream US production and consumption patterns to the rest of the world is Wal-Mart, the world's biggest retailer, and the second largest employer in the United States after the Pentagon. Its business motto is 'Everyday Low Prices'. Wal-Mart, one of the largest companies in the world, has $256 billion in annual sales, and if it were an independent nation it would be China's eighth-largest trading partner. Wal-Mart profits flow from a regime of low wages, tight labour discipline and centralized managerial control (even the temperature in each of Wal-Mart's more than 3,500 American stores is controlled from its headquarters in Bentonville, Arkansas). Its massive size and monopoly purchasing power allow it to push down supplier prices, which in turn forces low wages on the employees of the supplying companies at home and abroad.

As of 2003, 222 of the 400 billionaires in the world were Americans, and members of the Walton family who effectively own Wal-Mart were among the eight richest people in the world.[9] Exploitation of labour results in an enormous transfer of wealth and resources to this plutocracy, although the owners of Wal-Mart would no doubt argue that it exemplifies the efficiency of capitalism. Nonetheless capital accumulation does not necessarily mean that capital, or the key individuals that direct its activities, are becoming any more productive (or indeed productive at all). For example, between 1980 and 2000 the compensation of America's ten most highly paid C.E.O.'s rose 4,300 per cent, to an average of $154 million, partly thanks to stock options and other more or less legal ways of augmenting salaries, a rise that has no relationship to the relatively small increases in productivity measured in that period.[10] And any productivity gains there have been have not been shared: over the past decade, the proportion of Americans living in poverty has risen, per capita income for members of middle-class households has fallen, US real wages have stagnated and household indebtedness has increased rapidly.[11]

What we are seeing is a kind of revolution in the relationship between capital and labour in the US, which disciplinary neo-liberalism seeks to reproduce worldwide. Indeed, whilst the US working classes get everyday low prices at Wal-Mart they also get drawn into debt bondage and suffer from badly funded Federal social programs. They are paying much more of their income in taxes than was the case thirty years ago and they are much more likely than the rich to be tax-audited.[12] The unemployed are subjected to workfare whilst the affluent receive 'corporate welfare'. For example, the mid-1980s bail-out of the Savings and Loans industry was the largest social-ization of private debt in history, to the tune of approximately $500 billion – though whether such a bail-out could be mounted again today, given the US government's enormous debt levels, is far from certain.

Discipline and punish: at home and abroad

In the US, whereas there is socialization of risk for the affluent, risk is increasingly privatized for the majority, and the market disciplines that increasingly apply for the weaker members of society are supplemented by often arbitrary forms of coercion and abuse. These are administered with apparent impunity through the apparatus of the state – including its ancillary privatized mechanisms. Such mechanisms of discipline and punishment are increasingly controversial features of US supremacy.

Indeed the major growth industry in the US over the past twenty years has not been in high-technology, dot-com activities but in private forms of crime control and the development of the so-called prison industrial complex, with private prisons the most vibrant sector. This may not be sustained in the immediate future because of the intensifying fiscal crisis in many of the states of the American union, which may well lead to calls for shorter sentences; but the prison-industrial complex seems unlikely to be significantly run down.

Partly reflecting the wider trends towards the privatization of security and organized violence (including the privatization of warfare, as in the Iraq war), the USA now has the world's highest rates of incarceration of any major power – and the racial and gender composition of the US prison population is also striking.[13] Striking too are the consistent reports of abuses, brutalization and torture, similar to those reported against prisoners of war, e.g. in Iraq in Abu Ghraib and Guantánamo Bay, Cuba, and more broadly in an archipelago of gulags, including apparently many secret installations in a variety of countries. In the past twenty-five years the prison systems of more than forty states 'have been under some form of court order, for brutality, crowding, poor food or lack of medical care', with many of the worst cases in the USA in Texas, whose prisons were under federal court supervision during much of the time President G.W. Bush was state Governor, because of overcrowding, violence and abuses by guards (even allowing inmate gang leaders to buy and sell other inmates as slaves for sex).[14]

Given that in the USA unknown numbers of people have also been detained in contravention of their constitutional rights it should not be surprising that in the current military offensives US-held prisoners of war have been routinely denied their rights under the Geneva Convention. In 2003 Attorney General John Ashcroft selected Lane McCotter to help lead a team of prison officials, judges, prosecutors and police chiefs to rebuild Iraq's system of justice. McCotter, who had been forced to resign as Director of the Utah Department of Corrections in 1997 after an inmate with a schizophrenic condition died while shackled naked to a restraining chair for sixteen hours, was nonetheless put in charge of reopening the notorious Abu

Ghraib prison in Baghdad and training its guards. At the time, McCotter's company, Management & Training Corporation, the third-largest private prison company in the US, was under investigation by the Justice Department.[15]

Major General Geoffrey Miller, former head of the Guantánamo detention center, was also put in charge of detentions and interrogations in Iraq, and much of the work appears to have been carried out by both troops and private military contractors under the supervision of the CIA.[16] In 2002-03 leaks revealed that the Bush administration had requested senior lawyers from the Justice and Defense departments to establish justifications to allow torture to be used in the war on terrorism: 'administration lawyers concluded that Congress had defined both international and domestic prohibitions on torture very narrowly, saying that harsh treatment was torture only if interrogators *deliberately* afflict serious physical or mental harm over prolonged periods'.[17] At the same time, lawyers in the Bush Administration have consistently sought legal measures and arguments to provide for immunity for US personnel from the International Criminal Court.[18] These developments have provoked outrage in the US and worldwide.

ECONOMIC CONTRADICTIONS OF NEO-LIBERAL GLOBALIZATION

The current era of economic globalization is dominated by US efforts to extend the empire of civil society and to secure the world market for the rule of capital. The mechanisms used to bring this about include a more liberalized framework for trade and investment, a related world market in intellectual property, and a more integrated world capital market. Each of these mechanisms helps US corporations to maintain their access to foreign markets, supplies of foreign labour, raw materials and goods, as well as facilitating huge inflows of foreign capital into the US. Yet it is a risky strategy and contains the possibility of a global financial crisis.

New constitutionalism and the plutocracy

Recalling our earlier reference to the wealthiest Americans, we can note that the US plutocrats with the highest net worth have their money concentrated in software and computers (e.g. Microsoft, Oracle, Dell), in media and entertainment (e.g. Metromedia, Viacom) and in investment houses. The other main area of massive accumulation of wealth is retailing, as we have seen with the Walton family. Not surprisingly each of these areas is reflected in the emphasis given in US foreign economic policy to creating new governance structures – in effect, new constitutional arrangements in other countries that lock in the rights of capital whilst locking out democratic accountability and democratic control over economic policy-making.[19]

First, the US government obtained guarantees for foreign investment and access to global sourcing for its brands to feed the endless US appetite for inexpensive consumer goods – so the shelves of Wal-Mart stores will remain stacked with goods manufactured by cheap labour from China. This partly explains why the US was keen to facilitate China's entry into the WTO and to lock in Chinese commitments to full repatriation of profits, and eventually to get China to allow full foreign ownership of private enterprises, and investment and sourcing in China for American corporations.[20]

Second, to govern these arrangements US models have informed not only accounting standards but also legal concepts and disciplines, although, as we have noted, the US government often refuses to be bound by its own strictures on the rule of law. Nevertheless, the US constitutional mechanism of judicial review has been reformulated internationally in the creation of dispute resolution mechanisms, with binding enforcement rules, such as those provided for in NAFTA and the World Trade Organization. Under pressures from the USA, the IMF and World Bank now use conditionality to give institution-building and policy advice to borrowing governments on banking law, contract law, company law, and more generally on the role of the judiciary, and especially on judicial review mechanisms modelled on American jurisprudence. Other US legal principles and concepts such as transparency are at the heart of global trade and investment regulation.

Third, these initiatives have allowed the USA to secure access to foreign markets and to protect its firms' high technology and other intellectual property, so as to strengthen US-owned capital relative to foreign rivals.[21] In addition the USA has pressed other governments for changes in tax and bankruptcy policy, favouring higher indirect taxes, lower income and corporate taxes, as well as new legal protections for investors against expropriation.

A fourth strand of the strategy involves efforts to globalize US-style corporate governance structures for securities markets, with freedom of corporate takeovers or other transfers of ownership. US corporations thus find it easier to acquire overseas firms and assets previously shielded from foreign takeover. Indeed, the vast majority of foreign direct investment in the 1990s was through mergers and acquisitions, not new investment – giving control over new areas of production, but not necessarily expanding it.

Fifth, the US has also established a commanding lead in core technologies associated with the information, communications and other industries of the so-called new economy (including defence), as well as internationally entrenching the dominance of its huge entertainment/image complex, and of its pharmaceutical giants. The period of accelerated globalization of intellectual property rights really began in earnest when the USA succeeded in linking trade to intellectual property rights in the Uruguay Round trade negotiations in 1994, redefining intellectual property rights as commodities. American software, entertainment and pharmaceutical companies then successfully lobbied for an agreement with global coverage and enforcement mechanisms.[22] Of course, 'trade-related intellectual property rights' (TRIPs) actually have little to do with free trade, but involve locking in the rights of private monopolies over innovations through patents and other forms of protection.

In sum, the governance regimes of the world market have been reshaped in the past twenty years in accordance with the 'new constitutionalism' and disciplinary neo-liberalism. The US has initiated many of these changes, and its corporations and consumers have tended to benefit most directly, but by no means to the exclusion of powerful interests in the EU and elsewhere who have supported these changes. Yet this has been a process full of problems in terms of its capacity for reproduction. As capital has become more liberalized and globalized, the frequency and depth of economic crises has worsened. The 1997-98 global crisis was the worst since the Great Depression, with many millions of people impoverished, and it illustrated the destabilizing effects of the free movement of capital to the point where even neo-classical economists have come to question its value and efficiency.[23]

The new era of liberalized capital: financial and fiscal crises

In 1998 many large institutional investors, corporations and super-wealthy individuals were bailed out when their investments went sour, ostensibly to prevent a more general financial collapse such as the one posed by the bankruptcy of Long Term Capital Management triggered by the Russian bond default. LTCM was managing money for super-wealthy individuals and large private banks (i.e. the risks of large investors or depositors were socialized). By contrast, in financial crises the general pattern is for the costs of adjustment to be dumped on unprotected capital, unprotected workers and the most vulnerable members of society – i.e. their risks are privatized, so ordinary taxpayers and the poorer members of society meet the costs either way. Nevertheless, in 2004 the Bush Administration was pressing for more free trade agreements to prohibit controls on capital movements (even in the event of an economic crisis), along the lines of two model bilateral agreements recently made with Chile and Singapore.[24]

In this way, the US financial complex has been at the vanguard of restructuring and deregulation (or more accurately, liberal re-regulation) of the world financial system. This more liberalized system that emerged during the 1980s and 1990s helped recycle the trade surpluses of other nations (especially from China, Japan and South Korea, as well as from the European Union) to fund American expansion and massive US debts and payments deficits. Thus globalization has also allowed the US to avoid relying solely on domestic resources to pay for its foreign wars.

In contrast to the early post-World War II period of the *Pax Americana*, when the US funded global reconstruction, the US is now by far the world's biggest debtor, and according to the Congressional Budget Office, US government debts are growing very rapidly. There is even a growing consensus amongst economists that despite the huge depth and liquidity of US capital markets, the scale of US individual, corporate, state, federal and foreign debt is not sustainable, and this is reflected in the tendency for some central banks to switch out of dollars into euros.[25] By 2003 one estimate was that foreign investors had claims on the US for about $8 trillion of its financial assets, the result of ever-growing US balance-of-payments deficits, which had reached about 5 per cent of GNP and were still rising in 2004. This stands in contrast to the period 1960-76, when the US ran balance of payment surpluses totalling almost $60 billion.[26]

Moreover, the costs of an American military imperialism based on 'full spectrum dominance' and the 'war on terrorism' are bound to rise very rapidly, and will ultimately have to be met with an increase in funding from domestic resources – i.e. they will involve financial sacrifices, in no small part because US imperial policies command little consent from other countries, as the *Financial Times* noted in 2003:

> The US may bear the cost of [future] conflict largely on its own. Kuwait, Japan, Germany and Saudi Arabia shared most of the $60bn costs for the 1991 Gulf War. No such coalition of the wallets seems likely this time. In a unipolar world, the US's potential ad hoc coalition partners for each engagement would be in a powerful bargaining position, as the recent haggling with Turkey shows. Mr. Magnus [of UBS Warburg] says: 'In a world where all countries [in effect] belong to the non-aligned movement, the price to a major power of building a coalition increases.'[27]

Although US defence spending reached about 10 per cent of GDP at times in the 1950s, dropped to 5-6 per cent by the 1980s and fell to a low of 3 per cent by 2000, it rose rapidly again thereafter. According to an analysis by UBS Warburg any open-ended commitment to position military forces and make them capable of fighting throughout the globe, allied to the costs of new weapons systems, could mean that the military budget, 'encompassing homeland security, foreign aid and other nation-building programmes', could rise from 4-5 per cent of GDP to as much as 8-9 per cent over the coming years. The Warburg report argues that this would lower private sector growth, particularly since highly skilled workers are needed to design and direct 'smart bombs, unmanned drones and laser-guided missiles'. Larger resources for human intelligence would also be needed 'against an amorphous terrorist enemy' in countries such as Turkey, North Korea, Colombia, Iraq, Afghanistan, the Philippines, Djibouti, Yemen and Bosnia. The authors add:

> Taking the nation's best brains out of biotechnology research, investment banks and corporations and putting them into the State Department, the Central Intelligence Agency and the military is not a blueprint for continuing the high productivity growth of the 1990s.[28]

Thus US imperial ambition may well be curtailed by 'fiscal overstretch'. While the US Federal debt is officially put at $6.5 trillion, the fiscal crisis is worsening at the state level, and US Federal deficits are rising rapidly because of a combination of tax cuts which mainly benefit the affluent and increased military outlays. Looking further ahead, funding obligations for Medicare and Social Security payments continue to grow – their combined net shortfall is growing at about $1.5 trillion per year and will accelerate around 2010 when about 77 million 'baby boomers' begin to collect Social Security benefits, and in 2013 when they start to obtain Medicare benefits.

The extent of the fiscal crisis was revealed in a report by a Federal Reserve economist and a former Treasury official. It was immediately buried by the Bush Administration, but noticed by investors. Its main findings were presented in Congressional testimony:

> The government reports that the national debt in 2003 was about $3.8 trillion in the form of government 'debt held by the public'. But that number ignores massive imbalances in the Medicare and Social Security programs and … other programs. When the liabilities associated with those programs are taken into account, the nation's fiscal policy is currently off-balance by over $43.4 trillion in present value, a number that is not reported in standard budget documents …. That imbalance is over *11 times* the $3.8 trillion debt held by the public that the government officially reports. $35.5 trillion of this $43.4 trillion imbalance stems from Medicare … while Social Security accounts for another $7.2 trillion. The rest of the government … has an imbalance of only $0.68 trillion.[29]

In this context, the US government could encounter very immediate constraints, particularly if there is a serious decline, let alone a reversal, of capital inflows. By early 2004 foreign capital inflows of about $1.5–2.0 billion *a day* were financing the US external deficit. If this funding problem worsens the Federal Reserve will be forced to increase interest rates at a time when the oil price is also rising quickly, potentially triggering substantial defaults on mortgages and other financial securities, as well as further fiscal retrenchment.

Thus the next international debt crisis could take place not in the Third World but in the US. Whilst the USA has consistently pressed for freer capital mobility to facilitate inflows of capital into the USA, thus helping to fund its balance of payments deficits, its leaders may soon come to realize that this a double-edged sword: a crisis of confidence in the US economy could reverse these flows very rapidly indeed, with the US hoist on its own petard.

'FULL SPECTRUM DOMINANCE' AND ITS LIMITS

US military dominance thus relies on its ability to maintain the confidence of (foreign) investors. Yet if the 'war on terror' continues to be pursued indiscriminately, along with continued engagement in Iraq and the development of expensive weapons systems, the costs could shake that confidence. US expenditures already massively dwarf those of all its major allies and rivals – the US spends more on its military than the next twenty states combined.[30] It is worth bearing this financial constraint in mind as we consider some of the expenditures that finance its military strategy, and its potential future costs.

The achievement of 'full-spectrum dominance' (the ability to dominate simultaneously land, sea, air and space) was heralded by the Bush II Administration as the most important single strategic initiative for the US in the twenty-first century. Its central rationale is to protect 'US interests and investments', not only from traditional rivals, but also from 'new challenges', including those stemming from 'a widening gap between haves and have-nots' – something the Bush II Administration seems to have considered natural, or at least unavoidable.

To bring this about Secretary of Defense Donald Rumsfeld emphasized rapid reaction, mobility and flexibility of forces, partly based on high-technology innovation, with incentives for American capital to serve to revitalize the military-industrial complex. Rapid militarization of space is one of the central facets of this approach.[31] Another flank includes efforts to enlarge US capacities to engage in information warfare, including secret information agencies that report to the White House and the Pentagon, shielded from wider scrutiny, along with a transformation of the US military apparatus so that it is better equipped to engage in 'cyber-wars', and to control global communication nodes and networks.[32] As we shall see, US military and intelligence apparatuses have already established considerable control over strategic nodes within global communication networks.

New wars and an empire of bases

Full-spectrum dominance is the counterpart to the Bush Administration's concept of the new wars of the twenty-first century. As Rumsfeld articulated it, this entails 'all elements of national power: economic, diplomatic, financial, law enforcement, intelligence, and both overt and covert military operations.'[33] This totalizing perspective includes the need for not only sovereign power to override the existing rules of war, e.g. pre-emptive strikes against actual or potential enemies but also policing what the Bush II Administration came to call the 'arc of instability'. This apparently runs between the Andean region (in effect Colombia), across North Africa, the Middle East and Southeast Asia towards the Philippines and Indonesia, where many of the key oil reserves in the world are to be found.

The apparatus for policing this area also includes US allies subordinated to US command, e.g. in NATO, and use of the forces of many other countries. This is why the US increased its budgets for Foreign Military Financing by 27 per cent for 2003 making it the USA's largest military aid programme, at about $4 billion annually. Much of this goes to foreign military training for the global war on terror in countries previously restricted from receiving American aid because of their human rights abuses or possession of nuclear weapons, such as Uzbekistan, Pakistan and India.[34] Simultaneously, the Pentagon is also creating 'an elite secret army with resources stretching across the full spectrum of covert capabilities', following recommendations made by its Defense Science Board's 2002 Summer Study on *Special Operations and Joint Forces in Support of Countering Terrorism*.[35]

However, the main forces for policing world order are located in what Chalmers Johnson calls an empire of military bases. The USA has between 700 and 1,000 military bases around the globe (depending on how they are categorized and counted); it has a further 6,000 inside the US and its own territories. About 250,000 uniformed personnel are deployed overseas with an equal number of civilian officials, plus around 45,000 locally hired foreign personnel (this does not include the new deployments in Iraq, of about 140,000, nor the small army of private contractors working alongside them as part of the new US model of quasi-privatized warfare). At least four and possibly six new bases are currently being constructed in Iraq. Since September 11th 2001 US forces have built, upgraded or expanded military facilities in Bahrain, Qatar, Kuwait, Saudi Arabia, Oman, Turkey, Bulgaria, Pakistan, Afghanistan, Uzbekistan and Kyrgyzstan. With the discovery of greater oil deposits in West Africa the US is also seeking to establish new bases in that region. The Pentagon's *Base Structure Report 2003* shows that it currently owns or rents bases in about 130 countries.[36] So US imperialism is, after all, territorial, as empires necessarily are; its contemporary form of colony is the military base, allowing for rapid deployment and intervention throughout the globe.

'Future Image Architecture' and ECHELON

US strategic thinking holds that challenges to its primacy are likely to be diffuse and global. Therefore an additional goal of American military-intelligence apparatuses is the dream (some might call it a nightmare) of creating a global panopticon: a total surveillance system that can place both friends and enemies alike under total surveillance.[37] An ironic example of the mindset that accompanies this was given following the capture of the EP-3E spy plane by China in April 2001, when a veteran of US Navy surveillance remarked to journalists that an officer in his squadron had business cards inscribed with the motto: 'In God we trust. All others we monitor'.[38]

In fact, there are already growing links between the far-flung empire of bases and its 'homeland' – all maintained by sophisticated communication structures that integrate and distribute information virtually instantaneously, in a military form of space-time compression. Moreover, full-spectrum dominance presupposes control over, or at least the ability to decisively intervene in, global communication systems. As has been noted in a report by a Lieutenant Colonel of the US Army:

> Whereas the world wars used attrition (WW I) and maneuver (WW II), information age war emphasizes control. Whereas the world wars attempted to exhaust (WW I) and annihilate (WW II), cyberwar seeks to paralyze. And whereas the tools of the world wars were firepower weapons (WW I) and mechanization (WW II) produced in mass, the tools of information war are limited numbers of inexpensive computers linked via global communication systems.[39]

Indeed, with respect to many military and surveillance practices, the Bush II and Clinton Administrations display considerable continuity. In April 2001 it was announced that the secret National Reconnaissance Office of the US had been authorized to undertake a massive expansion of its spy satellite systems, partly because other nations such as Russia, France, India and closer American allies such as Israel and Canada have satellite surveillance systems of their own.

'Future Image Architecture' is the most expensive venture ever undertaken by US intelligence agencies. FIA will cost US$25 billion over twenty years – by comparison the Manhattan Project to build the atomic bomb during World War II cost $20 billion in inflation-adjusted dollars. Again, this system fits well with the Bush Administration's priority of developing and dominating the military uses of space and the use of cyber warfare.[40]

Needless to say such developments – involving the National Security

Agency (NSA) and other US intelligence agencies – have created concerns in the European Union and elsewhere, particularly given the extensiveness of American intelligence networks such as ECHELON, which ceaselessly trawls electronic communications across Europe. Tens of billions of messages are analyzed every day through 'data mining' software operating through Internet servers. ECHELON feeds the data into huge computers known as Dictionaries that automatically select communications using lists of target numbers, subjects and keywords.[41] Virtually all the messages that are selected by Dictionary computers are automatically forwarded to the NSA or other users without being read locally. ECHELON is designed primarily for non-military targets: governments, businesses, organizations and individuals. Since most nations make it illegal to spy on their own citizens, UK–USA arrangements may allow this to be circumvented.[42]

'Operations' in Afghanistan and Iraq

It is in this light that the use of US military power in Afghanistan and Iraq needs to be assessed and we should note that organized violence forms only a part of an overall strategic effort in the region. The full panoply of 'operations' devoted to 'regime change' in Afghanistan and Iraq have thus included: covert or clandestine operations (e.g. widespread use of CIA and Pentagon Special Forces); the mobilization of foreign bases, as platforms for the attacks; integration of battlefield and surveillance plans; financial aid (including military aid); efforts to gain support from 'coalition members'; the Middle East Partnership Initiative; the Middle East Free Trade Initiative; and investments in military education and training, including training of police. This has been accompanied by extensive use of propaganda, both of the 'white' variety (e.g. 'embedding' journalists within military units; use of US-controlled media and television stations in Iraq to represent news in ways supportive of the US war/occupation efforts) and also of the 'black' type: i.e. disinformation campaigns, efforts to discredit enemies or dissenters through deliberate falsifications.

As for why the United States decided to go to war in Iraq – especially given that there was no evidence of links to Al Qaeda, or of WMD, and thus no evidence of direct threats to the USA; and given that virtually all credible legal authorities pronounced that the war was an illegal act of aggression – suffice it to say that, while the war is linked directly to the USA's official policy on energy security, driven by its increasing dependence upon foreign and especially Middle Eastern oil, we need to probe deeper. The willingness to risk a great deal in terms of a loss of legitimacy and to provoke mass resistance, protests, and even holy and civil war, was not only about conquering Saddam and taking control of Iraqi oil, but was also linked to reinforcing

several of the main pillars of US supremacy: above all, the USA's long-term
geopolitical position, involving both its military basing strategy and its
commercial interests, including potential threats to dollar hegemony, and of
course its prerogative to pursue wars of impunity.

This geopolitical rationale clearly unites the Clinton and Bush
Administrations, both of which waged war against Iraq, although in the case
of Clinton it was linked to a strategy of containment, principally through the
sanctions regime and the policing (and bombing) of the no-fly zones in the
northern and southern regions of Iraqi territory. The fulcrum of US policy
in the region since 1945 has been Saudi Arabia, and concerns were being
raised about fundamentalists in Saudi Arabia years before the attacks on the
World Trade Center and the Pentagon. So the geopolitical rationale
predates Bush II; and as James Woolsey, the Director of the CIA during the
Clinton Administration, explained in Congressional testimony, insofar as oil
is involved it had to do with the fear that future oil revenues 'amounting to
hundreds of billions ranging toward trillions of dollars ... into this volatile
region ... will support much governmental and private activity that is not in
the US interest, to put it mildly.'[43]

Nonetheless, the outcome of the war in Iraq has not been anything like the
Bush Administration had hoped. A massive blow to US prestige and credibility, one much more powerful than that stemming from its defeat in
Vietnam, may be in the making. And since the Middle East is now the
fulcrum of geopolitics, such a failure by the US in Iraq would encourage the
belief that the world superpower could be defeated by national resistance
forces, and would be a potentially decisive moment in the relationship
between the US and the Arab world, if not the entire Muslim world. Indeed
Iraq shows that the global panopticon and massive military power associated
with the US military 'footprint' is far from all-seeing and omnipotent, and that
its 'sovereign prerogative' can be challenged by forces of national resistance.

FORMS OF RESISTANCE

So with the Iraqi resistance in mind we conclude with a hypothesis
connected to Antonio Gramsci's political maxim: 'pessimism of the intelligence, optimism of the will'. Pessimism of the intelligence presupposes that
we can identify that which is relatively permanent or structural, and that
which is contingent or ephemeral in an historical situation and therefore
move towards sober, grounded analysis of the movement of political forces,
and their tensions and contradictions. As Gramsci noted, political analysis
must be directed 'violently towards the present as it is, if one wishes to transform it'.[44]

Let us therefore start with a few final observations on the situation in Iraq, which is crucial for understanding the geopolitics of empire. The USA has sought to fully privatize the Iraqi economy (with the exception of oil, which is under direct US military and indirectly, financial control) so as to constrain the options of any future Iraqi government – whether it is one of the successive puppet governments or one that may eventually draw on a broader popular mandate. For example, the US will keep its military bases, and ports and other airfields are now under the ownership and control of foreign private military contractors who are answerable to the US – not to any Iraqi government. The UN has effectively supported this policy of expropriation and primitive accumulation, as have Germany and France, and to a lesser extent Russia, countries that claimed to be most opposed to the invasion. In practice, the US now also controls the world's second largest known oil reserves after Saudi Arabia. If the US is able to further consolidate its political and strategic hold over the Middle East it will extend US geopolitical power significantly.[45]

The USA's allies know this, and central aspects of world order hinge upon the future relations between the most powerful capitalist states/regions. There is continuing discord between the leaders of the Atlantic states and their populations, reflected in the massive demonstrations against the Iraqi war and occupation. Indeed, some commentators see Iraq as provoking the worst crisis in transatlantic relations since the formation of NATO. But we should recall that with respect to Europe, as Giovanni Arrighi once pointed out, in many countries since 1945 there has emerged an 'American party', i.e. a set of social and political forces that support US imperial strategy and that form the foundations of the transatlantic 'organic alliance'. These forces form a transnational historical or power bloc drawn from political and civil society under US leadership (and Japan was added to its inner circles in the 1970s with the formation of the Trilateral Commission). In Europe such 'American' forces have included socialist, social democratic, conservative and authoritarian parties and regimes, as well as churches, media, intellectuals and unions – forces that more or less favour the enlargement of the empire of civil society – an empire that has now radically expanded eastward into the Former East Bloc after the collapse of the USSR.

Indeed, while concerns about the USA's technological leadership and its militarization and dominance of space (e.g. the Missile Defence/Star Wars system) have provoked efforts by other states and consortia into developing military-industrial alternatives, the US works hard to prevent allies and rivals achieving technological autonomy, since this would undermine its own 'full-spectrum dominance'. Thus whilst the EU has invested 3.6 billion euros in the Galileo system (planned to be operational by 2004) to challenge the US Global Positioning System (under Pentagon control), the US succeeded in

2004 in forcing the EU to make Galileo inter-operable with GPS, on national security grounds.

However, besides promoting its own consortia in strategic industries (e.g. the Airbus), the EU has also begun to confront key US interests in competition policy (including mergers and acquisitions and challenges to US monopoly power, e.g. against Microsoft). And in 2000 the EU announced its Lisbon strategy of becoming the most competitive economic space in the world by 2010, thus challenging US global economic leadership in the future.

Nonetheless, while the EU is seeking in some respects to increase its relative autonomy, at the same time it is gradually moving towards US-style financial liberalization and corporate governance based on shareholder value, replacing corporatist arrangements with regimes determined by ownership of capital. In effect the EU is actively promoting further deepening of disciplinary neo-liberalism in a wider Europe, as it has already been doing in its reconstruction efforts in the states of eastern Europe. However, there is widespread opposition, even among the European middle classes, to disciplinary neo-liberalism because of the way it undermines the social and welfare provisions that have constituted the West European postwar order.

Massive transatlantic trade and investment links and deep and cross-cutting ownership structures suggest a relatively permanent and structural alignment of Euro-American linkages that may endure any short-term rupture over Iraq.[46] And European military development since 1949 has been within the NATO framework under US dominance, which seems likely to continue as NATO's eastward expansion proceeds further. Nevertheless, none of these transatlantic arrangements are permanent, and we should also take note of the fact that this seems to go against the grain of majority opinion in Europe – again the middle classes are crucial here – which would like to see a European capability less subordinated to US imperialism.

Other constraints on US supremacy also seem likely to grow. For example, there are signs that large countries from the South, including India, Brazil and China are cooperating to establish a countervailing bloc to reduce the advantages of the US (and the EU) in matters of trade and investment. So far they have pressed mainly for greater liberalization of trade, particularly in agricultural products which are heavily protected by the metropolitan countries, but tensions are likely to increase rather than abate.

For their part, a growing number of US leaders are concerned about their heavy dependence on foreign capital to finance government operations. By mid-2004 over 50 per cent of US Treasuries were in foreign hands. Chinese and Japanese central banks hold the lion's share – largely to support the dollar and thus protect their US export markets (resulting in an overvaluation of the dollar relative to the East Asian currencies of about 20 per cent). Leading

American economists are worried at growing risks of a highly leveraged global economy, particularly in the US and Japan, and at the huge international financial imbalances. This suggests that any effort to increase or even sustain the US supremacy project risks a worldwide destabilization of investments, debt crises, and bursting of the worldwide asset bubbles that have grown in the past ten to fifteen years.[47]

The financial world itself, gorged on the 'seductive opium' of borrowing in a regime of cheap money (historically low interest rates and a depreciating dollar), is now becoming very jittery at the prospect of rising interest rates in the US and a 'destructive decline in the dollar' because of a worsening US current account deficit.[48] This links to growing long-term constraints on US financial and monetary power, and with it the US capacity to finance full-spectrum dominance. Alternatives to the hegemony of the dollar in world currency markets, such the Euro, will be further strengthened by a dollar crisis. Nor should it be forgotten that the US pays its foreign military bills in dollars.

What all this suggests is that the war in Iraq may be seen not as the first of a new series of endless twenty-first century wars waged to maintain and extend disciplinary neo-liberal globalization, but as the first that showed significant limits of US power. This is not only because of Iraqi resistance, but because other forces constrain and challenge US supremacy, at least in its current form. Indeed, a potentially far-reaching indicator of this is global public opinion which shows severe damage to the already shaky legitimacy of the US worldwide, with a majority viewing the US as the major threat to a peaceful world order.[49] The lawlessness and illegitimacy of US power in Iraq partly explains why political opposition to empire will likely grow. Further limits and political challenges arise with each of the many revelations of torture and brutalization of Iraqis, degrading acts that reflect not only the failure of the US to quell resistance, but also its impunity and repudiation of international law, and the amorality of its 'power to decree the exception'.

Throughout the world, and indeed in the US, many people are concerned at the threat to their own security posed by current US policies, which appear to be having the opposite effect that was intended – actually strengthening the ranks of terrorist groups such as Al-Qaeda. Many others worry about the consequences of the militant liberalism being applied in Iraq and the way it seems to be part of the organized grand larceny of the Enron stage of capitalism. The generalized economic insecurity of a world of disciplinary neo-liberalism is superimposed on that caused by the war on terror and in Iraq.

This also explains why some US allies could either refuse to be further co-opted into extending the American military dominance project, or pull back from it, as did the Spanish government elected in 2004 in the immediate aftermath of the terrorist bombings in Madrid. Grounds for optimism exist, too, in the growth of new movements that seek alternatives to the insecurity, injustice and excesses of disciplinary neo-liberalism and US supremacy. These new movements include workers and peasants; forces associated with peace and the environment, and disaffected former members of organized parties of the left – forces that reject a civil society premised on corporate rule with its political, social and ecological mono-culture, and intensified frameworks of exploitation and dispossession; and they also attempt to articulate alternatives that can preserve political, economic, ecological, cultural and social diversity.[50] Ultimately these forces stand against the most fundamental and antagonistic contradiction of all those that US supremacy entails: the fact that for a growing proportion of the world's population the deepening power of capital expropriates and undermines the basic means of livelihood. These forces engage in transformative resistance and are forging new forms of political agency that might transcend the structures, limits and contradictions of US-led efforts to instantiate disciplinary neo-liberalism. They seek to lower the increasingly tattered flags of the empire of capital and raise their own banners, under the slogan 'another world is possible'.

NOTES

I thank Tim Di Muzio for invaluable suggestions and research assistance.

1   Stephen Gill, *Power and Resistance in the New World Order*, Basingstoke: Palgrave, 2003.
2   See Stephen Gill, 'Pax Americana: Multilateralism and the Global Economic Order', in A. G. McGrew, ed., *Empire*, Milton Keynes: Open University Press, 1994, pp. 67-95.
3   Justin Rosenberg, *The Empire of Civil Society: A Critique of the Realist Theory of International Relations*. New York: Verso, 1994.
4   Giorgio Agamben, *Homo Sacer: Sovereign Power and Bare Life,* Stanford: Stanford University Press, 1998. Schmitt was of course a Nazi theoretician. For Agamben the concentration camp reflects this exceptional nature of sovereign power.
5   James K. Galbraith, 'A Perfect Crime: Inequality in the Age of Globalization', *Daedalus*, 131, 2002. Cited by Tom Nairn on: http://www.opendemocracy. net/debates/article-3-77-991.jsp. Accessed 10 May 2004.
6   In 1973 Pablo Neruda published a collection just before he died, prior to the coup. *Incitement to Nixoncide and Celebration of the Chilean Revolution* contained images of the poet's expulsion from his house by an army of corpses, and a world flooded by 'a great urinator'.
7   See John Kenneth Galbraith, *The Culture of Contentment*, Boston: Houghton Mifflin, 1992, and Eric Schlosser, *Fast Food Nation: What the All-American Meal*

Is Doing to the World, London: Penguin, 2001. On basic livelihood issues see Philip McMichael, 'Food Security and Social Reproduction: Issues and Contradictions', in Isabella Bakker and Stephen Gill, eds., *Power, Production and Social Reproduction*, Basingstoke: Palgrave, 2003, pp. 169–89.

8   Mike Davis, *City of Quartz: Excavating the Future in Los Angeles,* New York: Verso, 1990.

9   L. Kroll, and L. Goldman, 'Billionaires – the World's Richest People', *Forbes* 171(6), 2003, pp. 87–142.

10   Paul Krugman, 'Plutocracy and Politics', *New York Times*, 14 June 2002, citing Kevin Phillips, *Wealth and Democracy: A Political History of the American Rich*, New York: Broadway, 2002.

11   See Stephen Gill, 'Social Reproduction of Affluence', in Bakker and Gill, eds., *Power, Production and Social Reproduction,* pp. 190–207.

12   David Cay Johnson, *Perfectly Legal: The Covert Campaign to Rig our Tax System to Benefit the Super Rich and Cheat Everyone Else*, New York: Portfolio, 2003.

13   Approximately 2.1 million are now in US jails, up from 330,000 in 1972. A further 5 million are under supervision within its criminal justice system. The US incarceration rate in mid-2000 was 702 per 100,000 people, whereas the rate for Japan was 40, Sweden 60, Switzerland 85, Netherlands, France and Italy 90, Germany 95, Canada, Australia and Spain 110, UK 125, South Africa 400 and Russia 699. The incarceration rate for young black males aged 25–29 years was an astonishing 13 per cent. See http://www.sentencingproject. org/news/usno1.pdf; also the special edition of *Social Justice*, 27(3), 2000; Christian Parenti, *Lockdown America: Police and Prisons in the Age of Crisis*, London: Verso 1999.

14   Fox Butterfield, 'Mistreatment of Prisoners Is Called Routine in U.S.', *New York Times*, 8 May 2004.

15   Butterfield, 'Mistreatment of Prisoners'. In an Orwellian moment, the Pentagon announced in 2004 it would rename Abu Ghraib 'Camp Redemption'.

16   Editorial, 'The Military Archipelago: the New Iraq Crisis', *New York Times*, 7 May 2004.

17   Edward Alden, 'Bush Team Accused of Sanctioning Torture', *Financial Times*, 8 June 2004.

18   Mark Turner, 'US Struggles to Win Immunity for its Troops', *Financial Times*, 9 June 2004.

19   See Stephen Gill 'Constitutionalizing Inequality and the Clash of Globalizations'. *International Studies Review,* 4(3), 2002, pp. 47–65.

20   Of course powerful interests throughout the OECD, notably the EU, also support new constitutional mechanisms.

21   John Braithwaite and Peter Drahos, *Global Business Regulation*, Cambridge: Cambridge University Press, 2000.

22   US corporations have influential organizations such as the powerful Intellectual Property Committee. Its members include many giant corporations. IPC coordinates with Japan's Keidanren and the Union of Industrial and Employers' Confederations of Europe to shape US negotiating

positions.

23   Jagdish Bhagwati, 'The Capital Myth: The Difference between Trade in Widgets and Dollars', *Foreign Affairs,* 77(3), 1998, pp. 7-12.

24   Edward Alden, 'US Backs Curbs on Capital Controls', *Financial Times*, 2 April 2003.

25   Felix Rohatyn, 'The Unbearable Expense of Global Dominance', *Financial Times*, 9 June 2003.

26   Niall Ferguson, 'The True Cost of Hegemony: Huge Debt', *New York Times*, 20 April 2003. Rohatyn (see note 25) estimates *net* foreign debt at about $3 trillion.

27   Alan Beattie, 'New Role May Be Too Costly for Americans to Bear', *Financial Times*, 14 March 2003.

28   Beattie, 'New Role'.

29   Kent Smetters, Testimony to Subcommittee on the Constitution of United States, House of Representatives, 6 March 2003. Emphasis in original.

30   US military spending projected for fiscal year 2004 was approximately $420 billion, up about $80 billion since 2001. The 2003 supplement for Iraq was $79 billion; the 2004 supplement for Iraq was initially $87 billion; then President Bush requested a further $25 billion in mid-2004.

31   US Space Command, *Vision for 2020*, Washington DC: US Department of Defense, 1997, http://www.gsinstitute.org/resources/extras/vision_2020.pdf.

32   D.J. Rothkopf, 'Business Versus Terror', *Foreign Policy*, May/June, 2002, pp. 56-64. Chairman of Joint Chiefs of Staff General Richard B. Myers was commander of US Space Command in the late 1990s and oversaw development of US military computer networks, and became a champion of cyber-war tactics. James Dao, 'Low-key Space Buff: Richard Bowman Myers', *New York Times*, 25 August 2001.

33   Donald Rumsfeld, 'Transforming the Military', *Foreign Affairs*, 81(3), 2002, pp. 20-32.

34   William Hartung et al., 'Operation Endless Deployment', *The Nation*, 21 October 2002.

35   The study encouraged the amalgamation of special ops, intelligence, cover and deception, information warfare, psyops, and covert forces from the CIA and military agencies – into entities called Proactive, Preemptive Operations Groups (P2OG). Parallel efforts were urged to improve and link information databases and networks. According to Rumsfeld, 'Our task is to find and destroy the enemy before they strike us'. Cited in William Arkin, 'The Secret War', *Los Angeles Times*, 27 October 2002.

36   Chalmers Johnson, *Sorrows of Empire: Militarism, Secrecy, and the End of the Republic*, New York: Metropolitan Books, 2004.

37   Stephen Gill, 'The Global Panopticon? The Neo-liberal State, Economic Life and Democratic Surveillance', *Alternatives*, 20(1), 1995, pp. 1-49.

38   Christopher Drew, 'Listening, Looking: Old Methods Still Work', *New York Times*, 14 April 2001.

39   William R. Fast, *Knowledge Strategies: Balancing Ends, Ways, and Means in the Information Age*, Washington DC: Institute for National Strategic Studies,

2001.

40   Joseph Fitchett, 'Spying from Space: US to Sharpen the Focus', *International Herald Tribune*, 10 April 2001.

41   Proof of ECHELON was found in 1998-99 by intelligence specialist Jeffrey Richelson, via the US Freedom of Information Act.

42   The UKUSA agreements of 1947 effectively subordinated Australian, Canadian, New Zealand and UK intelligence agencies to the US. Jeffrey T. Richelson and Desmond Ball, *The Ties That Bind: Intelligence Co-operation Between the UKUSA Countries,* London: Unwin Hyman, 1990.

43   R. James Woolsey, Testimony to U.S. House of Representatives Committee on National Security, Washington DC, 12 February 1998.

44   Antonio Gramsci, *Selections from the Prison Notebooks,* Q. Hoare and G. Nowell-Smith, eds. and trans., New York: International Publishers, 1971, p. 175, note 75.

45   Leaders of 'old Europe' complained that the US had failed to give their firms 'equal access' to lucrative Iraqi reconstruction contracts, many of which were reserved for friends of the Bush Administration (e.g. Halliburton and Bechtel).

46   US-EU trade/investment links, the biggest in the world, are about $600 billion annually. By 2001, cumulative US-EU direct investment topped $1.6 trillion, with the EU receiving 53 percent (or $726 billion) of all US direct investment abroad, and sending 72 percent (or $947 billion) of all direct investment into the US. Jeffrey J. Schott and Gary Hufbauer, 'Transatlantic Trade Relations: Challenges for 2003', Munich: Transatlantic Strategy Group, Bertelsmann Foundation, 2003, www.cap.uni-muenchen.de/download/2003/2003_Miami_ Schott_Hufbauer.pdf.

47   Deborah Brewster, 'Pimco Chief Says Global Outlook is Less Stable Than in Past 20 or 30 Years', *Financial Times*, 17 June 2004. Pimco is the world's biggest bond fund manager of about $400 billion in bonds.

48   Editorial, 'A Rosy Scenario from the OECD. Yet the Financial Markets tell a Different Story', *Financial Times*, 12 May 2004.

49   Christopher Marquis, 'World's View of U.S. Sours After Iraq War, Poll Finds', *New York Times*, 4 June 2003.

50   For elaboration see Gill, *Power and Resistance,* pp. xi-xiv; 211-22.

FINANCE AND AMERICAN EMPIRE

LEO PANITCH AND SAM GINDIN

'Remember the song, "We Are the World"? In matters of finance and politics, if not culture, we are becoming the world and much of the world wants to become us.' (Chairman of the New York Stock Exchange Richard Grasso, 1997)[1]

Richard Grasso's exultation expressed the hubris that has attended the global ambitions of American financiers for over a century. The actual rise to world dominance of American finance was, however, far from smooth or inevitable. The goal of 'building the world's capital for all time to come' in New York, already articulated in the late 19th century, looked set to be realized by the end of World War I.[2] Yet it was only a decade later that the Wall Street crash triggered the Great Depression and the breakdown of the international financial order. And while New York took its place as the world's principal financial centre at the end of World War II, this seemed much less important when the new Bretton Woods order had supposedly marginalized finance relative to production and trade. As the story of 20th century capitalism is usually told today, only the neoliberal 'revolution' of the 1980s and 1990s finally unleashed the forces that made Wall Street the central location of the world economy. And far from this marking the end of history, the scandal that enveloped Mr. Grasso in 2003 over his $150 million salary not only epitomized the venality of New York as the capital of global finance but also appeared to many to symbolize its fragility.

From this perspective, it is perhaps not surprising that puncturing the hubris of New York's financial elite has become a favourite game of critical political economists. Playing this game may be dangerous, however, insofar as it underestimates the material significance as well as the obvious salience of global finance in the American empire. With this in mind, this essay tries to come to a deeper understanding, first, of the actual historical process that led to the realization by the end of the 20th century of a global financial order with New York as its operational centre, and with the American imperial state as its political carapace; and, second, of the way in which finance and empire reinforce each other today.

We begin in Part I with the unique position of the American state at the time of the reconstruction of capitalism after World War II. We argue that this did not allow for the repression of finance, as many believe the Bretton Woods arrangements accomplished, but rather that the seeds planted at that time for a new liberal trading order both reflected and contributed to the influence and power of financial capital. Part II examines the two-decade long period of confusion and hesitation about whether, and if so how, the American state could manage the emerging global capitalist economy in the context of the inflationary pressures and class conflicts of the 1960s and 1970s. Part III addresses the central moment in the neoliberal reconstitution of the global capitalist order: the domestic economic discipline introduced by the US Federal Reserve under Paul Volcker (the 'Volcker shock') at the beginning of the 1980s – which built upon the privatization and internationalization of financial markets that had already occurred, and carried them further still. We show that at each of the turning points in the evolution of the international capitalist economy, the American state both registered and extended the power and depth of financial capital at home as well as abroad.

Part IV analyzes not only the crises and contradictions but also the synergies involved in the relationship between finance, production and American empire today. It makes three central points. First, the expansion of finance has not been something apart from, but rather integral to the deepening of accumulation, as seen in both the continued internationalization of production networks and – as part and parcel of this – the continuing strength of the American economy. Second, liberalized finance needs to be seen less as a new constraint on the US state and more as a developing mechanism through which the state addresses its goals – including its capacity to contain the depth, breadth and duration of the crises that are inherent in the volatility of liberalized finance. Third, it is wrong to see the financialization of the American empire as a symptom of its decline: the globalization of finance has included the *Americanization* of finance, and the deepening and extension of financial markets has become more than ever fundamental to the reproduction and universalization of American power. It is an American empire strengthened rather than weakened by its financialization that we need to confront.

I. THE POST-WAR ERA AS THE CRADLE OF
GLOBAL FINANCE

Most liberal and even critical political economists have emphasized the 'embedded liberalism' of the post-war era, stressing in particular what often has been called the 'repression' of finance.[3] In turn, the growth of untrammelled global financial markets over the past quarter century has usually been seen in terms of the 'liberation' of finance from its post-war constraints. But the 1980s did not suddenly launch the liberalization and Americanization of international finance. No less a practitioner of financial capital and American power than Paul Volcker has stressed the continuity: 'I take it almost as an article of faith (a faith that in this case can be backed by facts) that the United States, as the dominant power after World War II and for decades afterwards, was the driving force toward a liberal trading order and the freedom of international investment.'[4] Concentrating on what distinguishes the two eras leads to the neglect of the processes at work that led from the first era to the second, and the extent to which neoliberalism's spread in the 1980s and 1990s depended on the structures previously established. As a recent study of international banking puts it, '[t]he Bretton Woods years should be regarded in a number of respects as the cradle of the global financial order that eventually emerged in the two final decades of the last century.'[5]

This itself cannot be properly understood except in terms of the new type of imperial order that emerged in the decades after World War II.[6] It was defined above all by the American state successfully overcoming the earlier fragmentation of capitalism into rival empires. The unique informal empire it now fashioned was characterized, above all, by the US state's economic penetration of, and close institutional linkages with, the other advanced capitalist states. This was an imperial order very different from the one that had been characterized by the ties between the imperial states and their colonies in the pre-World War I era.

In rethinking today how capitalist globalization was relaunched in the post–World War II era, the American interest in such a project seems obvious enough: the exhaustion of the old empires during the war suggested new opportunities too tempting to ignore, and the explosion of American productive capacity brought a powerful immediacy to the issue of access to – and therefore reconstruction of – Europe's markets. More generally, the thirty-year crisis of capitalism and its declining legitimacy, in face of both Soviet Communism and the strength of the left in the West European labour movements, meant that more than just post-war economic reconstruction was at stake.

But why did Europe accept the American project? After all, hadn't liberalism proven a failure? And how could Europe possibly compete with the US economically – or, even if it accepted the need for American capital and technology for post-war reconstruction, how could it possibly pay for this? Wasn't inward, self-reliant development the only real option? Insofar as these questions have been neglected, it is in large part because of the assumption that the post-war order was in fact not, even tendentially, a liberal-capitalist one, but one that 'embedded' capitalist relations within a political and social regulatory framework designed to limit and control its logic and dynamics. In this narrative the 'repression' of finance in favour of production, and the adoption of Keynesian fiscal policies and the Bretton Woods rules and institutions for managing global adjustments, created the foundations for the establishment of distinctive national, welfare-state capitalisms, especially in Western Europe.

But the reality was very different. At the time of the entry of the US into World War II there was a broad consensus in American capitalist and state circles that a top priority for the post-war world would be the reconstruction of a global free trade system. 'We have profited by our past mistakes', Roosevelt said as early as September 1942. 'This time we shall know how to make full use of victory'. What he meant by this was that, unlike at the end of World War I, the US government would now 'conquer its allies in a more enlightened manner, by demanding economic concessions of a legal and political nature instead of futilely seeking repayment of its wartime loans.'[7] The editors of *Fortune*, *Time* and *Life* magazines, in a joint statement in 1942, called for a 'new American imperialism' whose goal would be 'to promote and foster private enterprise, by removing the barriers to its natural expansion', by creating 'an expansionist context in which tariffs, subsidies, monopolies, restrictive labour rule … and all other barriers to further expansion can be removed.' This vision was strikingly similar to what would later be called neoliberalism, in which 'universal free trade' was seen as 'the ultimate goal of a rational world.'[8]

This imperial vision was articulated just as the US Treasury was taking the initiative, in conjunction with the British Treasury, to develop the plans that eventually led to Bretton Woods. Roosevelt's Secretary of the Treasury, Henry Morgenthau, promised a 'New Deal in international economics'. Important to the final outcome were Keynes's influential attacks on financial orthodoxy in the context of the new 'facts on the ground' – the comprehensive war-time controls over currency and capital flows. But this should not obscure the compromises that were made with the bankers, reflecting the continuing importance of financial capital both inside and outside the state.

The key issue was what role capital controls would be allowed to play after the war. As far as the US itself was concerned, the outcome had already been prefigured before the war. The New Deal at home had meant corporatist regulation and suppression of competition between financial institutions, but not the suppression of financial capital as a powerful force in American society.[9] The fact that the New Deal at home never extended to controls over the international movement of capital meant that rhetorical bravado of the kind occasionally heard from politicians like Morgenthau, about 'driving the usurious money lenders out of the temple of international finance', should never have been taken too seriously.

By the time many of America's leading capitalists entered the government during the war, the bankers' adamant opposition to an international treaty re-establishing controls over capital movements was well understood. Harry Dexter White wrote a position paper for the US Treasury in 1941 which correctly recognized that any really effective international system of capital controls would require recipient states to cooperate in policing incoming flows of capital that had escaped the controls of other countries. This proposal, however, ultimately got nowhere, as did Keynes's attempt to secure at least voluntary multinational cooperation against currency speculation. To be sure, even the New York bankers were pragmatic enough to see that most countries – with the key exception of the US – would continue to require capital controls after the war. But they never relinquished their view that such controls should be only temporary. They were motivated by their concern to protect investors' rights and for investors to exert discipline on the fiscal policies of governments – and this would 'continue to be part of Wall's Street rhetoric for the remainder of the century.'[10] So while the Bretton Woods Agreement recognized that states could operate capital controls, what was more significant was the US state's own refusal to use such controls, and the expectation in both Washington and New York that other states would use them only for a transitional period of reconstruction.

How short the transitional period was initially expected to be was evident from the great pressure the US put upon the British to quickly make sterling convertible, and the open arms with which Wall Street received a wave of capital flight from Europe immediately after the war. Even when it was recognized that if this continued it would spell the end of European capitalist reconstruction (and thus that even currency convertibility, let alone the removal of capital controls, would have to be postponed), the American state was not prepared to make European controls more effective by controlling capital inflows to the US. Rather, the funds pumped into Europe under the Marshall Plan were provided on terms that were meant to reinforce what European finance was demanding of European governments, i.e. 'to balance their budgets, restore financial stability, stabilize the exchange rate at realistic levels and enhance mutual cooperation.'[11] The use of 'offsetting financing'

– which would become the primary means of coping with capital flight in the neoliberal era – had been discussed at Bretton Woods but was formally rejected there in favour of capital controls. Yet this is what the Marshall Plan in a certain sense amounted to, at a time when the new International Monetary Fund had insufficient resources to play much of a role.[12]

The Bretton Woods rules and international institutions like the IMF did allow more flexibility in national adjustments to international imbalances. But what was really crucial was that the American state's acceptance of (what it always saw as temporary and transitional) barriers to selected US exports and investments helped to incorporate the Western European (and Japanese) states into the new imperial order. It tolerated their undervalued exchange rates, and used its financial and military aid to facilitate their access to American equipment and technology, while at the same time encouraging European economic integration. An important study undertaken in the early 1950s by leading American bureaucrats and academics concluded that '... the inability to realize the goals of Bretton Woods policy except marginally inevitably shifted the center of gravity and the orientation of American foreign policy away from attempts to apply universal trade and monetary prescriptions.' By 1948 it was already clear that 'internationalist trade and monetary policies and universal inter-governmental agencies play a peripheral or waiting part', while American programs and government agencies 'occupy the center of the stage.'[13]

The American state did not so much dictate to the European states as structure their options in the post-war period so that the reproduction of European capitalism depended on its international integration. It thereby 'internationalized' these states in terms of their goals and consequent responsibilities. Given the challenge (and potential contradictions) facing Europe in rebuilding its infrastructure while also rebuilding its social relations, relying on Bretton Woods alone was doomed to fail. The overwhelming economic dominance of the US would have led to balance of payments crises that the newly formed IMF clearly could not handle; 'fixed' exchange rates would have had to be repeatedly adjusted; beggar-my-neighbour trade policies would have been revived. It was the intervention of the American state in shaping the pattern of European reconstruction which – far more then the 'repression' of finance via Bretton Woods, or the deployment of Keynesianism as a policy technique – made the postwar golden age of capitalist growth possible.

Marshall aid itself had obvious strategic, trade and ideological purposes apart from financial stabilization and economic growth, all linked to strengthening Europe's capitalist classes. The post-war balance of class forces meant that labour could not be repressed as it had been before, which made it all the more important that financial capital should be reinforced. How far this could be accomplished varied from country to country. But it was certainly expressed in the determination with which the Bundesbank and the Finance Ministry in Germany espoused neoliberal monetarist policies throughout the post-war period. And, in the UK, the Bank of England – even after its nationalization by the post-war Labour government – continued to represent the interests of the City of London, often in alliance with a UK Treasury increasingly obsessed with restraining union wage power under conditions of high employment. Meanwhile, the Bank of International Settlements, having been saved from Keynes's attempt at Bretton Woods to extinguish it, was preserved as a bastion of financial orthodoxy. It was turned to practical as well as ideological use when, with American support, it became the vehicle for running the European Payments Union mechanism in the late 1940s.

But all this paled beside the special place that American financial capital itself occupied in the world capitalist order. The outcome of the war had effectively put the world on the dollar standard, and the Bretton Woods Agreement had effectively ratified this. Although the dollar was nominally backed by gold, the day could already be foreseen when gold would be demonetized 'along with copper, nickel, silver, not to mention wampum and clam shells.'[14] The dollar already had a unique status: as reserve currency; as vehicle currency through which firms were generally invoiced and other currencies were exchanged in international commerce; and as store of value for financial assets (including for the issuance of public and private long-term bonds). And this status was based, above all, on the immense size, depth, liquidity and openness of the US domestic financial markets.

The New York bankers had considerable influence in the Treasury under the Truman administration, even though 'lingering New Deal suspicion of Wall Street [had] culminated in one last cannonade' in the form of an antitrust suit launched in 1947 by the Justice Department against the investment houses that handled 70 per cent of Wall Street underwriting. But when this suit failed in the courts a few years later, it was a 'watershed in the history of Wall Street' that 'finally freed the Street of its image as the home of monopoly capitalists … the investment bankers finally proved they were vital to the economy.'[15]

The post-war economic boom and the financial bull market through the 1950s provided the space for American finance, even while still operating within the framework of the New Deal regulations, to further deepen its markets at home and expand abroad. Financial institutions of various types across the country not only participated in the rapid growth of industry but also found ways to encourage and take advantage of rising consumerism to draw in the working classes, especially through consumer loans and state-backed mortgage securities. International portfolio investment recovered slowly in the 1950s, but New York's investment banks, far from suffering from their exclusion from commercial banking under the New Deal financial legislation, became unrivalled in terms of the role they played (and the fees they earned) in capital-intensive infrastructural 'project financing' and in the placement of corporate, state and World Bank bond issues.[16] Although interest rates were low during this period, rising volumes and stable spreads between interest charged and interest paid supported profitability. The profits of financial firms grew faster than non-financial profits through the 1950s and 1960s: between 1945 and 1952 the average annual growth in profits in finance was 18 per cent compared to 11 per cent in the non-financial sector; from 1953 to 1969 the comparison was 7.5 per cent vs. 4.5 per cent.[17] Robert Rubin, the future Secretary of the US Treasury who joined Goldman Sachs in 1965, recalls one of the old guard telling him in the early 1970s 'that we junior partners would be unlikely to ever do as well financially as the older partners had because there would never be another period as good as the one that had just passed.'[18]

In the new dollar-centred international financial system the relationship of the rest of the world, and especially of Europe, to American finance could not be limited for very long to borrowing through financial services located in New York. Before the war, the branches of American investment banks had acted mainly as diplomatic outposts for their home offices, but by the late 1950s and early 1960s they had become dynamic financial actors inside Europe. This involved the export of American banking techniques and expertise, and facilitated an explosion of foreign direct investment by American multinational corporations. And US commercial banks, barred since the New Deal from investment banking activity at home, also jumped at the chance to set up foreign branches in Europe so that they could conduct the full range of activities requested by their American clients – and soon were also wooing European companies. This penetration of Europe by American corporations and banks meant the implantation of American capital as a class force inside European social formations, whereby '... economic expertise, social norms, and cultural habits are transmitted by the investing firm. This ties the recipient economies into the broader social totality out of which the investment has come, thereby broadening the basis of social relations upon which it rests.'[19]

The emergence of the Eurodollar market advanced this process very considerably. Initially using loopholes in exchange control regulations to set up external dollar accounts for Soviet-bloc and Arab states which were wary of banking in New York, British merchant banks switched their international operations from sterling to the dollar to take advantage of currency convertibility and the loosening of capital controls in Japan and Europe at the end of the 1950s. This provided a completely unregulated international repository for the dollar at a time when rates of interest in New York were still limited by New Deal regulations. Encouraged by the British authorities as a way of maintaining the City of London as an international financial centre, the effect of the Eurodollar market's emergence was to move the City – and through it, European finance in general – more closely into the American imperial embrace. In this type of new imperial order, moreover, capital controls based on the distinction hesitatingly drawn at Bretton Woods between 'productive' and 'speculative' financial flows increasingly broke down. Not only the unregulated Eurodollar market but also the intra-firm transfers that characterize so much foreign direct investment lay at the root of the eventual abandonment of capital controls in the 1970s.

Perhaps most important, the form that capitalist integration had by now taken affected the social formations of all advanced capitalist states, so that, even while economic competition among the advanced capitalist states returned, any revival of inter-imperial rivalry was foreclosed. Taking Germany as an example, the trade patterns in place by the late 1950s were themselves a factor in limiting protectionism, but the penetration of American direct investment affected (amongst other things) the nature of German capital – not just directly (GM, Ford, IBM) but also via suppliers, banks, and customers. This was reinforced by German firms' consequent need to establish a countervailing presence in the US, all of which tended to create cross-border networks of finance and integrated production.

The point is not that a transnational capitalist class had emerged, operating in a transnational ether beyond states, but something more complex. The capitalist class of each country retained its distinctiveness, but both the capital historically rooted there and the foreign capital that established itself alongside it now depended on each other's states, and especially on the American state, to expand and manage the capitalist order.

II. FROM BRETTON WOODS TO NEOLIBERALISM: 'HESITATIONS AND FALSE STARTS'

Once we recognize the post-war period as the cradle of a new, globalizing and liberalizing American imperium, its implications for future developments become clearer. By the end of the 1950s the American state was not merely at the apex of a hierarchy of states, but was by now a qualitatively different kind of state from the rest, and was internationalized in a distinct way. To be sure, the US had not simply imposed itself on Europe; it required the active participation of European states in the transformation of capitalist order in the postwar period.[20] But while all the advanced capitalist states increasingly recognized (to varying degrees) the responsibility they had to participate in the management of international capitalism, they also recognized – and increasingly insisted on – the central role the American state had to play in this. Only the American state bore the burden – and had the accompanying capacity and autonomy – to take on the task of managing the system as a whole.

Yet how exactly the American state was to do this became the burning question of the 1960s and 1970s. It might have been thought that the provisions of Bretton Woods would really come into their own once the period of reconstruction was completed towards the end of the 1950s. As European economic competitiveness was restored and currencies were made convertible, the post-war dollar shortage turned into a dollar glut thanks to European and Japanese exports to the USA as well as American military expenditures and foreign investments. In this new context, the contradictions of the Bretton Woods framework, above all those involved in its treatment of the US state as equivalent to any other state, increasingly began to reveal themselves. The fact that the deep penetration of Europe by US capital at this time coincided with an emerging crisis of the dollar meant that the consolidation of the new structure of imperial power was sometimes obscured. It was a situation that proved confusing to all the main actors – including the Americans. The *sang froid* with which the Fortune editors had proclaimed in 1942 that the new American empire would not be 'afraid to help build up industrial rivals to its own power ... because we know industrialization stimulates rather than limits international trade' was no longer in evidence in 1960, as both the outgoing Eisenhower Administration and the incoming Kennedy Administration panicked over the new American balance of payments deficit.

The introduction in the early 1960s of American controls on the export of capital for the first time since the war was certainly not welcomed by the New York bankers, who instead demanded – as did central bankers in Europe – higher American interest rates to cope with the problem. But the fact that these controls were seen as temporary and were accompanied by further US encouragement of other states to remove their capital controls, showed how limited an about-face it really was; it actually had the effect of further encouraging American banks to set up as direct participants in the Eurodollar market. This was an effect the American state was well aware of and even encouraged, as it served to sustain the value of the dollar and provide access to European funds, as well as reinforce the international predominance of US banks. In any case, given the option for the holders of dollars of converting them into gold, the controls would had to have been much more stringent to stem the falling confidence in the dollar.

Yet balance of payments deficits did not have the same meaning for the United States as they did for any other state. This was not widely recognized at the time, but as an obscure paper prepared for the Federal Reserve of Boston in 1971 pointed out: '[T]his asymmetry appears to be appropriate, for it corresponds to an asymmetry in the real world'.[21] However, before this perspective could be universally accepted (especially amongst bankers), the fiction of a gold standard behind the dollar standard would have to be abandoned and replaced not only by flexible exchange rates but types of global financial markets that could sustain them. And it would have to come to be seen that, far from necessarily representing a diminution of American power, the outflow of capital and the balance of payments deficits were actually laying the basis for a dollar-based credit expansion and financial innovation, both domestically and internationally – what Seabrooke appropriately calls the 'diffusion of power through the dollar.'[22] Above all, it would be necessary for the American state, as the imperial state, to retain the confidence of the ever more dynamic and powerful financial capitalists in the face of the pressures on the dollar. All this implied addressing the deeper contradictions of the Bretton Woods arrangements for fixed exchange rates and tying the dollar to gold, which by then had become a barrier to the American state's capacity to navigate between its domestic and imperial responsibilities.

Especially important in this regard was the way class relations had developed in the advanced capitalist states during the Keynesian era. Under the near full employment conditions that had arrived by the early 1960s, the militancy of a new generation of workers drove up money wages and challenged managerial prerogatives, with negative implications for productivity. At the same time, new social justice political movements drove up the social wage, and the 'new left' that emerged from the rapid expansion of post-secondary education had radicalizing effects in the political arena. But this did not amount to the kind of fundamental class realignment that could have sustained policies to move beyond Bretton Woods–style controls on external capital flows, to democratic controls over investment itself. Without this, inflation was the inevitable result of the 1960s militancy – and it was exacerbated by a growing revolt in the 'third world', leading to increased military costs as well as rising commodity prices.

Because capital – and not least financial capital with its natural aversion to inflation – was also strong, the contradictions became intense. Finance felt doubly pressured in the 1970s. Not only was it affected by the general crisis in profitability, but the form this crisis took particularly affected financial assets. As industrial capital – supported by the state's accommodative fiscal and monetary policies – raised prices to protect its profits, the resultant inflation devalued financial holdings. Yet financial capital was not passive in this period. Matching the rise of the new left was a new generation of MBAs, 'bright and ambitious students... paying more attention to business strategy, product development, marketing, and costs, the stuff of business-school curricula.'[23] Amidst a wave of takeovers and mergers, banks competed to recruit this ambitious new generation who developed key innovations in financial services, building on the development of certificates of deposit that initiated the 'securitization' of commercial banking (i.e. the shift from depositing money in a bank to buying a tradable financial asset from it). This transformed the role of banking from direct credit intermediation (taking deposits from and loaning money to particular customers) to mediating the interactions of lenders and borrowers in depersonalized securities markets. The vast expansion of risk arbitrage and block trading for institutional investors soon followed, and it was out of this that, in turn, the revolution in derivatives and hedge funds so crucial to the globalization of finance eventually emerged.

The privatization and liberalization of finance, which is usually dated from the 1980s, actually begins much earlier, with the state playing a direct and active role. In the 1960s, the decline of American foreign aid created pressures on foreign governments to find ways to get access to private credit; and this occurred alongside the advent of the deregulated Eurodollar market and the expansion of private foreign direct investment as the major form of capital flows. Later in the 1970s, after the Americans ended the convertibility of the dollar into gold, leading to the end of fixed exchange rates, there was an explosion of new market-based securities designed to meet the need of traders to hedge against the risk associated with floating exchange rates. Meanwhile, as economic growth slowed down, not only was the increasing public debt of the advanced capitalist states financed through private channels, the American state also insisted on recycling petrodollars to the third world through the private banking system. The increased opportunities, greater risks, and especially intensified competition that flowed from this privatization of credit led to further dramatic innovations in finance, especially the magnification of the range of securities.

The impact on American financial institutions of inflation, low real interest rates and stagnant profits in the 1970s accelerated the qualitative transformations of these years, which increasingly ran up against the old New Deal banking regulations. This was what prompted the global 'financial services revolution' that Moran dates as beginning in the mid-1970s with the abolition of fixed rates on brokerage commissions on Wall Street.[24] Monetary instruments that had previously seemed exotic now became basic parts of the financial landscape: money market mutual funds, for example, emerged to account for $25 billion in assets by 1979 – and by 1981, they had further quadrupled. The assets of foreign banking offices in the US increased eight-fold in the 1970s (matching the growth of the Eurodollar market), while the assets of American banks abroad increased almost seven-fold, and portfolio flows amongst the G7 increased eleven-fold. By the end of the 70s, the foreign earnings of the five largest American banks accounted for over half of their total earnings. Nor should it be thought that these developments took place within a self-contained financial sphere divorced from production and trade. US trade actually doubled as a share of GDP in the 70s, and foreign direct investment amongst the G7 increased almost six-fold.[25]

As financial capital outgrew the cradle of Bretton Woods, however, it ran up against the militant labour and other popular forces of the period. Every advanced capitalist state had to deal with the underlying problem of class rela-tions in this period. Since none of them was about to repress financial capital, they had to curtail the power of labour. Social democratic governments in Europe tried to cope by wooing trade unions into corporatist arrangements for wage controls, a strategy that increasingly proved unstable as workers revolted against their own unions.[26] In France, where low union density and Communist strength in the labour movement ruled this out, de Gaulle tried to return to the gold standard as a way of imposing austerity at home. Going back to the gold standard had the added attraction of undermining the dollar internationally. In the end this led nowhere. In May 1968, after de Gaulle granted a huge wage hike to derail the general strike and induce labour away from the revolutionary ambitions of the students, he acknowledged that the gold standard would have denied him this flexibility and 'stopped daydreaming about a return to gold.'[27]

As for the US itself, the Nixon administration elected in 1968 was caught between the call for higher interests to reduce capital outflows and the polit-ical costs associated with the increased unemployment this would cause. As Gowa's study shows, when it finally terminated the dollar's link with gold in 1971 after two years of trying to 'muddle through', this was more an act of expedience than one conceived as a dramatic break with Bretton Woods.[28] Far from providing any long-term solution, it was a way to avoid addressing the underlying contradiction of class relations that lay at the root of the inflation and dollar crisis of the period, which nothing less than breaking both the New Deal framework and the domestic power of American labour would accomplish. Such a neoliberal solution was presaged by the measures the US Treasury and New York Federal Reserve Bank required of the British Labour government during the 1976 IMF crisis, leading to the explicit abandonment of Keynesianism even before the elec-tion of Mrs. Thatcher.[29] But the asymmetry amongst the capitalist states in the new imperial order was such that until the American state dealt with the problem at home, no such solution abroad could be stable.

In spite of the problems faced by the American state through the 1970s, no serious challenge surfaced to its international dominance. This was partly because, despite the incontrovertible *force majeure* the US displayed in ending the dollar's convertibility to gold, the American state still remained concerned not to play up its dominant position too much. As an interdepartmental group chaired by Volcker (then undersecretary for monetary affairs in the Nixon Treasury) said in a 1969 report, even while seeking 'a substantial degree of U.S. control [of the international monetary system] ... in the interests of facilitating international harmony the appearance of US hegemony should not be sought.'[30] But at a deeper level it was the American penetration of the other developed capitalist countries, and the dense institutional linkages that had evolved between them and the US, that determined that inter-state tensions were limited to renegotiating the terms of the imperial relationship, not questioning its essence. Within the third world, instances of attempted withdrawal from American-led global capitalism were contained (the American defeat in Vietnam had not led to any domino effect) or turned around (the overthrow of Allende being followed by the introduction of neoliberalism under Pinochet), while the recycling of petrodollars further integrated the third world into global financial circuits.

Yet the management of global capitalism remained problematic. What had not emerged were the disciplinary mechanisms needed to adjust national economies to the rhythms of international accumulation. An immediate barrier to such a development was that the American state itself had not imposed the necessary domestic discipline that would allow it to maintain the value of the dollar as the international currency, a failure that was manifested in inflation in the US, and turmoil in international financial markets. While the end to dollar-gold convertibility in 1971 temporarily increased American foreign policy autonomy and avoided drastic domestic austerity, it did not end the tension between the American state's imperial and domestic roles. It did not yet mark, as is sometimes suggested, 'the dawning of a new international regime for money and international relations.'[31]

In the context of the floating exchange rates, petro-dollar recycling, expanding financial markets, continued labour militancy and 'soft' monetary policy that characterized the 1970s, by the end of the decade the American state was scrambling to deal with double-digit inflation, a declining dollar and, above all, large outflows of capital. Even the sober Bank for International Settlements went so far as to speak of 'a genuine Dollar crisis';[32] and there was a degree of discontent on Wall Street 'not seen since the last days of the Hoover presidency.'[33] Looking back to his appointment as Chairman of the Federal Reserve at the end of the 1970s, Paul Volcker recalled 'all the hesitations and false starts, the uncertainty and questions' after a decade in which 'theorizing and empirical analysis about stable and predictable relationship[s] ... seemed to break down in the United States and other countries'.[34]

III. THE VOLCKER SHOCK: FINANCE AND THE RECONSTITUTION OF EMPIRE

It was in this context that the 'Volcker shock' of 1979–82 brought to a definitive end two decades of policy confusion and tension between the state's imperial and domestic roles, through what Volcker himself called a 'triumph of central banking'.[35] This triumph was political, not technical. Like the first panic over the value of the dollar that marked the transition between the Eisenhower and Kennedy Administrations in 1960, the Volcker shock also spanned the transition between two Presidents of otherwise very different temperaments, Carter and Reagan. Volcker was himself no more than a 'pragmatic monetarist' (having first worked in the New York Fed and the US Treasury under Kennedy and Nixon trying to patch up the holes in the Bretton Woods system). What the Volcker shock entailed in policy terms, as he admitted, was not 'very fancy or very precise'.[36] For all the pseudo-scientific econometrics that provided ideological cover for the operation, it simply involved limiting the growth in the money supply and allowing interest rates to rise to whatever level – and at whatever short term economic cost – was necessary to break the back of inflation and the strength of labour. The Federal base rate rose from an average of 8 per cent in 1978 to over 19 per cent at the beginning of 1981 and didn't consistently return to less than double digits until after 1984.

The Fed's brief embrace at this time of the Friedmanite goal of controlling the money supply was contradicted by the diversity of financial instruments that had already developed – and that would soon spread much further under the impetus of extremely high interest rates. As Greenspan later explained: 'Increasingly since 1982 we have been setting the funds rate directly. In the current state of our knowledge, money demand has become too difficult to predict ... As the historic relationship between measured money supply and spending deteriorated, policymaking, seeing no alternative, turned more eclectic and discretionary.'[37] The Federal Reserve now explicitly took responsibility for directly declaring an interest rate that would project an unwavering anti-inflationary commitment so as to become the global anchor of a dollar-based world economy. This gave it, as Volcker put it, a central 'role in stabilizing expectations [that] was once a function of the gold standard, the doctrine of the annual balanced budget, and fixed exchange rates.'[38]

The only possible alternative to this would have involved extensive American capital controls over Wall Street, with cooperation from the European states. The outflows of capital from the US that so worried American leaders by the late 1970s came from American investors as much as disenchanted foreigners. Because the flow went to the unregulated Eurodollar and Eurobond markets, the Fed had at one point proposed that reserve requirements be put on Eurodollar deposits, which in order to be effective would have required other central banks to do the same.[39] Yet this was nothing like the early wartime proposals for cooperative capital controls. With Nixon's rescinding of the temporary capital controls that had been introduced in the 1960s, the American state was now more adamantly opposed than ever to the use of capital controls.[40] But the rejection by the European central banks of an American proposal to set reserve requirements on Eurodollar deposits also indicated the lack of genuine interest on the part of European states for cooperative capital controls. Even on the few occasions when they themselves raised controls as a possibility during the turmoil of the 1970s, it was notable that the European (and Japanese) governments did not push the idea very hard. What they did push hard was that the Americans should apply discipline to themselves.

Indeed, given the degree to which capital markets were already internationalized, effective controls now implied not only a much more far-reaching intervention in financial markets than ever before, but intervention in trade and investment as well. Just as the internationalization of finance had earlier accompanied the internationalization of production, so any attempt to control finance by the 1970s would not be able to leave industrial capital untouched. Not even social democratic governments in Europe were inclined to seriously contemplate such a radical intervention, as was shown by the hostile treatment of Tony Benn's Alternative Economic Strategy in Britain in 1975-6, and the rejection at the same time of the German unions' much milder proposals for investment planning.[41] And however committed (or not) the Mitterrand government in France was to the radical programme on which it was elected in 1981, by then extensive controls on capital and investment had already been ruled out in Europe no less than in the United States.

Thus when the Federal Reserve acted as it did in 1979-82 to show the imperium's own determination to win the confidence of the financial markets through the radical use of monetary policy, it was endorsing the inclination of European governments. They had been trying to cope with inflation in their own economies by shifting away from Keynesianism and the commitment to full employment, since holding on to these seemed bound to take them in a much more socialist direction than they wanted to go. With global capitalism structured around the dollar as the international currency, and instability of the dollar creating instability everywhere else, the focus was on whether the American state could in fact maintain the value of the dollar in the face of domestic pressures, and thus meet its imperial responsibilities. Having dispensed with a gold-related standard (because the discipline involved had proven too rigid), and in the absence of a solution based on cooperative capital controls (because its de facto implications were too radical even for European social democracy), the issue became the capacity of the American state to act unilaterally to preserve its access to global resources while re-establishing confidence in the dollar.

With the Volcker shock, the US effectively secured acceptance by other states and financial capital of the asymmetric treatment of its external deficit because, indeed, '*it corresponded to an asymmetry in the real world.*' The way American banks had spread their financial innovations internationally in the 1960s and 1970s, especially through the development of secondary markets in dollar-denominated securities, allowed the American state – unlike other states – to substitute the sale of Treasury bills for a domestic pool of foreign exchange reserves and run its economy without large reserves. The only proviso, as Seabrooke notes, was that it maintained a liquid financial system and could attract buyers for its securities in the international markets. Rather than evidence of the origins of a collapse of American hegemony, as many commentators have supposed, 'the US's ability to constantly re-finance its debt obligations is not a sign of weakness but evidence of its great structural power in financial relations'.[42]

The Fed's policy thus placed the need to 'discipline ourselves' (in Volcker's own words) at the centre of both America's economic revival and its international role.[43] The reconstitution of empire, in other words, began at home. And crucial to this, for all the tensions between regions and fractions of capital that attended this restructuring, was that it produced no split either within the American ruling class or between the American and other ruling classes. By the end of the 70s, the non-financial sectors of capital had themselves generally come to acknowledge the need to give priority to fighting inflation and thereby to accept that strengthening financial capital was in their own interests. Far from fighting the emerging leading role of financial capital, industry leaders accepted the costs implied by a finance-led revival of domestic and international accumulation.[44]

Of course, the US-led attack on inflation was only effective in combination with the strong underlying capacities of the American economy: its technological base, depth of financial institutions, and the resources that came with its imperial role. In breaking the inflationary spiral in the US through breaking the economic power of labour, the American state not only won back the confidence of financial markets, but also put itself in the position to be able to tell other states – all too ready to blame the US for their own inflation – to likewise address their own balance of class forces. And by further liberalizing its own financial markets, it not only deepened the domestic strength and liquidity of these markets but supported their further internationalization. It was this that now crucially sustained the dollar as an international currency and made US government securities seem as good as (indeed, because they paid interest, better than) gold. The resolution of the crisis of the 1970s through the strengthening of the structural power of finance thus reinforced the capacity of the American state to revive global capitalism.

The means by which American inflation and the wage militancy of US labour were broken – high interest rates – also led to an inflow of capital, a stronger dollar, and greater public debt (the Reagan defence expenditures adding to the costs of the induced recession). The consequent increase in international holdings of highly liquid US Treasury bills not only had a major impact on furthering the development of massive secondary markets in bonds, but lay at the core of the reconstituted form of American imperial rule. It allowed the American state to consistently rely on global financial reserves to expand its – and capitalism's – global reach. As this direction was consolidated and international confidence in the US was firmed up, access to foreign capital became less dependent on offering a higher rate of interest. Foreign capital came to the US again because it was a safe haven in a world that had not yet generally followed the American example, and because of the prospect of profitable investment there, given the definitive defeat of the unions in the US. Over the four years from 1975-78, foreign direct investment in the US had totalled $18.5 billion; in the period 1981-87, it *averaged* $22.9 billion *per year*.[45]

The Federal Reserve's success in initiating this turn rested on how convincing it was in its determination that not just short-term, but also long-term inflation would be controlled. This introduced a new parameter in state policy that implicitly accepted lower rates of growth as a corollary to the priority of low inflation, so as to stabilize the dollar and assure its international role. But the Volcker shock's contribution to the new priority of 'breaking inflationary expectations' in the early '80s depended on something more fundamental still.

However it was articulated, the real issue was not so much finding the right monetary policy, as restructuring class relations. Breaking inflationary expectations could not be achieved without defeating the working class's aspirations and its collective capacity to act to fulfill them. Notably, once the government entered directly into the Chrysler bankruptcy proceedings in 1980, Congress insisted that Paul Volcker sit on the public board responsible for the negotiations with the company, its creditors and suppliers, and the union; and Volcker was indeed finally responsible for securing from the UAW, the highest-profile union in the US, the conditionality (wage cuts and outsourcing) attached to the loan that Chrysler was granted. Meanwhile, outside the purview of the Fed but by no means unrelated to its objective, was President Reagan's smashing of the Air Traffic Controllers' strike in 1981. Indeed, Volcker would later say that 'the most important single action of the administration in helping the anti-inflation fight was defeating the air traffic controllers strike.'[46]

It was on this basis that the American state regained the confidence of Wall Street and financial markets more generally. This proved pivotal to the reconstitution of the American empire by unleashing the new form of social rule subsequently labelled 'neoliberalism' – promoting the expansion of markets and using their discipline to remove the barriers to accumulation that earlier democratic gains had achieved. As vehicles for the most mobile form of capital, the new financial markets contributed strongly to the universal-ization of neoliberalism in the 1980s and 1990s. The deepening and extension of financial markets that had already occurred by this time – their domestic and international growth, their increasingly multi-dimensional and innovative ties to business, and their penetration of consumer savings – were central to this new form of social rule. The new global market in foreign exchange that had emerged when the gold standard was terminated in 1971 did not itself immediately lead to 'the active international market in finan-cial claims as a whole' that best defines the term 'global finance'.[47] This awaited the development of financial capital's new capacities in creating, assessing and selling new kinds of securities that would spread throughout the monetary system after the Volcker shock.

Crucial here was the increased international liquidity of credit and its contribution to the management of risk. This allowed for what Dick Bryan has called the international 'commensurability of value'.[48] Financial markets, especially through the invention of a large number of financial instruments called derivatives (swaps, options and futures not based on the trade in phys-ical products), put a price on the various dimensions of risk associated with exchange rates, trade, long vs. short-term investments, political develop-ments, etc. This vastly extended the basis for comparing the performance of assets not only across space and time but also across the various dimensions of risk themselves.[49] All this has become central to the dynamics of compe-tition and accumulation in global capitalism.

No less important was the imperial basis of this financialization, above all the full international acceptance, a decade after the dollar was freed from gold, of the dollar's continuing role as the fulcrum of the international financial system. Ultimately, the risks involved in international accumulation are contingent on confidence in the dollar and its material foundations in the strength of the American economy, and in the capacity of the American state to manage the inevitable volatility of financial markets. The post-war boom had reflected this kind of confidence in American power; the reconstitution of empire that began in the early 80s was about restoring it after the uncertainties of the 1960s and 1970s.

The turning point of the 'Volcker shock' thus represented a convergence of imperial and domestic responsibilities. Bound up with renewed capitalist confidence in the US was the free-market, anti-statist rhetoric of Reaganism and Thatcherism. This did not mean the end of regulation, of course – any more than Keynesianism had, conversely, meant the suppression of markets. When the Federal Reserve-supported Depositary Institutions Deregulation and Monetary Control Act (DIDMCA) was passed in 1980 right in the midst of the Volcker shock, it revealed by its very title the futility of any discourse cast in terms of a dichotomy between regulation vs. deregulation, or state vs. market.

Encouraging finance to spread its wings demanded new forms of state intervention to manage the uncertain implications of that freedom. A recent textbook on American finance casually notes, for example, that, 'the financial system is amongst the most heavily regulated sectors of the American economy.'[50] What was at issue was not deregulation but the form that regulation would take. Regulation was re-conceived to emphasize managing, as opposed to preventing, the volatility implied by more open financial markets: improving supervision, requiring self-regulation and, of course, setting interest rates and acting as lender of last resort. This was especially necessary since, alongside the enormous shake-out that interest rates approaching 20 per cent brought about in American industry in the early 1980s, an enormous shake-out in the financial sector also began at this time. Over 4500 banks – 36 per cent of the total – shut their doors between the end of the 70s and the early 90s, not including the Savings and Loans industry collapse, making the period what one Congressional study subsequently called 'undoubtedly the most turbulent years in US banking history since the Great Depression.'[51] The concentration and centralization of banking was offset by, as well as partly due to, the emergence of new financial institutions offering new instruments and services. The financial sector as a whole expanded explosively, both in the US and globally.

This was facilitated by a spate of legislation gradually allowing banks to operate in securities markets and non-bank institutions to engage in commercial property-lending (thus gradually reversing the provisions of the New Deal's Glass-Steagall Act long before it was formally repealed at the turn of the century). The legislation facilitating competition in the financial services sector was also designed to expand consumer credit markets. The American working and middle classes maintained their standards of living by working longer hours and going into debt. They often re-mortgaged their homes to do so, and commercial banks sold off the resulting debt in packages to investment banks which in turn repackaged them for sale in the derivatives market. On the other side of the ledger, commercial banks relied less and less on deposits for their funding and more and more on selling and trading securities. Meanwhile the New York investment banks famously made out like bandits. As Michael Lewis said in his Wall Street memoir, *Liar's Poker*: 'Had Volcker never pushed through his radical change in policy, the world would be many bond traders and one memoir the poorer …. A Salomon salesman who had in the past moved five million dollars' worth of merchandise through the traders' books each week was now moving three hundred million dollars through each day.'[52]

This trading in securities was so profitable that it not only swept across all the different sectors of finance but soon encompassed industrial corporations themselves. The New York investment banks, moreover, not only increasingly asserted their dominance in the City of London, but became significant actors in all other financial centres. Apart from the competitive advantages they enjoyed from having pioneered the innovations in securitized finance, they were also aided by the other financial centres' emulation of New York's 'big bang', and by the American state's own concerted actions aimed at the diffusion of its neoliberal regime. The fact that the major New York investment banks took the lead in providing financial services and advice for mergers and acquisitions in all the regional financial centres from Europe to East Asia meant that they came to play a significant role in transforming not only financial markets, but business practices generally, on US lines. Under these conditions, the widely-held belief of the 1980s that Japanese banks were poised to displace American financial dominance was soon shattered. Even the close industry-bank networks for which Japan and Germany were famous could not remain immune for long from the transformations this entailed. A truly global financial system 'based on the deregulation and internationalization of the US financial system', as John Grahl has put it, 'is neither a myth not even an alarming tendency, but a reality.'[53]

IV. FINANCE AND EMPIRE IN GLOBAL CAPITALISM

The historical account we have offered above challenges the conventional bifurcation of the second half of the 20th century into one era based on the suppression of finance (associated with the golden age of capitalism and a beneficent American hegemony) followed by another based on finance's liberation (associated with a decline of both the dynamism of capitalism and the hegemony of the American state). For all the attention that has been paid to the Volcker shock as a momentous turning point in contemporary capitalism, too little attention has been paid to the extent to which its great impact was conditional on the earlier strengthening of financial capital by virtue of its markets having become notably liberalized, with domestic and international developments reinforcing each other.

Many critics at the time insisted that the Volcker shock could not work. High interest rates would induce austerity in the short term, and not only block growth but also fail to reverse the competitive threat from Europe and Japan. Above all, it was argued, shifting power and resources to finance, a section of capital that was unproductive of surplus, would not only increase inequality but also limit long-term accumulation. How far can we say the dire predictions have proven correct? It is certainly the case that the defeat of labour and the reinforcement of financial capital's power since the early 1980s have led to stark and increasing inequality within the US, and between the North and the South. But this by no means entailed a decline in capitalism's dynamism. As we have argued at length elsewhere,[54] while it is true that giving priority to the defeat of inflationary expectations implied slower growth, that in itself hardly qualified as a crisis for capitalism. As Maddison has shown, average annual growth rates in the quarter century after 1973, while below those of the golden age, were still above every earlier period in world capitalism from 1820 to 1945.[55]

As for the implications of the relative increase in the role and power of financial institutions, there was an underestimation of how the deepening of capital markets, and the competitive pressures and mobility they generate, could lead to increased capital productivity and profit rates. They did this not just through their disciplinary impact on firms and governments, but also by reallocating capital and supporting the dissemination of technology across firms and sectors (more rapid exit of relatively inefficient firms, support for risky but innovative start-ups, dissemination of new technologies into old sectors). Both the decline in the rate of profit that signalled the end of the golden age and its subsequent recovery after the early 1980s have been convincingly linked, empirically, to corresponding decreases and then improvements in the 'productivity' of capital (i.e. the output per unit of capital stock).[56]

To be sure, this doesn't answer some larger questions about the contributions of finance to restructuring – questions made more controversial because of disputes about how to conceptualize 'finance'. Of course, credit creation in itself does not necessarily imply an increase in productive activity. But the historical development of financial institutions, accelerating from 1960 onwards, has included the expansion of services beyond the acquisition of savings and the provision of credit. A major change occurred in the very nature of what financial institutions do. As investment houses challenged the former dominance of banks, and as banks remade themselves to counter this threat, 'finance' evolved far beyond its classical role in credit provision and was placed directly at the heart of the accumulation process, essentially introducing a new sector that straddled credit and production. Forms of money themselves became commodities that could be packaged and sold to an unprecedented degree. Furthermore, these financial packages frequently came with new business services, including many previously performed by other sectors (accounting, payroll, information systems, consulting). And they included consumer services that, like Fed-Ex or fast food outlets, completed the delivery of a product or saved time in acquiring a product or service (ATM machines, credit cards). Financial institutions have, at the same time, been early and crucial players in the information revolution, providing the major market for computers and software, and developing key information technologies and systems for themselves and others.[57]

Moreover, the global spread of capitalism could not be sustained without overcoming barriers to managing risk. The development of markets that commodify risk was a response to this. It is clear enough that such markets include morally repulsive speculation, appalling waste, and conspicuous inequalities. They have also added new risks.[58] Indeed, their very necessity within capitalism is a reason to question the acceptability and indeed rationality of capitalism as a social system. But all of this does not erase their importance to *capitalist* development. The deepening of financial markets and the strengthening of financial institutions did increase volatility, but they were also crucial to limiting the negative effects of the very volatility that they engendered, contributing to capitalism's overall dynamism – which of course often works through crises – and supporting the durability of the system. Like transportation, risk management adds a cost to the final product, yet it is a cost that non-financial capitalists have had to accept as part of what makes the expansion of global accumulation possible. The larger share of overall profits that has recently gone to finance certainly includes speculative and rentier gains, but it also needs to be seen as representing in part a return for finance's contribution to keeping general profits higher than they would have otherwise been.

Finally, the deepening of financial markets has played a directly imperial role. It has made it possible for the American economy to attract global savings that would otherwise not be available to it. Those capital inflows are often seen as an imperial tithe the US imposes on other countries ignoring how much of this capital comes to the US for reasons of prudent investment and profitability. In any case, they have sustained the dollar at exchange rates that would otherwise have been lower, making imports cheaper for both American consumers (thus serving to support legitimation and reduce the reproduction costs of labour), and for American industry (supporting US competitiveness, while sustaining the level of American investment and reducing the costs of empire abroad). And it is not only the relative strength of the US economy that these financial markets maintain. They also contribute in other ways to making the empire easier to manage: the inflows of capital and imports of commodities to the US have allowed global savings to be channelled and global exports to be expanded, while mobile financial markets have disciplined and promoted the neoliberal restructuring of other economies, reinforcing the barriers to any attempt to delink them from the global system.

But while finance has proven to be 'functional' for both global accumulation and the American empire, this certainly does not mean that it is not attended by contradictions, let alone grotesque inequalities and injustices. This has been seen in a series of severe disruptions in the accumulation process, above all in the third world, ranging from repeated crises in Latin America to the massive East Asian crisis of 1997-98, while Africa has been in more or less perpetual crisis over this entire period. In our view, the ubiquity of crises over the past two decades is directly linked to the particular features of the way the crisis of the developed capitalist states in the 1970s was resolved. Neoliberalism was born out of a response to that crisis, and focused mainly on stabilizing the relationship between the American economy and the other advanced capitalist countries, even though it was other countries which eventually suffered the worst long-term effects.[59] The reconstitution of the American empire in the early 1980s through higher interest rates launched the third world debt crisis, and the subsequent promotion of neoliberal globalization left a debt overhang that has made it hardly surprising that every application of 'structural adjustment' has itself proved crisis-prone. Moreover, the shift to a greater reliance on markets, and especially volatile financial markets, has meant that the advanced capitalist countries themselves have not been immune from crises. These were registered in the Savings and Loan industry collapse and the stock market crash in the US in the latter 1980s, the exchange-rate crisis in Europe in the early 90s, Japan's decade-long deflation through the 1990s (with its stock and

property asset crashes being followed by bank insolvencies), and the bursting
of the American financial bubble in 2000.

Yet each of these crises was relatively contained in terms of its depth,
duration, and tendency to spread. How are we to understand this combination of volatility and resilience? The fact that crises are now such a common
event is only half the story. Though financial crises may be inevitable, in
certain circumstances they may, as Chris Rude has emphasized, also be functional to neoliberalism's reproduction and extension.[60] Analogous to the
impact of business cycles, but in a more extreme form and involving more
direct imperial intervention, financial crises may be exploited to reduce or
remove barriers to capitalist interests that 'ordinary' market or diplomatic
pressures could not dislodge. The other half of the story, then, is that over
this same period, the capacity to cope with these crises has also grown. The
development of this capacity involves an acceptance of the fact that crises
cannot, in the present stage of capitalism, be prevented. '[P]eriodic financial
crises of one sort or another are virtually inevitable,' Robert Rubin
concluded from his period as US Secretary of the Treasury in the 1990s;
equally inevitable, in his view, was that the US state would act as 'chief of
the fire department.'[61]

The ability of the American state to manage domestic and international
economic crises is based not just on the institutional learning and development that has occurred over time within the Federal Reserve and the
Treasury (supplemented by cooperation with their counterparts across the G-
7) and in international institutions such as the BIS, the IMF and the World
Bank, but also on the strength of economic structures outside the state. This
is what Greenspan means when he says that the existence of a complex of
financial institutions and markets can act as 'a backup' to one another 'to
mitigate financial crises', citing how capital markets 'were able to substitute
for the loss of bank financial intermediation' in the 1990 recession, and how,
conversely, during the 1998 crisis 'banking replaced the capital markets.'[62] To
this one might add the way Wall Street was mobilized by the Federal
Reserve in bailing out Long Term Capital Management in the shadow of the
Asian and Russian crises. And the durability of the American banking system
(and the importance of the spreading of risk through securitization) was seen
when the bursting of the stock market bubble of the late 90s, to the surprise
of many, did not register a crisis of any significance amongst major banks.

There are many today who think that the ballooning US trade deficit
portends a much more serious crisis waiting to happen, and one that is likely
to prove unmanageable because it implicates the empire itself and its
currency. But it is also necessary to put this prospect in historical perspective.
When the balance of payments deficit first emerged in the early 1960s, it led

to what now is generally seen as an excessive panic. Robert Roosa, on the other hand, speaking from his experience of trying to address the problem within the Treasury, concluded prophetically in 1970: 'Perhaps, by conventional standards, the United States would have to become a habitual renegade … barely able to keep its trade accounts in balance, with a modest surplus on the current account, with an entrepot role for vast flows of capital both in and out, with a more or less regular increase in short-term dollar liabilities used for transaction purposes around the world.'[63]

In the 1970s it was widely assumed that the American trade deficit would necessarily lead to American protectionism. There has certainly been plenty of nationalist sentiment in the US, but rather than withdrawing from world markets the American state has consistently used the threat of protectionism to beat down foreign opposition to the global neoliberal project, thereby transforming 'nationalist impulses into strategies for opening up other nations' markets.'[64] There has been a continuous deficit since the 80s and it has not alarmed investors, who seem to think that an American deficit is not necessarily an intractable problem.

Nevertheless, that deficit has now increased dramatically and remains at stubbornly high levels, in spite of recent decreases in the value of the dollar. The current account deficit, which had averaged 1.7 per cent of GDP between 1982 and 1997, subsequently increased markedly and by 2003 had reached almost 5 per cent of GDP.[65] Does this not signal a vulnerability to foreign creditors, especially in light of what is often seen to be a structural decline in American competitiveness, especially in manufacturing?

While American foreign direct investment continued to expand through the 1990s, manufacturing at home in that decade actually grew faster – much faster – than in any of the other developed countries.[66] Furthermore, the US led the rest of the G7 in the growth of exports right through the 1980s and 1990s.[67] The US trade deficit was thus not caused by a loss of manufacturing and export capacity but by the enormous importing propensity of a US economy which experienced much greater population growth, and had a much greater proportion of its population working – and working for longer hours – than any other developed capitalist economy. Imports contributed to lowering the cost of reproducing labour and obtaining both low and high-tech inputs for business, each of which facilitated low inflation at home as well as increased exports. There were, of course, particular sectors that were hit hard by the restructuring of American industry, but the overall picture has been one of a relatively strong capitalist economy which, while increasingly unequal and exploitative, has in overall terms held its own in exports, while being able to import ever more by virtue of its relative financial strength.

In considering whether the inflow of capital implies that the US economy is vulnerable to capital flight, it is once again important to note that over the last decade the inflows did not come in just as compensation to 'cover' the deficit, as imagined by those focusing exclusively on international trade statistics. The inflow of capital was mainly the product of investors being attracted by the comparative safety, liquidity and high returns that come with participating in American financial markets and the American economy generally. The dollar stayed at relatively high levels until recently because of that inflow of capital, and it was the high dollar that allowed American consumers and businesses to import foreign goods cheaply. Lately the inflow has mainly come from central bankers abroad, padding their foreign exchange reserves and limiting the decline in the value of the dollar relative to their own currencies.

All this precisely reflects how the new imperialism has come to differ from the old one. While financial markets in the old pre-world War I imperialism were quite developed in terms of the size of capital flows, they generally took the form of long-term portfolio investment, much of it moving only one way, from the imperial centres to the periphery. In contrast, international markets in short-term securities today are massive and, in the absence of the gold standard, it is American Treasury bills that stand as the world's monetary reserves. As well, the old imperialism limited the extent of manufacturing in the periphery, while the division of labour in the new imperialism has, by way of foreign investment and outsourcing, included the expansion of manufacturing in the third world (though cross-country variation is very substantial, 80 per cent of third-world exports by value are now manufactured products). This has not only contributed to the American trade deficit but as the trade surpluses, especially in south-east Asia, have been recycled into capital flows to the US, this has also contributed to making the imperial power itself, remarkably, a debtor in relation to some third-world countries. Yet at the same time these very developments sustain the American economy's ability to have privileged access both to the world's savings and to cheaper goods.

A major speculative run on the dollar is, of course, not impossible, but the form that the globalization of capitalism now takes makes this less rather than more likely. Global savings outside the US are now some $5 trillion, and as these savings are increasingly integrated into global financial markets and therefore available to the US, it only takes 10 per cent of those savings to cover a US trade deficit of $500 billion.[68] This makes that deficit look more manageable. The largest holders of the dollar in Asia and Europe (the respective central banks) are in any case anxious to block the dollar's collapse because this would threaten their exports to the US, and because it would devalue the dollar assets they hold.

The global economy has developed with and through the dollar as the dominant currency, and there is no evidence to date that the only other remotely serious candidate, the Euro, is about to replace the dollar in this respect. As of 2002, 65 per cent of central bank foreign exchange reserves were in dollars, as compared with only 15 per cent in Euros; the dollar was used in over 90 per cent of transactions in foreign exchange trading, as compared with under 38 per cent in which the Euro was used; almost 90 per cent of over-the-counter derivatives transactions globally involved the dollar, compared with only 42 per cent involving the Euro.[69] This is, however, primarily not an economic issue but an imperial one – and neither Europe nor Japan has shown either the will or the capacity to displace the US from its leading role in the capitalist world. In contrast to the old paradigm of inter-imperial rivalry, the nature of current integration into the American empire means that a crisis of the dollar is not an 'American' crisis that might be 'good' for Europe or Asia, but a crisis of the system as a whole, involving severe dangers for all. To suggest, as Arrighi does, that because the holders of American Treasury bills are now primarily in Asia we are therefore witnessing a shift in the regional balance of power, is to confuse the distribution of assets with the distribution of power.[70]

Although traditional Marxist theories of structural crises provide valid insights into the nature of these discontinuities, they sometimes tend to fetishize crises in the sense of abstracting them from history. As Arrighi once argued, the economic crisis of the late nineteenth century was rooted in a capitalism very different from that of the 1930s or the 1970s in terms of class formation, industrial and financial structures, and state capacities.[71] Clinging to the notion that the crisis of the 1970s remains with us today flies in the face of the changes that have occurred since the early 80s.[72] What kind of crisis of capitalism is it when the system is spreading and deepening, including through sponsoring another technological revolution, while the opposition to it is unable after three decades to mount any effective challenge? If crisis becomes 'the norm', this trivializes the concept and diverts us from coming to grips with apprehending the new contradictions of the current conjuncture.

We need to be careful not to try to counter the conservative conceit of the 'end of history' by renewing predictions of the implosion of global capitalism. A future beyond capitalism is possible, and increasingly necessary from the perspective of social justice and ecological sanity, but capitalism is still in the process of being made. The American state has a privileged position in today's 'making' of capitalism, albeit not an omnipotent one insofar as its rule must operate through other states. The nature of this empire – its complexity, its incompleteness especially with regards to the third world, the fact that it depends on other states and hence the social formations and class struggles within them, and the weight given in its functioning to inherently volatile financial markets – all these factors combine to create a context in which crises repeatedly occur. Yet alongside the developments that make such crises virtually inevitable has come a capacity – based on structures inside as well as outside the American state – to limit their extent, a capacity that is considerably reinforced by the relative weakness of working classes everywhere. That is, while capitalism is unable to avoid crises, it has so far proven able to manage them. This does not mean that it is no longer useful to speak of contradictions inherent in capitalism, but we must be careful not to make too much of their consequences unless they take the form of class contradictions that raise challenges to both capital (in terms of whether it can adapt and respond) and labour (in terms of whether it can develop the political capacity to build on the openings provided). We must dispense with a notion of 'crisis' as something that leads capitalism to unravel on its own; our theories of crisis must be politicized to integrate the responses of both states and class actors.

The openings for radical change in the present era of capitalism will generally revolve around problems of political legitimacy rather than any sudden economic collapse. In the third world, the neoliberal restructuring of states to support global accumulation has not led to coherent patterns of internal development. The pressure to open up their economies leaves these countries extremely vulnerable to financial crises, given the lack of depth of their financial institutions. The 'new financial architecture' promoted by the American Treasury after the 1997-98 financial crises to require transparency and accountability in the new market economies came to look increasingly hypocritical and implausible as a spate of scandals hit Wall Street. This has tended to delegitimate both the empire itself and those third world states, exacerbated by foreign takeovers of third world banking sectors. The restructuring of other states through direct military intervention, as in the case of Iraq, not to mention the unlimited 'war on terrorism' makes imperial rule more and more visible, and less and less perceived as legitimate.

In the developed countries, neoliberalism has also weakened those dimensions of the state that address legitimation; and as pressures mount in Europe for further 'reforms', the fact that this must be done without the US economy's luxury of access to global savings only intensifies the degree of exploitation that must be achieved in those countries. The American state depends on other states to develop popular backing for its imperial role, and this is becoming increasingly difficult for those states to secure. The economic costs of empire at home are correspondingly higher as popular forces abroad limit the ability of other states to share the military, economic and rhetorical burdens of empire. Meanwhile measures taken inside the US to secure support for this burden by creating paranoia and suppressing dissent (as in the Patriot Acts) are subverting the very freedoms the US is supposed to be fighting for – and this could become a major focus of debate inside the US itself. This might even coalesce with resentment at home as well as abroad against the instabilities and tribulations that volatile financial markets bring to people's daily lives.

The Left will not, however, go far in creating political openings out of such contradictions by waxing nostalgic about a previous golden age of capitalism, when empire was apparently beneficent and finance allegedly repressed. That the US state was not seen as imperial, and finance was not actually repressed, when the world's working-class movements were strong is part of the unfortunate legacy that we have had to contend with in recent decades. That is why, in trying to analyze the nature of global finance and American empire today, we began by tracing the actual historical process that brought us here. The way out of global capitalism and American empire will not be found in a return to a reformism modeled on the post-war order. The fact that the globalization of capitalism has left virtually no national bourgeoisies for labour to ally with, and few divisions to exploit between finance and industry, helps make the case for struggles at the level of the national state that are anti-capitalist as well as anti-imperial. While we cannot rely on renewed inter-imperial rivalries or financial crises spiralling out of control to clear the way to social transformation, the openings provided by the problems of neoliberal and imperial legitimacy provide an ample terrain for the development of new political strategies that do fundamentally challenge capitalist social relations.

NOTES

We wish to thank Greg Albo, Patrick Bond, Dick Bryan, Robert Cox, Dan Crow, Gérard Duménil, Travis Fast, David Harvey, Eric Helleiner, Colin Leys, Mike Lebowitz, Eric Newstadt, Chris Rude, Alfredo Saad-Filho, Donald Swartz, Bill Tabb and Alan Zuege for their comments on earlier drafts of this essay, as well as all those who participated in the Comparative Political Economy 'Empire Seminars' at York University.

1   Richard Grasso 1997, quoted in L. Seabrooke, *US Power in International Finance*, New York: Palgrave, 2001, p. 151.
2   'Today, there are no more worlds to find. Upon us is the responsibility never laid before on a people – building the world's capital for all time to come'. John DeWitt Warner 1898, quoted in André Drainville, *Contesting Globalization: Spaces and Places in the World Economy*, London: Routledge,

2004, p. 65.

3   Eric Helleiner, *States and the Reemergence of International Finance*, Ithaca: Cornell University Press, 1994. p. 3.

4   P. Volcker and T. Gyohten, *Changing Fortunes: The World's Money and the Threat to American Leadership*, New York: Times Books, 1992, p. 288.

5   S. Battilossi, 'Introduction: International Banking and the American Challenge in Historical Perspective', in S. Battilossi and Y. Cassis, eds., *European Banks and the American Challenge*, Oxford: Oxford University Press, 2002, p. 27.

6   For our understanding of the specific nature of the American empire today and a detailed account of its historical evolution, see Panitch and Gindin, 'Global Capitalism and American Empire', *Socialist Register 2004*, London: Merlin, 2003.

7   M. Hudson, *Super Imperialism: The Origins and Fundamentals of U.S. World Dominance*, Second Edition, London: Pluto, 2003. The policies the American state had adopted at the end of World War I, insisting on the repayment by its allies of its war loans, made the latter dependent on the German state meeting the heavy reparations payments imposed upon it – and at the same time made all the European states dependent on the loans of New York bankers to meet these obligations.

8   'An American Proposal', *Fortune Magazine,* May, 1942, pp. 59-63.

9   T. Ferguson, 'From Normalcy to New Deal, Industrial Structure, Party Competition and American Public Policy in the Great Depression,' *International Organization*, 38(1), 1984; Helleiner, *States and the Reemergence*, p. 31.

10   L. Seabrooke, *US Power in International Finance*, New York: Palgrave, 2001, p. 53. Seabrooke goes on to say: 'The rejection of capital controls on the dollar provides an obvious example of how Washington's and Wall Street's *interactive embeddedness* impacted upon the framework of international finance'. But 'embeddedness' in this sense, meant the very opposite of the repression of finance, let alone the decommodification of social relations that Polanyi meant by the term. On this, see H. Lacher, 'Embedded Liberalism, Disembedded Markets: Reconceptualizing the Pax Americana', *New Political Economy*, 4(3), November, 1999.

11   These are the words of W.F. Duisenberg, the first head of the European Central Bank, looking back on the occasion of the 50th anniversary of the Marshall Plan, in the context of recalling that 'before receiving that aid each recipient country had to sign a bilateral pact with the US … Along with the carrot thus came the stick. In many ways this is similar to the approach followed in later years by the International Monetary Fund in its macroeconomic adjustment programs.' Speech at dinner held by the President of the Netherlands Bank and the Bank for International Settlements, Washington, D.C., May 15, 1997.

12   In any case, the IMF was staffed with officials who shared the views of the US Treasury and thus employed the 'conditionality' of macroeconomic austerity from the beginning. See the opening chapters of M. Harmon, *The British*

Labour Government and the IMF Crisis, London: Macmillan, 1997. On 'offsetting financing' see Helleiner, *States and the Reemergence*, 1994, p. 61.

13   *The Political Economy of American Foreign Policy*, Report of a Study Group sponsored by the Woodrow Wilson Foundation and the National Planning Association, New York: Holt & Co., 1955, p. 213.

14   C.P. Kindleberger, *International Money: A Collection of Essays*, London: Allen & Unwin, 1981, p. 103.

15   R. Chernow, *The House of Morgan: An American Banking Dynasty and the Rise of Modern Finance*, New York: Simon and Schuster, 1990, p. 402; C. Geisst, *Wall Street: A History*, New York: Oxford University Press, 1997, p. 272.

16   'In reality, the Banking Act of 1933 … did the embryo US investment banks, operating (until then) mostly as subsidiaries of commercial banks, a big favour. As independent entities they were able to create and mould the business free from the restraints of the traditional slow-moving commercial banking culture. Put simply the US investment banks wrote the rules while everyone else … was busy trying to work out what investment banking was all about! With such a head start, it is hardly surprising that they remain so dominant.' (T. Golding, *The City: Inside the Great Expectations Machine*, London: Pearson Education, 2001). On the expertise of US banks in 'project financing' (going back to the role they began to play for oil companies in the 1930s), see R.C. Smith and I. Walter, *Global Banking*, New York: Oxford University Press, 1997.

17   US Bureau of Economic Analysis, National Income and Product Accounts, Table 6.16D. http://www.bea.doc.gov

18   R. Rubin (with Jacob Weisberg), *In an Uncertain World: Tough Choices from Wall Street to Washington*, New York: Random House, 2003, p. 81.

19   R. Germain, *The International Organization of Credit*, Cambridge: Cambridge University Press, 1997, p. 82.

20   Most theorists of 'hegemony', with their focus on consent and coercion among states, never quite capture the American penetration that structured this active participation. Poulantzas' notion of American 'penetration' is much richer, yet to the extent that American direct investment is crucial to his analysis, it does not explain the fact that Europe was already well-integrated into the American project before the wave of American investment that began in the mid-fifties.

21   Quoted in Hudson, *Super Imperialism*, p. 327, italics added. Kindleberger was one of the few economists in the 1960s who questioned the significance of the balance of payments crisis in the US, arguing that the deficit largely reflected the American supply of financial intermediary services through borrowing short term capital and lending long in terms of foreign direct investment – a 'trade in liquidity profitable to both sides'- rather than a trade deficit or over-investment abroad as was commonly understood. Kindleberger, *International Money*, p. 43.

22   Seabrooke, *US Power*, p. 68.

23   R. Sylla, 'United States Banks and Europe: Strategy and Attitudes', in S. Battilossi and Y. Cassis, eds., *European Banks and the American Challenge*,

Oxford: Oxford University Press, 2002, p. 62.

24   M. Moran, *The Politics of the Financial Services Revolution*, London: Macmillan, 1991.

25   The calculations in this paragraph are derived from 'Flow of Fund Accounts 1975-84, *Federal Reserve Board,* September, 2003; 'International Operations of US Banks', *Federal Reserve Board Bulletin,* 84/6, June, 1998; and 'International Capital Markets September 1998 – Annex V', International Monetary Fund, October, 1998. See also B. Cohen, *In Whose Interest?*, New Haven: Yale University Press, 1986, pp. 21-31.

26   See L. Panitch, *Working Class Politics in Crisis*, London: Verso, 1986, chs 4-6.

27   G. Arrighi, 'The Social and Political Economy of Global Turbulence', *New Left Review*, 20, 2003, pp. 35-6.

28   See Joanne Gowa, *Closing the Gold Window: Domestic Politics and the End of Bretton Woods*, Ithaca: Cornell University Press, 1983, esp. pp. 147, 166.

29   L. Panitch and C. Leys, *The End of Parliamentary Socialism*, Second Edition, London: Verso, 2001, chs. 5, 6.

30   Quoted in Gowa, p. 129.

31   P. Gowan, *The Global Gamble: Washington's Faustian Bid for Global Dominance*, London: Verso, 1999, p. 33.

32   Bank for International Settlements (BIS), *Annual Reports*, 1979, p. 3.

33   Geisst, *Wall Street*, p. 320.

34   P. Volcker, 'The Triumph of Central Banking?' Per Jacobssen Lecture, The Per Jacobsen Foundation, Washington, D.C., September 23, 1990, p. 5.

35   As a Federal Reserve paper later exulted: 'In the early 60s, the Federal Reserve was little known outside of the financial services industry and university economics departments. Twenty years later Fed Chairman Paul Volcker was one of the most recognized names in American public life.' M. Goodfriend, 'Monetary Policy Comes of Age: A Twentieth Century Odyssey', FRB of Richmond, *Economic Quarterly*, 83(1), Winter, 1997, p. 1. What follows is partly based on our personal interview with Volcker in March 2003, and draws as well on J. Woolley, *Monetary Politics: The Federal Reserve and the Politics of Monetary Policy*, Cambridge: Cambridge University Press, 1984, pp. 102-5; P. Johnson, *The Government of Money: Monetarism in Germany and the United States*, Ithaca: Cornell University Press, 1998; and C. Rude, 'The Volcker Monetary Policy Shocks: A Political-Economic Analysis', unpublished paper, Department of Economics, New School University, January, 2004.

36   Volcker, 'The Triumph', p. 5.

37   Alan Greenspan, 'Rules vs. discretionary monetary policy', Stanford University, Stanford, California, September 5, 1997, .

38   Quoted in Johnson, *The Government of Money*, p. 178.

39   J. Hawley, 'Protecting Capital From Itself: US Attempts to Regulate the Eurocurrency System', *International Organization*, 38(1), Winter, 1984.

40   Helleiner, *States and the Reemergence*, pp. 101-21.

41   Panitch and Leys, *The End of Parliamentary Socialism*, chs 4-6.

42   Seabrooke, *US Power*, p. 105.

43   Volcker, *Changing Fortunes*, p. 167.

44   This interpretation has been confirmed by our personal interviews with senior executives of the American auto corporations as well as with Paul Volcker. For the UK case, see C. Leys, 'Thatcherism and British Manufacturing: A Question of Hegemony', *New Left Review*, 151, 1985 (also based on interviews with industry leaders).

45   R. Guttman, *How Credit Shapes the Economy*, New York: Sharpe, 1994, p. 334.

46   Quoted in John B. Taylor, 'Changes in American Economic Policy in the 1980s: Watershed or Pendulum Swing?', *Journal of Economic Literature*, Vol.. XXXIII (June 1995), p. 778.

47   See J. Grahl, 'Notes on Financial Integration and European Society', paper presented to 'The Emergence of a New Euro-Capitalism?' conference, Marburg, Oct. 11-12, 2002, published in M. Beckmann, H.-J. Bieling and F. Deppe, *Euro-Kapitalismus und globale politische Ökonomie*, Hamburg, VSA Verlag, 2003, p. 1. By the end of the 70s, foreign exchange transactions were already ten times higher than that of trade, although this represented only a taste of the explosive growth to come.

48   D. Bryan et al., 'Financial Derivatives and Marxist Value Theory', School of Economics and Political Science Working Papers, University of Sydney, December, 2000.

49   See Adam Tickell, 'Unstable Futures: Controlling and Creating Risks in International Money', *Socialist Register* 1999, esp. pp. 249-51.

50   F.S. Mishkin, *The Economics of Money, Banking and Financial Markets*, Boston: Addison Wesley, 2000, p. 41.

51   A. Berger et al.., 'The Transformation of the US Banking Industry', *Brookings Papers on Economic Activity*, Vol. 1995, No. 2, 1995, p. 57.

52   M. Lewis, *Liar's Poker*, New York: Penguin, 1989, pp. 35-6.

53   J. Grahl, 'Globalized Finance: The Challenge to the Euro', *New Left Review*, 8, 2001, pp. 43-4. On the growth of American investment banks abroad, see R.C. Smith, *The Global Bankers*, New York: Plume 1990, pp. 45-6; Thomson Financial (http://www.thomson.com) offers the best data on these banks in mergers and acquisitions.

54   L. Panitch and S. Gindin, 'Rethinking Crisis', *Monthly Review*, 54(6), 2002; Panitch and Gindin, 'American Imperialism'..

55   See Angus Maddison, *The World Economy, A Millennial Perspective*, Paris: OECD, 2001, esp. p. 265.

56   G. Duménil and D. Lévy, 'The Profit Rate: Where and How Much Did It Fall? Did it Recover? (USA 1948-2000)', *Review of Radical Political Economy*, 34, 2002; G. Duménil and D. Lévy, 'Neoliberal Dynamics – Imperial Dynamics', Cepremap, Modem, Paris, 2003; M.J. Webber and D.L. Rigby, *The Golden Age Illusion,* New York: Guilford Press, 1996.

57   L. Klein, C. Saltzman and V. Duggal, 'Information, Technology and Productivity: The Case of the Financial Sector', *Survey of Current Business*, August, 2003; Berger et al., 'The Transformation'.

58   See Tickell, 'Unstable Futures', esp. pp. 251-7.

59   This was an outcome overdetermined by the fact that the American state in
      the post-war era had allowed European and Japanese reconstruction to take
      place via the kind of export-led development that built on and sustained the
      internal coherence of their domestic economies, while countries in the
      developing world (which had registered only as a secondary concern among
      the architects of Bretton Woods and later received no comparable assistance
      to Marshall Aid) had much more limited space and fewer possibilities to
      establish their own internal coherence. Attempting to create such internal
      coherence was out of the question for most developing countries, pressured
      and tempted as they have been to accept the promise of access to already
      developed technologies, rich markets and ready finance. If this was so even
      under the import substitution industrialization strategies permitted in the
      Bretton Woods era, it was all the more so under neoliberalism.

60   See Chris Rude, 'The Role of Financial Discipline in Industrial Strategy' in
      this volume.

61   R. Rubin, *In an Uncertain World*, pp. 213-5.

62   A. Greenspan, 'Mr. Greenspan asks whether efficient financial markets
      mitigate financial crisis', Remarks before the Financial Markets Conference of
      the Federal Reserve Bank of Atlanta, Sea Island Georgia, *BIS Quarterly
      Review*, 114, 1999, http://www.bis.org/index.htm.

63   Quoted in Hudson, *Super Imperialism*, p. 319.

64   C. Scherrer, 'Double Hegemony? State and Class in American Foreign
      Economic Policymaking', *American Studies*, 46(4), 2001.

65   *Economic Report of the President 2004*, Table B-1; US Bureau of Economic
      Analysis, *op cit.*, Table 4.1.

66   Manufacturing did of course grow faster in Asia, but the US maintained an
      impressive record vis-à-vis Europe and Japan. According to a US Department
      of Labor report, the average annual rate of growth in manufacturing between
      1990 and 2001 was 3.0 per cent in the US but only 2.2 per cent in France, 1.3
      per cent in Italy, 0.4 per cent in the UK, 0.3 per cent in Germany and 0.2 per
      cent in Japan. E.L. Chao, *A Chartbook of International Labour Comparisons:
      United States, Europe, Asia*, US Department of Labour, May, 2003, p. 21.

67   See World Trade Organization, *Trade Statistics, Historical Series*, August, 2003,
      available at www.wto.org. Note, however, that since 1998 there has been a
      lag in US exports in good part due to the relatively slower economic growth
      in Europe..

68   *World Development Indicators*, http://www.devdata.worldbank.org/dataonline/.

69   This data is derived from the BIS 2003 *Annual Report* and the BIS *Quarterly
      Review*, September, 2003.

70   G. Arrighi (with J. Moore), 'Capitalist Development in World Historical
      Perspective', in R. Albritton, M. Itoh, R. Westra and A. Zuege, eds., *Phases
      of Capitalist Development*, New York: Palgrave, 2001.

71   G. Arrighi, 'Towards a Theory of Capitalist Crisis', *New Left Review*, 111,
      1978.

72   Our analysis clearly differs in fundamental ways from Robert Brenner's *The
      Boom and the Bubble,* London: Verso, 2002. Apropos the argument being made

here, three such differences are especially important. First, while Brenner does give some historical specificity to the source of the crises of the early 70s – the limits to exit that followed the concentration of capital and the subsequent tendency to over accumulation – we argue that those limits were in fact not of a technical nature but of a political nature, as the escalation of factory as well as bank closures in the early 80s following the Volcker shock clearly shows. That is, even in analyzing 'market competition', the state must be brought into the analysis (and not only in regards to exchange rates). Second, and related to this, Brenner underestimated the capacity of the American state to restructure its domestic base, in part because he reduces the role of finance to an external, ad hoc, instrument that can only postpone 'real change'. Third, while Brenner rightly argues that an economically strong but politically weak working class could not sustain a profit squeeze in the face of capitalist restructuring, had he acknowledged that capital *did* in fact restructure and that the breaking of the working class was fundamental to that project, he might have provided a more credible interpretation of both the earlier crisis and capital's current success. But by insisting that the crisis never ended, he shifts attention away from working-class resistance as both a pivotal factor in causing the crisis and a target of its resolution at the end of the 70s and beginning of the 1980s.

THE ROLE OF FINANCIAL DISCIPLINE IN IMPERIAL STRATEGY

Christopher Rude

Financial instability has been a consistent feature of neoliberal global capitalism, and when this instability has taken the form of a major financial crisis, as it did in East Asia in 1997, the consequences for the economies involved have been severe. Economic contractions, leaving economies in ruin and populations traumatized by increases in unemployment, poverty, and inequality, have been the typical results. The liberalization and internationalization of capitalist production relations have created an economic system in which recurrent financial crises set the pace and rhythm of economic activity and change within the centre as well as at the periphery. This essay examines this financial and economic turmoil and the role that it plays under neoliberalism. It also explores the role that the state plays in regulating, but not eliminating, the turmoil. Some readers may find the argument surprising. It is that the financial instability and the economic hardship that it creates play an essential role in reproducing capitalist and imperial social relations. The financial instability is functional. It disciplines world capitalism.

We begin with a theoretical analysis. We argue that the financial turmoil is not a surface phenomenon but an expression of the way the law of value operates under neoliberalism; second, that the liberalized global financial system is not the source of the instability but has the task of managing and containing the deep-seated uncertainties that today disrupt the global accumulation process; and, third, that the financial and economic turmoil, as managed by the global financial system, reproduces capitalist and imperial social relations by disciplining and punishing subordinate classes and nations. The reproduction of capitalism and imperialism via persistent financial and economic instability is risky. If capitalism and imperialism are to be reproduced through financial turmoil, the global banking and financial system must be resilient enough to survive its own disorder, so that the subordinate classes bear the burden of the turmoil, and the banking and financial systems higher up the 'imperial chain' of national banking and financial systems must be more resilient than those lower down, so that subordinate nations and regions bear the cost. This is where the state comes in. The various national banking and financial systems are regulated and supervised and, where appropriate, supported by injections of official liquidity, in such a way that the damage caused by the turmoil is directed away from the dominant classes and the centre towards the subordinate classes and the periphery.

After examining the core features of the supervisory and regulatory regime organized under continued US domination by the early 1990s to ensure that financial and economic turmoil is managed so it extends and reproduces global capitalism, we then turn specifically to the 1997 Asian and 1998 Long-Term Capital Management (LTCM) crises to see how they affected the policies of the authorities – the G–10 central banks, G–7 ministries of finance, IMF, BIS, and other related bodies – that were responsible for managing the global economy.[1] The reforms that these authorities implemented in response to the two crises – the 'New International Financial Architecture' – did not change anything essential. The policy makers continued to believe in the rationality and efficiency of financial markets, reasserted their desire to create a fully internationalized global economy, and renewed their efforts to maintain the profitability of banking and finance. On the other hand, the Asian and LTCM crises did affect their views on the nature of neoliberal capitalism in significant ways. In particular, the policy makers came to see that financial crises were an inevitable feature of the neoliberal regime they had created and thus that the focus of their reforms should be on controlling rather than eliminating them. Contrary to those who believe neoliberalism implies a lack of regulation, moreover, the reforms that they implemented increased rather than decreased regulatory oversight of the global financial system, albeit in a decidedly neoliberal manner. In this, the authorities followed an old pattern: the liberalization and internationalization of capitalist production relations during the neoliberal period have always been accompanied by nearly continuous re-regulation of the global financial system in response to its recurrent financial crises.

The banking regulation, supervision, and lender-of-last-resort policies that have been in place since the early 1990s, and that were strengthened in the wake of the Asian and LTCM crises, have played a role in maintaining global capitalism under US domination as important as the role played by local police forces, or by the United States' military in Kosovo, Afghanistan, Iraq, and elsewhere. And, it is precisely because of the central role the of US financial authorities in the making of these policies as well as because the US banking and financial system is the strongest and most resilient in the world that, as we note in conclusion, the United States not only has the capacity to sustain its own massive current account deficit but also to reproduce its position at the top of the imperial chain.

THEORETICAL CONSIDERATIONS: FINANCIAL TURMOIL, RISK MANAGEMENT AND NEOLIBERAL DISCIPLINE

Financial crises and the economic contractions that follow are not haphazard events. Financial crises occur because imbalances build up between the financial system and the underlying macroeconomy – imbalances between stocks of financial assets and liabilities, on the one hand, and flows of national income, on the other – and they occur when these macroeconomic financial stock/income flow imbalances become unsustainable.[2] The 'function' of financial crises and the economic contractions that they create is to remove these imbalances between the financial system and its macroeconomic 'monetary base.' Under neoliberalism, there is a greater tendency for imbalances of this sort to appear. Stating the issue in classical Marxist terms, since the equity and debt instruments that make up the financial system exist as fictitious capitals – as discounted future expected profit streams – the financial and economic turmoil that characterizes neoliberal global capitalism expresses itself, in the first instance, in an increase in the tendency for the financial markets to over- and under-estimate future profits. The damage caused is not just economic bubbles but also the misallocation of capital.

But why has this occurred?[3] The internationalization of the circuits of capital has created a truly global economy, but not abolished the nation state. Due to the continued existence of a system of territorially sovereign national states and thus the continued use of different national currencies as mediums of exchange within each national territory, intrusions of essentially local factors – national currencies affected by domestically determined interest rates – disrupt the movement of capital through its global circuits. Regardless of whether it exists in its money, commodity, or productive form at the time, a capital is denominated in the currency of the nation whose space it occupies for the moment and thus must change its currency denomination as it moves from one national territory to the next. The point we are making is simple. A US multinational corporation operating a factory in Brazil, for example, pays its local labour force and purchases any locally produced intermediate products using Real. Not only that: the whole enterprise is accounted for in Real, including the depreciation of the capital stock. Inputs produced in another nation are accounted for in the currency of that nation.

Products sold locally earn Real; those sold elsewhere earn the local currency. A factory operating in another country is accounted for in the currency of that country. One of the tasks of the treasury department of the home office in the United States is to translate the foreign activities of the firm into US dollars in such a way as to maximize the firm's profits on a global basis. The financial assets that trade on the Euro and other external financial markets are the sole exception to this 'local currency' rule. But this is why they were created: they exist to help multinational corporations hedge their exposures and thus maximize their global profits in their home currencies.

Due to the uneven movement of capital through its global circuits, moreover, these nationally specific monetary/financial obstacles are different in different parts of the globe – and are subject to change. The financial obstacles that disrupt the global circuits of capital are themselves discontinuous as a result, because they are contingent and uncertain. Their contingency and uncertainty, in turn, makes the movement of global capital through its circuits contingent and uncertain. In the new neoliberal global economy there is thus no longer a single money commodity, as there was under the nineteenth century gold standard, functioning as a universal standard of value throughout the global economy. Nor is there a single state-backed national currency that can fulfill the same role, as the US dollar did under the Bretton Woods system until the early 1970s. Instead, there is a multiplicity of different national currency commodities that circulate internationally at changing rates of exchange against each other, and a parallel multiplicity of domestically determined and constantly changing interest rates – and this manifold of changing exchange and interest rates is itself continually being restructured by the foreign exchange and interest rate derivatives that make up the global money market.[4] As a result, the transformation of socially necessary labour time into prices of production has become a radically contingent process, since the monetary values in terms of which economic value is measured are different in different parts of the globe, change relative to one another across monetary areas as well as over time within each monetary space, and are also being continually transmuted through the use of derivatives. Deep-seated, persistent financial and economic turmoil is therefore a characteristic feature of neoliberal global capitalism because of the resulting increase in the uncertainty of the global accumulation process – which in turn increases the uncertainty of the profits of capital as a whole.

These contingencies and uncertainties exist because of the particular way in which capitalism became structured towards the end of the twentieth century as a world economic system divided into nation states, organized into three imperial or sub-imperial blocs, centred on the economies and currencies of United States, Europe, and Japan.[5] As the internationalization of the circuits of capital has taken place primarily among the countries of the centre, these contingencies and uncertainties arise chiefly in the centre rather than in the periphery: a capital faces greater uncertainties as it moves between any of the three major imperial-currency blocs than it does when it circulates within a single imperial-currency bloc.[6] But we must not hold the 'liberal-ized' global financial system itself primarily responsible for the financial turmoil that this situation tends to produce. The opposite is in fact the case: the global financial system has the responsibility for managing and containing the financial contingencies and uncertainties that disrupt the global accu-mulation process.

This last point is very important. The financial system still has to mediate between savers and investors, and to that end, global financial capital continues to fulfill the traditional tasks of collecting the idle monies in the hands of individual capitals, of bringing these individual money capitals together to form what David Harvey has called the 'common capital of the capitalist class',[7] and of allocating them to the most profitable investment outlets wherever they may be. Today, however, the financial system also has to manage the spatial and inter-temporal financial uncertainties that intrude into the operation of the law of value. The financial contingencies that global capital has to contend with as it moves through its circuits call for the use of the risk management techniques that the global financial system now provides, and the success of the risk management strategies employed affects the performance of the underlying economy fully as much as the way the aggregate global social capital is allocated.

The resulting transformation of the day-to-day operation of domestic and international financial markets has been profound. Indeed, most of the features of the global economy today that are alluded to under the rubric of 'financialization' can be explained in terms of the competitive struggle between individual capitals to profit from the global economy's need to hedge against the financial contingencies that would otherwise disrupt the international circulation of capital. These include dramatic increases in the trading volumes of both exchange-traded and over-the-counter securities; securitization (the transformation of mortgages and other apparently non-marketable assets into marketable securities); the extensive use of derivatives; hedge funds; increases in the financial activities of ostensibly non-financial corporations; the rise of the large multinational financial conglomerates that now dominate the global financial system; and the increase in the proportion of the social surplus transferred to finance.

Trading activity has risen in the stock, bond, foreign exchange, and money markets in every country because trading allows an individual company to pass onto another company a risk that it does not want to assume, and thus permits the spreading of the risk to whoever wishes to bear it. The advantages of securitization are similar. Securitization permits a bank to exchange the mortgages, car loans, credit cards, etc. it creates for cash or other securities. Derivatives – securities whose values are defined in terms of the performance of other securities – are used extensively because they allow a company to bridge the gaps between different spatial and inter-temporal uncertainties and thus allow it to restructure these exposures in any way it sees fit. Hedge funds exist to absorb the risks that the large multinational financial conglomerates do not want to bear. Multinational non-financial corporations engage in financial activities to manage their own exposures because it is less costly for them to do it themselves. In addition to other factors making for the concentration and centralization of capital, large financial conglomerates dominate the global financial system because their size and global scope allow them to transfer and so diversify their risks internally, using their own risk measurement and allocation systems to do so as efficiently as possible. And finance absorbs so much of the social surplus simply because its risk management activities are needed.

Several factors, however, limit the capacity of the international financial system to manage the risks of the global accumulation process. First, financial crises no longer function, as they did under the gold standard or the Bretton Woods system, fully to remove the imbalances that arise between a country's financial system and its monetary base. Since there is no stable monetary unit of value against which the fictitious capital values can be measured, the manner in which a financial crisis is resolved depends on the response of the monetary base. Changes in exchange rates and interest rates can alter the underlying macroeconomy so as to lessen or intensify a crisis or to keep it contained in a particular part of the globe – or they can create a financial contagion that spreads the turmoil elsewhere. The financial and economic turmoil thus never really disappears but assumes an essentially protean form, so that one crisis transmutes into the next. Second, the spatial and inter-temporal discontinuities that disrupt the international circulation of capital have a particularly profound effect on the circulation of global financial capital itself. The international financial system has to manage its own uncertainties as well as those of commercial and industrial capital – uncertainties that in any case essentially are irresolvable. Third, the competition between individual capitals to profit from the global economy's risk management needs cannot but lead to misallocations of these risks that increase the uncertainty of the accumulation process. Financial institutions can and do underestimate the risks they are assuming and thus take on too much risk relative to their capacity to manage it. The search for profits tempts them to underestimate the risks in whole regions of the globe and thus to misallocate their capital. Global financial capital therefore has a task that it will inevitably mismanage. This is why financial crises appear. Imbalances arise between the financial system and the underlying macroeconomy because the financial system cannot always contain the risks it is supposed to contain, and because competition leads individual financial capitals to take on risks they cannot bear.

Here is where the state comes in. The international economic system through which global capital moves as it completes its circuits is not just discontinuous; it is also fundamentally hierarchical. The national monetary spaces through which a capital circulates exist in relations of domination and subordination. The multiplicity of national currencies and domestically determined interest rates that disrupt the circulation of capital form a strict hierarchy, an 'imperial chain' of more powerful and less powerful national banking and financial systems. The liberalization and internationalization of capitalist production relations have not abolished the hierarchical and antag-onistic relationships that exist between the centre and the periphery of the world economy, between the imperial powers within the centre, and between capital and labour worldwide. They have simply altered the way in which these structures of domination manifest themselves.

The introduction of financial contingencies into the operation of the law of value has created a capitalism characterized by a deep-seated and persis-tent financial and economic turbulence, and in doing so, it has changed the way in which capitalism reproduces itself. The turmoil is not just an economic phenomenon. It both shapes and is shaped by the capitalist and imperial social relationships that constitute the world economic system and is thus essentially political. The turmoil maintains and restructures capitalist and imperial social relationships by disciplining and punishing the subordi-nate classes or nations involved just as surely as do the local police and the military. The weapons deployed are not billy clubs and bombs but financial crises and the ensuing stagnations.

Neoliberalism is not just an effort to privatize the reproduction of capi-talist and imperial social relations production, an attempt to turn over to the private sector many functions that had previously been considered legitimate functions of the state. Neoliberalism is a truly radical project to establish a kind of social control very different from that employed during the 'Golden Age' of Keynesian economics and US 'New Deal' imperialism. The disci-pline used during the Golden Age is probably best understood in terms of Gramsci's concept of hegemony, which he defined as consent plus force. This was a structure of domination where the dominant classes (in the centre if not in the periphery) and the dominant imperial power (the United States) were willing to make sacrifices of an 'economic-corporatist' kind. The subordinated classes and nations could consent to their subordination provided they could believe their short-term material interests would be met. State violence was still used when the consensus broke down, but as long as the consensus was maintained, the struggles that did occur were protracted polit-ical/ideological/cultural wars of position that took place in the first instance within the institutions of civil society.[8] The neoliberal project establishes a different form of domination, one where financial instability and economic insecurity replace compromise and consensus. The mechanisms of social control are much more direct. Global capital, under continued US domina-tion, can maintain the subordination of the dominated classes and nations using what amounts to a financial and economic violence, backed up by mili-tarized police action when economic intimidation breaks down. The manipulation of cultural symbols by the global mass media can fill any residual need for legitimacy.[9]

The introduction of new financial contingencies into the operation of the law of value has therefore given the global financial system new responsibil-ities. As the financial infrastructure of a capitalist and imperial world system, it must manage financial and economic risk and turmoil in such a way that they reproduce the hierarchical relations between the centre and periphery, between the imperialist powers within the centre, and between global capital and global labour. The global financial system must therefore have the crisis management capacities needed to contain and shape risk, and to calm and shape turmoil when it erupts into financial crises and recessions, and it does these things in very specific ways. The imperial chain of national banking and financial systems that make up the global financial system must be so orga-nized as to reproduce itself through recurrent financial crises. In this way, the burden of a crisis will not be borne by financial capital in the form of lower profits, bank failures, and insolvencies but by the subordinate classes in the form of unemployment, poverty, and greater inequality. This also means that the banking and financial systems higher up the imperial chain must have greater risk management capacities than those lower down. The 'ideal' neoliberal global economy is one where all of the harm caused by the insta-bility is transferred to the dominated classes and the periphery.[10]

CAPITAL'S REGULATORY REGIME

The policy regime that accomplishes all this is surprisingly simple. The core features of neoliberal global capitalism's supervisory and regulatory regime are, first, internationally uniform risk-based capital standards, devel-oped by the BIS's Committee on Banking Supervision, that permit the large multinational financial conglomerates that dominate the international finan-cial system to set their own capital requirements based on their own internal risk models; second, the principle, also promulgated by the Basel Committee, that home countries in the centre and not host countries in the periphery have the supervisory, regulatory, and lender-of-last-resort responsibilities for multinational financial conglomerates; and third, a division of labour between the IMF and the central banks in the centre according to quite different principles than the first two, whereby the IMF resolves financial crises in the periphery by imposing austerity, while the major central banks resolve financial crises in the centre by easing credit.[11]

The US authorities took the initiative in the development of the BIS capital standards. The initiative was taken in response to the difficulties that the Latin American debt crisis caused to the US banking system, and the capital requirements were initially designed to protect a bank against its credit risks. According to the original 1988 Basel Capital Accord, all internationally active banks, regardless of where they are headquartered, must maintain a capital reserve fund equal to 8 per cent of their risk-adjusted assets. The amounts of capital that a bank must hold in reserve to back up its particular portfolio of investments increase with the credit risks associated with its investments: the credit-risk weights of each of the bank's assets are determined by prescribed formulas, and off-balance sheet as well as on-balance sheet investments are subject to the capital requirements.[12] Since less creditworthy assets have a higher risk-weight, the capital requirements force financial institutions to allocate their capital according to the credit risks of their investments. Banks are penalized for making risky investments and rewarded for making safe investments. The banks must also maintain capital reserve funds sufficiently large to insure them against insolvency in the event that their counterparties are unable to honour their commitments. The capital requirements thus aim to make each financial institution strong enough to survive its own risk-taking.

The capital requirements under the 1988 Capital Accord went into effect at the end of 1992. The Accord was amended in 1996 to incorporate the market risks arising from banks' open positions in foreign exchange and traded debt securities, equities, commodities, and options.[13] In the amended Capital Accord, banks must hold capital against both their credit and their market risks, and the overall minimum capital ratio remains at 8 per cent. An important aspect of this amendment was that, subject to strict quantitative and qualitative standards and the approval of their supervisors, banks could use their own internal risk models for measuring their market risk capital requirements. The amended Accord thus created a two-tiered system of banks. The large multinational financial conglomerates that have the resources to set up and run their own internal risk-measurement and risk-management systems are allowed to determine their own capital requirements, and are expected in principle to set aside a capital reserve fund sufficiently large to protect them from insolvency at a predetermined probability. If properly enforced, the amended capital standards also imply that the supervisory and regulatory authorities of the major capitalist states work 'hand-in-glove' with their multinational financial conglomerates on a daily basis to monitor how the conglomerates measure and thus allocate their global market risks. The smaller and less sophisticated banks, which cannot quantify their survivability in this way, have their market risks determined by the 'standard measurement method' specified in the amendment to the Accord, and thus presumably require less attention – and help – from the regulators. Many of these smaller and less sophisticated banks are of course headquartered in the periphery.

Crucial to understanding how the capital requirements function is the priority that the authorities give to the capital requirements as the first of the 'Three Pillars' of the Capital Accord relative to the other two – market disclosure and discipline, and prudential supervision and regulation.[14] The emphasis is placed on the capital requirements that rely on financial institutions' internal risk-management systems. Market and disclosure discipline comes second. The authorities de-emphasize the traditional activities of official regulators and supervisors, who actively enforce externally determined regulations. The 8 per cent capital requirement is a minimum capital ratio. A bank's supervisor may require it to maintain a higher one. But the authorities may have no need to enforce any requirement that a bank have a higher capital ratio, due to market discipline. Since a bank's capital ratio is made public, it functions as a quick and easy measure of the bank's soundness. Banks with high capital ratios have easy access to both capital and credit. The markets punish banks with low capital ratios.

As for prudential supervision and regulation, after the failure of the Bankhaus Herstatt in 1974, the G–10 central banks determined that the home country, and not the host country central bank, has the ultimate responsibility for the foreign branch of an internationally active bank.[15] Until this time, the G–10 central banks had not determined how they should share the responsibility for resolving international financial crises. The first major decision of the Basel Committee concerned how these responsibilities should be discharged under a 'Condordat' (made public in 1983) that established that no foreign banking establishment should escape supervision, that the supervision should be adequate, and that the home country rather than the host country should be responsible for supervising the foreign branch. The agreements reached in the Condordat were subsequently revised and strengthened to become the 'home country rule' of international banking supervision, according to which the home country has the supervisory, regulatory, and lender-of-last resort responsibilities, on a global consolidated basis, for the internationally active banks that are headquartered there. Thus, the authorities of the imperial powers in the centre of the global economy, who have the greatest crisis prevention and management capacities and in whose countries the multinational financial conglomerates are headquartered, have the responsibility for supervising, regulating, and maintaining the liquidity of their multinational banks and investment houses no matter where they may do their business. The authorities in the centre are thus responsible for the behaviour of the branches of their banks in the periphery and so indirectly responsible for the banking and financial systems of the periphery in so far as the interests of their banks are involved. The regulators in the periphery are responsible only for their own banks and the few foreign branches these banks may have.

This prudential supervision and regulation aspect of the Basel Accord is related as well to the division of labour mentioned above whereby the IMF stabilizes a crisis in the periphery through a structural adjustment programme, while the major central banks stabilize a crisis in the centre by a monetary easing. The purpose of the IMF's austerity in the periphery is to prevent the turmoil that originates there from spreading to the centre. The purpose of the monetary easing in the centre is to end any turmoil that may appear there – regardless of its origin. This division of labour was not the product of a formal agreement, but originated informally in the 1980s during the Latin American debt crisis, for this was when the IMF was redesigned in order to impose structural adjustment programmes on the debtor nations, and when the authorities in the United States learned to ease or extend state credit to troubled firms to counter the 1987 stock market crash and resolve the ensuing US savings and loans crisis.

The G-10 central bankers who set up the BIS capital requirements in 1988 and revised them in 1996 were certainly not thinking in terms of the law of value as they tried to cope with the uncertainties and contingencies that intrude into its operation today. Still, it is no mere coincidence that the risk-based capital requirements encourage risk taking and risk management on the part of market participants. By forcing all internationally active financial institutions to allocate their capital according to the risks of their investments, internationally uniform risk-based capital requirements have created a global financial system designed to manage the risks of the accumulation process. Internationally uniform risk-based capital requirements also require every internationally active financial institution to hold a capital reserve sufficient large so that it can survive its own risk taking. By thus laying the ground for the solvency of every financial institution by means of rules intended to relegate bank failure to a low level of probability, the BIS Capital Accord designed a global financial system that is, in principle, also resilient enough to survive its own disorder.

The G-10 central bankers gave the global financial system another noteworthy property: risk-based capital requirements force financial institutions to cut back on their lending during a financial crisis. Since equity makes up the largest part of a bank's capital, the total value of its capital is largely determined by the value of its equity in the stock market and thus will fall sharply in any financial crisis that includes a stock market crash. Meanwhile, according to the formula set up by the Basel Committee, the volatility of a financial crisis increases the measured market risks of the financial conglomerates that use their own internal risk models to determine their own capital requirements.[16] During a financial crisis, therefore, the capital requirements become more burdensome just when the available capital is most likely to decline. To meet the capital requirements, the large financial conglomerates must decrease their investments, that is, cut back on their extensions of credit. In creating a global financial system designed to manage the risks of the global accumulation process and to be resilient enough to survive its own disorder, the G-10 central bankers also designed a global banking and financial system that in stabilizing itself, destabilizes the underlying macroeconomy.

The imperial chain of national banking and financial systems is maintained by way of two-tiered market risk capital requirements, the home country rule principle, and the contrasting crisis-management policies of the IMF and the major central banks. A multinational financial conglomerate headquartered in the centre of the global economy is able to use its own internal risk models to set its own market risk capital requirements, is supervised on a global consolidated basis by a strong and resourceful regulator, who will work with the multinational firm daily to increase the efficiency of its risk measurement and allocation methods, and can count on injections of official liquidity should the bank, despite all this, need it. A smaller and less sophisticated financial institution headquartered in the periphery, by contrast, must set its market risk capital requirements using the rule-based 'standard methodology', is supervised by a weaker (and perhaps very weak) regulatory authority, and will face an IMF-imposed structural adjustment programme should a financial crisis hit its country. The market discipline created by this system is obvious: the bank headquartered in the periphery is placed at a competitive disadvantage relative to the multinational financial conglomerate.

THE ASIAN AND LTCM FINANCIAL CRISES AS TURNING-POINTS

The amended Capital Accord went into effect at the end of 1997, just as the Asian crisis was reaching its climax. That crisis and the LTCM crisis that followed in 1998 were not the first financial crises of the neoliberal period. Federal Reserve Chairman Volcker's 1979 monetary policy shock did not just end the 1970s inflation, it also precipitated a Latin American debt crisis which would burden the US financial system and the Latin American economies throughout the 1980s. The debt crisis was followed by the US stock market crash in 1987, the US Savings and Loans crisis of the late 1980s, the meltdown of the Japanese financial system and economy in the early 1990s following the bursting of Japanese stock market and real estate bubbles, the European Monetary System's crises of 1992 and 1993, and the Mexican peso crisis of 1994-95. The Asian and LTCM crises were turning-points in the history of neoliberal global capitalism, however, for at least four reasons.

First, because of their intensity and global scope. The financial turmoil that began with the devaluation of the Thai baht in July 1997 spread swiftly from Thailand to Malaysia, the Philippines, Indonesia, and the Republic of South Korea (the other countries at the centre of the crisis), leaving economic devastation in its wake.[17] By the end of 1997, the Asian financial panic pushed these economies into a steep contraction, with Indonesia experiencing the largest decline. In doing so, the Asian crisis brought to an end what had hitherto been one of the longest periods of rapid growth ever to occur in the periphery: the 'Asian miracle' of the 1980s and early 1990s.

The Asian financial panic also reduced the profits of the multinational banks and investment houses that had invested heavily in Southeast Asia and South Korea. Japanese banks were hit particularly hard. Already burdened by the nonperforming loans that had appeared on their books due to the collapse of the 'bubble economy' in the early 1990s, Japanese banks had attempted to consolidate their investments worldwide by concentrating their foreign exposures in the countries that were now at the centre of the crisis. The losses they experienced on their investments there added to their already considerable burdens. The effect was to push any recovery of the Japanese economy into the indefinite future. The harm that the Asian crisis did to the profits of the large multinational financial conglomerates also led them to reduce their exposure to the periphery more generally, and this, in turn, had an immediate adverse effect on emerging market economies worldwide – an effect made worse because the authorities in the periphery were forced to adopt contractionary fiscal and monetary policies to counter the downward pressure on their currencies. By early 1998, signs of acute financial and economic stress began to appear in Russia, Brazil, and Argentina.

Following a period of calm in the spring and early summer of 1998, the financial turmoil resurfaced in the fall when, following the Russian default in August, the collapse of the LTCM hedge fund led to panic in the very heart of the world financial system. The unwinding of the fund's highly leveraged derivative positions caused the otherwise very liquid US Treasury market, positioned at the very apex of the hierarchy of global financial markets, to freeze up, causing a potential threat to the foundation of the entire system. For a moment in the fall of 1998, therefore, with the financial systems of the periphery already in crisis and the US Treasury market, typically the deepest and most liquid financial market in the world, in disarray, the global financial system really did seem on the verge of collapse.

Second, the Asian and LTCM crises were turning-points, because they were the first financial crises fully to reveal the neoliberal nature of the turmoil. Unlike the 1980s Latin American debt crisis, the countries at the centre of the Asian crisis were following policies entirely in keeping with the precepts of neoliberal thinking. Tight fiscal and monetary policies, low inflation, and high private sector saving and investment rates characterized all of the crisis countries before the crisis broke. They had also recently liberalized both their domestic financial systems and their capital accounts, thus dismantling the mechanisms that had previously allowed them to pursue activist industrial policies without interference from the international financial system. The proximate causes of the 1980s Latin America debt crisis, the 1993 EMS crisis, and the 1994–95 peso crisis were specific actions on the part of national governments in the centre of the global economy: the 1979 Volcker money supply shocks, the high interest-rate policy adopted by the recently reunited Germany, which was inconsistent with existing EMS parities, and another round of tightening by the Federal Reserve in 1994. The Asian crisis, by contrast, was a purely private sector phenomenon, an endogenously-determined asset boom-bust cycle, involving lending by G-10 banks – mostly in the form of increasingly short-term bonds – to private borrowers in the crisis countries, who, in turn, had used the monies for increasingly speculative purposes. Unlike previous financial crises, which were widely anticipated, the Asian crisis also caught international investors by surprise, and when they suddenly became aware of size of their impending losses, they withdrew their capital from the region in a panic. In the first half of 1997, foreign capital had continued to flow into the crisis countries on a massive scale; the swing from a capital inflow to an outflow in late 1997 was over 10 per cent of the GDP of the countries involved. In contrast to previous periods of acute financial turmoil, once the Asian crisis started to unfold and spread, it took on a dynamic of its own, which no authority, the IMF included, could stop or control until it had run its course – that is, until the imbalances that had built up between the financial systems of the afflicted countries and their underlying macroeconomies had been removed.

The neoliberal origins of the LTCM crisis are equally obvious. Ahead of the Russian default the LTCM hedge fund had reportedly adopted a set of very large and highly-leveraged trading strategies, mostly through the use of derivatives, that assumed credit spreads would narrow, equities would rise, and the volatility of the financial markets would fall. In taking on these positions, the firm was not attempting to guess the future direction of the market or the underlying macroeconomy. Instead, based on a presumably rigorous statistical analysis of past price movements, LTCM's strategy aimed at arbitraging price discrepancies: it purchased securities its theoretical model suggested were underpriced and sold and 'shorted' securities its model suggested were overpriced. The large banks and investment houses that were on the other side of LTCM's trades welcomed its complex arbitrage strategies. Before the appearance of LTCM, they had used other firms to unload their risks. However, due to its reputation for high standards and sophisticated risk-management systems, as well as to its size and global reach, LTCM came to play a very special role in the international financial system: it became the place where the multinational financial conglomerates believed their most complex risks would be most expertly managed.

Following the Russian default, however, when global financial markets began to move simultaneously in the same direction, with credit spreads widening, equity markets falling, and volatility increasing in every market, LTCM began to experience losses on every front. As the firm tried to reduce its exposures, it found that the attempt to do so aggravated its difficulties. The LTCM's counterparties made its situation worse by attempting to unwind their own positions. Soon the liquidity of the credit derivative, interest rate swap, US Treasury, and other fixed income markets where LTCM had been most active began to disappear. The crisis came to a head when LTCM reportedly could not make the margin call on a large losing 'short' position in the Treasury bill futures market. Had LTCM actually defaulted, the futures market clearing house might have collapsed, in which case the Treasury bill market would have become illiquid. Under these circumstances, the Federal Reserve Bank of New York organized a private support operation for the firm in late September 1998, as it had clearly taken on more risks than it could bear. However, the global financial system did not regain its ability to manage the risks of the accumulation process until the Federal Reserve restored the system's liquidity by easing interest rates in October.

The third reason why the Asian and LTCM financial crises were historical turning-points was that the turmoil they unleashed is still very much with us. Though the LTCM-related turmoil in the centre quickly abated following the Federal Reserve's interventions, the Fed's actions had little effect on the forces that the Russian default and LTCM's demise had set in motion in the periphery, forces that would eventually lead to the floating of the Brazilian Real in January 1999 and to Argentina's depression and subsequent default in December 2001. Moreover, the interest rate reductions that ended the LTCM turmoil helped fuel what Federal Reserve Chairman Greenspan had already called the 'irrational exuberance' of the US stock market. The consequences were the stock-market-bubble-driven recovery of the US in the late 1990s and hence the recession that occurred when the 'dot.com' bubble burst in 2000. Due to decisive countercyclical action on the part of the Federal Reserve, this time in the form of another round of interest rate reductions, the ensuing recession in the United States was mild. As of this writing in the summer of 2004, however, worries abound that the Fed's easing of credit allowed the financial turmoil to transmute into yet another stock market/housing bubble, whose collapse could end the recovery in the United States.

Finally, the Asian and LTCM crises were turning-points because of their political effects. The crises did succeed in reproducing existing class and imperial social relations. By bringing the Asian miracle to a halt and pushing any recovery in Japan into the indefinite future, the way the Asian crisis was resolved reinforced the economic victory of the United States over Japan that was initially accomplished with the collapse of Japan's 'bubble economy.' If there was an economy besides the United States that benefited from the Asian crisis, it was mainland China. With the end of the 'miracle' in Southeast Asian and South Korea and with Japan mired in stagnation, China became the centre of capital accumulation in Asia, even as millions of Chinese workers and peasants became 'redundant.' But by increasing unemployment, inequality, and poverty throughout the periphery, the Asian crisis put downward pressure on wages worldwide, thus increasing the global rate of exploitation. Meanwhile, the Federal Reserve's quick and decisive action, first to organize a private support operation for LTCM and then to lower interest rates, brought the LTCM crisis to a halt well before it could have any adverse effects on the position of the United States in the global economy.

On the other hand, the Asian and LTCM crises, and the Asian crisis in particular, caused many to question the merits of the neoliberal order. Due its severity, global scope and obvious neoliberal nature, the Asian crisis delegitimized neoliberalism as an historical project for many individuals throughout the globe, and in doing so, helped to launch the 'anti-globalization' movement. As combined with the subsequent LTCM crisis, it also led many of the policy makers who were responsible for managing the global financial system, and who had hitherto been advocates of neoliberalism, to express doubts about the viability of their previous efforts. The crises destroyed any lingering beliefs they may have had that the neoliberal order was not crisis-prone, and for a time made them doubt their ability to prevent and manage the crises they now believed would inevitably occur. In view of its failure to contain the contagion stemming from the Asian crisis, they questioned in particular the crisis prevention and management capacities of the IMF.

In this atmosphere, policies that previously had been seen as either irrelevant or radical were taken seriously. Capital controls, Tobin taxes, regulations placing quantitative restrictions on financial institutions' borrowing and lending, and other similar policies that earlier had been only discussed by the critics of neoliberalism suddenly had currency. For a time, as well, calls for a new and different regulatory institution, including a 'World Financial Authority', and for an international lender-of-last-resort received serious attention.[18] As the effects of the Asian and LTCM crises receded into the background, however, with the recovery of the US economy in the late 1990s, policy makers regained confidence both in neoliberalism and in their crisis management capacities. They lost interest in more radical and far-reaching reforms and began to devise measures that would instead strengthen rather than change the existing policy regime. By the time of the G-7 summit meeting in Köln, in June 1999, the essential features of the reforms that would be implemented under the rubric of the 'New International Financial Architecture' had already been largely agreed upon. They were conservative.

THE 'NEW INTERNATIONAL FINANCIAL ARCHITECTURE'

Six principles governed the reform measures that the G-7 leaders endorsed at that time.[19] They were, first, that improved transparency and better codes of conduct would reduce the severity of future financial crises; second, that more extensive banking and financial market regulation would have the same effect; third, that the more serious informational and regulatory lapses lie in the periphery rather than in the industrialized centre; fourth, that the economies of the periphery should continue liberalizing their capital accounts, albeit subject to its proper sequencing; fifth, that the integration of the same economies into international capital markets requires them to pursue austere monetary and fiscal policies; and sixth, that the steps that had already been taken to improve the available crisis management facilities and policies were sufficient to handle future financial crises.

Central to the reform measures endorsed by the G-7 at the Köln summit meeting was the belief that insufficient information contributed significantly to the Asian and LTCM crises, and thus that 'improved information will help [financial] markets adjust more smoothly to economic developments, minimize contagion and reduce volatility.'[20] To this end, the authorities took steps to make more timely and reliable information, mostly about developing countries, available to investors, and advocated the development and implementation of codes and standards of good practice for economic, financial, and business activities. They covered codes of good practice on fiscal transparency and in monetary and financial policy, as well as the codes and standards necessary for the proper functioning of the private financial system, including accounting and auditing, bankruptcy, corporate governance, insurance, payment and settlement systems, and the organization of securities markets.

The G-7 also stressed the need for improved regulation and supervision of the monetary and financial systems in both the centre and the periphery to deal with specific problems that the two crises had revealed. In the centre, the focus was on banks' dealings with hedge funds and similar operations in commercial and investment banks (proprietary trading desks) as well as on the regulation of offshore financial centres. The authorities also advocated measures to improve the management of lending to the periphery, especially of a short-term nature, to contain the foreign financing of risky investments there. For the periphery itself, measures were adopted concerning the need to manage the risks associated with the rapid growth of domestic credit, currency and maturity mismatches of assets and liabilities, the accumulation of large short-term borrowings in foreign currency, and the valuation of collateral during episodes of asset inflation.

The proposals adopted at Köln reflected the G-7 governments' commitment to financial market internationalization and liberalization. 'Recent events in the world economy', they argued, 'have demonstrated that a strengthening of the system is needed to maximize the benefits of, and reduce the risks posed by, global economic and financial integration.' By affirming the need for further internationalization and liberalization, the G-7 saw the problem of reforming the international financial architecture as largely one of filling in certain gaps in the provision of information, implementation of codes and standards, and regulation and supervision of financial markets and institutions. They shifted the burden of reform, however, away from the industrial countries to the developing world, for this was where the more serious informational and regulatory gaps supposedly were, and where greater openness to the international capital markets was still required. To this end, 'capital account liberalization should be carried out in a careful and well-sequenced manner, accompanied by a sound and well-regulated financial sector and by a consistent macroeconomic policy framework.' Though 'the use of controls on capital inflows may be justified for a transition period as countries strengthen the institutional and regulatory environment in their domestic financial systems', more comprehensive controls on inflows 'may carry costs and should not in any case be used as a substitute for reform.' Controls on outflows, the G–7 emphasized, 'can carry even greater costs.' The same commitment also shaped the kind of macroeconomic policies they stressed developing and emerging-market economies should adopt. Because of increasing international capital mobility, they warned, 'weak macro-economic policies and financial infrastructures [in developing markets] can be penalized more severely and more suddenly by investors.'[21] The recommendation was strong: developing and transition economies should have tight monetary and fiscal policies leading to low wage and final goods inflation and exchange rate policies that lead to sustainable current account deficits and external debt burdens.

The depth and severity of the Asian turmoil, coupled with the apparent inability of the authorities to contain it or its contagion, led to the recognition that the Asian crisis was new, and thus that the policies that had been designed to manage 'current account' crises in the periphery were inappropriate to deal with the 'capital account' crises that were the product of internationalized financial markets. The IMF introduced new and expanded lending facilities, and advocated orderly 'standstill' and 'workout' agreements for debtor countries and their creditors. To increase the involvement of the private sector in the prevention and management of emerging-market financial crises, the G–7 also advocated 'the use of market based tools ... aimed at facilitating adjustment to shocks through the use of innovative financial arrangements, including private market-based contingent credit lines in emerging countries and roll-over options in debt instruments.' They also stressed the importance 'of collective action clauses in sovereign debt contracts, along with other provisions that facilitate creditor coordination and discourage disruptive action' and encouraged 'efforts to establish sound and efficient bankruptcy procedures and strong judicial systems.' Finally, they warned that the resolution of a financial crisis in the periphery might require sacrifice on the part of foreign creditors to the periphery. The G–7 were quite explicit about the risks involved. They indicated that 'reducing net debt payments to the private sector can potentially contribute to meeting a country's immediate financing needs and reducing the amount of finance to be provided by the official sector;' and that since in 'exceptional cases, it may not be possible for the country to avoid the accumulation of arrears, IMF lending into arrears may be appropriate if the country is seeking a cooperative solution to its payment difficulties with its creditors'; and that in such exceptional cases, 'countries may impose capital and exchange controls as part of payments suspensions or standstills in conjunction with

IMF support for their policies and programs, to provide time for an orderly debt restructuring.'[22]

Certain features of the not-so-well-hidden imperial agenda of the G-7's reforms are easy to decipher. One does not have to believe that increased transparency and better codes of conduct will reduce the severity of financial crises to see that global capital would benefit from more accurate and timely information about the economies in the periphery or from uniform codes of conduct for the private financial systems there. Nor should the benefits that the countries involved would obtain from improved banking and financial market regulation and supervision blind us to the fact that capital would benefit from these as well. The interests of global capital are also clearly represented in the strong overall condemnation of capital controls, especially on outflows, and the requirement that the governments in the periphery adopt restrictive fiscal and monetary policies, as these will lower wages and cut inflation. It is not so obvious, however, why the authorities went out their way to warn investors about the risks of lending to the periphery, or why they took steps to 'involve' the private sector in the resolution of future financial crises there. Especially, given the severity of the LTCM crisis, it is also not clear why the authorities decided that the more serious lapses lay in the periphery and not in the centre.

An important BIS document on the Asian crisis contains the following statement about the regulatory framework that allowed the banks in the centre of the global financial system to weather that period of extreme turmoil:

> While significant risks existed, there were also significant risk mitigants that played an important role regarding banks' ability to limit the negative effects of the Asian crisis. Solvency [capital] requirements of G10 bank supervisors and regulators allowed banks to better weather the problems associated with Asian risks with fewer fears of insolvency than in the earlier debt crisis. For example, US banks' total cross-border claims accounted for 500% of their capital in 1982; in June 1997, total cross-border claims represented 108% of capital. Moreover, the foreign claims of G10 banks were also much better diversified than in past crises, in terms of both countries and types of counterparties.
>
> Disclosure of risks by G10 banks in some countries improved compared with past emerging market crises, but the G10 countries had a diversity of experience in the quality of their banks' disclosures. For those market participants that made their risks more transparent, they and their supervisors were better able to judge risks and temper their actions accordingly....
>
> Prudential supervision and regulation also assisted in protecting G10 banks from the Asian crisis. In particular, guidance by supervisory

authorities on internal controls, risk management systems, lending limits and country risks aided G10 banks in managing their Asian exposure. Those banks with sound country risk, market risk and liquidity risk management systems appear to have been able to avoid significant loss. Regulators and supervisors themselves took away lessons from the 1980s debt crisis, and applied them to their respective banks.[23]

In its analysis of the LTCM crisis, the BIS goes on to suggest that policy makers should learn the following 'tentative lessons from this experience:'

> Foremost is the realisation that the first line of defence at a time of market stress is sound risk management by market participants, which in turn requires a regulatory and monetary policy environment ensuring that market discipline effectively governs credit decisions and risk-taking. Policymakers should also appreciate that the fallout from last year's financial market strains was less pronounced on real activity in the industrial countries because a healthy commercial banking system was able to act as a substitute means of intermediating funds.[24]

Several themes run though these statements. They are, first, the importance that the G–10 central bankers gave to risk taking and risk management by market participants; second, the view that the more robust and resilient a nation's banking and financial system, the more able it is to survive and function in a financial crisis; third, the confidence the central bankers showed in the regulatory framework in place within the advanced capitalist nations ahead of both crises, a framework they believed had allowed their banking and financial systems to withstand the Asian and LTCM turmoil without too much damage; and fourth, the importance that the G–10 central bankers gave to the 'Three Pillars' of the Capital Accord – regulatory capital requirements involving the use of internal risk-measurement and risk-control systems, market disclosure and discipline, and prudential supervision and regulation – in maintaining the resilience of their banking and financial systems. The implications of the statements are clear. The authorities took the measures they did in establishing the 'New International Financial Architecture' to strengthen the existing BIS capital requirement regime. They thus warned investors about the risks of lending to the periphery and took measures to 'involve' the private sector in the resolution of future financial crises there to encourage risk taking and risk management. And the authorities determined that the more serious lapses lay in the periphery and not in the centre because of their confidence in the crisis management capacities of the regime they had already put in place in the centre.

CAN THE CENTRE HOLD?

But is the confidence of the financial authorities justified? There is a widely-held belief, not confined to the left, that a crisis of the dollar is now unavoidable, threatening the dominance of the US financial system and the imperial power of the US state that stands at the centre of the global capitalist order. At the root of the problem, according to this view, is the US current account deficit. The deficit is unsustainable, the argument goes, because every quarter's current account deficit means an equivalent increase in the United States' net debtor position, which is already massive. Eventually, foreign investors will get tired of purchasing US assets, and this will lead to a run on the US dollar. If this view were correct, the argument of this essay would be problematic, to say the least. It would be hard to maintain, as we have, that neoliberal global capitalism is a world economic system wherein the financial and economic turmoil is distributed internationally depending on the strength and resilience of the national banking and financial systems that make up the imperial chain, and in which persistent financial and economic instability reproduces capitalist and imperialist social relations by punishing and disciplining subordinate classes and nations.

But, in fact, the view that the US current account deficit must issue in a dollar crisis is mistaken. The relationship between the US current account deficit and the net change in the US net debtor position used in the argument is an accounting identity and has no explanatory power. What matters to foreign investors is not the total size of their investments in the United States relative to the total size of US investments abroad, which is what the US net foreign asset position measures. What matters to them is the share of their US investments in their portfolios and the expected returns on the various components of their portfolios. Standard portfolio theory implies that foreign investors will reduce the relative US share in their investment portfolios if and only if the risk-adjusted expected rate of return on US investments declines relative to the risk-adjusted rates of returns on their investments elsewhere; and that they will reduce their investments in the United States if and only if they anticipate losses on their dollar exposures.

The US national banking and financial system is the strongest and most resilient one of all and thus sits at the top of the imperial chain. This is why foreign investors, like US investors, are willing to hold dollar assets. The market that truly matters here is not the US stock market, but the US Treasury market. The US Treasury market is the deepest and most liquid market in the world because US Treasuries have the lowest credit risks. It is the market in which the Federal Reserve operates, and Treasury bills, notes, and bonds have the 'full faith and credit of the government of United States'. For these reasons, the US Treasury market is the foundation of the interna-

tional financial system. This both reflects and gives the United States tremendous power. For if the argument we have presented in this essay has any
validity, it implies that the global economic and financial instability is shifted
everywhere away from the United States.

This is why no proper understanding of the international economic system
can be had today without an understanding of the nature of imperialism
today. Neoliberal globalization is a historically radical capitalist project, an
attempt to discipline subordinate classes and nations through economic
intimidation. But since the attempt to maintain and extend capitalist social
relations through recurrent financial and economic crises is an inherently
risky venture, neoliberal capitalism is also a dangerous, even a radically
absurd, historical project: the global financial system is a chaotic system that
if left to its own devices might well collapse. This is why the centralizing,
organizing, and coercive activities of the capitalist state, and above all of the
US imperial state at the centre of the system, continue to play such an essential role. If financial instability is a means by which capital disciplines world
capitalism, capital had to find a way to regulate and control it, to make a
liberalized global financial system not just resilient enough to survive its own
disorder but also resilient in such a way as to maintain its fundamental hierarchical structure. The capitalist state, and especially the US imperial state,
disciplines the financial discipliners.

NOTES

1   This is largely based upon primary sources, above all the reports and working
    papers of the BIS's Basel Committee on Banking Supervision (herein cited as
    BCBS) from 1979 to the present.
2   This is how Marx understood financial crises. See David Harvey, *Limits to
    Capital*, New York: Verso Press, 1999, pp. 292-296. This is also one of the
    major themes of Lance Taylor's *Reconstructing Macroeconomics: Structuralist
    Proposals and Critiques of the Mainstream*, Cambridge: Harvard University Press,
    2004.
3   The analysis of the way in which the law of value operates in the neoliberal
    period presented in the following paragraphs takes its lead from Michael
    Rafferty, Dick Bryan and Neil Ackland, 'Financial Derivatives and Marxist
    Value Theory', Working Papers, School of Economics and Political Science,
    University of Sydney, 2000. Though their work is an attempt to give a labour
    theory of value interpretation of financial derivatives, the implications of their
    analysis of the spatial and inter-temporal discontinuities that disrupt the
    international circulation of capital are quite general. A theoretical justification
    of both approaches can be found in Duncan Foley, 'Asset Speculation in
    Marx's Theory of Money', in R. Bellofiori, ed., *Marxian Economics: A
    Reappraisal, Essays on Volume III of Capital, Volume 1: Method, Value and
    Money*, New York: St. Martin's Press, pp. 254-270, 1998.

4   Local national currencies are clearly obstacles to the international circulation
       of capital, but why interest rates? In a system of variable interest and exchange
       rates, interest rates and exchange rates are intrinsically linked by way of the
       interest rate parity condition, according to which the difference between the
       interest rates of two currencies is equal to the expected change in the relevant
       exchange rate. In the real world, any sharp distinctions between the obstacles
       caused by interest rates versus exchange rates are dissolved in the global
       foreign exchange and money markets.

5   See Gregory Albo, 'The Old and New Economics of Imperialism', in *Social
       Register 2004*, London: Merlin Press, 2003, pp. 88-113. China, however, may
       be taking over the leadership of the Far Eastern bloc.

6   If there is more uncertainty in the centre than the periphery, why are interest
       rates higher in the periphery than in the centre? Is not what is normally called
       a 'risk premium' on the assets of the periphery actually an 'imperial premium'?

7   Harvey, *Limits to Capital*, p. 284.

8   The argument that Gramsci's hegemony has a material basis is taken from
       Adam Przeworski, *Capitalism and Social Democracy*, New York: Cambridge
       University Press, 1985. He applied it to class compromises, but the same
       argument can be applied to imperial compromises, with the Cold War
       undoubtedly structuring this cultural war.

9   One can learn much from the post-modern analysis of the role of the media
       in neoliberal global capitalism provided one does not separate their analysis
       from the real material conditions of production. It is noteworthy that the
       millions of marginalized former workers and peasants that occupy the 'mega-
       slums' of the South watch TV. Thus Mike Davis's analysis in his 'Planet of
       Slums', *New Left Review*, 26, 2004 still needs to be read alongside Jean
       Baudrillard's *Simulations*, New York: Semiotext [e], 1983 or Guy Debord's
       The Society of the Spectacle, New York: Zone Books, 1994.

10   The 'mega-slums' are thus functional to neoliberal global capitalism and a
       product not just of its turmoil but of its turmoil as organized by its banking
       and financial market system.

11   Ethan Kapstein was the probably first to recognize the importance of the BIS
       and the Basel Committee in the governance of the global economy, although
       he analyzed only the implications of the capital requirements and the 'home
       country rule' principle, and not the division of labour between the major
       central banks and the IMF. See his 'Resolving the Regulator's Dilemma:
       International Coordination of Banking Regulations', *International
       Organization*, 43(2), 1989; and *Governing the Global Economy: International
       Finance and the State*, Cambridge: Harvard University Press, 1994.

12   The 1988 Accord is described in BCBS, 'International Convergence of
       Capital Measurement and Capital Standards', Basel: BIS, 1988. In the 1988
       Accord, each of a bank's assets has a prescribed risk weight and the 8 per cent
       capital minimum requirements applies to the value of the asset as this value is
       adjusted by its risk weight. A bank's claims on OECD central governments,
       for example, have a zero risk weight and the capital requirements pose no cost
       to the banks in terms of capital they can't lend out and make money from. A

fully secured residential mortgage has a 50 per cent risk weight and thus a 4 per cent cost – in bankers' language this is known as a 'capital charge'. Claims on non-OECD central governments have a 100 per cent risk weight and thus an 8 per cent 'capital charge'. The 'capital charges' for $1,000,000 in US Treasury bonds, a $1,000,000 residential mortgage, and a $1,000,000 loan to the government of Brazil are $0, $40,000, and $80,000, respectively.

13   The amended Accord is described in BCBS, 'Overview of the Capital Accord to Incorporate Market Risk', Basel, BIS, 1996. A bank using its own internal risk model to measure its market risk capital requirements does so using a 'value-at-risk' model that measures the losses that the bank can occur at a predetermined probability level. For a bank using the 'standard methodology', each of the bank's assets is given a risk weight similar to that used in the initial Accord, except that the risk-weights used here are designed to measure the market risk of each of the bank's assets.

14   The role of the 'Three Pillars' of the Capital Accord is explained in BCBS, 'Overview of the New Basel Capital Accord', Basel: BIS, 2003. These distinctions are also discussed by William White, 'New Strategies for Dealing with the Instability of Financial Markets', paper presented at the FUNDAD meeting, Budapest, 24-25 June 1999, and 'What have We Learned from Recent Financial Crises and Policy Responses?', BIS Working Papers, Number 84, Basel: BIS, 2000. White is the BIS's chief economist. The G-10 central banks have not yet reached a consensus about the New Capital Accord now under discussion. The major change that it would initiate would be a refinement of the measurement of credit risk, either through the use of credit rating agencies or banks' internal credit risk models.

15   BCBS, 'History of the Basel Committee and its Membership', Basel: BIS, 2001, p. 1.

16   Since a bank's capital requirements are determined by the probability distribution of the returns of its assets over the past year, the volatility of a recent financial crisis will increase the variance of the bank's probability distribution and thus increase its 'value-at-risk'.

17   The account of the Asian crisis presented here is taken from Christopher Rude, 'The 1997-1998 East Asian Financial Crisis: A New York Market-Informed View', in Barry Herman, ed., Global Financial Turmoil and Reform, New York: United Nations University Press, 1999, pp. 369-403. The account of LTCM troubles relies upon the BIS reports on the matter (BCBS, 'Banks' Interactions with Highly Leveraged Institutions', Basel: BIS, 1999; BCBS, 'Sound Practices for Bank's Interactions with Highly Leveraged Institutions', Basel: BIS, 1999; and Committee on the Global Financial System, 'A Review of Financial Market Events in Autumn 1998', Basel: BIS, 1999), Perry Mehrling, 'Minsky, Modern Finance, and the Case of Long Term Capital Management', Barnard College, mimeo, 1999, and market sources.

18   For a description of the World Financial Authority proposal, see John Eatwell and Lance Taylor, Global Finance at Risk: The Case for International Regulation, New York: The New Press, 2000.

19   These measures were presented in the statement by Group of Seven Finance Ministers, 'Strengthening the International Financial Architecture', Report of the Finance Ministers to the Köln Summit Meeting, 18-20 June 1999.

20   Ibid., paragraph 16.

21   Ibid., paragraph 1 and 30.

22   Ibid., paragraph 41, 43, 45, and 50. Most large international loans are syndicated loans. In the event of a default of an international loan, the problem frequently arises therefore as to how to coordinate the interests of the many creditors involved. Collective action clauses in loan contracts prevent creditors from negotiating with the debtors individually and thus facilitate the orderly workout of non-performing loans for the creditors as a whole.

23   BCBS, 'Supervisory Lessons to be Drawn from the Asian Crisis', Working Papers, Number 2, BCBS, Basel: BIS, 1999, pp. 15-16.

24   Committee on the Global Financial System, 'Review of Financial Market Events in Autumn 1998', Basel: BIS, 1999, p. 2.

HOLLYWOOD RELOADED:
THE FILM AS IMPERIAL COMMODITY

SCOTT FORSYTH

The features of the typical Hollywood film are now part of popular cultural discourse. 'High concept' films or blockbusters are defined by budgets of $100 million and up, with half as much again spent on massive promotion campaigns, plus investment in the most advanced technologies for elaborate stunts, explosions and computer-generated 'special effects'. Hollywood corporations are part of huge media/communication conglomerates linked with the electronics, real estate and even aircraft and armaments industries. Films are the strategic, leading edge – the 'tentpole' in the latest show-biz jargon – of an expanding circuit of consumable commodities including videos, television, internet, comics, novels, games, toys, clothes, fast food, theme parks and rides; entertainment industries are now the leading American export. For films, the circuit increasingly depends on remakes, prequels, sequels, series and franchises, all pre-sold, in an interconnected repetitive process that diversifies revenues and avoids risk – and in which most individual films actually lose money! Equally important, Hollywood defines, with its capital and technological innovation, what a film product now is; competitors are forced to compete on this level. And its industrial and cultural dominance is reinforced by control of financing, distribution, theatrical exhibition and production on an international scale.

Hollywood developed and even pioneered strategies of international competition from the 1920s onwards, but over the past twenty years a programme of focused reorganization has enabled it to recreate the oligopoly of the classic studio system on an international scale, consistently aided by the American state. Over the 1990s, assisted in myriad ways by state subsidies, lobbying and trade negotiations, Hollywood not only increased its market share in most of the world, but also dramatically increased its control of theatres and production capacity in most countries. Even with protection other countries' film industries have become not so much rivals as branch plants for Hollywood productions, suppliers of cheaper skilled labour, sources of capital, inspiration for innovative styles, exporters of new talent and stars. More than an evolution of earlier forms of cultural imperialism is involved here: what has happened is the material incorporation of other national film industries into what Miller calls an American-dominated international division of cultural labour.[1]

So the Hollywood film is a key commodity of American imperialism today, and its favoured genre is the 'action film'. Of course, films of action and spectacle have always been central in film history, but never so dominant as in the last twenty years of Hollywood's revitalization. The blockbuster can of course be 'polygeneric', mixing horror, fantasy, sci-fi, spy and police thrillers, war films, melodramas into the action film, making it a sort of metacategory for the dominant form of film today, with simple narratives and concise themes – quests, chases, revenge, war – and simple characterization, with plenty of occasions for stunts, fights, battles, and effects of all kinds, and clear resolutions. Globalized Hollywood can also organize itself around plots that skip from one cheap exotic location to another, from one diminished or dismantled national industry to another.[2] Naturally, this is also a terrain of fierce critical debate. Rarely have film critics so forcefully announced the death of the cinema, or so routinely denounced films as trivial products of an industrialized system Adorno could hardly have imagined. Some critics defend action films with populist connoisseurship and textual tracking of its vast repertoire, and some film scholars analyze action films as the latest in a lineage of films that have always indulged the pleasures of spectacle, thrills and 'attractions'; for them, America is once again simply entertaining the world with what the people want.[3] But what this essay seeks to emphasize is the way the action film by its very nature reflects the might of American capital, corporate organization and technology, all aimed at ensuring that this is indeed what the people want; and what its narratives and ideologies then embody and personify so forcefully – the celebration of American individualism and heroes, and of America itself, the resolution of good over evil, the repetitive crushing of the country's foes.

War films of all kinds have been especially prominent in recent Hollywood output, and the cinematic aesthetics of war permeate countless films in the action genre. The American military has an intimate relationship with these productions, showcasing military hardware, sanitizing scripts, and utilizing films, television and video games for recruitment and propaganda, and even military training. Some scholars even argue that Hollywood and the military industrial complex are converging. While the war on Iraq was still 'officially' on, 'gamers' – video and computer game fans – could join in with *SOCOM II:Navy Seals*. The Reaganite action hero, with some interesting variations, and even more, comic-book superheroes, remain central in countless action films; and the action film itself, despite the too-easy derision of most critics, has assumed a central role in the political economy of multi-national corporate filmmaking. And the ultimate Reaganite 'hardbody' is now in the Governor's mansion in California.[4]

It has become commonplace to observe that the American mass media's role in the war on terror and the invasions of Afghanistan and Iraq was both crucial and servile – a war staged for and through the key media giants. Overall, we can say that this representation of these wars – and it goes way beyond simply re-presenting them – constitutes a cultural event, a Debordian spectacle.[5] Hollywood contributes to, prepares this event and spectacle, and makes watching it comprehensible and enjoyable.

We can easily cite examples of how Hollywood helped us as spectators. When President Bush said he wanted Bin Laden 'dead or alive', everyone understood the evocation of the Western. We also knew the enemy, from the racist representations of Arabs in dozens of films over the years.[6] When Bush climbed out of a fighter plane on an aircraft carrier and strode manfully on the deck, we all remembered Tom Cruise in *Top Gun* (1986). When Bush taunted the crushed Iraqis, telling them to 'bring it on', we recognized the laconic idiom and grim humour of an American action hero.

If the first Gulf War could be understood as a videogame, the wars on Iraq and Afghanistan unfolded as sports shows, with CNN and FOX correspondents as jock cheerleaders in games that had predictable but still suspenseful endings. Indeed, the networks utilized all the aesthetics of mainstream television to deliver the wars as exciting, branded programming – logos, musical themes, star 'journalists' – and the media war called on the conventions of multiple genres – the war film, soaps, game shows, sports, radio talk shows. This is useful but perhaps inadequate. What actually governed the production and consumption of these wars was the prototype of the Hollywood film today; the organizing spine of the event was the polygeneric, capital- and technology-intensive action blockbuster – its dramas and narrative expectations, images, military spectacles, its weaponry fetishism, its fixation on media technology itself, and its triumph of American Good over all Evil.

At the level of performance and characterization, to appreciate President Bush on that aircraft carrier, we must really imagine the Imperial Presidency, not only its dignified and obvious association with state power and grandeur, but also its Hollywood representation – the President himself as the hero of the spectacle. We have been prepared for this by years of films of the American President – comedies, thrillers, murder mysteries – not to mention the Reaganite films which, several critics have argued, ultimately offered

Reagan himself as the hero of public fantasy. Bush's posturing as President evoked Harrison Ford in *Air Force One* (1997), literally killing the crazed ex-Soviet terrorists himself, or the flyboy President of *Independence Day* (1996) destroying alien invaders to make the world safe for America's national holiday.[7]

And of course it is the terror of September 11 that begins this new imperial action movie and overarches, sometimes explicitly, more often emotionally, all the wars that TV and Hollywood are now fighting. It is commonplace that we watched 9/11 as if caught in a movie. As Mike Davis and Slavoj Zizek brilliantly reminded us, it recalled images that Western culture had conjured up in countless films, books and comics.[8] Movie-goers have been traumatized enjoyably for years by the destruction of the mighty towers of Western capital, the war coming home from the always vanquished subaltern world, the triumphs of Progress and Empire answered by invasion, barbarism, apocalypse: America destroyed, or almost, again and again, by marauding Arab terrorists, Communists, bloodthirsty drug lords, rogue KGB officers with nuclear bombs, invading aliens.

On 9/11 neither Bruce Willis nor Arnold Schwarzenegger came to the rescue, and the narrative of revenge begun by that atrocious 'opportunity' (as the 'neocons' saw it) is still unfolding in the real world. American television has continued in an entertaining and craven fashion to cheerlead war with several didactically propagandistic 'movies of the week' – including *Saving Jessica Lynch* (2003), released even after the real private Lynch had disavowed the story of her heroic rescue by US special forces.[9] However, feature films operate on a much longer production schedule, so their ideological articulation with hegemonic politics has to be more complex and sophisticated. Indeed, Hollywood spokesmen reacted immediately to 9/11 with guilt – for all the disasters they had imagined, for all the atrocities and violence they had aestheticized, as if they themselves had conjured up the disaster. Movie premieres were cancelled or delayed, scripts were revised and Hollywood reported for duty. The Pentagon asked screenwriters to brainstorm terrorist scenarios in order to help preventive investigations, while producers met with Karl Rove, Bush's top adviser, to discuss the patriotic themes needed for the new day. We may be just beginning to view the fruits of the most explicit ideological enlistment since Hollywood's massive role in World War II. It is not surprising that Hollywood films resonate with the world-view of the American Right. What is more interesting is to see what part supposedly 'liberal' Hollywood plays in the new imperial patriotic campaign.

GOOD WARS AND HUMAN RIGHTS WARRIORS

The American leadership is anxious to drape their current wars in the mantle of the Good War. World War II is endlessly evoked in rhetoric and imagery to insist on an unequivocal equation between the USA and universal rights. This draws on a political – and cinematic – interpretation of World War II that has been important to the vindication and portrayal of US imperialism for decades. The war film of the 1940s has provided a range of conventions and narratives that remain lastingly influential; in particular, the male combat group, isolated and endangered, representative of America, connected by bravery and camaraderie. Epics from the 1950s to the 1970s – *From Here to Eternity* (1953), *The Longest Day* (1962), *Patton* (1970) – replayed those uplifting myths on a grand scale to mythologize America's singular role in the victory, and *Saving Private Ryan* (1998) represents its most successful updating. The film's opening – the horrific spectacle of the Normandy landing – shocked audiences, as key war films always do, with a new realism and explicitness. That violence, with all the resources of horror film special effects and digitally enhanced mayhem, secured our attachment to an egregiously sentimental tale of a combat unit's rescue of the surviving Ryan brother. It allowed a renewed celebration of the male combat group – the conventional multi-ethnic allegory for America itself – that had been undermined by the darker variations of the Vietnam film cycle of the 1970s and 1980s – *Apocalypse Now* (1979), *Platoon* (1986), *Full Metal Jacket* (1987). In *Saving Private Ryan* Spielberg's American 'brothers' fight for each other, not for any ideological or political aim, and the film concludes in the most spiritual, literally flag-waving celebration of America.[10]

While there have not been a large number of recent World War II films, *Saving Private Ryan* recuperated the war film in a way that could be readily evoked. It spawned a successful television miniseries, *Band Of Brothers* (2001), and a number of war films set in World War II. The most expensive and widely marketed of these was *Pearl Harbor* (2001). While this film premiered before 9/11, it aestheticized The Project for a New American Century's call for 'another Pearl Harbor' to impart energy to America's mission in the world. The Pentagon worked closely on the film with Disney Studios; the premiere was held on an aircraft carrier and recruiting booths were set up in theatres.[11] Notably, *Pearl Harbor* also offers a heart-warming sub-plot of a heroic black cook saving his hostile white fellow-sailors. The crimes of racism are raised to view – and then corrected by American democracy. It is worth recalling that this liberalism is integral to the classic Hollywood war films; however much they fit within contemporary and reactionary American nationalism, they were often the work of the Hollywood left, perceived as part of a national front against fascism. In Popular Front left nationalist logic,

World War II films often celebrate the 'citizen soldier' as a mythos for the collective heroism of the nation, whereas more recent films celebrate the professional warrior as an institutional embodiment of the state.[12] However, Hollywood films in general are likely to combine liberal and conservative themes and tropes, more likely to square ideological circles than follow a didactic line.

The conventions of the good war migrate easily to other wars. *We Were Soldiers* (2002) goes back to a key battle early in the Vietnam war to reverently celebrate the heroism of the American soldier, lovingly and spiritually nurtured by Mel Gibson's Colonel Moore – patriarch to his family and his soldiers. The film introduces itself as a 'testament' and carefully depoliticizes 'a war we did not understand'. It consciously 'forgets' more than ten years of Vietnam war films that had consistently questioned and de-romanticized, even if largely in apolitical terms, the American defeat; America's Colonel Moore simply fights wars because there are bad people in the world. The heroes in this film too 'fought for each other', once again reducing war to military professionalism and male bonding. More interestingly, the film is one of the few American films to humanize the Vietnamese enemy, pictured throughout as worthy and soldierly foes.

Black Hawk Down (2002) reduces the context even more dramatically. The disastrous American intervention in Somalia is told as the story of one helicopter crew on a wild rescue mission in Mogadishu. The film's superbly kinetic music video-style battle scenes valorize the stoic professionalism of its soldiers and focus the spectator on the most viscerally limited enjoyment. On the one hand, the film's refusal to provide any context or explanation for the battle we are excitingly thrust into is necessary for its reduction of the theme to a single combat group's battle to save each other, 'to leaving no man behind' as the highest good. On the other hand the stark imagery of this ugly, impoverished Third World outpost and its hundreds of faceless slaughtered Africans – background and fodder for the high-tech heroics of the First World – speaks more than allegorically about global imperialism now. Tom Doherty argues convincingly that both *We Are Soldiers* and *Black Hawk Down* are tales of moral rearmament and soldierly courage, despite debacle and defeat, that resonate with precision in the post-9/11 ideological discourse.[13]

Several recent war films reflect the recent opportunistic dusting-off of the ancient doctrine of the just war in service of imperialist aggression – in its new form as a doctrine of the right to wage 'pre-emptive' war, as in Afghanistan and Iraq.[14] In these films imperial soldiers are caught in wars whose grand motives are seen to be bogus or fraudulent, or beyond comprehension, but in situations that can be reduced to a moral dilemma – the saving of 'innocents'. In *Tears of the Sun* (2002) an intervention in an imaginary African civil war forces tough American professionals, led by the icon-ically grim and stoical Bruce Willis, into a *crise de conscience*. In a ponderously didactic morality lesson they rescue a group of innocent civilians from tribal massacre. Diplomatic niceties have rendered the Americans temporarily vulnerable but their massive superiority is reasserted in a climactic spectac-ular of F-18s. While the film is reverential in its human rights rhetoric, its Reaganite and Clintonite political message is that the Western decision to do 'good' must trump international law, the political context and – that old cliché – bureaucratic timidity. The happy Africans gratefully bless the Americans: 'God will never forget you, Lieutenant!' In *Behind Enemy Lines* (2001) an American pilot crashes behind Serbian lines in a fictionalized Balkan war and is hunted by Serbian paramilitaries who are busy conducting an ethnic massacre. The film casts NATO and France as those favourite Reaganite villains, bureaucrats and appeasers, whose delay in organizing a military rescue lends the film what little suspense it can muster. Finally, a feisty American officer defies his NATO superiors and America saves both its hero and the cause of human rights.

The most interesting of the human rights warriors are in *Three Kings* (1999). It is one of the few films to be set in the first Gulf War and it offers a cynical, derisive picture of official American motives and actions; the role of the media is particularly mocked. The band of rogues who set out to steal Hussein's gold bullion eventually give up the fortune in order to rescue an endangered group of innocent civilians caught between the American invaders and Hussein's brutal power. The film was marketed, and received, as unconventional, even 'oppositional' but it is still a fantasy of human rights imperialism. The fault in the Gulf War, it says, was failing to go all the way to liberate Baghdad, allowing our hands to be tied by venal politicians. It is a prescription for the next war on Iraq. There are good and bad colonial subjects and the West must intervene for the good; the film is about what one critic astutely labelled the 'neo-colonial mission'.[15]

A number of films do work against the upbeat glorification of America's military destinies and 'manly warriors'. *Buffalo Soldiers* (2002) recalls anti-war comedies like *MASH* (1970) and *Catch-22* (1970). Set on a base in peace-time West Germany, these American heroes are specialists in graft and drug and arms dealing. Nothing is sacred and the heroes' careless machinations end in mayhem and dozens of deaths. But the satire is finally just toothless cyni-cism, mockingly suggesting that what these deranged crooks need is a good war! An earlier film, *The Siege* (1998), even casts doubt on the war on terror as a noble war. This liberal attack on militarism also revels in chillingly premonitory images of deranged Arabs bombing New York and the martial law imprisonment of thousands of Arab Americans. The terror is gradually exposed as blowback for CIA machinations in the Middle East: 'we're the CIA, something always goes wrong'. On the one hand this echoes the popular suspicion of the CIA that had been popularized in the anti-war movement and featured in paranoid spy thrillers throughout the 1970s. On the other hand American liberalism is so pallid that the film needs the FBI to rescue democracy in another implausible but cheerful rehabilitation of the American state. These films disturb the exciting story told in most recent war films, but they clearly are not part of a significant cycle of anti-war films. They have little connection to that powerful lineage in film history. For all the liberal angst and dissent, it is still the pro-war action spectacle that is emblematic of Hollywood today.

RAINBOW RAMBOS AND SUPERVILLAINS

In 1990, Chief of Staff Colin Powell could joke that he '…was running out of villains', but throughout the 1990s Hollywood provided him with a dizzying variety of them – crazed Arabs, evil Latin drug lords, brutal Russian Mafiosi, rogue KGB-ers, supervillains intent on world domination, monsters from space – in a cinematic lineage that reaches back to the silents, Fantomas, Dr. Mabuse and Dr. Moriarity. In recent years, old Nazis are still a reliable menace but Cubans and North Koreans are appearing with opportunistic regularity too. In the popular comic book films, villainy is often some pure, supernatural Evil, fitting enemies for a spiritually-defined America battling evildoers all over the world. And at the center of the action film is the hero, usually a lone wolf rebel, always up to the challenge of these villains, and also revised and updated in recent years.

Rambo played a key part in defining America's modern action hero: he cinematically refought the Vietnam disaster as a good war, joined the Mujahadeen to slaughter the Soviets in Afghanistan, and entered American political discourse. The Rambo films were brutally simplistic but always more complex politically. Rambo was a dark Other, the enemy of the American state as much as of America's enemies: the infamously hard killer that America needs but cannot tolerate, coded as Native, Hippie, or victimized working class.[16] Few contemporary films address that complexity but many, not surprisingly, attempt to recreate the Rambo phenomenon. Vinn Diesel in XXX (2003) is the most manufactured new Rambo. His character, X, is presented as a rebel the CIA needs – an unlikely combination of extreme sports, heavy metal, tattoos and muscles – but he has been constructed with synergetic marketing in mind. This new Rambo confronts supervillains who are a particularly jumbled meshing of contemporary anxieties – Russian army deserters, drug lords, ravers, anarchists – all pursuing a dastardly plot with biological weapons that will unleash a destructive utopia/dystopia of 'absolute, beautiful freedom'. Of course, X stands up for the 'old stars and stripes' and saves the world.

Arnold Schwarzenegger in *Collateral Damage* (2002) is a more plodding update but the film is also more explicit in its Reaganite didacticism and its opportunistic articulation with the immediate military and geo-political agenda of the US state. The film's release was delayed by post 9/11 sensitivities but a year later the movies were back to the grim fun of the catastrophic destruction of American cities and Arnold, as a humble fireman, becomes a citizen vigilante out to avenge the death of his wife and child, travelling to Columbia to battle a fictional version of the revolutionary FARC. This action hero as family man becomes agent of the CIA's covert intervention in the third world that has been held back by liberal wimps in Washington. The film does make a slight effort to consider the costs of US interventions in Latin America, and even raises the issue of American atrocities there; but Latin American revolutionaries are finally equated with madness and terrorism. With neocolonial finality, the hero exacts a satisfyingly brutal vengeance on the rebellious Third World.[17]

Perhaps the most notable thing about these heroes and dozens like them is their colour and diversity. They are not just white hulks, but include a host of African American stars – Denzel Washington, Wesley Snipes, Samuel L. Jackson, and a long list of rap singers – women warriors (*Lara Croft: Tomb Raider*, 2001 and *Lara Croft: Tomb Raider: The Cradle of Life*, 2003, *Charlie's Angels*, 2000 and *Charlie's Angels: Full Throttle*, 2003, *Kill Bill Volume 1*, 2003 and *Volume 2*, 2004), kids at CIA summer camp (*Agent Cody Banks*, 2003, and *Agent Cody Banks: Destination London*, 2004), and Latino kids (the *Spy Kids* series). Even James Bond's superhero skin is saved by an equally suave, invincible female African American spy (*Die Another Day*, 2003). Perhaps most striking, major Asian stars are featured in a growing cycle of international hit thrillers – Chow Yun Fat, Jackie Chan, Jet Li – not to mention any number of mutants and superheroes from Batman and Spiderman to the X-Men. Even complete idiots can save the world in the many successful and toothless parodies of the already smirkingly self-parodic spy films – the popular *Austin Powers* series, *Johnny English* (2003), *I Spy* (2003). This diversification of the hero can be seen as a politically neutralized kind of identity politics: the remnant of the civil rights campaigns is feebly echoed in the X-Men's pursuit of justice for mutants, and the women's movement becomes the frothy girlpower of the Angels. Significant social and demographic changes are certainly reflected in, and may even mildly subvert, these popular film genre conventions. But the diversification of heroes also reflects the enhanced role of marketing in contemporary Hollywood, with demographically overlapping targets and multiple identification positions and modes of consumption. Finally, the shift reflects global Hollywood's pursuit of international markets and the incorporation of the stars and styles of other national cinemas, from Hong Kong to Japan to Mexico. Hollywood has been keeping up with postmodern cultural studies.

In fact, this 'rainbow' casting allows all these heroes to play the same roles in these action films' predictable challenges. The ideology of individualism trumps liberal and conservative ideologies and allows all the new Rambos to battle, in their routinized rebelliousness, for America, literally or symbolically, for Good against Evil, just as before. Liberalism is incorporated effortlessly by action films' formal and ideological inventiveness.

While these heroes usually stand for America, their motives are often simplified to mere revenge, the most efficient convergence of character and narrative. Revenge is very cinematic. Yet even in such simplified narratives there is often some disturbance of the simple celebration of America the Good. Bad as so many of them are, action films' continued success is partly due to the fact that some of them contain a minimal degree of ambiguity, contradiction, or even critique. In these films imperialism is not all fun; the dark side of America is involved as well. Ideologies in film are never mono-lithic, always capable of contradiction and ambiguity, even dissonance and critique. Denzel Washington's Creasy in *Man on Fire* (2004), for example, is tormented, suicidal and alcoholic as well as a globetrotting CIA assassin; he fears God will never forgive him for his crimes. Bizarrely enough, however, the film then gleefully follows the story of the brutal revenge of torture and slaughter he exacts – presumably the sort of mayhem he is tormented by – against Mexican gangsters and crooked cops. To take another example, *The Sum of All Fears*, another plodding idealization of heroic CIA agents in the influential Tom Clancy series, nonetheless returns us to the enduring enter-tainment value of the destruction of American cities with the film's set-piece nuclear destruction of Baltimore. By the time the film was released in 2002, Hollywood's sensitivity had evidently returned to pre-9/11 levels.

Another element of dissonance in the imperial action film comes from the spy thriller which despite its imperial roots has always contained a critical, even leftist side, from anti-Nazi Popular Front thrillers to ambiguous, paranoid films about the Cold War. The spy is the favourite adventurer of contemporary empire. James Bond and the Angels hopscotch around the world happily blowing things up in exotic locations. Current and former CIA hitmen travel to foreign backdrops to kill countless foreigners in *Man on Fire, Bad Company* (2002), *Mission Impossible 1* and *2* (1996, 2000), *The Bourne Identity* (2003) and many more. The spy is inherently capable of deceit and betrayal and in *Mission Impossible* or *The Bourne Identity*, paranoia is more than reasonable and the enemy most to be feared is the one within. In *Spartan* (2004), venality and corruption go right up to the White House; as the President's daughter puts it, 'I was raised by wolves'. Even a film designed to rehabilitate the institutional reputation of the CIA, *The Recruit* (2003), ends with betrayal within by the very father figure who embodies the agency's 'ideals'. Some films have even gone beyond paranoia to critique. *The Quiet American* (2002) is a thoughtful version of the Graham Greene classic mockery of American good intentions. Johnny Depp's cheerfully psychotic CIA agent in *Once Upon a Time in Mexico* (2003) is more than darkly comic in its portrayal of the murder and catastrophe America can bring. The film memorably concludes with the imagery of popular insurrection against a CIA-engineered coup! *The Beach* (2000) is a bitter, if superficial, critique of the despoliation of the third world by Western tourism.

Several cop thrillers also show city police, those other personifications of the state's monopoly of violence, in a problematic light. In *Training Day* (2002), the corrupt character of a charismatic cop indicts the war of occupation the police are conducting against America's inner-city 'third world'. *Dark Blue* (2003) is a similar exposé of police corruption, by implication at the level of the police as a repressive institution. Both films conclude with liberal salvation, but the reversal of conventional cop hagiography is still notable.

Then we have *The Matrix* series of films. Their popularity opens up the cultural possibility of what the science fiction critic Peter Fitting calls 'critical dystopian' films. The original, *The Matrix* (1999), in particular, proposed a monstrous version of technophobic paranoia, a world of media technology gone mad, and humanity reduced to bodily slavery. It imaginatively indicted modern capitalism as 'the desert of the real'. Notably, the second and third films in the series, *The Matrix Reloaded* (2003) and *The Matrix Revolutions* (2003) dissipate this intriguing concept in New Age messianism.[18]

THE AESTHETICIZATION OF COERCION: CONCLUSIONS

The critical element in the action film remains a minor theme in Hollywood. The action film – especially the war versions I have largely focused on – is always blatantly political, always about international power, and mostly uncritical. I have argued that such films offer a national allegory of America – beleaguered in a dangerous world of multiple threats and enemies. On the other hand, as Fredric Jameson suggests, many convoluted spy thrillers and their mad super-villains with their nefarious plans for world destruction offer a picture of global capitalism, and all its unseen violence, manipulation and havoc, as a subtext, in a culture where it is easier to imagine the end of the world than to picture capitalism itself.[19] Certainly, action films are constantly imagining the end of the world as a cinematic spectacle, and very rarely name capitalism or imperialism. More narrowly, what we have in so many films is a representation of the power of the imperialist American state, 'the power of armed oppression' in Engels' phrase,[20] with its military functions and institutions heroically personified and familiarized by professional warriors, citizen soldiers and vigilantes, who are also quite often rogue heroes for an increasingly militarily defined 'rogue state'.

But Hollywood's version of imperialist militarism is populist fun, enlisting us all in an imperial project that requires popular consent. The action film displays, over and over, the immense technological and military capacity of America's media and state, over and over, an aestheticized representation of coercion that plays an important role in securing consent. For Hollywood's USA is a benevolent friend to the world as well as a bringer of revenge. The conclusion of *Independence Day* says it clearly. The American president, and a squad of heroes, have destroyed the invaders' command ship and developed a superior technological response to the aliens' apparently invincible technological prowess. They share it with the rest of the world as we skip to locations all over the globe and a series of quickly sketched national stereotypes follow American orders in defeating the invaders. The images illustrate Hollywood's, and American-led globalization's, ability to dominate, incorporate and orchestrate the world's consumption of America; it is the symbolic performance of imperialism.

As viewers we can enjoy imperialism as a spectacle – we can track and enjoy the generic confluences and convergences, the sideshows and tangents. And this brings us back to the imperial role of culture today: Hollywood is emblematic of America's cultural and ideological domination; and the Hollywood action movie is the key output of the vast media conglomerates that have been crucial to American globalization and its ability to remake the world in its own mad image.

Despite this apparent triumph, however, the new globalized Hollywood has financial, aesthetic and ideological fault lines. On finance, Hollywood's venerable lobbyist Jack Valenti has issued dire warnings about the escalating production costs of the blockbusters that ensure Hollywood's domination. Massive interconnected webs of synergy can be houses of cards and one bloated imperial commodity flop can bring down a corporation. The huge media conglomerates that buttress Hollywood's global domination have also been rocked by tumultuous and volatile mergers, takeovers and collapses, as the hi-tech and stock market bubbles burst in the early years of this century. Faced with this, Hollywood has increasingly relied on foreign investment to offset its own aversion to risk. But since the blockbuster strategy is actually risk-filled, it is uncertain if its access to foreign capital will remain secure.

Imperial Hollywood may be in danger of imperial overreach.

Aesthetically, these films – built on audience research and technological gimmickry and sold by total control of marketing and exhibition – have been condemned by critics and cinephiles as the trivializing death of the cinema. This may be exaggerated but this phase of Hollywood filmmaking has opened up an aesthetic vacuum that art cinema, nationally-rooted films and even politically militant features and documentaries may be able to fill. Indeed, Hollywood's domination has not been total or entirely homogenizing: Hollywood's need to internationalize itself should allow a contested terrain of alternatives to develop.[21] There are also indications that the action film may move beyond the trivial. Film studies have focused on the development of 'action auteurs'; the stylistic innovations and spiritual meditations of John Woo, the mixing of feminism into male-fixated genres by Kathryn Bigelow, the wild homages to Asian cinema by Quentin Tarantino. These artists may bring an unexpected weight, albeit likely depoliticized, to films designed for so-called passive consumption, and may indicate some resilience in the always necessary relative autonomy of cultural producers within the mighty culture monoliths.[22]

Then there is the vulnerability of ideology to political realities. Some have speculated that blatant American triumphalism will become a hard ideological sell as America's imperial adventure in Iraq continues to founder and massive anti-American and anti-imperialist politics continue to develop. Hollywood's international domination has also brought an unprecedented dependence on foreign audiences, and finding ways to appeal to foreign viewers has become important for corporate strategies. Explicitly didactic Reaganite-Bushite films are unlikely to be common. Hollywood will most likely shape imperial ideology allegorically; action heroes will increasingly do battle in fantastic worlds of Good and Evil, or be set in long-ago days of imperial glory.[23]

Hollywood has indeed 'Reloaded' in the last decade, in corporate structure, in control of production and markets, in defining film by out and out commodification. These imperial commodities dominate global culture and celebrate America's triumphs, formally and ideologically, and the fact that many such films feature humanitarian concerns, guilty angst or multicultural heroes only serves to get liberal viewers to buy into their main message. But recall that *The Matrix* proposes the future of capitalist modernity as a nightmare of the military-industrial-media complex gone mad; one critic argues that, implicitly, the Matrix is Hollywood. Cracks along the fault lines of capital, global production and aesthetic and ideological contradictions may make Hollywood's imperial commodity subject to the kind of disaster and collapse it so pleasurably imagines and expensively constructs on screen.

NOTES

1   See in particular, Toby Miller et al., *Global Hollywood*, London: BFI, 2001; Aida Hozic, *Hollyworld: Space, Power and Fantasy in the American Economy*, Ithaca and London: Cornell University Press, 2001; Janet Wasko, *Hollywood in the Information Age: Beyond the Silver Screen*, Cambridge: Polity Press, 1994; Justin Wyatt, *High Concept: Movies and Marketing in Hollywood*, Austin: University of Texas Press, 1994. On Hollywood's historical international strategy, see John Trumpbour, *Selling Hollywood to the World: US and European Struggles for Mastery of the Global Film Industry 1920-1950*, Cambridge, New York: Cambridge University Press, 2002; for an overview of critical concepts of culture and imperialism, see John Tomlinson, *Cultural Imperialism: A Critical Introduction*, Baltimore: The John Hopkins University Press, 1991.

2   Miller et al., in *Global Hollywood* provides several powerful illustrations; Prague has become Hollywood's second European production location after the dismantling of the large state studio and the unemployment of a highly skilled film work force, pp. 71-72; *The Beach*, a film condemning Western tourism, was produced with the coercive co-operation of the Thai government in violating its own environmental regulations in order to produce a more picture-perfect paradise, p. 197.

3   For a considered critical analysis of action films, see Jose Arroyo, ed., *Action/Spectacle Cinema*, London: BFI, 2000; for critical opprobrium, see Robin Wood, *Hollywood from Vietnam to Reagan and Beyond*, New York: Columbia University Press, 2004.

4   On the convergence of Hollywood and the military-industrial complex, see Hosic, *Hollyworld*; on the importance of war films, see Tom Pollard, 'Hollywood's War Machine', in Carl Boggs, ed., *Masters of War: Militarism and Blowback in the Era of American Empire*, New York and London: Routledge, 2003.

5   For a useful analysis of media in the recent wars, see Paul Rutherford, *Weapons of Mass Persuasion: Marketing the War Against Iraq*, Toronto, Buffalo, London: University of Toronto Press, 2004.

6   See in particular, Jack Shaheen, *Reel bad Arabs: how Hollywood vilifies a people*, New York: Olive Branch Press, 2001.

7   On Reaganite cinema, see Andrew Britton, 'Blissing Out: the Politics of Reaganite Entertainment', *Movie*, 26/27, 1985; Douglas Kellner and Michael Ryan, *Camera Politica: The Politics and Ideology of Contemporary Hollywood Film*, Bloomington: Indiana University Press, 1990; Robin Wood, *Hollywood from Vietnam to Reagan and Beyond*; Susan Jeffords, *Hard Bodies: Hollywood Masculinity in the Reagan Era*, New Brunswick, NJ: Rutgers University Press, 1994; Michael Rogin, *Ronald Reagan, The Movie and Other Episodes in Political Demonology*, Berkeley: University of California Press, 1987; Chris Jordan, *Movies and the Reagan Presidency*, Newport, CT: Praeger, 2003; also, Scott Forsyth, 'Evil Empire: Spectacle and Imperialism in Hollywood', in *Socialist Register 1987*, London: Merlin Press, 1987 and 'Hollywood's War on the World', in *Socialist Register 1992*, London: Merlin Press, 1992.

8   See Mike Davis, 'The Flames of New York', in M. Davis, ed., *Dead Cities*, London: Verso, 2003; Slavoj Zizek, *Welcome to the Desert of the Real*, London: Verso, 2002. For a useful overview, see Chris Sharrett, ed., *The Apocalyptic Idea in Postmodern Narrative Film*, Washington, DC: Maisoneuve Press, 1993.

9   For the CIA's involvement in television production, see Doug Saunders, 'When the CIA is Happy, It's not a Good Sign', *The Globe and Mail*, October 18, 2003, Linda McQuaig, '9/11 Movie Paints Bush as Hero', *The Toronto Star*, June 1, 2003.

10   On the conventions of the Good War film, see Tom Pollard, 'Hollywood's War Machine', p. 316.

11   See Chalmers Johnson, 'American Militarism and Blowback', in Boggs, ed., *Masters of War*, pp. 124-125.

12   On radicalism and wartime Hollywood, including the combat film, see Paul Buhle and Dave Wagner, *Radical Hollywood The Untold Story of America's Favourite Movies*, New York: The New Press, 2002, pp. 201-260. See R. Claire Snyder, 'Patriarchal Militarism', in Boggs, ed., *Masters of War*, pp. 261 for an interesting discussion of these categories of citizen and warrior in American military history and ideology.

13   For an excellent discussion, see Tom Doherty, 'The New War Movies as Moral Rearmament: *Black Hawk Down* and *We Were Soldiers*', *Cineaste*, XXVII(3), 2002.

14   On human rights imperialism, see Amy Bartholomew and Jennifer Breakspear, 'Human Rights as Swords of Empire', in *Socialist Register 2004*, London: Merlin Press, 2003.

15   See the excellent close analysis in Lila Kataeff, '*Three Kings*: Neocolonial Arab Representation', *Jump Cut*, 46, (Summer) 2003, www.ejumpcut.org. She observes '... the film personalizes an intervention in the affairs of a colonized nation by using the logic of the colonizer to attempt to solve the problems of the colonized.'

16   Kellner and Ryan's *Camera Politica* offers a compelling account of Rambo as a working-class victim articulated with right-wing populism.

17   Schwarzenegger's star persona, and perhaps political potential, has been carefully constructed from film to film, see the case study in Jose Arroyo, ed., *Action/Spectacle Cinema*, pp. 27-58.

18   For an interesting discussion which concludes that the Matrix is our watching Hollywood, see Osha Neumann, 'Selling The Matrix', *Radical Society*, 29(1), 2002, pp. 73-83.

19   Frederic Jameson, 'Postmodernism, Or the Cultural Logic of Late Capitalism', *New Left Review*, 146, 1984, p. 88; also, see Frederic Jameson, 'Reification and Utopia in Mass Culture', *Social Text*, 1(Winter), 1979, pp. 130-48.

20   Friedrich Engels to Philip van Patten, 1883, *Marx and Engels Correspondence*, Moscow: International Publishers, 1968, www.marxists.org/archives.

21   Recent Hollywood films that take up rather daring political subjects include *Bulworth* (1998), *Cradle Will Rock* (1999), *The Gangs of New York* (2002); political documentaries have reached significant audiences recently, including *Bowling for Columbine* (2002), *The Corporation* (2003), *The Fog of War* (2004).

Michael Moore hopes to bring down the Bush government with his new film *Fahrenheit 9/11* (2004). Hollywood has partially managed this competition by creating its own divisions for independent and art films.

22   For a case study of Woo, see Arroyo, ed., *Action/Spectacle Cinema*, pp. 59–82; for a critical discussion of Bigelow, see Yvonne Tasker, 'Bigger than Life', in Arroyo ed., *Action/Spectacle Cinema*, pp. 195–199.

23   Recent trips to past empires and epics include *Master and Commander: The Far Side of the World* (2002), *Pirates of the Caribbean* (2002), *The League of Extraordinary Gentlemen* (2003), *The Last Samurai* (2003), *Hidalgo* (2004), *The Alamo* (2004), *Gladiator* (2001), *Troy* (2004). A more contemporary, Rambo-style example is presented in *Bad Boys 2* (2003); these cops organize their own invasion of Cuba, along with anti–Castro terrorists, recalling, and correcting, the Bay of Pigs fiasco.

FEEDING THE EMPIRE: THE PATHOLOGIES OF GLOBALIZED AGRICULTURE

HARRIET FRIEDMANN

When the negotiations at the World Trade Organization collapsed in the fall of 2003, it was because a coalition of governments from the global South insisted that the governments of the global North meet their commitments under the 1995 Agreement on Agriculture to reduce their farm subsidies and export subsidies, as a condition for negotiating on further rights for multinational corporations, notably investment and intellectual property rights. Agriculture had been explicitly excluded from the General Agreement on Tariffs and Trade (GATT) when it was founded in 1947, so reaching the Agreement on Agriculture (AoA) was one of the great accomplishments of the WTO when it was founded in 1995. But it was mainly an agreement in principle, full of exceptions and exclusions, and few of its promises have yet been kept. Subsidies remain the most divisive issue, and rifts between North and South have now started to overshadow the long-standing rifts on trade issues within the North. In fact, the AoA is now an obstacle to completion of the larger WTO agenda. At the same time, an intersecting mix of new issues, including food safety, genetic technologies and intellectual property, affecting both North and South, are at least as intractable. They pit corporate interests, which now link agriculture and food intimately with the chemical sector, against a range of farm, citizen, indigenous, and consumer groups, and raise jurisdictional questions about the WTO relative to other international institutions.

In this essay I argue that agriculture and food have all along invisibly underpinned relations of property and power in the world system. Now they have finally emerged as key points of conflict in international organizations. A perspective on power and wealth different from the usual one, which emphasizes agriculture as an industry, may indicate alternative paths out of the present impasse of global rule-making. With this goal, I explore in turn (and in brief) the past, present, and possible futures of agriculture, and the social forces at play in determining the conditions under which any possible future will unfold. At the heart of any solution to today's global agricultural impasse the dilemma, I conclude, is an appreciation of 'livelihoods' and 'habitats', that is the living foundations of all human societies: healthy human bodies and relationships and earthly cycles of air, water, soil, and organisms.

FOOD REGIMES UNDER BRITISH AND US HEGEMONY

The present impasse over global rules for agriculture goes deeper than inter-state conflicts. It reflects profound changes in social relations across the whole spectrum of activities related to production and consumption of food, and all on a world scale. To analyze these relations, I adopt the concept of 'food regime', which refers to a relatively bounded historical period in which complementary expectations govern the behaviour of all social actors, such as farmers, firms, and workers engaged in all aspects of food growing, manufacturing, services, distribution, and sales, as well as government agencies, citizens and consumers.[1] Complementary expectations cannot be taken for granted. They exist only at certain times, and work best when they seem 'natural' and are therefore based on norms and rules that are at least partly implicit. Rules for food regimes have been far more implicit than those governing, for example, money or war. Two food regimes have existed so far: the first centred on the Atlantic trade between England and the Americas, which was consolidated after 1870, but also included settler regions that have since declined, such as the Danube Basin and Punjab in British India; the second expanded after World War II to include all the former colonies of Europe, but excluded the Soviet bloc until its collapse, and hinged on the US as rule-maker and – consequently – dominant exporter. The current dissension over food and agriculture stems from structures built in successive food regimes since 1870, and was precipitated by events of the early 1970s, which launched a long unresolved crisis.[2]

The Settler-Colonial Food Regime

The Settler-Colonial Food Regime, which emerged at the height of British global supremacy from 1870 to 1914, created the first price-governed market in an essential means of life. Since 1500 long-distance trade had connected inter-dependent and specialized regions, and grain from agricultural regions exporting from Baltic ports had eventually facilitated the expansion of classes of waged workers, relying on the purchase of food, in Western Europe. However, all governments were still in thrall to the ancient belief that subjects hold rulers responsible for a reliable supply of food. The beginning of the end of this came in 1846 when despite rebellions of rural producers unable to compete in increasingly worldwide food markets, and of urban dwellers still believing that there were 'just prices' for food,[3] the British Parliament took the epochal decision to remove import protection from its domestic farmers by repealing the 'Corn Laws'. This was made possible by the fact that Britain, the dominant power of the time, had created a trans-oceanic market in basic foods (and an ideology of Free Trade to justify it).[4]

The new food regime created an enduring pattern of regional specialization based on the interests and power of the main importer, Britain. Specialized export regions, now re-defined as the world's 'breadbaskets', were established in the Settler-Colonial food regime through the investments by British capital in railways and the violent expulsion of indigenous peoples from their land and their replacement by expanding settler states.[5] The regions settled by European wheat farmers and cattle ranchers included leading members of the present-day Cairns Group of major agricultural exporting countries (led by Australia and Argentina, and including Canada), which at the WTO today promote the complete liberalization of trade in food. Also created as export-dependent regions at this time were those areas feeding the ports on the Baltic and Black Sea, plus Siberia and Northwest British India (these were eclipsed when this food regime collapsed between the First and Second World Wars) and the vast plains area of the United States (which became dominant, however, only in the subsequent food regime). Brazil (an ambivalent Cairns Group member, and key leader of the South at the WTO) would become a major exporter only in the last days of the later food regime. The most important fact to note is that in the Settler-Colonial food regime power and wealth resided in the importing countries, which exported capital and labour to 'improve' (or as we would now say 'develop') lands taken by force from indigenous peoples.

The Settler-Colonial regime also laid the basis for a later industrialization of agriculture, paradoxically through inventing the modern 'family farm'. Unlike peasant agriculture in Europe and elsewhere, settlers on newly surveyed land were put there to serve capital as well as states. After 1870 railway and shipping capital was made profitable by the monocultural export farming of settlers. The poverty of the settlers, who emigrated to escape economic marginalization or political repression, chiefly in Europe, combined with their frequent inexperience in dry grassland farming and the absence of wood or other forest resources, ensured that they would produce as much as possible of what was demanded and buy as much as they could afford, such as barbed wire fencing and mechanical harvesters, as well as goods for personal use.

States achieved maximum efficiency in holding territory against indigenous resistance, or against competing states (e.g. along the US–Canada
border) by settling immigrants on the largest feasible land areas. This ensured
that in the newly settled wheat and livestock export regions labour and not
land would be in short supply (a reversal of the European experience), and
that labour would be provided by the 'self-exploitation' of patriarchal settler
families.[6] Emigration from Europe served the increasingly explicit interests
of European governments in political stability and cheap food, as economic
modernization rendered both villagers and urban workers marginal and
sometimes unruly. The Settler-Colonial food regime thus unfolded via three
mutually reinforcing effects of government policy: emigration from Europe,
settlement of lands converted from indigenous use to commodity production
of European staple foods, and long-distance shipment of low priced wheat
and meat.

A final legacy of the Settler-Colonial regime was the globalization and
simplification of a wheat-beef diet. Wheat, like beef, was once the preserve
of elites, while ordinary people ate 'coarse grains' such as barley, rye, and oats.
As more and more people in Europe and the settler regions entered food
markets, their nutrition was compromised, not only by low wages (a matter
of quantity) but also by lack of variety relative to the garden and wild foods
that at least thriving peasantries had enjoyed.[7] Their diets became simplified,
and tastes shifted towards other colonial imports of sugar, coffee, tea and
cocoa,[8] while opium-based 'medicines' blunted hunger and its effects. In the
1880s a small segment of English workers (and a larger segment in the US)
gained wages that allowed them to aspire to middle-class tastes, such as bread
and roast beef. In the same years, steel roller mills began to manufacture
white flour from hard wheat imported from settler regions, and refrigeration
allowed unprocessed meat to be shipped across the ocean. Workers had more
to eat but the quality of their diet declined as white bread, industrial beer,
sugared tea and jam, and (to some extent) canned foods, lowered its nutri-
tional content.

This directs attention to what Polanyi calls the 'natural' substance of
society. Despite the agro-ecological reality that sustainable food production
relies on an agronomy that preserves and even increases soil fertility, the
Settler-Colonial food regime created an illusion of paradise in which this
reality did not apply – and a corresponding way of measuring productivity.
Monocultures and large land areas per farm created the perception of
increased productivity in settler areas based on two temporary phenomena:
low prices, thanks to the 'mining' of the natural fertility of lands never before
farmed; and a shift in measurement from yields per unit of land to yields per
person. Low prices and soil mining led to an economic and ecological cata-

strophe (the Great Depression and the Dust Bowl) that within less than half a century ended the Settler-Colonial food regime. For consumers, depression and two world wars renewed fear of scarcity, as trade collapsed and prices soared, and as people who had come to depend on their wages for food could no longer revert to personal or geographical ties to the remaining farms.

At the same time ordinary people continued to experiment in relation to changing conditions, but locally, both in growing food, and in what they ate. In many small farms, gardens, and kitchens, people altered systems of mixed cultivation and invented new flavours by incorporating plants and animals that had become available only after colonialism. In Europe, these included potatoes (for fish and chips), maize (polenta), peppers and tomatoes,[9] while in the Americas cattle, mangoes, grapes and many other Old World domesticates entered into cultivation and cuisines. These, too, provided a legacy available to be appropriated by industrial agriculture and food manufacturing, but also for the continual reinvention of farming and cooking.[10]

The collapse of the Settler-Colonial food regime left four enduring legacies which helped to shape new relations of power, property, and trade in the subsequent regime: a labour shortage in agriculture; deeply commodified farms; measures of efficiency based on land-extensive monocultures; and the globalization and 'democratization' of a diet based on wheat and beef.

The Mercantile-Industrial Food Regime

After the prolonged crisis of the Settler-Colonial food regime, which staggered and finally collapsed through the depression and another world war, the United States led the way in creating a new food regime. As the undisputed new hegemon the US had the power and the wealth to protect its domestic policies, and the vision to foster complementary accommodations in the interests of other governments. US post-war economic strategy was explicitly oriented towards re-establishing free trade but as regards agriculture, its situation was unlike that of 19th century Britain in that it faced resistance to free trade by US farmers, who were key to the electoral success of the governing Democratic Party, and had inherited a dependence on exports from the Settler-Colonial regime. Then, in 1947, a convergence of circumstances led to the adoption of a new set of implicitly mercantile rules, institutions and practices in agriculture. The Cold War began, inspiring a new constellation of food policy and foreign policy. US Cold War foreign policy included both dismantling European empires and attracting newly independent governments into a US-centred trading system to compete with the Soviet bloc; until 1972 the US and its allies actually maintained an embargo on trade with the Soviet Union and its allies. Also in 1947 the

World Food Board meeting, led by the US and Britain, rejected plans that had been made during the war for the multilateral regulation of agricultural exports and imports, and agriculture was explicitly excluded from the General Agreement on Tariffs and Trade.[11] Free Trade in agriculture, key to British hegemony, gave way under US hegemony to managed agriculture within the Free World.

Thus in pursuit of both domestic and foreign policies the US led the way in creating a new food regime based on mercantile principles: governments set prices and other conditions for domestic farmers, controlled the distribution (and prices) of food to the poor, and managed imports and exports. Although the mercantile character of 'export subsidies' (or 'dumping') and related 'domestic subsidies' is now recognized in WTO disputes, it was long disguised in the costumes of domestic welfare and foreign aid ('food stamps' in the US and a variety of schemes initiated by postcolonial governments, especially those in receipt of 'food aid'). In one sense food aid really was an innovation, specific to the new monetary regime of fixed exchange rates, and took the form of 'concessional sales' of food, purchased in nonconvertible currencies.[12] It began with Marshall Aid, of which a full 40 per cent consisted of food, feed and fertilizers, and which created economic foundations for the former colonies of Britain, France, etc. to reorient their trade from the old empires to the United States.

European governments welcomed Marshall aid for its role in rebuilding their agriculture – mainly wheat and livestock – on 'modern' lines, and because the US supported a massive import substitution project for wheat (and sugar beets) via the 1957 Common Agricultural Policy (CAP), which has endured as a centre-piece of European integration. Governments in the former colonies welcomed subsidized exports because cheap food fostered alliances between ruling elites that distributed it and urban populations that received it, lowered world prices even for non-recipients, and provided a model for governments to intervene directly in their own agriculture and trade. Cheap food also fitted well with the shared belief in 'development' – also first articulated in 1947[13] – by encouraging a shift of labour from 'backward' peasant agriculture to 'modern' industry. Less powerful and wealthy export countries, such as Canada, Australia, and Argentina (which much later formed the Cairns Group), compensated for the loss of exports to the US by creating marketing boards and managing food supplies, both to stabilize domestic agriculture and to cut back production in face of growing US export shares.

New patterns of regional specialization and trade emerged in the Mercantile-Industrial food regime, fostering a 'modern' diet based on wheat and beef. First, US export dominance, far from being a natural result of US resources or efficiency, was based on its unique capacity to use tax revenues to buy vast quantities of domestic wheat and accept payment for exporting it in, for example, pesos or rupees. Similarly, far from lacking land, labour, or skills to feed their own people, in 1947 most of the former colonies of Africa and Asia, as well as of Latin America, had sufficient domestic food supplies, and many exported food. Under the norms of the new Mercantile-Industrial food regime they accepted subsidized imports, sacrificing their domestic peas-antries and encouraging a taste for wheat among their own urban consumers.[14] Second, during the Allied Occupation Japan changed its imports from Asian rice to US wheat and animal feeds. Third, also with US encouragement, Europe adopted US-style farm support and related trade policies in order to change its historic situation as a food importer. True, an import substitution model required higher levels of import protection and domestic agricultural subsidies than were required in the US. But in less than three decades the CAP reversed Europe's trading position from importer to exporter, and also led to the subsidizing of exports of government-held surpluses. Europe ulti-mately came to compete with the US in world wheat markets, leading in the 1980s to conflicts verging on trade war, and to a shift in the perception of what was involved from 'food aid' to 'dumping'.[15]

The new patterns of international specialization that unfolded in the fifties and sixties reflected and encouraged a deepening of commodity relations through industrial technologies and capitalist firms. US government subsidies for agricultural commodities, including the recently introduced soybeans, supported efforts by machinery and agrochemical corporations to encourage farmers to specialize far more than before. The most significant step was to separate crops from livestock, and offer industrial inputs to replace the complementary functions of plants (as food for livestock) and animals (as power to pull equipment and as the source of manure to fertilize crops). Giant corporations emerged selling farm machinery powered by fossil fuels, and chemical fertilizers and manufactured feedstuffs based on maize and soymeal. Intensive livestock operations in turn encouraged the conversion of grain farms from producing food for human consumption to producing animal feeds, particularly soybeans and maize.[16] The new monocultures, however, provided feasts for crop predators of all kinds, and as insects, diseases, fungi and weeds adapted to manufactured pesticides, they required ever greater quantities to be applied. Eventually the main applications of genetic technology to crops would be those designed to increase the toler-ance of feed crops (soybeans and maize) to ever greater applications of the herbicide glyphosate.

Within the mercantile framework of the food regime, governments in most regions encouraged the industrialization of agriculture on the US model, often by importing industrial inputs from the US. In contrast to the labour scarcity and early specialization typical in settler regions, where industrial agriculture was invented, in Europe and the ex-colonial regions industrial monocultures confronted labour-intensive and ecologically-adapted mixed farming or peasant systems.[17] While European feedstuff manufacturers supplied inputs for most domestic intensive livestock operations, they used as raw materials maize and soy, at first imported almost entirely from the US. The producers of the specialized crops supported by the CAP dispensed with the use of animals in favour of industrially produced tools, chemicals, and feedstuffs. The Third World, where peasantries persisted despite pressure from cheap world grain supplies, undertook its own modernization (and sometimes import substitution) in the sixties and seventies through the Green Revolution. High yielding varieties of rice, wheat, maize, and potatoes led to the introduction of monocultures in place of mixed farms and required industrially-produced, often imported, inputs. In post-colonial settings the marginalization of peasant farms through imports and the industrialization of agriculture led to the shedding of farm labour that could not easily be absorbed elsewhere, and compromised traditional agronomic systems and the many foods, medicines, and ecological services they had provided. Vitamin A, for example, a micronutrient contained in many of the food plants destroyed as weeds in the conversion to monoculture, became a more significant deficiency. Eventually genetic modification would be undertaken to insert Vitamin A in rice.

Meanwhile, on the sales side, industrial farmers supplied new customers. Individuals and local retailers gave way to food manufacturing corporations and supermarkets. While small farms had supplied canneries in the first food regime, now they had to become larger and more specialized in order to enter into long distance supply streams or enter into contracts with ever larger firms.[18] Most significantly, there was a proliferation of new manufactured edible commodities composed of many substitutable raw materials, such as 'fats', 'sweeteners', 'thickeners', and 'flavours', and eventually of chemically synthesized substitutes for organic food sources.[19] Food manufacturing and, later, service industries transformed diets, beginning in North America. Instead of the form that had characterized human diets for thousands of years, based on a starchy staple complemented by a variety of (mostly) plants providing flavours and proteins,[20] the Mercantile-Industrial food regime introduced a manufactured diet whose main components are fats and sweeteners, supplemented with starches, thickeners, proteins, and synthesized flavours.[21]

But industry and technology inevitably outgrew the mercantile framework, which constrained the freedom of agrobusinesses to source agricultural raw materials, and to sell edible commodities, anywhere on the globe. While still content to accept subsidies,[22] in the 1980s agro-food corporations joined efforts, led by governments which could not compete in the mercantile game, to end government management of agricultural commodities. The turning-point was the world food crisis of 1972-73.

THE CONTINUING CRISIS OF THE MERCANTILE-INDUSTRIAL FOOD REGIME

The Mercantile-Industrial food regime rested on trading blocs that had been created and sustained by Cold War embargoes. The defining feature of the regime – government-held surplus agricultural commodities – were like a lake whose elevated level depended on the dam between the rival political blocs. Suddenly, in 1972 and 1973, the dam was breached when the US, as part of its new policy of détente, sold vast quantities of agricultural commodities to the Soviet Union.[23] A torrent of grains and soybeans flowing from the Free World to the Soviet bloc ended an era of surplus stocks that had begun in 1947. As in the oil crisis of the same years, grain and soybean prices tripled, and even though surpluses quickly returned in response to the high prices, they changed from a source of power to a liability. The sudden food scarcity undermined each of the convergent expectations that under-pinned the regime.

The US quickly lost its dominant position. Panicked by organized protests by consumers angered by high meat prices, and by farm organizations incensed at the windfall profits captured by the grain trading companies, Congress slapped an embargo on soybean exports. Japan, which depended on US exports for the source of vegetable protein in its national diet, protested. The US quickly reinstated shipments but the damage to Japanese confidence had been done, and Japan invested in new sources. As a result, Brazil became the first of several major export competitors with the US.[24] Relative earnings were greater for Brazilian soy exports, which in contrast to US raw bean exports were mainly processed in Brazil by joint ventures between Japanese investors and the Brazilian government.

Europe simultaneously reduced its imports of US feedstuffs and became an aggressive competitor in wheat exports. Europe was able to diversify its imports of maize and soybeans by turning to the New Agricultural Countries.[25] This contributed to the growth of commercially-priced at the expense of subsidized shipments. At the same time, Europe increased its exports of CAP wheat in direct competition with those of the US, thus intensifying mercantile competition to the point of a near trade war. The US government urged farmers to respond to high prices by removing limits on acreage to encourage maximum production (these limits had contained surpluses within manageable limits, as well as promoting soil conservation).

In the 1980s and '90s the US intensified its state-supported export strategies. Ironically, after paying cash for early US shipments, the USSR lost its ability to pay, in part because of the costs of the renewed Cold War arms race in the 1980s. The US, faced with competition from both commercial and CAP-subsidized exports, chose to shift its concessional shipments away from the South and to the USSR and, after its collapse, to Russia. By now the US gained no advantage from these exports other than being able to dump surpluses. The economy was now manifestly hooked on agricultural exports. A new way of talking about food exports emerged, explicitly centred on agriculture as a source of US power.[26] This debate reflected a loss of hegemony, in which that power had been real, invisible and widely accepted as beneficial.

Meanwhile, the Third World was abandoned by the new food regime. Development, which in practice meant industrialization, had created widespread dependency on imports of energy and food. When both became scarce in the early 1970s it led to recession in the capitalist world and shifted wealth to oil-rich governments, which in turn lent to governments in the South and Eastern Europe. At the same time, prices for exports from the South plummeted, as food industries developed substitutes for the raw materials produced in the former colonies, notably sugar and tropical vegetable oils. Several major substitutes, such as high fructose corn syrup and maize and soy oils, were relatively cheap because of US commodity programs. The South borrowed, and transnational banks lent, with little prospect of repayment, and within a decade the Mexican default officially launched the debt crisis.

Structural Adjustment policies, widely imposed on indebted countries by, first, the International Monetary Fund, and then the World Bank, forced debtors to adopt policies that worsened the conditions inherited from the now dying Mercantile-Industrial food regime. Most of the items in the standard list of 'conditionalities' that emerged during successive debt renegotiations after the Mexican default of 1982 had negative effects for food security. The abolition of food subsidies exposed poor consumers to higher and less stable prices, leading to 'IMF riots'.[27] Convertibility of currencies led to the failure of local industries and the reduction of government expenditures led to fewer public employees and more poor consumers, especially in urban areas. The abolition of agricultural subsidies undermined the remaining peasant sectors, sometimes still quite large, and the dismantling or disempowering of government marketing boards (and other instruments for managing agricultural production and trade) exposed domestic food producers to even more intense competition by commodities from the

North – which continued to benefit from both production and trade subsidies. The conditions set by Structural Adjustment Programs were meant to increase export earnings to repay debts, both by increasing traditional exports (such as sugar and coffee, despite chronically low prices), and by introducing 'non-traditional' exports (such as 'counter-seasonal' fruits and vegetables, the expansion of cattle production for the hamburger industries, aquaculture of fish and shellfish, and flowers). In the well-publicized case of cattle grazing in the Amazon, poverty encouraged a new round of settler expansion at the expense of the original inhabitants of the area, and of a tropical forest ecosystem that was even more quickly degraded than the grasslands of the Settler-Colonial food regime had been.

POLICY RESPONSES: HOW TRADE SHIFTED THE AGENDA FROM FIGHTING HUNGER TO ADVANCING PROPERTY RIGHTS

Within a decade there was a dramatic shift in policy responses to the troubles of the Mercantile-Industrial food regime. The United Nations, which had languished under the Mercantile-Industrial regime, was resuscitated at the moment of crisis. The first response was multilateral and inclusive of the South; indeed it was focused on the problem of world hunger. The Food and Agriculture Organization (FAO) called a World Food Summit (WFS) in 1974 to address the sudden spurt in the numbers of hungry people caused by the price rises. Attending states declared that 'every man, woman and child has the inalienable right to be free from hunger and malnutrition in order to develop their physical and mental faculties' and committed themselves to achieving this right universally within a decade.[28] The Summit created the World Food Council to upgrade the desultory activities of the World Food Program, the International Fund for Agricultural Development and the FAO Committee on World Food Security.

Thus the 'right to food' and 'food security' were now defined as goals after decades of assuming that such issues could be left to industrial agriculture. Multilateral institutions were upgraded (and European and OPEC bilateral aid was expanded) to fill in for the drastically reduced bilateral US 'concessional' flows. The aim of food aid became more consistently 'humanitarian'. Even US food aid legislation was changed to convert it from sales to grants in the wake of revelations that allocations had been used in unauthorized support of the US war in Vietnam.

The commitments undertaken in 1974 were far from met. Indeed, over twenty years later, in 1996, the WFS adopted a more modest target of 'reducing by half the number of undernourished people by no later than the year 2015.'[29] And five years after that the WFS declared that the estimated reduction required in the number of the hungry by eight million per year would have to be increased to twenty-two million in order to achieve the same target, and feebly called on governments to meet their commitments.[30] The inclusive and multilateral focus on hunger reduction had been sidelined, along with the more comprehensive initiatives of the New International Economic Order promoted by the United Conference on Trade and Development in the shape of the Brandt Commission report, *North-South: A Project for Survival.*

Instead trade, now defined far more comprehensively than in the past, replaced food security as a dominant objective. The neoliberal project that took shape during the 1980s had specific goals for agriculture and food, specifically their inclusion for the first time in trade agreements. The Uruguay Round of the GATT began in 1986 against a background of debt-enforced 'adjustment' in the South and dangerous trade conflicts over agriculture in the North. The South was already converting from domestic to export agriculture, under double pressure to open its domestic markets to subsidized food from the North and to increase export earnings through exporting 'non-traditional' (mainly luxury) products to the North. Sometimes this meant the conversion of African or Caribbean land and labour to supply *haricots verts* to France, or carnations to Canada; other times it meant the monocultural production of 'improved' and standardized traditional crops for export, such as tomatoes from Mexico.[31] In the North, the US and the European Community were caught in disastrous export competition; the US was pressing a reluctant Japan to remove import barriers; and the US and other exporters attacked European restrictions, notably on the use of hormones in beef production, as ploys designed to protect not consumer health but domestic livestock producers. Smaller exporting countries that could not afford to play the competitive subsidy game formed the Cairns Group to press for an Agreement on Agriculture that would subordinate all agricultural policies to the single criterion of outlawing 'trade distortion'.

Amidst the many cross-cutting national interests and alliances (extending, as we shall soon see, to new issues and institutions as well), the US was caught between its attachment to the old GATT as a useful tool for shoring up its mercantile advantage (and supporting other strategic goals), and the possible advantages of a new multilateral institution to press its interests as a dominant food producer. In anticipation of agreement, Europe (and to some extent the US) began to restructure domestic farm subsidies to 'decouple' production from trade and link them to social, environmental, and rural development goals. But subsidies, including export subsidies, remained high in both the US and Europe. Food safety issues remained unresolved, and continue to rankle, as a WTO ruling forces the EU to pay $180 million per year to the US for the right to retain the ban on beef hormones, and complex issues of 'traceability' have replaced the expired EU moratorium on GM foods.

While US and CAP policies were deeply institutionalized, agrofood corporations – the *industrial* half of the regime – began to chafe at the *mercantile* rules and practices that had spawned them. By the 1980s the interests of these corporations had become far more complex than trade alone, and included rules on intellectual property, a concept which was itself widened to cover living organisms; production methods, including new genetic and other technologies; and reorganizations enabling them to source and sell globally. One wave of corporate mergers concentrated food manufacturers into giant enterprises linked to tobacco. Another wave of mergers linked agricultural chemical companies with both grain traders and seed companies. Just as food and agriculture were becoming a branch of the chemical industry, genetic engineering became a leading-edge technology. Profits from control over seeds thus drove the private sector agenda of research in genetic applications – an extension of the earlier agenda driving conventional breeding towards hybrids rather than open-pollinated varieties.[32] In particular, Monsanto Corporation sought to extend the profits on its herbicide glyphosate beyond the life of its patent by substituting patented seeds genetically engineered to tolerate increased applications of the chemical (increased applications were necessary as weeds developed resistance). After US courts accepted Monsanto's arguments and overruled the Patent Office to allow patenting of life forms, the US pressed to 'harmonize' the WTO agenda in that direction.[33] More than three quarters of GM crops planted on 52.6 million hectares in 2001 were designed for herbicide tolerance.[34]

While the corporate agenda increasingly focused on intellectual property as the driver for the global reorganization of agriculture, it was the unwillingness of governments of the North to abolish their domestic farm and export subsidies that inspired the alliance of South states, led by Brazil, India and the newly admitted WTO member China, to refuse to negotiate further. The G20 (whose numbers are in constant revision) may not hold together beyond that veto. This is partly because of their ambivalence about liberalized trade; although food security and viable peasant sectors are increasingly appreciated for a variety of reasons, the deep changes wrought by structural adjustment seem to have narrowed the alternatives to exporting, and the failure of the North to open its agricultural markets is experienced as hypocrisy that is vulnerable in the WTO. At the same time Venezuela, an oil-exporting country free from debt collection conditions, is pursuing food security against American pressures for a Free Trade Agreement of the Americas and the severe threats from multiple forces at home, also supported

by the US. Brazil, whose Workers' Party was elected on a Zero Hunger plat-
form, may be large enough to challenge the whole system of perpetual debt.
At the same time, social movements in both North and South are growing
more sophisticated in understanding old issues, such as hunger and land
reform, and linking them to new issues, such as control over seeds and
knowledge, health, and agroecology.

NEW ISSUES AND INSTITUTIONS

New issues have complicated the politics of hunger and agricultural trade
today. Parallel to the WTO and the FAO, three new processes unfolded in
the 1990s. First, the Earth Summit of 1992 set a new agenda and created a
crosscutting set of inter-state alliances. Responding to social movements and
scientific findings, the UN made two agreements – both of which remain to
be ratified by enough governments to come into effect, but which also
provide a focus for alternatives to emerge for food and agriculture. The
Climate Change agreement has not so far been attached to agrofood issues,
but this may change with increasing attention to the unsustainable dependency on fossil fuel energy involved in both industrial agriculture and
long-distance transport ('food miles').[35] More immediately, the Convention
on Biological Diversity (CBD) introduced a 'precautionary' approach,
shifting the burden of proof for safety to exporters. This has been a focal
point for organizing against GM crops and has created new alliances. In
particular, since most of the world's genetic diversity, including the wild
ancestors of most food crops, is in the South, concern about loss of biodi-
versity and conditions for sustaining it give the South an advantage in genetic
'resources'. Thus well-endowed Ethiopia has taken leadership at the CBD,
and Brazil has conflicting alliances, protesting against industrial agriculture at
the CBD while promoting exports in the Cairns Group. Environmental
issues have thus complicated trade agendas and offer alternative foci for
shaping the future of food and agriculture.

Second, the health risks associated with industrial agriculture, manufactured foods and fast foods have led to international disputes and rising citizen
concerns. New strains of bacteria, antibiotic resistance, and new animal
diseases transmissible to humans, are all associated with industrial agriculture.
Unknown effects of chemical additives, as well as highly publicized findings
of the harmful effects of altered ingredients (such as 'trans-fats') in processed
foods, and the alarming rise in obesity and related diseases worldwide, are
associated with industrially produced diets. A cascade of crises has brought
food and agriculture into the public's consciousness. Some, such as the recent
discovery of BSE in a Canadian cow, inaugurated complicated trade negotiations over bans among (at least) Canada, the US, and Japan. Thus, who

should decide on risks, and what criteria should dominate, are in dispute both nationally and internationally.

Governments in the North have always exercised control over imports on safety and health grounds, and applied elaborate national food safety regulations to do so. It has often been used as a hidden protection for domestic producers (e.g. a longstanding US ban on Argentine beef on grounds of hoof-and-mouth disease). The 'precautionary principle', which emerged from the early politics of air pollution,[36] is now inscribed in the European Constitution. It is often supported by Japan, and sometimes by states in the South, and has come to play an important role at the WTO through Sanitary and Phyto-Sanitary measures and the WTO-sanctioned food standards body of the UN (the Codex Alimentarius, a joint body of FAO and the World Health Organization). In both venues, the US leads the opposition to 'precaution' under the competing rubric of 'sound science'. Where the former acknowledges uncertainty and the political nature of risk assessment, the latter emphasizes expertise as the arbiter of risks and thus presupposes an objectivity based on formal knowledge. It is important to note that many scientists object to the use of science to make policy decisions, such as whether a genetically modified crop is 'substantially equivalent' to one that is not, and to justify risks imposed on citizens without democratic discussion.[37]

Third, social movements have proliferated around all these issues, including some very new ones related to indigenous rights and knowledge, and have increasingly engaged in discussions seeking common ground across national and social divides. In 'parallel summits' of non-governmental organizations and social movements at the FAO and other UN organizations, and since 2001 at the World Social Forum, the politics of hunger have found new strength by allowing people from North and South to discuss policies related to price, access, safety and health. Other participants in these meetings are new international organizations of small farmers, including indigenous farmers, such as Via Campesina, and movements for land reform, notably the Landless Workers Movement in Brazil. Agricultural discussions increasingly link North-South issues, such as the appropriation of genetic materials found in the South by corporations using patents acquired in the North. The intellectual property rights governed by the WTO are now regularly disputed legally, patent claim by patent claim. They are also challenged in principle by the proponents of alternatives, including the democratic regulation of the commons, bioregional reorganization of farming systems to follow watersheds and other natural features, and the promotion of cultural diversity clearly resting on livelihoods evolved in specific places.

CONCLUSION: THE PROSPECTS FOR LIVELIHOOD

As a bureaucratic language evolves to reflect these pressures from below (such as the 'multifunctionality' of agriculture), conflicts over language (e.g. a 'right to food' versus 'food sovereignty') reflect unresolved issues in popular movements. Nonetheless, a new vision of 'livelihood' may be taking shape in global consciousness. A case in point is the recent decision by Monsanto to withdraw its application to the Canadian government to approve GM wheat due to 'lack of demand'. Whence comes this 'lack of demand'? European and Japanese government resistance rests on public opposition, which stiffens governments' resolve in international negotiations. Consumer resistance, which is surprisingly high in the global South (as shown in the refusal of GM food aid), is lower in North America. Yet the coalition in Canada resisting GM wheat linked interests that otherwise tend to be opposed – farmers, environmentalists, and the Canadian Wheat Board.[38]

Two successive food regimes and their crises have reflected Polanyi's 'double movement' between periods of freeing market forces and periods in which regulation is renewed in response to damage done to people and their habitats. The free trade of the Settler-Colonial food regime integrated the world's agriculture and food, but after fifty years collapsed in social and economic catastrophe. The government-managed systems of the Mercantile-Industrial food regime spawned corporations and rising agricultural regions eager to reinstitute Free Trade. This time the cumulative effects of the two regimes has widened the scope and scale of the agrofood system to the point of destroying all the wild places that previously absorbed ecological shocks of agriculture. And it has deepened commodity relations to the point where virtually nowhere can people feed themselves without resort to increasingly global markets.

An increasingly transnational public dialogue is taking place over how to promote human and ecosystem well-being. A promising concept to make the human and natural substance of society into a program for public policy at all levels is that of 'ecological public health' proposed by Tim Lang and his associates in the UK.[39] Health is the avenue through which citizens all over the world are discovering the fundamental connection between human health and ecosystem integrity. Whether it is this or another concept or concepts that brings into focus an alternative to a trade- and property-centred agenda, certain issues will have to be decided. Who owns knowledge? Who owns plants? Who owns genes? What applications of genetic knowledge serve the well-being of all? How are risks assessed, and who decides which risks are worth taking? Who is responsible for unanticipated problems, such as genetic pollution or loss of pollinating insects or allergic reactions to unknown components of altered foods? What kinds of accounting and money systems might foster something new at the limits of specialization, industrialization, and homogenization, a web of human food systems based on diversity, ecological awareness, justice, and democracy?

In answering these questions I find it useful to adopt Polanyi's focus on both the human and the natural substance of society, and to interpret agriculture in terms of *livelihood*, or social provisioning, conceptually re-linking human activities with needs, and social relations with habitats. The re-emergence of agriculture into the centre of policy conflicts offers the possibility of correcting the curious blindness of the development era to the ineluctable relationship between society and nature, and of making agriculture the fundamental point from which to assess what is right and wrong about current and future global rules and relationships.[40]

NOTES

1   Stephen Krasner, 'Structural Causes and Regime Consequences: Regimes as Intervening Variables', in Stephen Krasner, ed., *International Regimes*, Ithaca: Cornell University Press, 1983, pp. 1-22, 355-368.
2   Harriet Friedmann, 'International Relations of Food', in Barbara Harriss-White and Sir Raymond Hoffenberg, eds., *Food: Multidisciplinary Perspectives*, Oxford: Basil Blackwell, 1994 (also *New Left Review*, 197, 1993, pp. 29-57).
3   Charles Tilly, 'Food Supply and the Public Order in Modern Europe', in Charles Tilly, ed., *The Formation of National States in Western Europe*, Princeton: Princeton University Press, 1975.
4   *The Economist* was founded to argue for free trade, which it continues to do.
5   William Cronon, *Changes in the Land: Indians, Colonists, and the Ecology of New England*, New York: Hill and Wang, 1984; and *Nature's Metropolis: Chicago and the Great West*, New York: W.W. Norton, 1991.
6   The concept of self-exploitation is taken from A.V. Chayanov, *The Theory of Peasant Economy*, edited by Daniel Thorner, Basile Kerblay and R.E.F. Smith, Homewood IL: Richard D. Irwin, for the American Economics Association, 1966. See also Harriet Friedmann, 'Patriarchal Commodity Production', in Alison MacEwen Scott, ed., *Rethinking Petty Commodity Production*, special issue of *Social Analysis*, 20, 1986, pp. 47-55.
7   Robert McC. Netting, *Smallholders,Householders: Farm Families and the Ecology of Intensive, Sustainable Agriculture,* Stanford CA: Stanford University Press, 1993.
8   Sidney W. Mintz, *Sweetness and Power: The Place of Sugar in Modern History*, New York: Viking, 1985.
9   Alfred Crosby, *The Columbian Exchange: Biological and Cultural Consequences of 1492*, New York: Praeger, 2003.
10   See the contrast and relation between High Modernity and Metis in James C. Scott, *Seeing Like a State: How Certain Schemes to Improve the Human Condition have Failed*, New Haven CT: Yale University Press, 1998.
11   The US also failed to ratify the International Trade Organization agreement

of 1948, largely to protect its agricultural import quotas.

12   In 1954 US Food for Peace (PL480) legislation created a system of sales abroad, in inconvertible currencies, of surplus US government-held stocks of agricultural commodities (mainly wheat), which had resulted from US farm programs set up to stabilize commodity prices for US farmers. Both Marshall aid and PL480 aid mostly took the form of 'concessional sales' in inconvertible national currencies. European and Japanese economies were devastated (and Great Britain indebted to the US) after World War II, and for more than a decade were not able to earn enough through exports to make currencies convertible with dollars. The Third World never aspired to convertibility in these years, because overvalued currencies were key to import substitution in industry. Concessional sales meant that the US held accounts of francs, yen, pesos or rupees in each recipient country, which could be spent only in that country. It was reasonably considered 'aid', but at the same time gave the US resources to use in its own interests in these countries, a situation that later contributed to loss of legitimacy (see 'enduring crisis' section below). See Harriet Friedmann, 'The Political Economy of Food', and Robert E. Wood, *From Marshall Plan to Debt Crisis: Foreign Aid and Development Choices in the World Economy*, Berkeley: University of California Press, 1986.

13   Gustavo Esteva, 'Development', in Wolfgang Sachs, ed., *The Development Dictionary: A Guide to Knowledge as Power*, London: Zed, 1995.

14   The most notorious case may be Nigeria, a colossal policy failure documented by Björn Beckman and Gunilla Andræ in *The Wheat Trap: Bread and Underdevelopment in Nigeria*, London: Zed Press, in association with Scandinavian Institute of African Studies, 1985.

15   Humanitarian food aid, in the form of gifts rather than loans, was a minor part of US PL480 shipments. It is now distinct. Multilateral humanitarian food aid, particularly through the UN World Food Program, has also become more important.

16   See Daryll E. Ray, Daniel G. De La Torre Ugarte and Kelly J. Tiller, *Rethinking US Agricultural Policy: Changing Course to Secure Farmer Livelihoods Worldwide*, Agricultural Policy Analysis Center, University of Tennessee, 2003. Available at http://www.agpolicy.org.

17   Netting, *Smallholders, Householders*.

18   This has been extensively studied through 'commodity chain analysis', pioneered in agriculture by William Friedland, Amy E. Barton and Robert J. Thomas, *Manufacturing Green Gold: Capital, Labor, and Technology in the Lettuce Industry*, Cambridge: Cambridge University Press, 1981. A recent example is Deborah Barndt, *Tangled Routes: Women, and Globalization on the Tomato Trail*, Toronto: Garamond, 2002.

19   See David Goodman, Bernardo Sorj and John Wilkinson, *From Farming to Biotechnology: A Theory of Agro-industrial Development*, Oxford: Basil Blackwell, 1987 and the popular book by Eric Schlosser, *Fast Food Nation: The Dark Side of the All-American Meal*, Boston: Houghton Mifflin, 2001. The first true manufactured food in this sense was margarine, which unlike butter or plant-based oils, could be manufactured from any fat. The margarine industry first

used cottonseed oil and lard, which were cheap byproducts of textiles and meatpacking. It soon encouraged government commodity programs in soy to create a stable supply of oil. Then, to complete the circle, a byproduct of soy oil was soymeal, which fostered the growth of intensive livestock feed industries. Soymeal required a grain complement for animal feed, and to supply the livestock industry, vast acreages switched to a simple rotation of maize and soy. See Jean-Pierre Bertrand, Catherine Laurent and Vincent LeClercq, *Le Monde du Soja*, Paris: Editions Decouverte, 1983.

20   Sidney W. Mintz, 'Eating and Being: What Food Means', in Harriss-White and Hoffenberg, *Food*, pp. 102-115.

21   Ibid., and Goodman, Sorj and Wilkinson, *From Farming to Biotechnology*.

22   Export subsidies were paid to grain trading companies, not to farmers. See Dan Morgan, *Merchants of Grain*, London: Penguin Books, 1980.

23   In 1968 Canada had sold wheat to China, which was by then hostile to the Soviet Union, but both countries were marginal players in the Mercantile-Industrial food regime.

24   US export share fell within a few years from a virtual monopoly to about two-thirds.

25   A frequently noted feature of the period was the emergence of Newly Industrialising Countries (NICs). NACs were their counterpart in undercutting US dominance in the food regime. See Friedmann, 'International Political Economy of Food'.

26   The idea of 'green power' referred to control over world food exports.

27   John Walton and David Seddon, *Free Markets and Food Riots: The Politics of Global Adjustment*, Oxford: Blackwell, 1994.

28   http://www.fao.org/wfs/index_en.htm.

29   Ibid.

30   http://www.fao.org/DOCREP/MEETING/005/Y7106E/Y7106E09. htm#TopOfPage.

31   Barndt, *Tangled Routes*.

32   Jack Ralph Kloppenburg, Jr., *First the Seed: The Political Economy of Plant Biotechnology, 1492-2000*, Cambridge: Cambridge University Press, 1988.

33   Lawrence Busch, 'Workshop on the Politics of Genetically Modified Seeds, Masters in International Relations', Toronto, University of Toronto, January 2003.

34   Erik Millstone and Tim Lang, *The Atlas of Food*, London: Earthscan, 2003, p. 44.

35   For example, transporting one kg of asparagus from Chile to New York emits 4.7 kg of carbon dioxide (Millstone and Lang, *Atlas of Food*, p. 67); Lang is the originator of this useful measure. For a local application, see Stephen Bentley, 'Fighting Global Warming at the Farmer's Market: The Role of Local Food Systems in Reducing Greenhouse Gas Emissions', A FoodShare Research in Action Report, Toronto, January, 2004.

36   Maarten Hajer, *The Politics of Environmental Discourse: Ecological Modernization and the Policy Process*, Oxford: Clarendon Press, 1995.

37   Royal Society of Canada Expert Panel on the Future of Food Biotechnology,

Elements of Precaution: Recommendations for the Regulation of Food Biotechnology in Canada, February, 2001, available at http://www.rsc.ca/foodbiotechnology/indexEN.html.

38   Andre Magnan, 'Strange Bedfellows: Contentious Coalitions and the Politics of GM Wheat', unpublished manuscript, Department of Sociology, University of Toronto, April, 2004.

39   See, for example, Tim Lang and Michael Heasman, 'Diet and Nutrition Policy: A Clash of Ideas or Investments?', *Development*, 47(2), 2004, pp. 47-63.

40   Colin Duncan, *The Centrality of Agriculture: Between Humankind and the Rest of Nature*, Montreal: McGill-Queen's Press, 1996.

REVIVING THE DEVELOPMENTAL STATE? THE MYTH OF THE 'NATIONAL BOURGEOISIE'

VIVEK CHIBBER

Speaking at a meeting with domestic bankers in the fall of 2003, in the wake of the calamitous implosion of his country's economy, Argentine President Nestor Kirchner announced his intention to rescue the Argentine economy from the ruins of neo-liberalism. But, he declared, 'it is impossible to build a national project if we do not consolidate a national bourgeoisie'.[1] In fact, this speech was only one among many he made following his inauguration in May, stressing the need for a 'national capitalism'. Kirchner has not been alone in this. In Brazil, the rise to power of Luis Inacio Lula da Silva and the Worker's Party has revived talk of a social pact between labour and capital, and the possibility of carving out a space for Brazilian development through an alliance with 'national' industrialists – represented, most pointedly, in the choice of textile magnate Jose Alencar as Lula's Vice-President. And both Kirchner and Lula follow in the wake of Venezuelan President Hugo Chavez, who, in the face of open hostility from the United States, has railed against neo-liberal orthodoxy, exhorting developing countries to reclaim the legacy of national development models.

All this talk of national capitalisms and social pacts alludes to an era that appeared to be buried, once and for all, under the weight of the Washington Consensus. This was the half-century of 'developmentalism', spanning the years of the Great Depression to the debt crisis of the 1980s. In the immediate aftermath of the debt crisis, it did seem that the drive toward liberalization and privatization had acquired an irresistible force in the developing world. There was an ineluctable quality to the dismantling of the policy apparatus handed down from the years of development planning, enough to make even the mention of 'national projects' seem somewhat quaint. But matters are different today. After the dismal economic record of the quarter-century under neo-liberal hegemony, the experience of the 1950s and '60s has gained respectability – as indeed it should. For despite its somewhat ignominious end, the developmentalist era out-performed its successor on most every measure.[2] Politically, the dismal record of neoliberalism has meant a steady loss of legitimacy in the South. Thus, it is not altogether surprising to find a revival of the ambition to construct national development.

The call for a return to a kind of 'developmentalism' is not only to be found among political elites. It also emanates from a powerful and articulate wing of the anti-globalization movement – critical intellectuals, NGOs, and trade unions. In a period when free market policies have little credibility, but labour is not strong enough to pose a serious challenge to private property, some kind of statist development project appears to many to be the 'transitional programme' of our time. Defending a space for national capitalist development, under the direction of domestic groups, at least seems consistent in *principle* with conscious direction of the economy – even if under the hegemony of the national bourgeoisie.

This nostalgia for the bygone era is certainly understandable. In many respects, I am sympathetic to it. But we also have behind us a half-century of experience with just such models of development, models which relied upon, and fostered the growth of, domestic capitalists. It may, therefore, be of some relevance to turn to the historical record, in order to examine closely the political preconditions for, and consequences of, developmentalist projects.

I have already noted that in many crucial respects the record of the developmentalist years is superior to that of the years that followed. But any acknowledgement of its successes must also take account of its internal contradictions, since these contributed powerfully to the model's eventual disintegration. In fact, I will argue that the economic weaknesses of the model can in large measure be explained by the kind of political alliance that was required to support it; in particular, by the ways in which capitalists were able to impose limits on the scope of state power. Further, the political conditions which made the developmentalist alliance possible at all required concessions from workers which may well, in current conditions, be unacceptable. Hence, even if national development projects of the kind alluded to may be possible, they may not be *desirable* – at least not to progressives. The whole matter turns on the nature, the interests, and the power of the class to which Kirchner made his overture upon taking office in 2003 – the national bourgeoisie.

Three sets of expectations have traditionally been associated with national capitalists, especially within the Marxist tradition, where they are sometimes elevated to the status of historic 'missions'. The main expectation is that, because they derive their profits from the domestic market, national capitalists have an interest in the expansion of capitalist relations, and in rapid economic growth; hence their status as the linchpin of national development strategies in the modern era. Deriving from this are two other putative interests. They are expected to spearhead, or at least accede to, the abolition of pre-capitalist relations, since this is the precondition for the spread of capitalism. This was the basis for the expectation, among Marxists of the Third International, that the bourgeoisie was a natural ally in the 'anti-feudal' stage of liberation movements. A final expectation was that this class would also have a natural interest in opposing imperial economic encroachment – again, because of its dependence on the domestic market. In this, the national bourgeoisie was inevitably contrasted with the local 'compradors', who, because of their links with metropolitan firms, were seen as irredeemably tied to imperial interests.

Political and economic developments over the past decades have called all this into question. National capitalists showed very little inclination to participate in attacking feudal landed classes. Further, that there was a clear separation between the 'national' and 'comprador' wings of the domestic bourgeoisie has also been called into question. No doubt, there were distinct interests associated with different relations to metropolitan firms. But capitalists seem to have been happy to play both roles simultaneously – trying to protect their domestic market, while striving for lasting ties with metropolitan firms. Interestingly, while both of these roles have been thrown into doubt, the fount from which they spring – the assumption that national capitalists are a natural ally for initiating rapid development – has not been questioned. If anything, the trend in recent scholarship has been to press it into service even more. And it is present in many of the declarations of the anti-globalization movement.

It is this assumption about the national bourgeoisie – its status as the natural social force for rapid development – that needs to be challenged. Over the past decades a quite powerful set of myths has come to obscure the real experience of twentieth century capitalism in developing countries, papering over the actual dynamics, the roles played by key actors, and their interests. This essay aims to make a start in clearing away some of these myths. If developmentalism is to be revived, these are myths from which it needs to be free.

THE BASIS OF DEVELOPMENTALISM AND ITS WEAKNESS

Three 'stylized facts' are taken for granted in most discussions of post-war development strategies. First, that these strategies were centered around the idea of rapid industrialization, a massive push to catch up with the developed countries and the industrial frontier. In this, they sought to repeat the successes of the previous generation of late developers – Germany, Japan, Russia – which had also placed industry at the center of their economic strategies. At the core of the mid-twentieth century initiative was the process of import-substitution, aimed at fostering the growth of local industries by a two-step process: first, by limiting the entrance of imports through the erection of tariffs and quantitative controls, in order to create a market for local firms; and second, by providing support for the rapid growth of these firms through a process of heavy subsidization. Subsidies and tariffs were the chief instruments through which the domestic capitalist class cleared out a space for itself to grow, protected from competition from the more advanced countries.

The second 'stylized fact' is that the industrialization drive was undertaken as a 'common project' between political elites, state managers and the domestic capitalist class; to this, some add a measure of inclusion for labour as well. The critical members of the power bloc, of course, are taken to be the newly emerging industrialists and political elites. For the industrialists, the reasons to support such an ambition are obvious; what was remarkable was their dramatic ascent into the domestic ruling bloc in so many countries at around the same time, especially when landed elites were still very much in place, and had exercised a vice-like grip on power for decades. Indeed, the *political* eclipse of landed oligarchies in South America, South Asia, and parts of the Middle East, even though they still maintained considerable economic power, is one of the more remarkable aspects of the story.

The third generally accepted notion is that, within the alliance between the state and business, the state took the role of senior partner. Hence the common description of rapid industrialization projects as 'state-led development'. One explanation for this points to the youth and small size of the local industrial sector, the generally uneven and quite patchy development of markets, and the shallowness of financial markets; for these reasons states had to take the lead in initiating industrialization. Another view places the source of state dominance not on the weakness of capital per se, but on its weakness *relative* to the elephantine development of the state – as a peculiarity of the post-colonial inheritance (Alavi's 'overdeveloped state'),[3] or a legacy of statist traditions, as in post-Ottoman Turkey. Two interpretations emerge from this general assumption, depending on where the emphasis is placed as to the source of state dominance. In some cases capitalists are taken to have abdicated some of their autonomy to state managers, in recognition of their need for the latters' guidance and assistance in the industrialization process; in others, they are simply seen as being in no position to resist when planners and political elites impose the new strategy upon them. In this case, the state is seen as a paternalistic agent, shepherding local entrepreneurs onto an accumulation strategy which is, in any case, consistent with their interests.

The notion that rapid industrialization strategies were 'state-led' is arguably one of the pillars of development literature. What is difficult to reconcile with this view, however, is the indisputable fact that, over the course of the developmentalist era, these states found themselves struggling to achieve what they had taken to be their central mission – directing the flow of domestic private investments into sectors with high social returns, and away from those in which returns on investment may have brought enormous private profits, but were of less developmental significance. In South America, the Middle East, and South Asia, state-led strategies did bring about a transformation of the economy in the generally desired direction. But this was achieved haltingly, at enormous public cost, with much of the work being done by public enterprises, and often resulting in highly inefficient private sectors. The most visible signs of the expense at which it was achieved was the expanding fiscal burden on these states – as they had to absorb much of the losses incurred by the private sector, while at the same time continuing to funnel public resources to the private sector in the form of subsidies; and a growing imbalance on the external account – as the enormous inflow of imported capital goods was not balanced by a flow of investment into exportable lines, with which the external debit could have been balanced.

The question therefore arises: if the developmentalist era was indeed *state-led*, then what explains these states' weakness relative to the tasks at hand – leading to the eventual collapse of developmentalism, and its replacement by neoliberalism? Why was the quality of state intervention so much below what was needed to push local industry to the technological frontier? The most compelling answer would appear to be that, if state managers did not succeed in their mission, it was because they lacked the *capacity* to do so. And this is plausible. Industrial policy requires a certain level of institutional capacity on the part of the policy apparatus. There is no warrant at all to assume that states come equipped with this, especially in developing countries. Simply embarking on an interventionist development strategy does not, therefore, mean that the state will have the institutional muscle to succeed. So perhaps the reason industrial policy met with at best patchy success was that political elites were not able to equip their states with the right kind of policy apparatus.

It is indisputable that developmental states in much of the South lacked the institutional capacity needed for industrial policy to fully work. This has been the main discovery of a veritable avalanche of case studies over the past decade or so. But this simply raises the next, and quite obvious, question. If *dirigisme* requires some degree of state-building, then why did political elites not build the necessary institutions? I will argue that the main source of resistance to building strong and supple policy apparatuses turned out to be the national bourgeoisie itself. I should make clear at the outset that I am using this term in the sense handed down by its originators, the Marxists of the Second and especially the Third Internationals: it refers to the segment of local capitalists who are oriented to the domestic market, seek autonomy from metropolitan control, and ally with the state around industrialization.

Given this description, it may seem paradoxical to suggest that national capitalists opposed state-building for rapid development. Certainly, theorists at mid-century did not expect this, and much of the current literature on developmentalism has taken it as so unlikely that its very possibility has not been explored. For those coming out of the Marxist tradition, it was always that *other* segment of the bourgeoisie, the compradors, who were the villains of the story. These were the local capitalists with close ties to metropolitan capital, often based in trading and speculative activities, other times in agri-exports, but always suspect in their commitment to national development. The national bourgeoisie was suspect on labour issues, to be sure – and why wouldn't it be? But on allying around an impeccably bourgeois model of development, they were not only taken to have been reliable, but were expected to be the pivot on which the whole game turned.

THE NATIONAL BOURGEOISIE AND THE STATE

The key to understanding the vicissitudes of post-war development strategies is that state managers didn't simply nurture domestic firms by offering them protection and subsidies; these measures were part of a larger policy package, central to which was an attempt at *capitalist planning*. While capitalists did certainly have a direct and immediate interest in the former, this was not so clear cut with respect to the latter. Indeed – and this is the crucial point – the institutionalization of import-substitution made it rational for capitalists to resist, and reject, any attempt at genuine economic management. So, far from reinforcing each other, as political elites expected them to, and as students of the era have taken them to, import-substituting industrialization and state management of industrial development were in deep tension with each other. And this in turn implies that there was also the possibility for real conflict between the two central actors of the developmentalist drama, state managers and the national bourgeoisie. Opposition to strengthening the policy apparatus thus did not need to come from bureaucrats or from landed classes – it issued from the very agent the policies were meant to favour.

The motive that animated political elites in South America, India, and parts of the Middle East at mid-century was to industrialize their economies as rapidly as possible. There was plenty of experience to show that, if left to their own, industrialists had no proclivity to invest in those lines that were best for long-term growth. Products that yielded high individual profits were often those which had little or no social returns. The point of industrial policy and planning was in part to encourage firms in a direction that brought the two kinds of returns in line with each other. It was aimed at ensuring that investments were consistent not only with immediate profits, but also with national economic development. For the most part, planners intended to use 'soft' methods to prod firms in the desired direction – subsidies, cheap loans, tax breaks, etc. But industrial policy also included an irreducible element of coercion to compel them, where necessary, and to ensure that public monies were being utilized in the desired fashion. It was taken for granted that, in return for the subsidies that were being funnelled to them, industrialists would have to submit to a certain measure of accountability – they would have to accept being disciplined.

For planners, the need to discipline private firms was a natural feature of import-substitution. For capitalists, however, the incentive structure pointed in a different direction. As is well known, the immediate effect of import-substitution industrialization (ISI) is to protect domestic markets from competition from imported foreign products. But the exclusion of imports meant that in many manufacturing lines local markets came to be dominated by a small number of producers. This was partly because of the small size of the local market, but it was also because the scale requirements of modern manufacture called for larger outlays of fixed capital, and hence, firms with considerable market power. There was thus an enormous advantage to being the first entrant in any new line, as it was relatively easy to hold off the threat of potential competitors. Further, this advantage was reinforced by other peculiarities of ISI, one of which was to intentionally limit the number of producers in any sector by administrative means – precisely because of the small market, policy makers tended to be wary of the possibility of excessive or 'ruinous' competition.

The consequence of this state of affairs was that, once the threat of external competition was extinguished, local capitalists were given virtual monopo-listic control over their markets. And this in turn meant that, for any such dominant firm, the compulsion to innovate and invest in best-practice tech-niques dissipated – since it had markets handed over to it. Given this production regime, the subsidies flowing to firms from the state did not need to be reinvested to upgrade existing plant and equipment. Market dominance obviated the need to minimize costs. It made better sense, instead, to use the resources to start operations in altogether new lines and acquire a 'first-mover' advantage there. What made this especially attractive was that industrial firms in the leading 'late developing' countries were typically part of large, diversified business groups, which had expertise in numerous sectors, and maintained diverse investment portfolios.

For the national bourgeoisie, ISI thus presented the possibility of enormous gains. The problem was that, in order to maximize these gains, it made good sense to accept ISI's subsidization components, while rejecting the ambitions of state managers to control what industrialists did with the subsidies. The critical factor underlying this resistance to discipline was the attenuation of competitive pressures in ISI. It may be wondered why firms would resent demands made by the state to perform at competitive standards, which, in many respects, was certainly in their interests. The reason is that, with the entry of international competitors blocked by protectionist measures, and with internal competition muted owing to the small size of the market, firms were under no systematic pressure to constantly upgrade their operations. With each influx of newly acquired credit or subsidies from the state, managers felt no compulsion to increase the efficiency of existing undertakings, since there was no imminent threat of losing market share. Hence, while state policy agencies granted subsidies to firms on the basis of a development plan with particular priorities, business houses made their own investment plans, based on their prognoses and their priorities, which often did not coincide with those of planners. For this very reason, they regarded the disciplinary component of ISI as an unacceptable encumbrance; in order to exploit their opportunities fully, firms would need maximum latitude to make their own decisions as to which sectors they would expand into, where new investments would be made. The best way to use ISI was to encourage the state's commitment to subsidies, while insisting that private capital should have the maximum latitude in their actual disposition.

In sum, whereas planners saw ISI and industrial policy as two sides of the same coin, for capitalists, ISI generated an incentive to *reject* the discipline of industrial policy. Those institutions intended to further the subsidization process were supported by capital; but dimensions of state-building aimed at enabling planners to monitor and regulate firms' investment decisions were stoutly resisted. At the surface level, the conflict between the national bourgeoisie and the economic planners was not always apparent. It was common to find industrialists joining the chorus calling for planning, economic management, and the like. But what they meant by this was a process in which public monies were put at their disposal, and at their behest. To them planning meant the socialization of risk, while leaving the private appropriation of profit intact. Business groups in these countries accordingly waged a campaign in which they called for, and supported, central coordination of economic policy while at the same time fighting strenuously against measures which would give planners any real power over their investment decisions.

THREE HISTORICAL CASES: INDIA, TURKEY, BRAZIL

These lines were more clearly drawn, and the dynamics were visibly played out, in the region where the political elite had the clearest and deepest commitment to a state-led development model – the Indian subcontinent.[4] Under Nehru's leadership, the Indian National Congress began formulating an agenda for post-colonial planning a full decade before the departure of the British. The leading lights of the business community, for their part, not only announced a commitment to participate in post-independence planning, but even called for it, also before full autonomy was achieved. What became clear very quickly, however, was that the two groups had very different conceptions of the appropriate range of power to be enjoyed by the state. Business groups launched an all-out offensive against all instruments designed to give teeth to the planning apparatus, while clamouring all the while for more subsidies and more protection. State intervention in industrial development would be tolerated, but only if it was on the invitation of business groups – not at the discretion of planners. The campaign, waged through an intense lobbying effort and backed by an investment slowdown, was largely effective. The new government did install a planning apparatus, but one in which the central Planning Commission had little power to oversee, let alone directly influence, private investment.

The gestation of a planning regime was not nearly as long in Turkey. Whereas in India the commitment was enunciated more than a decade before its initiation, the turn to planned industrial policy was rather rapid in the Turkish case, where it was first proposed at the end of the 1950s, and installed less than five years later. It is true that Kemalist *etatism* can be traced back to the 1920s, intensifying in the years after the Great Depression. But state protection and promotion of industry was rolled back in the 1940s, so much so that the industrial sector's weight in the economy declined from 18 per cent of national income at the end of the 1930s to less than 12 per cent by 1952. It was only in the late 1950s that the liberalizing interregnum ended, and import substitution was put back on the agenda, this time with an eye toward planned development. The movement was quick. A restructuring of the state apparatus was initiated, somewhat hesitantly, in 1958; it accelerated in 1960 after a military coup removed the Democratic Party from power, and was completed before the middle of the decade. As in India, domestic capitalists were in favour of both ISI and central coordination of economic policy. The new military junta thus had considerable autonomy to design the institutions for industrial policy and restructure the state around them

On the advice of well-known experts like Jan Tinbergen and Alvin

Hanson, a State Planning Organization (SPO) was established as a nodal agency for economic policy. Tinbergen and his supporters within the Turkish state proposed that the SPO should have powers not only to draw up plans, but also to ensure that all allocative decisions were in line with plan priorities. They signalled that the direction of investment would have to be very different from that which firms had been choosing over the past decade; further, they proposed that state enterprises, which had been used since the 1930s as a milch cow by private firms, should be rationalized in a way that would pressure the latter to upgrade their own operations. All this pointed in the direction of a planning regime committed to streamlining accumulation for national capital – which naturally entailed imposing discipline on the proclivity for speculative and short-term gains.

What immediately emerged, however, was that the industrialists had a very different conception of planning. Under pressure from business, state enterprise reform was put in cold storage; proposed tax reforms aimed at enhancing compliance from the very wealthy and increasing national savings came under violent criticism; efforts to elicit information from firms regarding their investment plans met with stiff resistance; and most centrally, initial attempts to steer the flow of investment toward more strategic sectors and away from those preferred by local firms came to naught. Seeing the writing on the wall the planners in the SPO issued a collective resignation in late 1962. The planning apparatus remained formally in place, as in India, but was never given the power to oversee effective control over local industry. In fact, in studies of Turkish economic policy, one comes across the argument that the decline of the planning regime set in as early as 1965 – only three years after the SPO was installed!

In India and Turkey capitalists attacked, and then rolled back, what were rather radical designs at state restructuring. The Brazilian experience was different, in that the political leadership never had the same level of commitment to planning, and hence never drew up comparably ambitious blueprints to which capitalists had to respond. Import substitution was consolidated after 1930, under the first Vargas regime. But the post-war dispensation witnessed, as in Turkey, an initial retreat on that front, as the Dutra administration liberalized controls and international trade. It was only with the return of Vargas in 1950 that ISI was consolidated, only this time with more explicit talk of central coordination and some planning. But while post-war Indian and Turkish leaders moved to install nodal planning bodies with sweeping powers – which then came under attack – there were no direct parallels in Brazil. This was because a decade-long, and quite intense, campaign by domestic capital had already made it clear that a planning regime would not be tolerated.

Brazil also contrasts somewhat with India and Turkey, in that its developmentalism was shaped in part by a powerful wing of capitalists linked to foreign, especially American, capital. This current coexisted with a newly formed stratum of capitalists, led by Roberto Simonsen and Euvaldo Lodi, who personified the so-called national bourgeoisie. Simonsen in particular led a long struggle to legitimize ISI and an interventionist industrial policy in the eyes of Brazilian industrialists. But he had to fight a constant rearguard action against the liberal wing of local capital which, in alliance with US firms, demanded a minimal regulation of industrial investment. The point to note, however, is that the narrow space for development planning was not simply a reflection of this split within the local bourgeoisie, or of the weakness of its nationalist segment. It is that, when it came to the state's power to demand compliance from local firms, or to restructure investment patterns, or to punish speculative profit-making activities – it lost the support of even the nationalist wing of the business class. Simonsen himself announced the prudential limits to state planning in the same text in which he defended state intervention, warning that planning must never restrict 'private initiative', or come into competition with it through public investments.[5] The reality of these limits was made very clear when state managers dared to transgress them. When the state did move to discipline business practices after the war – through anti-monopoly legislation, inquiries into price-gouging, and the like – it was firmly rebuffed by the national capitalists themselves.

In this context, efforts to restructure the state around the needs of industrial planning tended to be hesitant and episodic, always careful not to trigger an attack. Brazil was unusual among developmental states in never having a real nodal agency for planning. If ever one was proposed, it was always with utmost hesitancy, and short-lived. A National Economic Council was promulgated in the 1946 Constitution, which was initially slated to have wide-ranging powers over development planning, but though the provision was allowed to pass, the Council was rendered toothless.[6] Instead of genuine planning bodies with effective powers, state managers resorted to decentralized and ad hoc policy agencies, assigned particular tasks – islands of planning in a sea of hostility. The Brazilian developmental state in fact never even aspired to the same range of power over local capital as did the Indian or Turkish variants. It was slower to consolidate, weaker in is foundations, and more timid in its ambitions – at least with reference to state-building. Underlying this was a far more hostile national capitalist class than in the other cases.

THE ROLE OF ORGANIZED LABOUR

It is important to note that in none of these cases was capitalist intransigence driven by the fear of an energized Left. In the early 1960s the Turkish labour movement was no threat at all. The military junta that came to power in 1960 had no truck with unions, and the return of the Republican party soon thereafter did not herald an opening for unions to gain in power. In Brazil too, while unions were given new-found legitimacy by Vargas, starting in 1930, they were quickly subordinated to a labyrinthine corporatist state structure in the Estado Novo, and marginalized even further under the Dutra administration. In neither case did domestic firms have to worry about a political elite under the influence of an energized and mobilized working class.

Of the three, it was only in India that there was any real sign of a threat from labour when developmentalism took off. But this threat was swiftly eliminated by Nehru and the Indian National Congress. Almost immediately after Independence, the labour movement was split by the creation of a new union federation allied to the Congress party, a federation constitutionally committed to industrial peace and the planning regime. Within a few years, aided by the ruling party's patronage, it emerged as the most powerful wing of the labour movement, and in so being, largely abdicated independent political action.

The marginalization of labour was in part an attempt by political elites to curry favour with the national bourgeoisie. It was hoped that a narrowing of the political space would allay any fears that business might have of a slide from capitalist to socialist planning. But it was also driven by the political elite's own disdain for labour, and their abiding belief that national development could not be trusted to the labouring poor. Policy would be trusted to the natural leaders of the nation – industrialists and state managers. It never seems to have occurred to this group that an alliance with a mobilized labour force might have bolstered their leverage against a resistant business class.

On the other hand, it cannot be denied that the ease with which unions were sidelined was partly due to some of their own choices. There was a tendency to be seduced by all the talk about planning and coordinated development. Even more, labour leaders were aware of their weakness as a social force and accepted with alacrity their incorporation into state structures. There was a hope that their formal incorporation into the state and its planning bodies would make up for their lack of power on the shop floor. This, of course, turned out to be a fantasy. Once they demobilized, the balance of power shifted even more decidedly toward business, narrowing further the political space, and increasing the ability of capital to set the terms for policy and state-building.

THE PATHOLOGY OF DEVELOPMENTALISM

The examples provided above are simply meant to illustrate the basic principle: in the paradigmatic 'state-led' industrialization strategies, the actual power that states were able to accumulate was severely limited, and it was limited because of a very firm hostility on the part of national capitalists. Planners could very well funnel resources to firms, and attach to them stipulations and conditionalities regarding their use – but they had little chance of ensuring their enforcement. Capitalists were able to divert funds away from targeted sectors and into their own preferred lines. To give just two examples: a survey of Turkish planning from 1968 to1980 revealed that, of the total subsidies received by firms, less than 20 per cent was invested in accordance with plan directives.[7] Similarly in India, at the height of planning, not only were plan targets consistently under-fulfilled, but no less than 25 per cent of all subsidized investments ended up in lines that had been banned outright by the planners.[8] The only sectors to which investment did flow readily in these countries, and in fact exceeded plan targets, were consumer goods – which were typically a low priority for the planners. State managers could go on making their forecasts and draw up plans with high-minded rhetoric, but the fact was that they had very little ability to ensure their actualization. Capitalists, on the other hand, comfortably ensconced in a protected and highly subsidized environment, could take the money and divert it to the sectors that they favoured.

This generated a political economy in which accumulation proceeded at a fairly rapid pace for close to four decades. But it did so in a fashion that progressively undermined the conditions of its own existence. On the one hand, state expenditures grew at a faster pace than incoming revenue, a direct consequence of the asymmetry between subsidization and planning in ISI. Not only was the state expected to continue its commitment to subsidies and transfers to private firms, but, as the latter ignored plan signals and diverted investment elsewhere, the slack had to be taken up by state enterprises, which increasingly came to embody a safety net for the private sector: providing cheap inputs, purchasing private sector products at inflated prices, and moving into lines capitalists considered unattractive. All this was supported, in the last analysis, by a continual drain on the public exchequer. Hence, even when the economy grew at an impressive clip, it was in a race with the fiscal deficit, which often grew even faster.[9]

This fiscal drain was paralleled by an increasing imbalance on the external account. Although ISI is today pilloried by neoliberals as a withdrawal from the world economy, the fact is that its onset generated a further integration into world markets – ironically, by an escalation of imports. It is true that imports of consumer goods were blocked, but the acceleration of domestic production in turn required a growing inflow of imported capital goods. In principle, however, the upward trend in capital imports was to be balanced by commensurate increases in exports. Here again, we encounter a pervasive myth among exponents of the Washington Consensus, viz. that ISI consistently ignored the importance of exports. In point of fact, by the late 1950s a large number of import-substituting countries implemented export promotion programs, in explicit recognition of the importance of exports for further growth. Indeed it was none other than Raul Prebisch, the apostle of ISI, who stressed this as an imperative at the close of the decade.[10]

The problem was not resistance from *planners*, but from *firms*. The strategy in ISI was to oversee a transformation of the industrial structure, and as a part of that, to change the composition of exports, from primary goods to higher-value manufactures. But again, precisely because of their inability to discipline capital, states failed in this ambition. Safe behind their protective barriers, capitalists simply preferred the inflated domestic market to highly competitive export markets. Time and again export promotion efforts came to naught thanks to the persistent lack of interest on the part of local firms. Exports thus either remained dominated by traditional products, or moved into higher value lines very slowly; in either case, they were simply unable to generate the revenue required to offset the growing import bill. States were thus confronted with a choice: either slow down the rate of investment to bring it into line with the external account, or forge ahead on a precarious route, hoping to acquire the needed revenue through borrowing. Many opted for the latter in the seventies, when the world was awash in petrodollars – only to finds themselves bankrupted a decade later.

The weakness of state planning apparatuses thus played a critical role in the unravelling of national development projects in the 1980s. This is not to say that there were no other causes of the economic crises. But it is remarkable how, as time passes, the blame has come to be laid on bureaucracies and planners – leaving the role played by business entirely unacknowledged. There is something of an irony in this, since, in essence, developmentalism amounted to a massive transfer of national resources to local capitalists. The aims of industrial policy in the post-war period can be understood as a sort of implicit contract: public funds would be funnelled to firms in the short term, on the understanding that the state would, in exchange, hold them accountable to certain performance standards. So over the medium term, the community would gain from the initial coddling of local capitalists. But with states left weak and fractured, the equation was reversed. Capitalists were able to initiate a half-century long primitive accumulation, socializing their risks and losses, while privately appropriating the gains. The end result was that there was development and industrial growth – but at an enormous cost to the public.

THE SECRET BASIS OF THE KOREAN MIRACLE

Korea is perhaps the one case where local capitalists *did* ally with political elites around state-led industrialization.[11] In Korea, just as in India and other late developers, institutions for development planning had to be built anew, especially those which would be used to discipline capitalists. But unlike their counterparts, Korean industrialists did not react against the state-building effort. Instead, they joined in the project. Why did they do this, while capitalists elsewhere did not?

The basis for the alliance with the state lay in the fact that Korean economic strategy after 1960 grafted export-led industrialization (ELI) onto ISI, and in doing so, generated a different set of incentives for the national bourgeoisie. At the core of export-led industrialization was a commitment by firms to direct at least a part of their product at export markets. So unlike firms in ISI, which produce for an insulated domestic market, producers in ELI were thrown into the vortex of international competition. This created a corresponding difference in political incentives with regard to the state. Whereas firms in ISI could ignore the demand for investing at peak levels of efficiency, their counterparts in ELI could not, for fear of losing position in export markets, where competition was far more severe. So while firms in ISI had an incentive – once they had already taken the state's money – to resist state demands for productivity enhancing investment, those in the latter had an incentive to comply with such demands, precisely in order to survive in export markets. Further, the Korean *chaebol* needed the state's assistance to unpack technology, coordinate investments between complementary sectors, impose uniform quality standards, and so on, without which export success would have been highly unlikely. So unlike the case in ISI, firms in ELI had an incentive to abide by the state-building project, for a strong state was an important ingredient in acquiring success in export markets.

Korea was not alone in putting greater emphasis on exports at this time. This change was attempted in a number of countries in the early 1960s, but it failed time and again, against resistance by local producers. Why should they hazard the highly competitive export markets, when they had the comfort of guaranteed profits at home? The shift was made possible in Korea by a highly fortuitous circumstance, which brought together factors unavailable to other countries. First, and perhaps most importantly, Japanese firms were entering Korea at this time to set up partnerships with Korean producers around an export strategy. They brought with them extensive sales and marketing networks, as well as plentiful lines of credit – precisely what firms in India, Turkey, and Latin America lacked. Korean capitalists thus had a critical entry barrier removed, as they were shepherded into lucrative export markets, with networks of clients ready and waiting. But while partnership with the Japanese firms could offer them entry into US markets, surviving in those markets required more – it needed the helping hand of the Korean state, in the manner described in the preceding paragraph. Park Chung Hee's ascension brought to power a ruthless regime, but one which, to Korean capitalists, was desirable precisely because it was committed to building a state capable of coordinating their success in export lines. When Park signalled that he was going to push for an export strategy as well as for a developmental state, he found a ready ally in the Korean national bourgeoisie.

With this partnership secure, the results of Korean developmentalism were very different from those elsewhere. Because the state was able to effectively steer the flow of private investment and to ensure its effective utilization, state enterprises did not have to pick up the slack as they did in Latin America and India. Further, because of the effectiveness of state intervention, industrial growth was very rapid, making for a spectacular rate of economic growth, which kept state revenues high. These two factors contrasted with the outcomes in our other cases, and in turn greatly eased the fiscal burden. Hence, while state expenditures in Korea expanded rapidly, this rarely resulted in high deficits, since revenue expansion was able to keep pace. On the external front, again, the state was able to steer investment toward newer, high value lines, and in particular, toward tradable goods. This made for a very different outcome than in Latin America; in Korea the import bill and external debt rose very rapidly, but export rates increased even more rapidly, allowing the country to escape constraints on its external and financial sectors.[12]

The arrival of the Japanese was crucial in inducing Korean capitalists to turn to export markets, which in turn made them willing to abide by Park's switch to ELI, which in turn made them ally with Park around building a developmental state. Capitalists in India, Turkey, or Brazil did not have the benefit of patrons like the Japanese firms. Indeed, foreign investors in India – mainly British and US multinationals – went out of their way to *discourage* exports, reinforcing reliance on domestic markets. The secret of Korean success in building a powerful developmental state is thus the anterior switch to a different accumulation model, export-led industrialization, which created an incentive for the bourgeoisie to accept the state-building project. In India and elsewhere, conditions conspired to present ISI as the only viable accumulation model; the cost of this was that the model undermined the conditions for effective state intervention, since it pitted capitalists against the state. The conditions which allowed Korean capitalists to make the switch, and hence accept a developmental state, were simply not available elsewhere.

THE MYTHOLOGY OF THE NATIONAL
BOURGEOISIE

The claim that the national bourgeoisie is an unreliable agent of rapid development goes against some deeply held convictions, not least among Marxists. During the period when the concept gained currency – the years of the Third International – it was *agrarian* classes that were the major cause for concern on the Left. The extent of capitalist production in agriculture, the economic classification of rural producers, the political orientation of the peasantry toward socialist parties – these were issues that exercised the minds of European, and soon afterwards, Asian Marxists. To be sure, there were areas of ambiguity with regard to industrial capitalists too. On two issues in particular – their orientation towards the imperial powers, and toward alliances with labour – capitalists were seen either as straightforwardly unreliable, or as 'vacillating' (as Stalin would so delicately put it). But when it came to the interests of national capitalists with respect to industrialization, there was a general understanding that they were firmly in favour of it. More confident still was the appraisal of the relation between modernizing political elites and national capitalists – they were seen as natural allies, collaborating on a shared project of domestic development. So much so, that figures like Ataturk, Nehru, Vargas, and later, Peron, were frequently presented either as direct representatives of the 'national bourgeoisie', or, if the latter was considered to be too weak, as their de facto guardians. In any case, while room might have existed for tension between modernising elites and domestic capitalists on some issues, Marxists rarely if ever considered that there would be tensions around the process of domestic capitalist development itself.

What explains this? Why did Marxists so rarely consider the possibility that capitalists would revolt against core elements of a developmentalist project? One quite natural reason was that the historical experience of twentieth century state-led development was yet to come. Hence, the antagonism between economic planners and capitalists on state-building had not been witnessed. It is true that there was the experience of early modern mercantilism, and of the nineteenth century's state-led developers – Germany, Japan, and of course Russia – to draw upon. But it is critical to register that, on the issue that divided the bourgeoisie and the state, this generation of late developers differed a great deal from those of the twentieth century. State intervention in Germany, Japan, and others of the Victorian era had very few measures aimed at regulating and monitoring the investment activities of private firms. The role of the state was far more passive, having been confined basically to the tasks of subsidization and protection. The politics of state-building therefore differed commensurately, focusing on the accretion of institutional capacity for raising revenue, and not for disciplining capital. Naturally, in this context the ties between planners and industrialists were not nearly as strained. When theorists as late as mid-century considered the likely dynamics of development planning, they had behind them a historical experience which simply did not offer a good guide to what they should expect.

There was also a second weakness in Marxist thinking on this matter, however, which had to do with political theory. Early theorists of development worked with a fairly one-sided understanding of the state and its relation to capitalist interests. For this generation, the capitalist state was an institution which basically *reflected* ruling-class interests – it was a state at the service of the rising capitalist class. It posed a problem and a potential threat to capitalists only if it was under the influence of *another* class – declining landlords trying to shore up their power, a growing and mobilized working class, colonial or imperial rulers, etc.. In these scenarios, it would be natural for the bourgeoisie to cavil at any strengthening of state capacity, in that it would be at the service of forces hostile to them. The state's orientation was taken to reflect the balance of political forces. It is not surprising, then, to find that Marxists gave little consideration to the tensions that state-led development would actually give rise to. The national development project was supposed to be led by and in the interests of the national bourgeoisie. There was thus, on this theory, no room for tensions between them and the state – after all, it was *their state*.

If we move from this instrumentalist view to one which allows for some independence of the state from capital, the conflicts surrounding developmentalism become less mysterious. The very fact of the state's relative autonomy meant that its powers were not under the direct control of the national bourgeoisie. The state of the mid-twentieth century was also very different from that of the mercantilist era, or of the Victorian years. It was endowed with a set of technical and administrative instruments which made an interventionist strategy far more worrying to domestic capitalists. The distinctive feature of development planning, what distinguished it from the interventionism of the nineteenth century, was that it was aimed at directly reducing industrialists' autonomous power over investment. If instrumentalist state theory were true, then this would not have posed a problem – capitalists would, through their control over the state apparatus, ensure that intervention was restricted to those instances where they called for it, and they would ensure that its claws were never drawn against them. But precisely because of the state's genuine, albeit limited, independence from their control, capitalists regarded the whole enterprise as fraught with danger. They therefore adopted the strategy of encouraging and fostering the broad developmental agenda, while at the same time pruning away the elements which might encroach on their investment prerogatives.

Given these liabilities – the difference between first and second generation developmentalism, and the commitment to an overly simplistic understanding of the state – initial arguments about the national bourgeoisie were unable to anticipate its contradictory position in the development process. What is interesting is that it was not simply the theorists of development who missed the structural basis for this conflict. State managers too seemed to have laboured under the impression that, since their agenda was devoted to strengthening national capitalism, it would elicit the support of national capitalists. Of course, they did not believe the instrumentalist story about state power, since they were quite aware of the independence of their initiative and often regarded capitalists with quite a bit of disdain. But they do seem to have thought that, given the bourgeoisie's own declarations in favour of rapid development, they would cede to state managers the autonomy they needed to build the needed policy instruments, and then to use them. This is one reason political elites moved with such alacrity to marginalize and demobilize labour. It was only partly done to gain the confidence of their business classes; the other reason was that it was just taken for granted that the active and hegemonic members of the 'modernizing bloc' would be the state and capital, the natural partners in the venture.

Capitalists had a very different idea. Rather than ceding to state managers the autonomy to build a powerful planning apparatus, they set about *decreasing* it. This was what the attack on state discipline was all about. If elites were, in fact, to build the appropriate policy instruments, they would have to *usurp* the needed autonomy – having it ceded to them was not on the cards. The irony is that the very force which might have boosted their power over capital, and generated enough independence from it to push through their reforms, was the very force that they took pains to demobilize – labour.

CONCLUSION

Looking back today from the ruins of the neoliberal revolution, it is understandable that there may be a certain nostalgia toward the developmentalist era, and toward that storied class, the national bourgeoisie. The intervening years seem to have left us with a sturdy mythology about that period, one in which states had the power and the vision to navigate a path to autonomous development, in which the business class hitched its wagon to the national project, and labour had a place at the bargaining table. There is some truth to this story. Considerable progress was in fact made by the developing world in the era of developmentalism, much more than in the quarter century of neo-liberalism. States did play an important role in this, and national capitalists did collaborate with policy-makers to some degree in planning a development path. Nothing in this essay is meant to question that.

What is important to recognize is that, while there was a social bloc that cohered around developmentalism, the fate of the whole project cannot be understood if we ignore the enormous contradictions and costs that it brought in train. Capitalists simply would not countenance the installation of policy instruments that would have enabled planners to hold firms accountable to plan priorities. And in the absence of such instruments, state guidance turned out to be a quite different creature than originally intended. Instead of being the embodiment of capital's commitment to national development, it became a conduit for a monumental transfer of national resources into the pockets of local industrialists. Industrial structures did change slowly, but not at a pace or in a direction that would offset the growing drain on the exchequer, or which would bring in revenues fast enough on the external account. Slowly, the project unravelled as an accumulation model – but at little cost to national capitalists.

Korea was unusual in escaping this route. But here too, it was the internal dynamic of the accumulation model which led to a turn to neo-liberalism. An exceptionally united capitalist class had, by the early 1990s, outgrown its need for state support as a condition for export success. The partnership that had supported the developmental state therefore dissolved, and the chaebol began calling for a dismantling of the planning apparatus. The end of the developmental state was not brought on by the IMF or the US in the aftermath of the 1997 crisis. That was only a denouement to the critical events. The old apparatus had fallen into disrepair much earlier under the pressure of the chaebol, and it was in fact its prior dismantling that brought on the crisis. The point worth noting is that even in Korea, where there was some kind of business support for a national development project, indeed, where this partnership with capital was crucial to the project's success, capitalists remained in the alliance only so long as state intervention was a central precondition to their profitability.

For most countries, a key political consequence of the project was the organizational enfeeblement of the labour movement. This was in some measure engineered by political elites, partly because of their own paternalism toward, and distrust of labour; it was also demanded by capitalists as a condition for their (promised) cooperation with the interventionist regime. But it is impossible to ignore the fact that this whole process was hugely enabled by labour's own seduction by the rhetoric of national development and planning. Too often, unions reposed an altogether unwarranted confidence in the state's ability to protect their interests, to discipline the capitalist class, and to manage class conflict through an adroit manipulation of plan priorities. Labour was in many cases too eager to take its place at the table, so to speak, and to agree to the corporatist structures that are common to industrial relations in developing countries. The long-term consequence of this demobilization was a steady enfeeblement of the working class as a political actor. Hence, when the turn to neo-liberalism came, labour lacked the organizational muscle and experience to fight effectively against it.[13] Ironically, it was the very absence of such opportunities for inclusion that may have contributed to the Korean labour movement's extraordinary development and radicalization. Whereas unions in many countries coming out of ISI remained dependent on state support, the Korean unions established a militant independence early on, and mobilized at a level that has few parallels in the developing world. While they were unable to block the onset of liberalization, they have been able to intervene in the transition to a new accumulation model with considerable force.

So while the nostalgia for the developmentalist era is, to some extent, understandable, a more sober assessment suggests different lessons. The last time political elites and subaltern classes looked to the national bourgeoisie for spearheading a development project they got something less than they wanted, and much less than they deserved. If left to its devices, there is no reason to think capital will react differently on another occasion. Indeed, if the reasoning of this essay is correct, the resistance to state intervention will most likely be even stronger in future.

It is not clear how the ongoing process of economic integration affects the very possibility of national projects. For some, globalization makes any such idea quite implausible, since it has so completely integrated domestic firms with multinational corporations. But while the fact of cross-national integration is indisputable, its extent is very much a matter of debate. It is even less clear whether this process, even where it has progressed considerably, makes national projects unworkable. What this essay has argued is that, to the extent that developmental projects are possible, their advocates will be well advised to take a hard look at the experience of their predecessors. Future national development strategies will have to generate a new kind of politics capable of extracting concessions that were rarely even demanded last time around – concessions over investment flows, the movement of capital, labour standards, and much else. In an era where the political momentum is in precisely the opposite direction, this is no mean task. But that is no reason to continue labouring under the influence of myths that are demonstrably false, and with hopes that are sure to be dashed.

NOTES

1   Quoted in Raul Zibechi, 'Globalization or National Bourgeoisie: an Outdated Debate', *Focus on Trade*, 94 (November), 2003.

2   For a good comparison of the two periods, see Mark Weisbrot, Robert Naiman and Joyce Kim, 'The Emperor Has No Growth: Declining Economic Growth Rates in the Era of Globalization', Center for Economic and Policy Research Briefing Paper, May, 2001.

3   Hamza Alavi, 'The State in Post-Colonial Societies', *New Left Review*, 74, 1972.

4   See my book, *Locked in Place: State-Building and Late Industrialization in India*, Princeton: Princeton University Press, 2003.

5   Ricardo Bielschowsky, *Brazilian Economic Thought (1945-1964): The Ideological Cycle of Developmentalism*, unpublished Ph.D. Dissertation, University of Leicester, 1985, pp. 392–393.

6   Sonia Draibe, *Rumos e metamorfoses: um estudo sobre a constituição do Estado e as alternativas da industrialização no Brasil, 1930-1960*, Rio de Janeiro: Paz e Terra, 1985, pp. 306, 321. I would like to thank Cesar Rodriguez for summarizing portions of this book for me, as part of our research on Brazilian development.

7   Vedat Milor, 'Planning the Market: Structural Transformation of the Economy in Turkey, France, and Korea, 1950-1990', unpublished manuscript, p. 295.

8   See my 'Bureaucratic Rationality and the Developmental State', *American Journal of Sociology*, 107(4), 2002.

9   For Latin America, see Christian Anglade and Carlos Fortin, *The State and Capital Accumulation in Latin America*, Volumes 1 and 2, Pittsburgh: Pittsburgh University Press, 1985 and 1990.

10   See the account in Cristobal Kay, *Latin American Theories of Underdevelopment*, New York: Routledge, 1987.

11   This section summarizes arguments developed elsewhere. See my 'Building a Developmental State: The Korean Case Reconsidered', *Politics and Society*, 27(3), 1999 and 'Bureaucratic Rationality'.

12   See Jeffrey Sachs, 'External Debt and Macroeconomic Management in Latin America and East Asia', Brookings Papers on Economic Activity, Number 2, 1985, pp. 523–573.

13   For a good account of this dynamic, see Nicola Christine Pratt, *The Legacy of the Corporatist State: Explaining Worker's Response to Economic Liberalization in Egypt*, Durham: University of Durham, Centre for Middle Eastern and Islamic Studies, 1998.

BANDUNG *REDUX*: IMPERIALISM AND ANTI-GLOBALIZATION NATIONALISMS IN SOUTHEAST ASIA

GERARD GREENFIELD

Fifty years after the Asia–Africa Conference was held in Bandung in April 1955 the 'Spirit of Bandung' continues to be redeployed and rediscovered, attributed to gatherings as diverse as the World Conference Against Racism,[1] the World Social Forum (WSF), and the Asian–African Sub-Regional Organizations Conference (AASROC), whose preparations for the celebration of the 50th anniversary were seen as a coordinated response to globalization by marginalized states.[2] Indeed, this 'Spirit of Bandung' is deemed more relevant than ever by Left nationalists, pan–Asianists and 'Third Worldists' seeking to restore or reinvigorate a unified front against US-led globalization and/or US imperialism.[3] The powerful and very public condemnation of imperialism and racism by nationalist 'Third World' leaders at the Bandung Conference is, it seems, the kind of political response needed today. The perceived radicalism of Bandung – bolstered by the CIA's attempts to disrupt what it saw as 'an impending Communist Conference in 1955'[4] through political assassination – has been written into the history of 'Third World' opposition to US imperialism. But in reviving the Spirit of Bandung in the fight against US imperialism it is important to ask whether such a unified voice of opposition really existed and – more importantly – whether it really challenged the US empire.

While the denunciation of US imperialism at Bandung is often attributed to Indonesia's first President, Sukarno, he made no direct criticism of the US at the time. In his opening address to the Conference delegates, Sukarno warned of a resurgent colonialism in 'its modern dress',[5] but remained preoccupied with colonialism of the old order. The only explicit reference to a new imperialism at the Conference was made by Brigadier-General Carlos P. Romulo, Special and Personal Envoy of the President of the Philippines to the US, who warned of 'a new super-barbarism, a new super-imperialism, a new super-power.' Yet this 'new super-imperialism' imposed by a system that was 'inherently expansionist' referred not to US capitalism, but to Soviet and Chinese Communism.[6] Similarly, the delegations of Turkey, Iran, Iraq, Pakistan and Sri Lanka defended US foreign policy and denounced China's support for Communist insurgency overseas. Mahmoud Muntasser, head of the Libyan delegation, alluded to external ideological threats posing 'a danger menacing the sovereignty of nations' that was 'more dangerous and of much stronger effect' than colonialism since it embodied 'all the disadvantages of classical colonialism, and, in addition, intellectual slavery.'[7] Mohammad Fadhil Jamali, leading the Iraqi delegation, identified Communism as one of 'three international forces' threatening world peace after 'old-time colonialism' and Zionism. Describing Communism as 'a subversive religion', he said that it threatened 'a new form of colonialism, much deadlier than the old one.'[8] In this context references in the Final Communiqué of the Asian-African Conference to 'abstention from interference in the internal affairs of one country by another' must be understood not only as a response to old and new forms of colonialism, but also to Communist expansionism.[9] Chou En-lai, Prime Minister and Foreign Minister of the People's Republic of China, was forced to abandon his prepared speech and instead appealed to Conference delegates to disregard distinctions between Communists and nationalists.[10]

Far from representing a united front against racism, neo-colonialism and imperialism, the Bandung Conference was characterized by divisiveness and conflict within Asia and Africa that not only undermined the ability of Third World nationalists to contest the US empire, but reaffirmed the legitimacy of US imperial ambitions. In the nationalist condemnation of the 'new super-imperialism' by Thailand's Minister for Foreign Affairs, Prince Wan Bongsprabandh, the 'threat of infiltration and subversion, if not aggression itself' was used to rally support for the use of military aggression against North Vietnam (and in the same speech Buddhist texts were quoted at length to give ideological legitimacy to the use of military force).[11] It was in this context that Thailand's Minister for Foreign Affairs also conveyed US President Eisenhower's 'greetings' to the Bandung Conference – a message that was interpreted as both measured consent and a veiled warning.[12]

The presence of the US state at Bandung – expressed through those states already operating within its informal imperial network (particularly Thailand, the Philippines and South Vietnam) – is inseparable from the historical legacy of the Bandung Conference. Within a decade the US would use this imperial network to escalate its military aggression against Vietnam and support a military coup in Indonesia. Six months after Sukarno's celebration of the 10th anniversary of the Bandung Conference under the banner of 'never retreat',[13] US-trained military leaders deposed Sukarno and orchestrated the massacre of more than a million people who were members or alleged members of the Indonesian Communist Party (PKI). The site of the Bandung Conference, Gedung Merdeka (Freedom Hall), became a military command center and hundreds of local PKI leaders and those accused of PKI sympathies were imprisoned in its basement, where they were tortured and killed.[14]

That Sukarno himself was in many ways unprepared for this had to do with the same ambiguities that were present at the Bandung Conference. His passion for neologisms had produced the term NEKOLIM (neo-colonialism, colonialism, imperialism) – a term that tended to deny the contradictions and fundamental differences within these systems of global power. It was at once a useful political slogan and useless theoretical tool. It lacked the historical and political subtleties and theoretical insights needed to inform political action.[15] The use of neologisms and slogans to simplify concepts and dissolve capitalism's complexities and contradictions led Sukarno to articulate radical anti-imperialist positions without any reference to class or capitalism. Sukarno's Left nationalism not only saw the primary struggle as one between nations, but through the ideology of 'Marhaenism' (national self-reliance) that accompanied NEKOLIM, it also denied the relevance of class struggle within Indonesia.

Notably, Sukarno also conflated pre-1945 colonialism with imperialism after the war, effectively obscuring the emergence of a new and unique American informal empire. Frustration with Sukarno's worldview was expressed by the revolutionary writer, Pramoedya Ananta Toer, in his speech to the Lekra Congress in Palembang in March 1964. Emphasizing the centrality of US imperialism, Pram advanced an indirect criticism of Sukarno's narrow concern with the reinstallation of British colonialism in Malaysia:

> Drag those 'Malaysian' neo-colonialists by their ears and put them in the defendant's seat. Pull off their mask and you'll see the true face of British imperialism with all its greed. But don't stop there. Pull off this mask too, and you'll see the truest face: US imperialism.[16]

Pointing to the new locus of power in the world, Pram observed that 'without US imperialism, other imperialisms will fall like leaves'.[17] Yet it is precisely because NEKOLIM obscured the intricacies and dynamics of the new imperialism that Sukarno continued to target former and new colonial powers equally, responding primarily to formal modes of empire.

It was only with the escalation of US military aggression in Vietnam that Sukarno focused more directly on US imperialism (although this did not necessarily mean a clearer understanding).[18] For its part, the US fully recognized that overt military intervention in Indonesia would be viewed as an act of *formal* empire. American officials were concerned that their actions would be labelled as a case of NEKOLIM and that this would expose their role in supporting the military coup.[19] Ironically, it was precisely because the new kind of imperial power they exercised was qualitatively different from colonial power that they could be relatively confident of being able to hide their role and protect their interests. Political alliances secured through military training programs and the promise of arms shipments via countries already integrated into the US empire in the region (particularly Thailand and the Philippines) escaped the NEKOLIM label. This demonstrated precisely why colonialismm and the new imperialism should not have been conflated by their opponents. It was through its confidence in the informal imperial alignment, especially military and security 'inter-service relationships', that the US government was able to provide the Indonesian army with 'shooting lists'[20] naming thousands of PKI leaders and organizers. A perceived threat to American imperial interests was thus eradicated – a pattern that would be repeated for the next fifty years and continues to this day.

Five decades after Bandung, the paradoxical reaffirmation of US imperial interests by Third World nationalists was re-enacted by Thailand's Prime Minister, Thaksin Shinawatra, who used the 'Spirit of Bandung' to launch a new regional formation, the Asia Cooperation Dialogue (ACD), in June 2002.[21] In his speech to the inaugural meeting of the ACD in northern Thailand, Thaksin described the new regional initiative as 'a confidence-building process for Asian countries, a confidence that is to be built upon *the Spirit of Bandung*'. Thaksin emphasized the need to promote this 'Asian consciousness' by quoting at length a marketing book on corporate branding. But the most remarkable aspect of this revival of the 'Spirit of Bandung' was the way in which Thaksin sought to add legitimacy to the ACD by citing its prior approval by the US President and the President of the European Commission:

> I met with them and informed them about the ACD initiative even before it was finalized. I was delighted that both leaders fully understood and concurred with me about the importance of strengthening our regional cooperation.[22]

Just as Thailand's Minister for Foreign Affairs conveyed the US President's 'greetings' to the Bandung Conference in 1955, this invocation of US approval in 2002 once again serves as a reminder of where imperial power really lies.

Stripping away the myth from the reality of the 'Spirit of Bandung' is not merely a necessary exercise in historical revision. It is also important because this myth reproduced in nationalist forms of anti-globalization politics that reinforce rather than contest the US empire today. This is especially clear in Thailand and Indonesia. Using the example of ruling-class appropriation of anti-IMF populism in Thailand, I argue that the reorganization of the Thai state on a Chief Executive Officer (CEO) model represents part of a wider process, i.e. the making of an 'interior' bourgeoisie and the transnational-ization of domestic capital from within the 'Third World'. This is illustrated by the strategies of the transnational agri-food conglomerate, Charoen Pokphand, and its role in the CEO-based reconstitution of the Thai state as part of a process of alignment with the US imperial state. Making sense of this requires a critical understanding of the interior bourgeoisie and chal-lenges the distinction between 'national' and 'foreign' capital implicit in Left nationalist responses to globalization.

The essay then goes on to examine the limits of 'localism' and 'localiza-tion' in anti-globalization movement struggles. The 'defence of the local' runs the risk of appropriation and re-deployment by nationalist politicians and, especially, the interior bourgeoisie, and thus may contribute to coun-tering and undermining working-class militancy. After examining recent developments from this perspective in Thailand, the essay concludes by returning to Indonesia and the 'Spirit of Bandung' to show how Sukarno's ideology of 'Marhaenism' is being used to contain radicalism and channel popular resistance in ways that deploy the rhetoric of anti-capitalism without challenging capitalism. Important parallels may be seen between its combination of community and self-reliance and the alternatives advocated by some segments of the anti-globalization movements. While these alter-natives differ in substance, they share the rhetoric of self-reliance and defence of community interests and may be appropriated and re-deployed by ruling-class interests seeking to utilize popular discontent with globalization in ways that legitimate and reinforce their own integration into global capi-talism and the American empire.

NATIONALISM AND THE LEFT IN THAILAND

While the mass mobilizations that occurred in response to the Asian economic crisis of 1997-98 broadened the base of anti-globalization move-ments, the revolutionary potential of these protests and their limitations remain subjects of debate among activists. What these movements did show was the primacy of nationalism as the reference point for popular discontent with globalization, whether understood primarily in liberal terms as corpo-rate globalization or in more radical terms as capitalist globalization or imperialism. Across a broad political spectrum, the IMF emerged as both symbol and source of the injustice and social devastation wrought by the crisis and its aftermath. According to many activists and academics on the Left, the crisis was engineered by the IMF to extend its domination over the countries in this region. In Thailand one of the most important Left critiques to enter the public debate on the causes and consequences of the crisis are the *Globalization Series* and *Local Knowledge Series* of the *Visions Project*. These series of publications condemn the IMF and World Bank as agents of US imperialism, while advocating localizing alternatives to the prevailing world order.[23]

Writing under the penname Yuk Si-ariya,[24] the Director of the Visions Project, Tienchai Wongchaisuwan, explains the crisis of Thai capitalism using a world-systems framework, locating globalization as part of the hegemonic project of the US imperial state. Tienchai argues that former Prime Minister Chuan Leekpai assisted the expansion of US hegemony in the 1990s by seeking US government support and declaring loyalty to the IMF. Tienchai's concern with the loss of national pride leads him to place greater emphasis on Thailand's 'begging' for US assistance and the imposition of American culture than on the political economy of American power. According to Tienchai, this 'loyalty to the IMF' contrasts with the disobedience of Malaysia and Indonesia, who 'were acting like the recalcitrant children of the IMF'.[25] Tienchai contends that, like its Southeast Asian neighbours, Thailand should have developed 'an independent strategy and standpoint' from which it could negotiate with the US, thereby challenging US hegemony and limiting the damage done by the IMF. Whether Thailand could have done this remains unexplored – a weakness exacerbated by Tienchai's emphasis on Chuan's failure as a national leader rather than offering a critical understanding of the neoliberal regime and ruling-class interests in Thailand. Furthermore, the central concept of US hegemony is largely dealt with in institutional and pseudo-cultural terms, with US hegemonic ambitions rooted in a 'wild west' culture of expansionism and domination, without reference to capitalism or any obvious capitalist imperative.[26]

The desire for an independent strategy to emerge from a correct set of policy choices, unrelated to the structural power and interests of capital, is a recurring weakness in the Visions Project. Insofar as capital is incorporated into the analysis at all, it is premised on a foreign-national dichotomy according to which national capital becomes virtually synonymous with the nation.[27] This is partly due to the treatment of capitalism in Thailand as underdeveloped or peripheral, operating within the inter-imperialist rivalry of Japan, China and the US. According to Tienchai: 'The deeper the crisis in Thailand and Asia in the future, the more Asian countries, especially

Japanese capitalists, China and the NICs [Newly Industrializing Countries] will lose.' He concludes that: 'The end result will be that American capitalists will enter and buy up assets at rock bottom prices and at the same time the American state will expand its influence, replacing China and Japan.'[28] The underlying assumption is that Thai capitalism, operating within the sphere of Asian-regional capitalism, existed outside the US empire prior to the Asian crisis and was subjected to imperial realignment only through the US state's use of the IMF to impose neoliberal restructuring and financial liberalization. Such an ahistorical approach ignores far-reaching US geopolitical and economic involvement in the reshaping of the Thai state and Thai capitalism in the decades prior to the economic boom of the 1980s and early 1990s.

Well before Chuan went begging cap in hand to the US, the military regime of Field Marshall Sarit Thanarat, who took power in the coup of 1958, reconstituted the Thai state as part of its integration into the American empire. Under what Peter Bell describes as the US role in the Thai 'nation-building' process, the US government was directly involved in creating major state agencies such as Thailand's Budget Bureau, National Statistical Office, National Economic Development Board, and Board of Investment.[29] This facilitated an influx of US capital that was further reinforced by Thailand's role as a strategic military and economic base for US imperialist aggression against Vietnam. Thus, while some historians interpret Sarit's political project as a process of making the state more 'Thai',[30] a more accurate interpretation is that the Sarit coup 'brought into line the strategic interests of the US, the dictatorial aims of the Thai military, and the commercial ambitions of domestic capital.'[31] The US military and economic support for the Sarit dictatorship and the direct role of US agencies in reorganizing the Thai state signalled an early phase of imperial alignment.[32]

In the absence of this historical context, Tienchai's analysis of US imperialism tends to present the Thai ruling class as devoid of strategic interests and the capitalist class as seemingly relegated to comprador status.[33] Capitalists in Thailand appear to have no stake in the globalization project overseen by the US imperial state and are driven to support globalization only due to an ideological shift imposed under US hegemony. Tienchai subsequently argues that 'as a theory and strategy' globalization 'has played a direct role in gearing the Thai ruling class and Thai technocrats to believe in currency liberalization and stock market deregulation, liberalization of information and entertainment, which will bring disaster to all Thai people.'[34] Such an argument neglects the process by which capitalists in Thailand and other Asian countries renegotiated, domesticated and redeployed neoliberal ideology as part of their own class strategies directed at working-class militancy. The class strategy of domestic capital is precisely to utilize neoliberalism to undermine working-class power, while at the same time using populist nationalism to mobilize working-class discontent against the IMF.

Ultimately Tienchai's analysis depicts globalization as a strategy of class war between the capitalists of the US, Germany and Japan (although China is a global power in his analysis, Tienchai avoids attributing it with a capitalist class), a class war that does not involve working classes at all.[35] Conforming with the dominant liberal and Left view expressed by NGOs and social movements, the working class are viewed only as victims of globalization and victims of the crisis. The prevailing orthodoxy in social movements, NGOs and the intellectual Left is to deny the role of working-class struggle in forcing capital 'to develop strategies of control and containment', thereby avoiding any risk that workers may be 'blamed' for the crisis.[36] As Ji Giles Ungpakorn, a founding member of Workers' Democracy in Thailand, has argued:

> The dominant ideological response among organized workers and Left-wing intellectuals to the crisis, and the manner in which governments handled economic policy, was in the form of Left Nationalism. This ideology is a mirror image of ruling class nationalism and a sign of the current ideological weakness of the Thai Left.[37]

'THE THIRD TEXAN': ANTI-IMF POPULISM AND THE CEO STATE

This convergence of Left nationalism and ruling-class nationalism is illustrated by the anti-IMF populism utilized by the *Thai Rak Thai* (Thais Love Thais) Party in its electoral victory and in Prime Minister Thaksin's attacks on the IMF. In a televised address to the nation on 31 July 2003, Thaksin announced that the final instalment of Thailand's debt to the IMF – incurred at the time of the Asian economic crisis – had been paid. Describing the damage done to Thailand by IMF policies imposed through loan conditionality, Thaksin congratulated Thai citizens on this 'victory' for the people and declared that: 'We shall never go back to the days of the IMF again as long as I am in office.'[38] This nationalist stance illustrated precisely the anti-IMF sentiment mobilized by the Left and utilized by the Right to bring Thaksin's *Thai Rak Thai* to power two years earlier.

A week after his anti-IMF speech Thaksin permitted the CIA to arrest an Indonesian national, Riduan Isamuddin (Hambali), in Thailand for suspected terrorist activities links to Jemaah Islamiah (JI). Hambali was already in US custody outside of Thailand when Bush made the announcement of his arrest and the US$10 million dollar reward, and only afterwards did Thaksin make his own announcement to the Thai public – an act that led Thai human rights groups to accuse Thaksin of turning the country into a 'US colony'. The real reward came in October at the APEC Summit, when Bush praised Thaksin for his 'good work' in capturing Hambali and announced that Thailand would be given 'major non-NATO ally status' – which includes access to depleted uranium anti-tank rounds and US government loan guarantees for private banks financing arms exports.[39] This nexus of free trade and state terror was further demonstrated by the commitment to finalize a US–Thai Free Trade Agreement (FTA) as yet another reward for Thailand's role in the exercise of US imperial power. Indeed, Thaksin's address to the US-ASEAN Business Council in Washington in December 2001 aptly summarized Thailand's role in the informal empire: 'Throughout the colonial era, the global wars of the 20th century, and the conflicts within Asia, Thailand and the United States have remained close friends and allies. That will not change in the dawn of the 21st century.'[40]

The identification of the populist-nationalist Thai leader with the US empire is symbolized by Thaksin's response to receipt of the Sam Houston Humanitarian Award in October 2002 at Sam Houston State University in Texas, where he gained his doctorate in criminal justice in the late 1970s.[41] Referring to the fact that James Baker III and former President George Bush were recipients of the award in earlier years, Thaksin declared that:

> Although I am the first Asian to get the award, you may count me as the third Texan. I consider myself a Texan – at least in spirit.[42]

In many respects this mix of Texas-trained police commander and billionaire corporate CEO turned Prime Minister encapsulates precisely the nexus of US imperial power in the region, with Thailand as deputy sheriff and an internationally-integrated site of capitalist accumulation. However, to ensure the continuity of his regime the Third Texan must maintain political legitimacy through a nationalist agenda that at times appears to challenge US interests. While this may appeal to Left nationalists in Thailand who see potential for challenging US hegemony, the situation is far more complex. As Leo Panitch and Sam Gindin have argued, the hegemonic power of the US empire does not necessarily entail 'a transfer of direct popular loyalty to the American state itself.' In fact, 'the greatest danger to it is that the states within its orbit will be rendered illegitimate by virtue of their articulation to the imperium.'[43] In this sense, the Thaksin regime's nationalism, particularly its appropriation of anti-IMF populism, plays an important role in maintaining its legitimacy. Whereas Left nationalists have set aside discussion of capitalism in favour of US imperialism, the Thaksin regime clearly extends nationalist ideological legitimation to the capitalist system itself. In his anti-

IMF speech, for example, Thaksin reiterated the inseparability of capitalism and nationalism: 'I have said on many occasions that under the capitalist and democratic systems, there is one common element among all the successful capitalist countries, that is, a sense of nationalism.'[44]

One of the most remarkable aspects of the *Thai Rak Thai* Party's ascent to power in 2001 was its ability to draw into its ranks prominent figures from NGOs and social movements, as well as former Communist Party of Thailand (CPT) cadres. Once again nationalism plays a central role in explaining how ex–CPT cadres could end up joining a political party led by Thaksin, one of the wealthiest capitalists in the country. As Ji Giles Ungpakorn observes:

> On the one hand, the vast majority of ex–CPT sympathizers firmly believed that socialism died along with the Cold War and therefore they have managed to put their beliefs behind them. On the other hand, those who still believed in some form of socialist society were just as comfortable working alongside a party run by nationalist businessmen as those who no longer believed in socialism. This is because the Stalinist politics of the CPT always emphasized the importance of nationalism and class alliances with 'progressive capitalists' over and above class struggle, especially in (what the CPT called) 'the national stage' of the Thai revolution.[45]

These broad political alliances enabled *Thai Rak Thai* to channel nationalist sentiment into a comprehensive political project aimed at radically reorganizing the state to better serve the interests of 'progressive capitalists'. Central to this is the Thaksin regime's establishment of the corporate Chief Executive Officer (CEO) model of governance as the basis for running the country. As a former CEO of his own telecommunications conglomerate, Shin Corporation, Thaksin has aggressively promoted himself not as Prime Minister of a country, but as CEO of Thailand Inc. A crucial element of this strategic reorientation of state institutions under the CEO model is the reconstitution of provincial governments, with the establishment of 'CEO Governors' in 30 provinces. This was widely seen as a consolidation of Thaksin's own power, bypassing key segments of the state bureaucracy. As Weerayut Chokchaimadon has argued:

> [T]he CEO arrangement gives power to each governor to interfere in activities of local administrative bodies – *tambon* (sub-district) and provincial organizations, and municipalities. From now on, these bodies will not have the local autonomy and freedom of thought to devise programmes based on local knowledge and needs. The governors will decide what must be done and how, based on national goals drawn up by Thaksin and his people .... Thaksin even ordered all

ministries to change rules to aid these governors in asserting their power. The governors now control the money, which used to be allocated by the ministries. They can reshuffle personnel. They can now run their local anti-drug and anti-mafia campaigns, not the central government. This appears to be decentralization, but with Thaksin pulling all the strings in Bangkok, the plan shoves aside the bureaucracy.[46]

Weerayut concludes that Thaksin is treating Thailand as 'just another company' and since 'Thaksin didn't run Shin Corp as a democracy', neither will he run the country democratically.[47] While criticisms such as those expounded by Weerayut expose the authoritarian ambitions of Thaksin and point to the political and ethical shortcomings of the CEO governor model, there is a tendency to neglect the transformative effect of CEO-ization on the state and the particular interests it serves. The CEO-ization of the state is a form of flexible decentralization that consolidates central control over the provinces through a harmonized local state management system. At the same time it enforces competition between the provinces for new injections of capital.

This model is explicitly based on the corporate strategies of the agribusiness conglomerate Charoen Pokphand (CP), which uses intra-firm trade and competition to increase productivity, maximize profits and maintain flexible centralized control. This application of CP's corporate structure to the state coincides with the relocation of capital within Thailand and the financialization of agriculture, intensifying the compulsion for provinces to compete against each other. As Pasuk Phongpaichit has argued, a key aspect of the CEO model promoted by Thaksin is 'broadening and deepening the extent of the domestic capitalist economy'.[48] In this context, Pasuk quotes Thaksin's assertion that: 'Capitalism needs capital, without which there is no capitalism. We need to push capital into the rural areas.'[49] For corporations like CP, this expansion into rural areas is facilitated by the use of its own CEO governance structures by state regulatory authorities and enables the implementation of its export-oriented agri-food strategy. This is based on CP's nationalistic vision of Thailand as the 'Kitchen of the World', now entrenched as one of the most important economic policies of the Thai state.

The role of the Thaksin regime in supporting the accumulation strategies of individual capitals such as CP is further illustrated by its orchestration of a cover-up and manipulation of the avian influenza (H5N1) outbreak in 2003-04. Despite a potentially serious threat to the legitimacy of the Thaksin regime, government officials refused to recognize the outbreak of H5N1 in Thailand in an effort to protect the poultry export industry and therefore the interests of CP. With 1.6 billion broiler chicks sold each year and control of a highly profitable chicken feed industry, CP's interests were threatened by the avian flu pandemic already recognized in neighbouring Vietnam, Cambodia, Laos and southern China. As the outbreak worsened, the government turned the crisis into an opportunity for CP by attributing the source of the epidemic to small-scale farming. The closed systems of large-scale factory farming used by CP and its contract farmers were promoted as a solution. Forestalling a serious impact on CP's poultry business, the government moved to replace small farmers with CP's closed factory farms, boosting the corporation's control over poultry production and chicken feed, and increasing its sale of broiler chicks in the domestic market.[50]

The dominance of CP in rural Thailand is increasingly matched by its urban presence, as the owner of Lotus supermarkets and 7-Eleven convenience stores, and its global power. Although its name is relatively unknown, CP is the largest supplier of animal feed in the world and the fifth largest agri-food corporation, operating over 300 companies in twenty countries. Ranked among *Forbes* magazine's annual list of dollar billionaires, the CEO of CP, Dhanin Chearavanont, exercises extensive political influence in securing the corporation's overseas interests. As a major investor in animal feed,[51] agrochemicals, food processing, motorcycles, seeds and supermarkets in China, Dhanin maintains close ties with the political leadership in Beijing.[52] Similar ties are maintained with the Bush family, including the hiring of former President Bush Sr. as a consultant, and the creation of joint venture businesses with Neil Bush, the brother of George W. Bush.[53] CP also made political donations to both the Republican and Democratic parties in the US to encourage support for China's WTO accession.[54] At the time of the 2000 presidential elections in the US, the Executive Vice President of CP, Sarasin Viraphol, was quoted in the Beijing *People's Daily* as saying that Thailand's interests would be better served by a Bush administration, especially by its stance on free trade and China.[55]

The reorganization of the state through CP's CEO model also illustrates the privatization of the functions of the state. In his book on *The Asian CEO*, Korsak Chairasmisak, Vice Chairman and Chairman of the Executive Board of Directors of CP and CEO of 7-Eleven, points out that CP's 7-Eleven chain convenience stores were the main outlet for public distribution in Bangkok of the draft Constitution of 1997. Faced with the legal requirement that the draft Constitution be made available to the public within forty-five days, it was determined that 7-Eleven stores, with two million customers a day, had greater access to the public than any state agency.[56] It was of course in CP's interests to ensure the smooth passage of the new Constitution since it was no less than 'a charter for Thailand's modern capitalists.'[57] This relationship to the state is set to continue, as the CEO-ization of the state brings government agencies even closer to the management and operational mode of 7-Eleven stores. For Korsak this forms the basis of the future of local, national and global governance:

> I myself have a vision of the contemporary world being led by 1,000 or so largest corporations spreading their branches all over the world. These corporations will have a lot of influence on socio-economic policy of many countries as well as on the life of ordinary people.[58]

In describing the political process of achieving this vision, Korsak suggests that CEO-ization is primarily concerned with the realignment and concentration of political and economic power. Describing elected politicians as having 'symbolic meaning', and using the case of Japan, Korsak states that:

> [A]ll that the Prime Minister can do is persuade his country's businessmen to increase investment. Whether or not an investment is made, and how much it will be, the final decision is with the CEO of the enterprise in question. The CEO is the one who has been given a mandate to 'act' for people from other societies. The CEO has been entrusted with the control and management of world productive resources, such as manpower, capital and technology. The CEO, as a result, comes to possess tremendous power to direct the trend of our world.[59]

In a commentary published in *Matichon Weekly* in March 2004, a leading progressive academic, Nidhi Aeosrivongse, raises a series of questions about a 'new nationalism' taking shape in Thailand under globalization, linking this to the CEO transformation of the national polity.[60] While posing the question of whose interests are served by this new nationalism, Nidhi observes that global competitiveness is now used to define the nationalist credentials of a Thai corporation, a change that is reshaping 'the spirit of Thai nationalism'. Devoid of historical or cultural roots and geared solely towards what appears to be a singularly corporate victory in the global arena, this new nationalism raises serious questions including, Nidhi adds, whether there is in fact any 'nation' involved in this new nationalism.[61]

Arguments by critics of the Thaksin regime such as Nidhi tend to support the view that the populist nationalism that brought Thaksin to power is being remade under the Thaksin regime. Yet *why* this is taking place, and the broader political and economic context of these changes, remain unclear. Whether it is the remaking of populist nationalism or the imposition of the CEO model, it seems necessary to move the analysis beyond institutions, policies and political personalities to understand the social conflict and structures of power underpinning these changes. For this we need to situate corporate strategies and political processes within an under-standing of class struggle, capitalism and the dynamics of the American empire.

NATIONALISM AND THE INTERIOR BOURGEOISIE

The construction of a new nationalism rooted in a CEO model of gover-nance is much more than an authoritarian grab for power in the interests of big business. It constitutes a deliberate strategy to undercut working-class power by further internationalizing domestic capital, deepening capitalist expansion internally, and reorganizing the state to be a more effective agent of that capital. It is in this sense *a class strategy*, undertaken not only in the interests of fractions of domestic capital seeking deeper integration into global circuits of capital, but *against* the struggle of the subordinate classes to contain the reach of capitalist accumulation and set barriers to the maximization of profit. It is precisely because the subordinate classes are engaged in struggles that challenge ruling-class interests that a populist nationalism (combined with selective political repression) is necessary. Just as the Third Texan must rail against the IMF to maintain the current political regime, the CEO-based reorganization of the state and the advancement of the interests of fractions of capital (exemplified by transnational conglomerates like CP), must continue to be framed in a nationalism that recognizes and supports 'progressive capitalists.'

The experience of Thailand suggests that class strategies of 'nationalist' capitalists are inseparable from Left responses to globalization and imperialism that invoke a nationalist defence of 'domestic' or 'national' capital. The particular anti-globalization alternatives informed by this kind of nationalism implicitly rely on a national bourgeoisie that should and can contribute to the struggle against US imperialism. It seems that this ideological position can only be maintained by assuming a continuation of classical imperialism and denying the political and social realities of the new imperial order, particu-larly the internationalization of capital in the 'Third World'.

Two ideological blind spots in particular have important implications for political action (or inaction). The first concerns the apparent paradox of a domestic capitalist class at once nationalistic and internationalizing. The second concerns the implicit belief that the domestic capitalist class still constitutes a 'national' bourgeoisie, and that globalization – as Tienchai argues – is essentially a class war between capitalists in the advanced capitalist countries. The fallacies of these positions cannot be countered by labelling these nationalist capitalists and their state representatives as nothing more than comprador capitalists abusing popular anti-globalization sentiment. Even less useful are moral judgments about the fabrications of these nationalists. Such contradictions are inherent in the very nature of capitalist classes and the class strategies they employ. As Nicos Poulantzas noted, 'There can be no doubt that bourgeois policy vis-à-vis the nation is subject to the hazards of its particular interests: indeed, the history of the bourgeoisie is one of continual oscillation between identification with and betrayal of the nation.'[62]

It is when the bourgeoisie oscillates towards identification with the nation that we find a convergence with certain kinds of anti-globalization nationalism; an alliance that seeks to defend the national bourgeoisie against the neoliberal policies of the IMF and US hegemony. However, rather than being victims of global capital, sections of the 'national' bourgeoisie are themselves able to internationalize, becoming transnational capital *without becoming foreign-owned or dominated*. Yet this change also means that their material interests become inextricably tied to those of the American empire and are *systemically* represented by the US imperial state. In other words, if domestic capital internationalizes and emulates the logic of global capital, then it requires the US imperial state to pursue its role in managing global capitalism. It also requires international capital to be internalized within every other state – a process involving what Panitch and Gindin refer to as 'the reconstitution of states as integral elements of an informal American empire'.[63]

Viewed in these terms, the radical reorganization of the Thai state through the CEO-ization model may be understood as a class strategy to remake the state in a way that better serves the interests of transnationalized fractions of domestic capital, and at the same time functions more effectively vis-à-vis the US imperial state. This may explain why individual capitals represented by transnational conglomerates such as CP pay tribute to the US state and seek both direct and indirect forms of representation to it. These forms of representation differ from institutional linkages with other states because only the US state is viewed in global terms. As we noted in the previous section, CP executives explicitly tied their interests to the US state not because of their investments in the US, but because of investments in China. Through its strategic alliances and joint ventures with transnational corporations like the US-based agribusiness transnational, Monsanto, and the UK-based global retailer, Tesco, CP has also internalized the interests and accumulation patterns of specific fractions of international capital. In this way, the interests of *nationalist* fractions of domestic capital are inextricably bound up with the US imperial state's effective management of global capitalism.

To make sense of this nationalistic, transnationalized domestic capitalist class that defends the nation *and* aligns itself with the American imperial order, it is important to recognize the social changes that have remade the national bourgeoisie into an 'interior' bourgeoisie. In his overview of Poulantzas' concept of the interior bourgeoisie, Bob Jessop explains that:

This 'interior' bourgeoisie is neither totally dependent on foreign capital – as is the comprador bourgeoisie, which lacks its own base of accumulation and is economically, politically, and ideologically subordinated. Nor is the 'interior' bourgeoisie sufficiently independent to play a leading role in any genuine anti-imperialist struggle (as is the national bourgeoisie). This intermediate position does not mean that the interior bourgeoisie lacks all measure of independence. On the contrary it has its own economic foundation and bases of accumulation at home and abroad and it still exhibits its own specific, national political and ideological orientations in opposition to American capital.[64]

This suggests two critical dimensions of the interior bourgeoisie: integration with, but not dependency on, circuits of foreign capital, and possession of 'its own economic foundation and bases of accumulation at home and abroad'. Although Poulantzas applied the concept of the interior bourgeoisie to advanced capitalist countries, the explanatory power of this concept may be useful in developing a more critical understanding of transnationalized fractions of domestic capital originating within 'developing' capitalist countries today.[65] The fractions of capital represented by CP, for example, clearly have their own economic foundations and bases of accumulation at home and abroad, while at the same time they are integrated into circuits of global capital. What this suggests is that the internationalization of capital (accelerated under the globalization project) does not simply produce a dependency of 'national' capital on 'foreign' capital, but involves a more complex process that includes the internationalization of domestic capital and the 'localization' of foreign capital. What appears as 'national' capital operates according to the logic of global capital, *in its own interests*, and without the bonds of dependency that characterize the comprador capitalists under classical imperialism.

Proponents of Left nationalism and localization especially tend to underestimate the extent to which the financialization of industrial capital has transformed the 'national' bourgeoisie. The assumption that financial markets and finance capital flows operate in separate spheres from production and circuits of manufacturing capital permits a nationalist identification with domestic manufacturing capital. What this suggests is that while certain industries, such as telecommunications and finance, are understood to be globally integrated, domestic manufacturing and agribusiness are seen as more clearly divided between foreign and local control. But this fails to recognize the way in which the financialization of industrial production and agriculture has transformed the patterns and boundaries of accumulation. Rather than being an intrusive force, international finance capital may in fact be internalized within domestic capital.

As a conceptual tool the concept of the interior bourgeoisie helps unravel the apparently paradoxical policies, strategies and actions of the state and fractions of domestic capital. More importantly, it suggests that the struggle by domestic capital against US hegemony (epitomized by resistance to the neoliberal project of the IMF) is a struggle *within* US hegemony, not against it. While neoliberal policies do threaten the interests of particular fractions of domestic capital, they also form part of the transformative pressures that remake some segments of the domestic capitalist class as an interior bourgeoisie. What this means is that 'nationalist' resistance of domestic capitalists to neoliberal integration into global circuits of capital is in fact a struggle to secure better terms for integration. Moreover, it involves an *internal* reorganization to emulate global capital more effectively. Against this background the mobilizational politics of nationalism forms part of a class strategy to reinvent the bourgeoisie as an interior bourgeoisie, whose internationalization of capital requires a more effective national state that gives it access to the US imperial state. Thus nationalist resistance may occur *within* the process of imperial (re)alignment.

THE LIMITS OF LOCALIZATION

It is increasingly clear that a more critical approach to 'localization' as an alternative to capitalist globalization is needed. The 'local knowledge' alternatives advocated by the Visions Project, for example, focus exclusively on the threat posed by 'foreign' capital, and look to 'local' capital to defend national interests. This in turn generates implicit support for the capitalist imperative of competition against foreign capital as a more effective means of defending local culture from imperial domination. An example of this is the position articulated in the Vision Project's *Local Knowledge Series* regarding the domestication of the genetic mapping and engineering of rice. This is seen as necessary in order to protect local rice varieties and to compete internationally as a rice-exporting nation.[66] Yet this 'alternative' neglects the role that genetic engineering plays in the commodification of living organisms – a process integral to the very logic of capitalism.

The broader relevance of this for anti-globalization movements lies in the fact that capitalism appropriates the defence of the 'local' as a means of re-legitimating itself. This is epitomized by the solidaristic call by Korsak Chairasmisak, the CP executive and 7-Eleven CEO cited earlier, for Thai family shopkeepers to become owners of a 7-Eleven convenience store as a means of resisting the pressures of transnational corporations: 'We will support them to become strong enough to withstand competition from foreign multinational corporations who have begun to cast an eye on Thailand's retail business.'[67] The fact that 7-Eleven (headquartered in Texas with 26,000 stores in 18 countries) is itself a multinational corporation is obscured, as it is reinvented as a local company challenging the interests of foreign multinationals. This is indicative of the challenges posed by the local-ization strategies of international capital. Given this challenge, it also serves as a sobering reminder to those activists advocating local alternatives to glob-alization and/or US imperialism that localization strategies should be rooted in a more coherent class analysis. In the absence of class analysis, and with the persistence of the false dichotomy of 'foreign versus national' capital, the radical defence of the local risks incorporation into capitalist localization strategies – class strategies that will fragment or demobilize popular resistance.

The limits of localization are even more apparent when proponents of globalization and supporters of the US empire are themselves advocating localization. A leading public intellectual and policy advisor, Chai-anan Samudavanija (who was the first to translate the term 'globalization' into the Thai language),[68] states unequivocally that

> America needs a Global Strategy for the age of globalization. Such a global strategy must be able to address the basic strategic objective that defines the American Agenda.[69]

This, he maintains, would benefit Thailand, insofar as its interests would be represented in the American Agenda. Yet at the same time Chai-anan shares with many Left-liberal academics and activists a belief in localization as a means of promoting 'the empowerment of individuals, decentralization and participation', thereby counter-balancing the social and economic impact of globalization and a shift in political power, where 'transnational operations replace the state in controlling and directing economic activities at all levels' and 'elites – political, military and technocratic – lose their most fundamental power over the private sector, namely their regulative authority.'[70] This leads Chai-anan to depict the rise of transnational power in a way that converges with the neo-Marxist Visions Project, where glob-alization has 'empowered international regimes such as the World Trade Organization and the International Monetary Fund' which then used the Asian economic crisis 'to lay down conditions and guidelines for economic recovery.'[71]

The significance of Chai-anan's synthesis of localization and globalization within the US imperial order is not the appropriation of political ideas, but the way in which this translates into political action. As mass labour protests against the privatization of the Electricity Generating Authority of Thailand (EGAT) escalated in the first quarter of 2004, with 50,000 workers taking to the streets on 3 March, Chai-anan was brought in by the Thaksin govern-ment as the new chairperson of EGAT to negotiate a settlement with the union. Depicted in the media as someone who 'wears the same shirt' as the workers,[72] Chai-anan attempted to appease the unions by agreeing to halt the privatization of EGAT. Confusion followed as the unions declared victory against privatization while Thaksin reaffirmed that privatization would go ahead. Chai-anan immediately denied that there was an agreement to stop the privatization and claimed that an alternative process of gradual privatization was formulated. In response, the EGAT union continued its protests and threatened strike action.

The struggle over EGAT privatization demonstrates an important political dynamic in the resistance to the Thaksin regime's neoliberal agenda, and signifies an important break in the ruling class use of populist-nationalism. When Thaksin declared a people's victory in his anti–IMF speech in July 2003, he asserted that Thailand's freedom from 'binding obligations' to the IMF signified an end to the forced privatization of state enterprises to repay national debt. Yet in the same speech he reaffirmed that privatization would proceed through *national* means, by listing these public utilities on the Stock Exchange of Thailand (SET). The listing of public service utilities on the stock exchange would ensure that 'accountability can be monitored by the capital markets' and that they would emulate capitalist enterprises in the private sector.[73] Through this shift the Thaksin regime attempted to contain workers' resistance to privatization within the parameters of anti–IMF nationalism, and by removing the IMF from this equation he believed that resistance would dissolve. It was very significant in this context that the workers' unions and labour groups saw through this and recognized the continuity of the neoliberal project within the Thaksin regime's nationalist agenda, and responded with organized mass protests against continued privatization through SET listings. In this sense the anti-privatization movement offers renewed possibilities to break from the Left nationalism that characterized the responses to the Asian crisis, broadening the struggle beyond anti–IMF nationalism and targeting the specific ruling-class strategies that seek to co-opt or marginalize working-class militancy.[74]

Despite such possibilities, for this to become a major challenge to global capitalism and American empire, the interconnections between globalization, corporate domination, racism, capitalism and imperialism need to become coherent elements of a worldview central to the collective understanding of a mass movement and its aspirations, not merely slogans to march under. The relationship between alternative globalization, anti-globalization and anti-imperialist movements and populist nationalism is often based on broad coalitions, tactical alliances that seek to use nationalism – rooted in discontent with the global status quo and the sense of vulnerability and insecurity associated with globalization – to gain support for more radical responses.

Regardless of the ideological justification (where 'pragmatism' seems to be the most pervasive), the strategic implication of appeals to national sovereignty, self-sufficiency, self-reliance and so forth is essentially the same. Such a narrow understanding of the US imperial order in terms of economic domination (expressed in terms of US transnational corporations) risks advocating alternatives that reinforce the logic of capitalism and therefore supporting the very system the US imperial state is managing. More importantly, it risks mobilizing working–class people in ways that promote the very kind of populist nationalism that capitalists are using to negotiate the terms of their imperial assimilation.

BACK TO BANDUNG:
THE SUBSTANCE OF SLOGANS

Perhaps nowhere in Asia is this seen more clearly today than in Indonesia where, as with the anti–IMF mobilizations in Thailand, there is massive anger and frustration over the vulnerability and uncertainty generated by accelerated globalization and intensified US military aggression. Yet this popular anger and frustration is also subject to being managed and utilized by ruling-class interests.

Among the twenty-four political parties contesting the July 2004 elections in Indonesia, no less than six laid claim to the legacy of Sukarno, including three separate political parties led by his daughters Megawati, Rachmawati and Sukmawati. The reinvention of Sukarnoism as a *nationalist* political programme included the revival of a key element in the political mythology of Sukarno, founded on the legendary meeting of Sukarno and the peasant-farmer, Marhaen, that gave rise to his doctrine of 'Marhaenism', or self-reliance.[75] The denial of class struggle was one of the primary ideological goals of Sukarno's invention of Marhaenism, premised on his rejection of the Marxist concept of the proletariat as inappropriate to the Indonesian context. According to Sukarno, Marhaen was 'not a member of the proletariat, for he does not sell his [sic] labour-power to another without participating in the ownership of the means of production.'[76] Therefore Indonesia did not have a working class, but had a mass of 'destitute people' who owned the means of production but still lived in poverty. This ideological shift was not simply a matter of redefining class struggle in terms of the 'little people' or 'the destitute people' of Indonesia. Marhaenism identified them as *the nation*, effectively defining class struggle out of the equation.

In rallying public support for her party (now called the Indonesian Nationalist Party Marhaenisme), Sukmawati Sukarno reasserted the relevance of Marhaenism in the 21st century in the context of globalization but was unable to define its contemporary meaning or explain the specific social and economic policies that it would entail.[77] Like Sukarnoism more generally, Marhaenism is being used for its symbolic power, channelling popular discontent into support for *ruling-class* nationalism. This strategy for managing the discontented masses extends to the more progressive versions of Marhaenism, epitomized by the Partai Nasional Bung Karno (PNBK, Brother Karno National Party) created in 2002. Renamed Partai Nasional Banteng Kemerdekaan (Freedom Bull National Party) to meet legal requirements banning the use of personal names in the 2004 elections, PNBK advocated 'progressive revolution' based on the ideology of Marhaenism and the advancement of 'Indonesian socialism'.[78] As with other nationalist political parties, no clear economic agenda for achieving self-reliance was presented, let alone a vision of 'socialism.' Rather, social democratic reforms (social welfare and subsidies) were offered to the masses in the hope of tapping the populist nationalism generated by larger political parties like Megawati's PDI (Indonesian Democratic Party).

As a mobilization strategy used by fractions of the Indonesian ruling class, Marhaenism offers significant potential because its lack of substance is combined with a broad reach across the political spectrum. Radically interpreted as a domesticated Marxism appropriate to Indonesia, Marhaenism also informs Left nationalist responses to globalization and US imperialism. Doctrinal legitimacy for these radical interpretations is found in the *Marhaen Declaration* of 1964, which added an overt anti-capitalist line to its populist nationalism, calling for the removal of landowners and capitalists from the Indonesian Nationalist Party (PNI). Although the purge never materialized, this anti-capitalist rhetoric plays an important role in binding Marhaenism to anti-imperialist and anti-globalization positions today.[79] According to Mohammad Samsul Arifin, 'The genuine Marhaenist says, as long as there are practices of imperialism, colonialism and feudalism in the world, this doctrine remains relevant.'[80] The power of Marhaenism, it is argued, is that while it shares a revolutionary agenda with Marxism, the latter focuses on the working class while Marhaenism 'widens its constituency to almost all people in the community'.[81] Thus a revolutionary agenda is asserted, but without class or class struggle. The radical anti-globalization and anti-imperialist struggle is – once again – perceived as a struggle of nations. Susilo Eko Prayitno, a member of the presidium of the Indonesian National Student Movement (Gerakan Mahasiswa Nasional Indonesia, GMNI) describes Marhaenism as a Marxist theory 'born in the struggle to abolish capitalism, colonialism and imperialism'.[82] Notably, GMNI was among a dozen student organizations that held mass protests in Jakarta in February 2003 to advocate 'Tritura', the 'three demands of the people',[83] including the reduction of prices, the prosecution of corrupt politicians, and 'building a self-reliant nation'. It is this last demand that is perceived as a Marhaenist response to capitalist globalization and US imperialism.

Just as the distinctions between US imperialism and pre-1945 European colonialism were blurred by Sukarno's slogans, in which colonialism, neo-colonialism, imperialism and neo-imperialism were used interchangeably and without concern for either historical specificities or the political-economic dynamic of these systems of global domination, so today does the juxtaposition of neoliberalism, globalization, capitalism and imperialism (preceded by 'no!' or 'down with!') fail to enhance our understanding and chart a clear path for collective action. In the aftermath of the Asian economic crisis, mass mobilizations against the WTO and IMF have frequently invoked the kind of populist nationalism that attributes all social, economic and cultural ills to the institutions that police the global order while depicting the *nation* as the victim. Such an approach radicalizes the discourse of liberal Left responses to globalization but without making the necessary shift in political analysis or moving towards the kinds of revolutionary collective action required.

In a statement published in *Pembebasan* (Liberation), the monthly publication of the Central Leadership Committee of the People's Democratic Party (KPP-PRD), imperialism is associated with colonialism and 'blatant colonization' in ways that tend to obscure US empire rather than providing critical understanding and reference points for action:

> We are currently faced with a picture of a world that is in motion, culminating in a clash between imperialism against its enemies. Make no mistake, the demands of capitalist development up until this most recent stage (imperialism), require that they plunder the world's wealth, by what ever means – ferociously and blatantly. The occupation (colonization) of Afghanistan, then Iraq, adds to the series of subject countries, or countries subjected to fulfill the needs of imperialism. But the backlash and resistance to this – in its various forms – is an objective law that they also cannot deny. Exploitation by international corporations is immediately followed by resistance against it; their consolidation in a number of world forums (the IMF, WTO, World Bank, World Economic Forum and so on) is constantly blockaded by demonstrators who oppose them.'[84]

Disregarding the broad political spectrum that characterizes the anti-corporate populism and lesser anti-capitalist sentiment of these demonstrations, the KPP-PRD concludes that victory is assured: 'Over time this link in the chain of world *colonialism* will be evermore weakened by crisis, and the resistance it faces.'[85]

In a statement issued two months earlier, the KPP-PRD referred to the way in which 'the interests of global imperialism' are served through the debt trap in the Third World. It is 'the global imperialists' who 'will force these nations to open up their domestic markets through the WTO thus making it possible for the capital of global imperialism to control and take over, one by one, the assets of these nations.'[86] Thus the concept of imperialism is not used to explain the dynamics of global capitalism, but to add radical language to NGO and social movement concerns with corporate control and Third World debt. A common assumption underlies it: the nation, not class, lies at the heart of this struggle. This radical critique of imperialism, divorced as it is from class struggle, cannot be seen as inherently anti-capitalist.

The roots of such radical nationalism and anti-imperialism are far more complex than contemporary social movements often recognize. When the anti-colonialist mass organization, Serikat Islam, was radicalized towards the end of 1917, concerns expressed by local merchant capitalists prompted its leadership to clarify that the object of opposition was 'sinful capitalism', by which was meant *foreign capitalism*.[87] A quarter of a century later, faced with the prospect of losing the war and an indefinite Allied occupation of Indonesia that could facilitate European re-colonization, Japanese naval intelligence forces in Java created a school for Indonesian nationalists in October 1944 called *Asrama Indonesia Merdeka* (Dormitory of Free Indonesia). With the appointment of a radical nationalist connected with the underground PKI as its head, the school was dedicated to teaching Marxism-Leninism and 'students were taught to see Indonesia's fight for independence in terms of an international struggle against capitalist imperialism.'[88] Thus classes on Lenin's theory of imperialism were held under the auspices of the Japanese Imperial Navy! These examples are offered only to indicate some of the historical specificities and complexities of both imperialism and anti-imperialism. It is precisely the tendency to de-historicize globalization and imperialism that leads to a dangerous over-simplification of the challenges we face today, prescribing political action that is based more on slogans than substance.

The fact that the concept of 'imperialism' has been revived within anti-globalization movements in one sense presents new possibilities for a shift from anti-corporate populism to anti-capitalism. However, it is necessary to question whether specific events – notably US military aggression against Iraq – have led activists merely to graft anti-war and anti-Bush sentiments onto the anti-globalization movement's critique of transnational corporate control, producing the right set of slogans but with little substance. The use of the term 'US imperialism' does not in itself indicate any significant radicalization of the anti-globalization and anti-war movements. The 'Bush + Bombs + Big Corporations = US IMPERIALISM' formula may serve an immediate political purpose, but it may also diminish the possibility of understanding the deeper roots of US imperialism, blending liberal assumptions with revolutionary language in ways that undermine strategies of resistance.

Certainly in Southeast Asia today we see the concept of US imperialism being used as a means of identifying capitalism as foreign, thereby obscuring domestic capitalism and the material interests and class strategies of 'local' capitalists who are thus able to identify themselves with the nation. Similarly, the use of the idea of self-sufficiency in a reinvented Sukarnoism threatens to appropriate the demands of the anti-globalization food sovereignty movement. This presents severe political risks for the Left. It threatens to occupy and de-radicalize critical social spaces of resistance by reinventing the division between foreign and local capitalisms and defending local capitalists. If the target is the logo, then an image shift is often sufficient to answer those demands. Thus even the cultural symbols of globalization and US domination (variously seen as Americanization and 'cultural' imperialism) can be localized.[89] As a McDonald's restaurant poster in Indonesia reads: '*In the name of Allah, the merciful and the gracious, McDonald's Indonesia is owned by an indigenous Muslim Indonesian.*'

NOTES

This essay began in Bandung and ended in Bangkok, and during the course of this journey numerous people provided crucial support and advice. In particular, I wish to express my gratitude to Varoonvarn Svangsopakul for her invaluable assistance with translation from the Thai language. Thanks also to Awang Awaludin and Gody Utama for their assistance in Bandung, and Greg Albo and Peter Rossman for providing critical references. Of course, the views expressed here and any errors are solely my own.

1   See for example, Samir Amin, 'World Conference Against Racism: A People's Victory', *Monthly Review*, December, 2001.

2   'Asia-Afrika Berada pada pasai Posisi Marginal dalam Globalisasi', *Kompas*, 31 July, 2003; 'AASROC Merekonstruksi "Jembatan" Asia-Afrika', *Pikiran Rakyat*, 2 August, 2003.

3   Throughout the essay I refer to both globalization and US imperialism when discussing the targets of opposition of resistance movements and Left activists. This distinction is needed to reflect the variations across the broad Left, where opponents of US imperialism are not necessarily opposed to global capitalism and where resistance to globalization does not automatically translate into direct opposition to US imperialism. In my own view, globalization and neoliberalism are specific political projects under the aegis of the American empire to facilitate expansion of global capitalism and break working-class power. They are class strategies, and are not systems in and of themselves.

4   Supplementary Detailed Staff Reports on Foreign and Military Intelligence, Book 4, Final Report of the Select Committee to Study Government

Operations with Respect to Intelligence Activities (US Senate), April, 1976, p. 133. Quoted in William Blum, *The CIA: A Forgotten History – US Global Interventions Since World War 2*, London and New York, Zed Books, 1986, p. 108. In a fascinating note on this, Blum discusses evidence concerning CIA involvement in the bombing of a chartered Air India plane transporting members of the Chinese delegation to the Bandung Conference. It is also interesting to note that the current Bandung Conference Museum in Merdeka Hall, Bandung, includes photographs and a brief explanation of the tragedy, including photographs of the timing device used in the bombing, but makes no reference to possible US involvement.

5   'Address by the President of Indonesia', Centre for the Study of Asian–African and Developing Studies, *Collected Documents of the Asian-African Conference, 18-24 April, 1955*, Jakarta: Agency for Research and Development, The Department of Foreign Affairs, 1983, p. 7. It should be noted that while Sukarno addressed the Conference in an opening speech, he did not formally attend the meeting. It was actually on the 10th anniversary of the Bandung Conference in April 1965 that he famously pronounced those who thought imperialism dead to be 'madmen' and proclaimed: 'Imperialism is not yet dead, the struggle against colonialism and neo-colonialism is not yet over!' 'After Ten Years Still Onward, Never Retreat', in *Ten Years After Bandung*, Jakarta: Government Printing Office, 18 April, 1965, pp. 32-33.

6   'Addresses by Delegations – Philippines', *Collected Documents of the Asian-African Conference*, p. 98.

7   'Addresses by Delegations – Libya', *Collected Documents of the Asian-African Conference*, p. 83.

8   'Addresses by Delegations – Iraq', *Collected Documents of the Asian-African Conference*, p. 65.

9   'Addresses by Delegations – Pakistan', *Collected Documents of the Asian-African Conference*, p. 90.

10   'Addresses by Delegations – China', *Collected Documents of the Asian-African Conference*, pp. 44-47.

11   'Addresses by Delegations – Thailand', *Collected Documents of the Asian-African Conference*, p. 111.

12   'Eisenhower Sends US Greetings', *Indonesian Observer*, 20 April, 1955.

13   Sukarno, 'After Ten Years Still Onward, Never Retreat', pp. 32-33.

14   In the official history of the Museum of the Asian–African Conference, it states: 'After the abortive coup of G30S/PKI (i.e. the Communist Party), Gedung Merdeka was taken over by the military and a part of the building was used as a prison for the communist political prisoners.' *Reference Guide: The Museum of the Asian-African Conference*, The Museum of the Asian-African Conference, Bandung, 1992.

15   In 1966 Sukarno announced before the US Congress: 'May God give us, America and Indonesia, the best friendship which has ever existed between two nations.' This speech is recorded in archival video footage reproduced in the documentary film, *Mass Grave*, Lexy Junior Rambadeta & Off Stream, 2001.

16   'Kenapa kebudayaan imperialis Amerika Serikat yang harus dijebol?' (Why does US Imperial Culture Need to be Smashed?), speech by Pramoedya Ananta Toer to the closing ceremony of the Lekra Congress, Palembang. Reprinted in *Harian Rakjat*, 15 March, 1964.

17   Ibid.

18   As Edward Masters, who served at the US Embassy from 1964–68, pointed out: 'We were in effect public enemy number one at that time. We had replaced the British.' See the interview in the documentary, *Shadow Play: Indonesia's Years of Living Dangerously*, Thirteen/WNET, 2002.

19   The US Department of State sent a telegram to the US embassy in Jakarta reminding them that it is 'essential that we not give Sukarno and company opportunity claim that they [are]about to be attacked by NEKOLIM and that we not give Subandrio and the PKI citable public evidence that USG [US Government] supports Army against them.' The telegram then states unequivocally that: 'Army clearly needs no material assistance from us at this point', and goes on to explain that the informal imperial network of the US was sufficient, since years of Indonesian–US 'inter-service relationships' developed through military training programs, security and economic linkages 'should have established clearly in minds [of] Army leaders that US stands behind them if they should need help.' 'Telegram From the Department of State to the Embassy in Indonesia', Washington, 6 October, 1965. National Archives and Records Administration, RG 59, Central Files 1964-66, POL 23-9 INDON. http://www.state.gov/r/pa/ho/frus/johnsonlb/xxvi/4445.htm.

20   Evidence concerning the US government's provision of 'shooting lists' or 'death lists' of PKI members to the Indonesian military was reported in *South Carolina Herald-Journal*, 19 May, 1990; *San Francisco Examiner*, 20 May, 1990; *Washington Post*, 21 May, 1990; and *Boston Globe*, 23 May, 1990.

21   As a wealthy Southeast Asian capitalist nominated 1992 ASEAN Businessman of the Year, Thaksin was seen as the most appropriate host for the inauguration of the ACD, and has emerged as a 'model' leader among ruling classes in the region.

22   Opening Statement by Thaksin Shinawatra, Prime Minister of Thailand, at the Inaugural Meeting of the Asia Cooperation Dialogue, Cha-Am, Thailand, 19 June, 2002. Emphasis added.

23   A useful explanation of the background to the Vision Project and its Globalization and Local Knowledge series of publications may be found in Craig J. Reynolds, 'Thai Identity in the Age Of Globalization', in Craig J. Reynolds, ed., *National Identity and its Defenders: Thailand Today*. Chiang Mai: Silkworm Books, 2002, pp. 322-33.

24   As Craig Reynolds explains, the penname Tienchai uses implies 'a dream of a better Thailand' based on 'the epochal "Yuk Si-ariya" or "Age of the Mettaya Buddha", the Buddha who is to be reborn in this world long after the religion of Gautama Buddha has come to an end. The saving message of Dhamma will again right the world after the upheavals of the Age of Darkness, the Kaliyuga.' Ibid.

25   Yuk Si-Ariya, 'American Imperialism and the War to Usurp Hegemony', in

Phitthaya Wongkun, ed., *Wikrit Asia* (Asian Crisis), Second Edition, Bangkok: Amarin Publishing/Witthithat Project, 1999, pp. 49-51.

26   In explaining the cultural roots of US hegemony, Tienchai cites as the definitive text Robert Frank's and Phil Cook's *The Winner-Takes-All-Society*, New York: Free Press, 1995.

27   It might be argued that Tienchai's theoretical approach suffers from what Richard Bryan describes as 'the neo-marxist adherence to a nationalist taxonomy of capital' that leads to a false dichotomy of foreign and national capital, and an inability to perceive 'the contradiction *within* the internationalization of capital.' Richard Bryan, 'The State and the Internationalization of Capital: An Approach to Analysis', *Journal of Contemporary Asia*, 17(3), 1987, p. 256.

28   Si-ariya, 'American Imperialism and the War to Usurp Hegemony', p. 53.

29   Peter F. Bell, 'Thailand's Economic Crisis: A New Cycle of Struggle,' in Ji Giles Ungpakorn, ed., *Radicalizing Thailand: New Political Perspectives*, Bangkok: Institute of Asian Studies, Chulalongkorn University, 2003, pp. 55-57.

30   Thak Chaleomtiarana, *Thailand: The Politics of Despotic Paternalism*, Bangkok: Social Science Association of Thailand, 1979, pp. 140-141. Sarit gave prominence to a perceived Chinese Communist threat, and his chief adviser, Luang Vichit's study on Thai races depicted Communism as 'un-Thai', with the ideological-racial nexus of Communism and ethnicity excluding the possibility for Thai to be Communists.

31   Pasuk Phongpaichit and Chris Baker, *Thailand: Economy and Politics*, Second Edition, Bangkok: Oxford University Press, p. 131.

32   Sarit's loyalty to the US empire was satirized in Khamsing Srinawk's 'The Peasant and the White Man', where a peasant farmer's dog – old Somrit (bronze) – is taken away by a white man who promises to train Somrit as an obedient guard dog. This parodies Sarit's return from the Walter Reed hospital in the US. In the story, the dog returns alienated from the peasant farmer, refusing to eat simple food. The farmer has to feed him better food and dress himself better to please the dog, but Somrit – forgetting who raised him – turns and bites his master. Khamsing Srinawk, 'The Peasant and the White Man', in *The Politician and Other Stories*, Third Edition, Bangkok: Silkworm Books, 2001, pp. 70-80.

33   Tienchai's analysis of US imperialism in *Asian Crisis* draws heavily on the work of James Petras, whose essay 'The Asian Crisis and US Hegemony' was translated by Tienchai and published in a *Globalization Series* volume. (Pittaya Wangkul, ed., *Wikrit Asia* (Asian Crisis), Second Edition, Bangkok: Amarin Publishing/Witthithat Project, 1999, pp. 23-30.) Referring to the resurgence of 'neo-colonial' rule, Petras argues that 'the IMF entry means the return of US hegemony and the decline of Asian capitalism as an independent and competitive economic pole.' Again the central dynamic is 'division and conflict between national capitalism and states' and 'the continuing power exercised by imperial countries over the "newly industrializing countries".'

34   Si-ariya, 'American Imperialism and the War to Usurp Hegemony', pp. 59-60.

35   Ibid., p. 61.

36   Ji Giles Ungpakorn, 'A Marxist History of Political Change in Thailand', in Ji Giles Ungpakorn, ed., *Radicalizing Thailand: New Political Perspectives*, Bangkok: Institute of Asian Studies, Chulalongkorn University, 2003, pp. 28-29; Bell, 'Thailand's Economic Crisis: A New Cycle of Struggle,', pp. 41-74.

37   Ungpakorn, 'A Marxist History of Political Change in Thailand', p. 29.

38   'Repayment of the Final Instalment of Thailand's Debt under the IMF Programme', Speech by Thaksin Shinawatra, Prime Minister of Thailand, Government House, Bangkok, 31 July, 2003.

39   The Thaksin regime further escalated the US-led 'War on Terror' by massacring 108 Muslims in the southern city of Pattani on April 28, 2004, including the execution of 32 people who had sought refuge inside the 400-year-old Mosque.

40   Quoted in *The Nation* (Bangkok), 28 February, 2004. This quote was used in an article concerning Thaksin's angry response to a US State Department report on human rights violations in Thailand. In his response Thaksin declared that such criticism rendered the US 'a useless friend'.

41   Not long after receiving this award for 'notable contributions to humanity' and 'empowerment of others toward equality for humankind', Thaksin authorized a 'war on drugs' that gave legitimacy to greater police violence and led to more than 2,500 deaths in a few months.

42   Thaksin was the fourth after Secretary of State James Baker III in 1993, former Polish President Lech Walesa in 1996 and former President George Bush in 1998. Quoted in Michael Graczyk, 'Thai Prime Minister Gets Texas University's Highest Award', The Associated Press, 23 October, 2002.

43   Leo Panitch and Sam Gindin, 'Global Capitalism and American Empire', in *Socialist Register 2004*, London, Merlin Press, pp. 32-33.

44   'Repayment of the Final Instalment of Thailand's Debt under the IMF Programme', Speech by Thaksin Shinawatra, Prime Minister of Thailand, Government House, Bangkok, 31 July, 2003.

45   Ungpakorn, 'A Marxist History of Political Change in Thailand', pp. 32-33.

46   Weerayut Chokchaimadon, 'Thailand Faces Prosperity and Contradictions', *The Nation* (Bangkok), 25 September, 2003.

47   Ibid.

48   Pasuk Phongpaichit, 'A Country is a Company, a PM is a CEO', *Seminar on Statesman or Manager? Image and Reality of Leadership in Southeast Asia*, Centre for Political Economy, Chulalongkorn University, Bangkok, 2 April, 2004.

49   Ibid.

50   Chanida Chanyapate and Isabelle Delforge, 'The Politics of Bird Flu in Thailand', *Focus on Trade*, No. 98, April, 2004. The intervention by the Vision Project's Tienchai Wongchaisuwan in the debate on the avian flu crisis in Thailand manifests the same shortcomings that his neo-marxist analysis of the Asian crisis entails. Again writing under the pen name Yuk Si-ariya in a regular column in *Matichon Weekly* (Issues 1229-31, March, 2004), he addresses the issues of H5N1 and biotechnology not in the context of capitalism, but in terms of 'chaos'; and while alluding to the government

cover-up 'benefiting exporting companies' and the 'deception concerning the closed farming system', he ignores the strategies of capital (not least CP's) and their relationship to the Thai state.

51   This includes 106 feed mills in China employing 60,000 workers.

52   CP's investment license in China is Number 0001, indicating the early move into China under the name of Chia Tai. In April 2003, twenty-one workers at a Chia Tai poultry processing plant in Shandong Province died in a fire that exposed the brutal labour regime imposed by CP in its factories in China. Workers were ordered to remain at their posts during the fire and several died there, more fearful of punishment by the factory managers than the fire itself. See 'Twenty-One Lives Lost in 5 April Blaze at the Qingdao Zhengda Food Factory', *China Labour Bulletin*, 12 April, 2003.

53   Dan E. Moldea and David Corn, 'Influence Peddling, Bush Style', *The Nation* (US), 23 October, 2000. As a series of newspaper reports (and full page advertisements by CP's telecommunications subsidiary) in the Thai press show, CP hosted former President Bush visit to Thailand in January 1994 after his visit to China, providing the context for calls for a softer US stance on China and promotion of China's WTO accession.

54   '10 Years After the Kader Factory Fire: Thailand's CP Group and Corporate Responsibility', *Asian Food Worker*, May-June 2003, pp. 1; 6; 'CP and Rights', *The Nation* (Bangkok), 15 May, 2003.

55   'Thailand Benefits From Bush's Policies if He Wins in Election', *The People's Daily* (Beijing), 10 November, 2000. These interests are now articulated through the head 'CEO Ambassador' based in Washington who is directly answerable to Thaksin as CEO of the country.

56   Korsak Chairasmisak, *The Asian CEO in Action*, Bangkok: Post Books/DMG Books, 2003, p. 140. Another example of 7-Eleven undertaking state functions is the use of stores across the country by the Ministry of Commerce to distribute price-controlled supplies of sugar during a critical shortage.

57   Ungpakorn, 'A Marxist History of Political Change in Thailand', p. 17.

58   Korsak, *The Asian CEO in Action*, p. 131.

59   Ibid., pp. 43-44.

60   Notably, in Kasian Tejapira's categorization of 'globalizers' versus 'communitarians' in Thailand, Nidhi was classified among the 'communitarians' who challenged 'globalizers' such as Chai-anan Samudavanija. Kasian Tejapira, 'Globalisers vs. Communitarians: Post-May 1992 Debates Among Thai Public Intellectuals', paper prepared for Annual Meeting of the Association of Asian Studies, Honolulu, 11-14 April, 1996; Kasian Tejapira, *Wiwatha lokkanuwat* (Debates on Globalization), Bangkok: Phujatkan Press, 1995.

61   Nidhi Aeosrivongse, 'Thai Nationalism Under the Trend of Globalization' [in Thai], *Matichon Weekly*, Issue 1229, 5-11 March, 2004, p. 33.

62   Nicos Poulantzas, *State, Power, Socialism*, London and New York: Verso, 2000, p. 117.

63   Panitch and Gindin, 'Global Capitalism and American Empire', p. 17.

64   Bob Jessop, *Nicos Poulantzas: Marxist Theory and Political Strategy*, London:

Macmillan, 1985, p. 172.

65 See also Achin Vanaik, 'The New Indian Right', *New Left Review*, 9, 2001.

66 Anut Aphaphirom et al., *Teknoloyi patiwat lok su sangkhom khwamru lae yangyun* (Technology Transforms the World: Towards the Knowledge Society and Sustainable Society), Bangkok, Witthithat Project, 2000, pp. 180-82. Cited in Reynolds, 'Thai Identity in the Age of Globalization', p. 325. This localizing alternative is easily susceptible to appropriation by CP as a 'national' company that is rapidly establishing its dominance in Thailand's rice production and trade, while expanding its strategic partnership with Monsanto – the world's largest genetic engineering corporation. Moreover, it is a long-term strategy of Monsanto, Syngenta, Bayer CropScience and other agro-chemical/genetic engineering corporations to undermine opposition to genetically modified (GM) crops by first introducing GM rice varieties through national research institutes in Asia, then enforcing farmers' dependency on patented seeds and pesticides in later stages. See Varoonvarn Svangsopakul, 'Monsanto Offers False Promises', *The Nation* (Bangkok), 29 November, 2003.

67 Korsak, *The Asian CEO in Action*, p. 146.

68 Globalization was first translated into Thai by Chai-Anan Samudavanija who used the word *lokanuwat*, although it 'came to be synonymous with the concept of unbridled, often unethical, opportunism.' Following the intervention of the Royal Institute of Thailand the word *lokaphiwat* was established as a more appropriate translation. Pasuk Phongpaichit and Chris Baker, *Thailand's Boom and Bust*, Chiang Mai: Silkworm Books, 1998, p. 55; Reynolds, 'Thai Identity in the Age of Globalization', pp. 317-18.

69 Chai-anan Samudavanija, *Thailand: State-Building, Democracy and Globalization*, Bangkok: Institute of Public Policy Studies (IPPS), 2002, p. 198.

70 Emphasis in the original. Ibid., pp. 191-192; 194.

71 Ibid., p. 199.

72 Watcharapong Thongrung, 'Govt Position on EGAT Uncertain after Chai-anan Comments', *The Nation* (Thailand), 27 April, 2004.

73 'Repayment of the Final Installment of Thailand's Debt under the IMF Programme', Speech by Thaksin Shinawatra, Prime Minister of Thailand, Government House, Bangkok, 31 July, 2003.

74 A reversion to nationalism was apparent when union leaders declared the wave of go-slows and strikes launched on 28 April as 'patriotic leave from work'.

75 It is still debated whether Sukarno really met a peasant-farmer called Marhaen. Some argue that Marhaen is merely the term for 'peasant' in Sundanese – the language used in the region where the meeting was supposed to have taken place.

76 Sukarno, *Autobiography as Told to Cindy Adams*, Indianapolis, 1963, pp. 61-62; quoted in J.D. Legge, *Sukarno: A Political Biography*, Third Edition, Singapore, Archipelago Press, 2003, p. 85.

77 *Tempo*, No.15/IV, 16-22 December, 2003.

78 *Rikiran Rakyat* (Bandung), 16 February, 2004.

79 'In the name of Bung Karno', *Tempo*, No.15/IV, 16-22 December, 2003.

80   Moh Samsul Arifin, 'Tiga Sukarnoputri, Marhaenisme, dan Pemilu 2004
      (Three Sukarno Daughters, Marhaenism and the 2004 Election)', *Sinar
      Harapan*, 9 January, 2004.
81   Ibid.
82   Susilo Eko Prayitno, 'Marhaenisme dan Membangun Dunia Baru
      (Marhaenism and Developing a New World)', April, 2003.
83   Notably this *Tritura* originates in the 'three demands of the people' in the
      military-coordinated anti-Communist protests in the 1960s, calling for a ban
      on the PKI, the purging of PKI members from the Cabinet and lower prices.
84   'Build the Power of the Poor to Resist the Colonialists' Invasion', *Pembebasan*
      (Liberation), No. 7, April, 2003.
85   Emphasis added. Ibid.
86   'Reject the War against Iraq, Evict the Colonists and their Allies, Isolate the
      Puppet Regime of Mega-Hamzah', statement issued by the Central
      Leadership Committee of the People's Democratic Party (KPP-PRD), 24
      February, 2003.
87   George McTurnan Kahin, *Nationalism and Revolution in Indonesia*, Ithaca, New
      York: Southeast Asia Program Publications, Cornell University, 2003, pp. 72-
      73. Originally published by Cornell University Press in 1952.
88   Ibid., pp. 116-117.
89   For the use of 'McDonaldization' to connote a 'cultural massive attack against
      local cultures', which unfortunately but rather typically leaves the economic
      dimensions less clearly understood, see I. Wibowo, 'Globalisasi dan
      Kapitalisme Global (Globalization and Global Capitalism)', *Kompas*, 27 April,
      2002.

THE MEDIA MATRIX: CHINA'S INTEGRATION INTO GLOBAL CAPITALISM

Yuezhi Zhao

On October 8, 2003, in a lecture at the central Party School in Beijing, Rupert Murdoch, the transnational media baron who once proclaimed that satellite television would bring an end to authoritarian regimes everywhere in the world, cajoled top Chinese leaders to liberalize China's media market. Murdoch not only assured China's party bosses about the compatibility between market liberalization and the maintenance of their political power, but also claimed that 'China has the potential not only to follow the examples of the US and the UK, but to improve upon those examples to achieve a level of success all its own.'[1] Did Murdoch go too far in pandering to Chinese ears? How plausible is a Chinese success 'all its own' in this critical area of global power? If China can achieve a level of success 'all its own,' what role will there be for the sort of transnational capital symbolized by Murdoch, whose presence in China is already such that 'Murdoch' was among the top twenty 'keywords' of the Chinese media industry in 2003?[2]

The realm of communication and culture, defined broadly to include both physical networks and symbolic content ranging from media texts to language itself, provides a crucial vantage point for examining current global power relations. This is not only because 'soft power,' i.e., the power of ideological and cultural persuasion, plays an important role in US global dominance, but also because the communication and culture industries are themselves now important sectors of the global economy.[3]

But notwithstanding the American right's fear of 'China Rising', and projections of China as the US's next imperial rival, it is more plausible, at least at the current historical conjuncture, to view China as a regional power being integrated into the 'informal American empire' described by Panitch and Gindin.[4] Just like the American empire itself, however, there is no guarantee that China's current path of integration is sustainable.

CHINESE CULTURE BETWEEN THE IRON FIST OF
THE PARTY AND AMERICAN SOFT POWER

As Panitch and Gindin argue, it is 'not through formal empire, but rather through the reconstitution of states as integral elements of an informal American empire, that the international capitalist order [i]s now organized and regulated.'[5] Although the reconstitution of the post-revolutionary Chinese state as an integral part of this new global capitalist order began with Deng's 'reform and openness' program in the late 1970s, a key moment in the Chinese state's external reconstitution had already occurred earlier, in 1972, when, on the basis of its anti-imperialist foreign policy and its support for the non-aligned movement, China secured a UN seat as the legitimate representative of the Chinese nation. Then, in the same year, The People's Republic of China welcomed Nixon to Beijing and allied itself with the US against the Soviet Union.

The Nixon visit was also a pivotal moment for the Chinese media's capitulation to American 'soft power'. In particular, the technological and professional sophistication of the three US television networks that beamed live satellite reports of Nixon's visit back to US audiences stunned the Chinese and had a powerful demonstration effect. So, if the Soviet bloc first introduced television to China, it was US commercial networks that led to the fledgling Chinese television industry becoming the most powerful mass medium integrating China with global consumer capitalism.[6]

The Chinese communication and culture system thus became an integral component of the global capitalist system at the very beginning of the 'reform and openness' process, beginning with the airing of transnational advertisements on Chinese television in 1979. By the early 1980s, the Chinese state had prioritized the development of the telecommunication networks in coastal areas in order to facilitate transnational capital's access to cheap labour in China. Until the late 1970s the post-revolutionary socialist state had resisted Western culture in an attempt to develop a non-commercial national culture. Now the same state champions the commodification of communication and culture and the reshaping of these industries in the image of their transnational counterparts. Since the 1980s, the reformed state has been promoting 'informatization' as a central part of its development strategy and a key aspect of its integration with transnational capitalism.[7] By the early 2000s, the state was promoting the market-oriented development of the more sensitive cultural industries, ranging from news operations to video game installations, as new sites of economic growth.

To be sure, the Chinese version of the neo-liberal logic of liberalization and privatization is distinctive. The restructuring of China's national communication and cultural industries has two explicit objectives: ideological legitimation as well as capital accumulation. Liberalization has occurred predominantly within the state-owned sector, characterized by the proliferation of market-oriented media outlets within the traditional Party-state structure. Domestic private capital has been restricted largely to the peripheries of the communication and cultural industries. Even today, there are no privately-owned basic telecommunication service providers, just as there are no private newspapers or broadcast stations. Foreign penetration and global integration – from the importation of television programs to foreign direct investment in media and cultural production – has been carefully managed by the Chinese state, first on an ad hoc basis, and most recently through provisions in China's WTO accession. In addition to major concessions in the film industry, discussed below, China's WTO accession opens up its telecommunication services, advertising, and the distribution and retailing of audio-visual products, books, newspapers and magazines to foreign investment. The Chinese contribution to the recent wave of consolidation in global media markets has taken the form of state-engineered re-centralization and conglomeration within the Party-state sector.[8]

Now, after a quarter century of accelerated capitalistic development, China's communication and culture industry has emerged as one of the fastest growing and most profitable sectors of the Chinese economy. The Communist Party state itself is the dominant domestic capitalist, ready to do business with transnational media barons such as Rupert Murdoch and create the necessary internal legal and regulatory conditions for sustaining domestic and transnational capital accumulation, and acting as a 'responsible' state within global capitalism.

This, then, was the context within which American 'soft power' grew in the Chinese cultural realm throughout the 1980s and 1990s. While the pro-democracy movement in 1989 articulated its political aspirations in terms of American liberal democratic ideology, the suppression of that movement created the preconditions for the ideological dominance of neoliberalism in China,[9] and for the flourishing of commercialized popular culture. By 1997, the naturalization of American 'soft power' had reached a point where former Party General Secretary Jiang Zemin openly expressed admiration for the Hollywood blockbuster *Titanic*, while in 2003 Qinghua University professor Liu Jianming declared that the American culture industry represented 'advanced culture' and that the global popularity of Hollywood represented the triumph of the 'advanced culture' of one nation over the 'backward culture' of others.[10]

Perhaps the most ironic example of this process of 'inner colonization' is that while the Chinese branch of Murdoch's global satellite TV empire is known in Mandarin as *Xingkong Weishi* (Star-Sky Satellite Television), China

Central Television, the state television network, uses English – 'CCTV' – as its logo and acronym. As Wu Mei, a Macao-based communication scholar, has noted, the pervasiveness of English signs in the Chinese national media and public spaces is an obvious sign of cultural subordination.[11]

However, any conceptualization of cultural domination in terms of exclusive *American* cultural power is inadequate. As Herbert Schiller, one of the most eloquent critics of American cultural domination, has noted, a more diversified pattern of global media ownership and media flows means that the current pattern of domination, 'though still bearing a marked American imprint, is better understood as "transnational corporate cultural domination".'[12] In fact, Japan, Korea, Hong Kong and Taiwan – countries and territories that have already been integrated into the informal American empire – have played an important role in the transmission of transnational capitalist cultural values and forms to China. In newer cultural markets such as video gaming it is Japanese and Korean products, not American products, which dominate the Chinese market.

Thus, instead of celebrating cultural diversity and the limits of 'Americanization' in terms of 'glocalization' and 'indigenization',[13] it is more useful to think about cultural domination in terms of the penetration of capitalistic cultural relations in national cultural spaces in general. As Dan Schiller and I have argued, the transnational cultural industry is willing to 'parasitize', rather than flatten, cultural differences – whenever such variations give hope of profitability.[14] Or as Leslie Sklair puts it, the leading actors of the global capitalist cultural system

> have no particular interest in destroying or sustaining local cultures apart from the drive for increased profitability. Where local or national agents threaten profitability capitalists certainly destroy them, as colonial powers have done in the past wherever local enterprise interfered with their expansionist plans. Economic globalization has changed this to some extent by making it easier for globalizing corporations to integrate local partners into their cross-border networks and to take advantage of local partners and resources, an advantage that can be shared with local elites.[15]

The most insidious form of capitalist cultural domination is thus when a national media system internalizes the discourses of transnational capitalism. This kind of cultural hegemony does not have to involve the direct participation of American capital or American-originated media content, or for that matter, Japanese or Korean media capital or content. The most telling evidence of capitalist cultural hegemony is rather to be found in the discursive orientations of China's national news media, a realm that is formally still under the control of the Chinese state.

Chinese news coverage of two recent major events is illustrative. The first concerns China's WTO entry. Chinese press coverage of the US–China WTO agreement in 1999 naturalized neo-liberal globalization and systematically privileged transnational corporate speech and the imperative of US-led transnational capitalism. It not only relied on the US Embassy and American media for the content and interpretation of the WTO agreement, but even served as a propaganda organ for transnational corporations and their spokespersons. Meanwhile, not a single article in a sample of nearly 500 news stories and commentaries that I examined gave even a ceremonial voice to Chinese workers or farmers.[16] In the words of Wang Hui, the Chinese state and the media it directed 'undertook a long and one-sided campaign to publicize the WTO negotiations' and Chinese media reports 'corresponded with the American media on the same issue'.[17]

The Chinese media's coverage of the US invasion of Iraq in 2003 is an even more telling example. Here was an event in which the Chinese state articulated its opposition against American imperialism. On the surface, the Chinese media relayed the official position, to the extent that internet posts by American apologists inside China even attacked CCTV for its anti-imperialist pronouncements. However, a closer reading shows that coverage of the war was profoundly contradictory. A deeper level of submission to American imperialist power overshadowed official anti-war pronouncements. To begin with, the Chinese state allowed no room whatsoever for popular expression of anti-war sentiments in the Chinese media, just as there was no such expression on Chinese streets. Second, instead of engaging with fundamental questions regarding the legitimacy and justice of the war, or the validity of the Bush Administration's war claims, the Chinese media, following the lead of the American media, focused on military strategies and tactics, and the endless display and analysis of American weaponry. To do so, they relied heavily on American media for pictures of the war supplied by the Pentagon. As a result, a brutal imperialist war was turned into a reality television show displaying American military might and imperial reach.[18] Here, the penetration of American 'soft power' was manifested in the Chinese television's submission to the technological and discursive logic of American commercial television, and the imperial war as a news spectacle[19] – despite the Chinese state's official, and no doubt serious, opposition against the war. It should also be noted that, the intensive coverage of the war on Chinese television was the result of a deliberate decision on the part of state officials and CCTV top management, in an attempt to make CCTV 'China's CNN', and to strengthen the position of domestic media vis-à-vis transnational media corporations in the context of China's WTO entry. This included the launching of a CNN style 24-hour news channel. Apparently,

Chinese media officials and CCTV management believed that the way to win the Chinese audience was to mimic CNN's format and style, and to make transnational media footages available to a domestic audience who had increasingly demanded such material.

CULTURAL INTEGRATION AND TRANSNATIONAL CLASS FORMATION: TWO CASE STUDIES

The accelerated re-organization of the Chinese communication and culture industry in the context of domestic political authoritarianism and global integration also sheds light on class formation within China and beyond its borders. As Panitch and Gindin have argued, American foreign direct investment directly affects the class structures and state formations of other core countries.[20] The penetration of American capital as a social force tends to undermine the formation of 'a coherent and independent national bourgeoisie' and considerably diminishes 'the likelihood that domestic capital might challenge American dominance – as opposed to merely seeking to renegotiate the terms of American leadership.'[21] The emerging patterns of cultural production and consumption in the globally integrated film and magazine industries in China are indicative of this dynamic of transnational class formation.

The Film Industry

Film was introduced into China from the West, and before 1949 Hollywood dominated the Chinese film market.[22] The Maoist regime not only ended Hollywood's fortunes in China, but also developed a strong indigenous national film industry. In the early 1980s, Chinese films enjoyed enormous popularity, but as the 'reform and openness' process deepened a number of factors – political control, under-investment, competition from commercialized state television, and drastic social stratification and audience market fragmentation – combined to undermine the viability of the domestic film industry organized under the planned economy. By the early 1990s, the Chinese film industry was in deep crisis. Annual attendance at theatres dropped from 21 billion in 1982 to just under 4.5 billion in 1991.[23]

Hollywood, meanwhile, tried to re-enter the Chinese market as soon as US-China diplomatic relations were restored in 1979. Chinese audiences, isolated from Hollywood for nearly thirty years, necessarily had some catching up to do. Hollywood's re-entry into China thus began with public screenings, especially on state television, of cheap Hollywood classics, with Rupert Murdoch's 20th Century Fox playing a leading role in supplying them. By 1985, when the Hollywood blockbuster, *Rambo: First Blood*, was released in China and caused a national sensation, China's re-engagement with Hollywood had already intensified significantly. By 1994, under the double pressure of Hollywood and the film distribution and exhibition arms of the domestic film industry, China had decided to accept an annual importation of ten first-run Hollywood films on a box-office revenue-sharing basis. Driven by profit considerations and the sensibilities of middle class urban viewers, who had come to regard seeing the latest Hollywood blockbusters as part of their global cultural citizenship entitlement, the state-controlled film distributor and cinemas, as well as the mass media, enthusiastically promoted Hollywood movies, while ignoring domestic productions. In 1995, the 'most glorious year' for the Chinese film box office take, thanks to Hollywood imports, more than seventy domestic films were denied distribution to theatres.[24] By 1998, when the Hollywood blockbuster *Titanic* garnered a record one quarter of the year's total Chinese box office revenue, domestic Chinese film production, which had ranged between 100 and 130 annually since 1980, had dropped to a record low of 37. The prestigious Xi'an Film Studio had to lay off more than 10 per cent of its workforce.[25]

In response the more entrepreneurial Chinese filmmakers, in an attempt to secure commercial success and circumvent political control, not only gradually adopted Hollywood narrative styles, formulas, and business models, but also increasingly looked to the global market. The success of film-makers such as Chen Kaige and Zhang Yimou on the major international film awards circuits in the 1980s and early 1990s, and the inclusion of their films in the 'foreign' section of major video rental chains in North America, signalled the beginning of the selective incorporation of a Chinese film-making elite into an American-dominated global film industry that was becoming increasingly multicultural. Over time, these film-makers have grown increasingly independent of the domestic film infrastructure and gained the support of transnational film investors and distributors.

Zhang Yimou's 2003 Hollywood-style martial arts blockbuster *Hero*, for example, widely hailed in both Chinese and global media as Asia's response to American cultural imperialism, was funded by Miramax; the most commercial of the younger generation of filmmakers, Feng Xiaogang, made a cross-cultural hybrid called *Big Shot*, starring the Canadian actor Donald Sutherland and featuring a plot that glorifies Hollywood financial and cultural power. Feng readily admitted that Columbia Tristar, which invested in the film, influenced some artistic decisions in an effort to crack the US and global markets. As Stanley Rosen commented in early 2003:

> Sony recently announced its plans to invest $100 million in China's music and movie industries within three years. Sony chairman Nobuyuki Idei expects China to become the company's second-

largest market by 2008. In short, China's national film industry is becoming increasingly transnational …. Purely domestic productions, with no transnational appeal, may be doomed to play to mostly empty theaters.[26]

It is within this context that one must understand the significance of China's WTO entry provisions with regard to the film industry. Although the audio-visual sector was excluded from the final GATT agreement that created the WTO, the powerful Hollywood lobby secured major gains through the bilateral US-China WTO agreement that took effect in December 2001. Under the agreement, China committed to quadruple film imports to forty films per year upon accession. The number will increase to fifty by 2005, of which twenty could be first-run Hollywood blockbuster movies. It reduced tariffs on audio-visual imports, opened up its consumer market for audio-visual products to foreign distributors and, most importantly, allowed foreign investors to own up to a 49 per cent share in companies that build, own and operate cinemas in China. A full-scale restructuring of the film industry in China – from production to distribution, exhibition and consumption – has been under way since China's WTO entry. Major transnational entertainment conglomerates such as Time-Warner have teamed up with domestic Chinese partners to establish production facilities and revamp the Chinese cinema infrastructure. Moreover, they have managed to secure new terms of market openness far beyond the original terms set in China's WTO accession agreements. In December 2003, the Chinese state issued new rules allowing foreign investors to hold an up to 75 per cent stake in joint venture cinemas in seven of China's largest cities, effective January 1, 2004. In reporting this new rule, *The People's Daily* cited a Chinese film official as saying that 'the new regulation makes China a more attractive place for foreign cinema giants.'[27] Just as Zhang Yimou had to depend on Miramax's investment to make his 'Chinese' blockbuster *Hero*, the interests of others in the Chinese film industry, including Chinese state regulators who believe that Hollywood should help improve the domestic Chinese productions, are now increasingly linked to transnational capital. The post-WTO liberalization of film distribution and exhibition markets has also put pressure on the Chinese state to increase co-productions and import quotas. The top executive of a newly-established film distribution firm, for example, has called for an increase in film import quotas and the reclassification of Hong Kong and Taiwan films as 'domestic productions' so as to increase the number of Hollywood imports.[28]

This is not to say that the Chinese state and China's domestic capital have no global ambitions of their own. Dan Schiller has documented a series of initiatives on the part of Chinese communication industries to expand their global reach in information and communication technology manufacturing and service provision – from computer maker Legend's overseas expansion, to CCTV's English channel's distribution in three major US cities through the cable systems of Time-Warner and News Corporation.[29] The Chinese state is also trying to compete on its own terms in the global cultural industries by developing its own technological platforms and standards, including an alternative to DVD called EVD, which will supposedly allow domestic manufacturers to 'shake off their previous dependence on foreign technologies.'[30] While these developments are significant and will likely increase China's presence in the global cultural market, Schiller rightly concludes that 'China is nowhere near mounting a bid to up-end US political-economic power in communications and information.'[31] The pattern of integration between the Chinese film industry and Hollywood suggests that any notion that China can achieve success 'all its own' in the global market is far-fetched. Rupert Murdoch, whose investment in Chinese communication and culture markets ranges from audio-visual production to satellite broadcasting, internet websites and broadband cable networks, in all likelihood knew this very well when he lectured Party leaders in Beijing. Indeed, what was really significant was not what he said but the very fact of his lecturing to the Chinese leadership: it signified the emergence of a new form of class alliance between transnational capitalists and China's ruling elite.

The Magazine Industry

If the global integration of the Chinese film industry provides a case study in transnational class formation in the realm of production, the pattern of integration in the Chinese magazine industry provides a case study of this development from the angle of consumption.[32] Foreign investment in the media sector assumes a double role in class formation: it affects class structure not only in the socio-economic sense, but also in the cultural/ideological sense by providing cultural capital for particular social strata. The first US-China business joint venture in China was between International Data Group (IDG) and the Chinese state, established in the tightly protected print media sector as early as 1980, and remains one of the most successful foreign investment stories in China, with terms far exceeding the scope of foreign operation in the Chinese cultural sector outlined in the WTO accession agreements twenty years later. As the post-Mao leadership made information technology the key sector in its development strategy, IDG publications made available up-to-date technical information and championed the ideology of globalization through information technologies. This was especially true of *China Computerworld*, the Chinese version of IDG's flagship publication, which provided the right cultural product for the right audience at the right time. It fitted in perfectly with the information and cultural needs of a Chinese technocratic elite gearing up to constitute itself as the Party's new social base and as the 'representatives' of the 'advanced productive force,' as Jiang Zemin would later characterize them.[33] Their job, of course, was to transform the domestic economy around information networks and integrate it with the global capitalist information system. With *China Computerworld* as China's most authoritative and highest circulation IT publication, by 2002 IDG's publishing empire in China encompassed twenty-two titles, including *Digital Fortune*, which boasts a readership profile of individuals between 25-45 years old with 'an annual income above 100,000 RMB' and a 'global perspective;' and *Digital Power*, which again caters to 'young, successful people with higher level of education' who promise to 'have considerable spending power and social status.'[34] Although these publications do not command the ideological significance of, say, a Chinese version of *Reader's Digest*, their role in integrating the Chinese techno-cultural elite with global informational capitalism has nonetheless been profoundly significant.

Once IDG had established a cozy relationship with the Chinese state and helped to create a Chinese middle class based on the information economy, it teamed up with transnational consumer magazine publishers such as the Hearst Corporation to enfranchise this class as part of the transnational consumer market through the provision of consumer advertising and lifestyle tips. Other domestic and foreign collaborative ventures in consumer magazine publishing have also flourished. Since the late 1980s Chinese versions of transnational consumer and lifestyle magazines, including *Elle*, *Cosmopolitan*, *Esquire*, *Harper's Bazaar*, *Good Housekeeping*, *Auto Fan*, *Golf* and many other American, European, and Japanese titles, have competed keenly for the affluent urban middle-class market. Instead of being isolated and deprived by a tightly controlled domestic publications regime, members of China's affluent consuming elite are now served with the best of all consumerist worlds through the Chinese magazine industry's advertising, management, and copyright cooperation agreements with transnational publishers. Although hard news titles are still not welcome, as the *New York Times* noted, 'foreign magazines about fashion, technology and business are increasingly popular.'[35] Soon, young Chinese men will have the chance to taste some long forbidden fruits of Western consumer culture. While America's *Playboy* has long expressed an interest in going to China,[36] it looks as if its British counterparts will set their feet on China first. The *New York Times* reported on April 18, 2004: 'Britain's bawdy "lad mags" *FHM* and *Maxim* – which have been wildly successful by peddling women in barely anything, frat-boy humor, sexual innuendo and the occasional fashion top to twenty somethings – are now planning their own Chinese editions.'[37]

The resulting Chinese consumer and lifestyle magazine market is thus truly transnational – that is, transnational consumer culture embellished with various national tastes. *Trends Traveler*, for example, has a copyright arrangement with the American-based *National Geographic Traveler*, and picture and text exchange cooperation with the French magazine *Guide Moncos* and the Taiwanese magazine *To Go*. Combined with local content, *Trends Traveler* is a feast of appealing pictures and stories catering specifically to the university-educated high-income urban white-collar traveller aged between twenty-five and forty.

The content of the magazine's November 2002 issue serves as good case study of the cultivation of transnational class identities and sensibilities. As a Chinese transnational traveller and sophisticated cultural connoisseur you visit Scotland to learn its 'history in a bottle'; you take 'the classic petit-bourgeois trip' to the Louvre, the British Museum, and the Metropolitan Museum of New York; you idly surf the Internet to discover the pristine South Pacific Islands, and the next thing you know you are in your 'final Eden' at Royal Islands, where there is 'no meeting, no telephone, no newspaper, and no Internet.' You do see your native Chinese cities and villages, but these are the sites of cultural relics and contemporary consumption and leisure, not the cities of laid-off and migrant workers. These are the timeless Chinese villages of charm celebrated by the classic poets, without traces of economic dislocation or environmental degradation. Just as you will encounter local drinkers in a Scottish bar, you encounter your fellow Chinese as exotic 'others', including the innocent rural children who hide behind adults upon encountering a stranger, and the village women who do their laundry while leisurely chatting with each other in the open stream.

In this world constructed by transnational media capital and the Chinese state media bureaucracy the possibilities of consumption and cultural enrichment are endless and your personal 'Eden' is everywhere you go. You are told where to spot Mao statues in Changsha, the capital of Mao's home province, and are advised to seize the dusk light to capture photo images of the exotic Hui'an women with 'a feudal head and a democratic belly' (these mysterious women observe an exotic dress code, covering their heads and exposing their belly buttons). In this world, Mao's statues have become historical relics, and ideas such as democracy have become adjectives describing an aesthetic. As these magazines help the Chinese consumer elite to globalize their lifestyles and to connect themselves with their counterparts in Paris, New York, and Tokyo, they also coach them to view China through the transnational tourist's eyes and to construct new discursive relationships with their fellow Chinese citizens in lower social classes with non-dominant ethnic status.

Instead of trying to reach potential readers in the lower social strata, domestic magazines, facing increasing competition for the same thin layer of affluent urban consumers, are attempting to globalize themselves, a strategy that fits in well with both the state's objectives and the transnational mobility of the state's top media management personnel. The popular women's magazine *Nu You* (*Women's Friend*), for example, has been hand-picked by the state authorities for overseas expansion. Following the launching of an Australian edition in Sydney in 2001, a North American edition debuted in Vancouver in November 2003, targeting the city's small but affluent community of ethnic Chinese professional and business class women. The transnational mobility of its deputy editor, who has emigrated to Canada but plans to return to China once she acquires a Canadian passport, fits such a strategy perfectly.[38]

Meanwhile, China's hundreds of millions of rural women, who are worthless as consumers to both domestic and transnational capital, are currently served by a tiny magazine partially supported by the Ford Foundation. Under-consumption by China's vast rural population of 900 million and the urban working class continue to exacerbate the country's crisis of over-accumulation. Although the Chinese state, as part of its massive deficit financing of infrastructure projects, has invested in communication infrastructure in remote regions, especially in Xinjiang and Tibet, in the interests of national integration, there has been little attempt to increase the cultural industry's reach in rural or under-served urban markets. The ability of the US cultural industry to develop a strong domestic market and enfranchise the diverse US immigrant population was crucial to its eventual global expansion and universalistic appeal. In contrast, the Chinese cultural industry, while dreaming of achieving global market success, has not been able to, indeed, is perhaps unwilling to, reach China's vast numbers of internal migrants and the urban poor, not to mention the rural population.[39]

CLASS, NATIONALISM, CULTURAL POLITICS IN CHINA

This last point needs to be taken a step further. The expansion of the Chinese media as a component of the penetration of China by the transnational media industry has made it less relevant to the politics of China's internal class system. It serves transnational class interests, which are in reality shared by only a small fraction of the Chinese population, and if anything tends to aggravate the contradictions of the emergent Chinese economy within global capitalism. The implications of this need to be spelled out more clearly.

The Chinese segment of the transnational class is closely intertwined with the Chinese state, and relies heavily on its integrationist strategy to sustain its privileged position. At the same time, members of this class have developed extensive transnational linkages: Party General Secretary Hu Jintao's naturalized US citizen daughter works for J.P. Morgan; the municipal official or the middle-class professional most likely has a single child in a Western university or ESL school; an increasing number of the Chinese middle class travel to Sydney and Vancouver for their Chinese Spring Festival holidays.

To maintain their privileged position in the Chinese political economy and sustain an FDI and export-oriented pattern of economic growth, the Chinese ruling elite adopts macro-economic policies that help sustain US consumerism and militarism through the massive purchasing of US Treasury bonds,[40] while failing to enact substantive social reforms to secure domestic social peace. Members of China's ruling elite rely on the Chinese state to continue to provide them with the conditions for their social reproduction and they have responded to state attempts to curb their excesses (through anti-corruption campaigns, for example) by voting with their feet – obtaining foreign passports and sending their wealth and families abroad. The staggering volume of capital flight is thus the other side of the story of the FDI-driven and export-oriented Chinese 'economic miracle'. Beginning from the late 1990s, the amount of capital flight, mostly in the form of illegal transfer of state assets, has increased dramatically, approximating, and even surpassing the inward flow of FDI to China: from US$36.476 billion in 1997, to US$ 48 billion in 2000, compared with US$47 billion inward FDI for the same year.[41] This reached a record high of US$48 billion between September 2002 and February 2003 alone,[42] compared with an inward FDI of US$53.5 billion for the entire year of 2003. Still, it is very likely that these figures, cited in various academic and journalistic sources, understate the actual volume of capital fight. The same period has witnessed not only the massive exodus of private entrepreneurs, government officials and/or members of their families to the US, Canada, Australia, and other countries through immigrant and/or student visas, but also the phenomenon of government officials absconding with huge amounts of financial assets to foreign countries. By June 30, 2003, the five most heavily afflicted provinces of Guangdong, Henan, Fujian, Liaoning, Jiangsu, and the three metropolitan areas of Beijing, Shanghai, and Tianjin recorded that a combined total of 4,288 government and state enterprise officials had fled abroad, and that another 2,709 had disappeared (most likely also to foreign countries).[43] The flip side of the coin of this dimension of transnational class formation, of course, is the flight of tens of thousands of Chinese farmers to the West through international human trafficking networks and their enslavement in the sweatshops in New York, Los Angeles and other global cities.

Though transnationality is an increasingly important aspect of class reconstitution in a globally integrated China, this reconstitution is also characterised by fragmentation, localism, and particularism inside China. To begin with, class power in China is constituted politically and culturally, as well as economically, as witnessed by the prominent role of corruption and the currency of terms such as 'the capitalization of power,' 'official-entrepreneurs' and 'knowledge capitalists'.[44] Second, the Chinese economy is largely bifurcated along the rural-urban divide. The average real income of China's rural residents is about a sixth of that of their urban counterparts.[45] Consequently, the most significant line of social division is still one between the rural population and the urban population. This division is further compounded by profound regional differences and gender inequality. Third, within the urban sector of the Chinese economy, there are sharp divisions among different economic sectors and forms of ownership. Fourth, as the Chinese economy shifts from a production-driven to consumption-driven model, politically privileged access to prime consumer goods such as urban housing has played a crucial role in the pattern of class formation.[46]

The resulting transnational and multi-faceted nature of class formation in China has given rise to extremely complicated articulations of nationalism and class politics. On the one hand, a hegemonic bloc consisting of transnational capitalists, globalizing Chinese political, economic and cultural elites, and the urban-based middle class whose members are customers of both domestic and transnational capital, has assumed a dominant position in Chinese culture over other classes. The suppression of class discourse and containment of social conflicts, the cultivation of consumerism and market authoritarianism, tempered by a middle-class reformism ('caring for the weak groups'), constitute the official agenda of mainstream Chinese media and culture. A state-centered nationalist discourse of building a strong and powerful China through strategic cooperation with the US dominates elite media discussions of foreign affairs. By early 2004 Colin Powell felt able to celebrate the best US-China relationship since 1972, stating that the US 'welcomes a global role for China' on the condition that 'China assumes responsibilities commensurate with the role.'[47] Elite Chinese media discourse demonstrated itself to be on the same page by debating how to become a 'responsible global power' under American leadership and promoting the new foreign policy orthodoxy of 'great power cooperation.'[48]

On the other hand, the restructuring of the Chinese political economy under the hegemony of global capitalism has not been smooth, and it continues to be marked by divisions within elite politics and internal ideological contradictions, grassroots unrest and popular nationalistic sentiments, as well as cultural and ecological crises. Together with global economic uncertainties regarding the sustainability of the US economy, with which the Chinese economy is now deeply intertwined, these factors pose profound challenges to the Chinese state as an effective player within the American imperial order.[49]

Intra-elite conflicts and ideological contradictions have accompanied every step in China's integrationist trajectory in the past quarter century. In fact, Deng's reform program itself was inaugurated through the suppression of the Maoist left within the party. Since then, the anti-capitalist and anti-imperialist legacy of the socialist state has expressed itself in the 'anti-spiritual pollution' and 'anti-bourgeois liberalization' campaigns of the 1980s, the crisis of 1989, and left-wing ideological backlashes in its aftermath. Ideological struggles have continued in covert debates about the capitalistic nature of the reforms and left opposition to the Party's embrace of capitalism, all the way to the 16th National Congress in November 2002.[50] Although attrition has thinned the ageing communist old guard and elite contestations are being suppressed in the interest of regime legitimacy,[51] the Communist Party cannot afford to renounce its anti-capitalist and anti-imperialist ideological legacies altogether. Instead, it has to continue to draw upon these legacies to sustain its ideological legitimacy, for example, by continuing to denounce US hegemonism in its foreign policy pronouncements and by producing 'main melody' cultural products glorifying Mao and the Communist Revolution.

The reform process has also been met with vibrant forms of social contestation at the grassroots level. Localized protests by laid-off workers, impoverished pensioners, overtaxed farmers and urban residents displaced by real estate developments have become a permanent feature of the Chinese political scene, and the scope and frequency of these protests are intensifying. Although state repression, class fragmentation, media censorship and the short-circuiting of communication between the various segments of China's vast underclass have so far succeeded in containing and marginalizing these struggles, the Party state must continue to impose a brutal labour discipline so as to maintain 'a flexible work force that actually grows cheaper by the year'[52] if China is to continue to entice transnational corporations to produce these. This will necessarily exacerbate class conflicts. Similarly, the opening up of the Chinese agricultural sector within the WTO framework will accelerate the displacement of Chinese farmers, and it is highly unlikely that village elections and the Party's new policy of improving rural income, announced in early 2004, will alleviate rural discontent. Although current regime protesters tend to focus on immediate economic interests and target local officials and business operatives, working-class protests in the Northeast cities of Daqing and Liaoyang in spring 2002 demonstrated increased organizational sophistication and expressed explicit political demands. As one authoritative study of farmers' movements in Hunan province has noted, such movements have not only generated their own cultural resources and communication channels, but also produced their own organizational and political demands, including the establishment of independent farmers associations and 'the emancipation of modern serfs.'[53] Thus as transnational tourist magazines construct images of idealized and objectified Chinese farmers in a picture-perfect countryside, real Chinese farmers are increasingly asserting their own political subjectivity as agents of social change. Despite state repression, class conflicts are bursting out into the national consciousness on a frequent and unpredictable basis.[54] These intensifying social tensions, when articulated with popular nationalist and anti-imperialist sentiments, may create an explosive political situation.

The growing transnational cultural penetration of China, as well as reaching only a small segment of the population, has also been accompanied by a rise in Chinese nationalism, both official and popular. On the one hand, the Party has to resort to Chinese nationalism as a key component of its legitimating ideological discourse, while its territorial logic compels it to defend Chinese sovereignty in the face of American imperialist provocations and to contain Taiwanese and ethnic minority nationalisms. On the other hand, more and more Chinese are experiencing and/or becoming aware of the political and cultural contradictions of American imperialism – from the US's backing of Yelstin's autocracy in Russia, to the 'accidental' bombing of the Chinese Embassy in Belgrade in May 1999, the collision of a US surveillance plane with a Chinese fighter jet off Hainan Island in April 2001, and the imperialist adventure in Iraq. In East Asia, the revival of right-wing Japanese nationalism has also provoked strong responses on the Chinese side. Similarly, commercially-driven media outlets have found nationalism a highly profitable motif – to such an extent the Murdoch-invested and Hong Kong-based Phoenix TV cried 'China can say no' (to the US bombing of the Chinese Embassy in Belgrade) more quickly than CCTV, which has had to temper its sensationalism to the ruling elite's strategy of avoiding confrontation with the US.

As revealed by popular books and internet postings, the most vocal form of popular nationalism tends to be linked to political authoritarianism and contains neither a critique of global capitalism nor substantive class analysis. However, there are forms of popular nationalism that are critical of global capitalism and class domination at both the intellectual and popular levels. On the one hand, 'new left' intellectuals well tuned to the neo-Marxist and post-colonial literature have developed critical analyses of global capitalism and China's role in it.[55] On the other hand, perhaps as the ultimate 'dialectic' of the Chinese Revolution, the lived experience of global capitalism and American imperialism has led some Chinese intellectuals, workers, and farmers to reclaim as their own the anti-capitalist and anti-imperialist themes of the Communist Party. Within this context, Mao has re-emerged as an anti-capitalist and anti-imperialist political and cultural symbol for millions of disenfranchised Chinese workers and farmers, rather than a disembodied object of tourist attraction for the readers of *Trends Traveler*. No amount of liberal taunts made against China's laid-off workers and displaced farmers and their few intellectual allies for 'totalitarian nostalgia' can deflect popular quests for social justice and equality. The overwhelming popularity of an anti-imperialist and anti-capitalist play entitled 'Che Guevara', which brought together leftist cultural producers, university students, and ordinary workers in various Chinese cities in 2000, signalled the emergence of a new form of leftist cultural politics and a new form of internationalism and revolutionary idealism beyond the margins of the globally integrated Chinese cultural market.[56]

Class and nationalistic politics, of course, do not exhaust the forms of popular struggles in China. The rise of Falun Gong as a quasi-religious transnational cultural movement underscored the complicated intersections between class and identity politics and revealed the profound cultural contradictions of China's hyper-modernity and its global integration.[57] That China's accelerated integration with the West, the spread of Hollywood movies and the rise of the internet should have nurtured a nativist, conservative, and anti-modernist discourse such as Falun Gong, not only exposes the limits of capitalist cultural hegemony but also raises disturbing questions about the supposed emancipatory nature of globalized communication networks.

The more recent SARS outbreak, meanwhile, demonstrated the ecological contradictions of China's global integration, and it may well be the prelude to more serious environmental and health crises. Already, in the eyes of Canadian journalist Jan Wong, a globalized and globalizing China has 'failed the world' by covering up an epidemic bred in its dangerous soils. A population- and factory-dense 'third world city with all the usual sanitation problems, but one where many residents are rich enough to travel frequently and far,' and a 'hybrid of gleaming skyscrapers and farmers' markets selling live chickens and snakes … fringed by traditional peasant farms where people and pigs live cheek by jowl' – such is the Guangdong metropolis of Foshan, 'ground zero in the SARS outbreak.'[58] Such ecological and social conditions, coupled with a 'centuries-old tradition of bureaucratic secrecy and xenophobia' and a desire to sustain its lucrative tourism industry and expanding foreign investment, according to Wong, led to the initial cover-up of the outbreak by the Chinese state and the national media system.

This analysis, however, conceals the profound contradictions of global-ization and China's integration. After all, the infectious Chinese doctor who travelled to Hong Kong for a family wedding and stayed in a three-star hotel symbolized the increasing mobility of the rising Chinese middle class, in other discursive contexts a prized consumer and a favoured agent of social stability and democratization. Similarly, Foshan, one of the famed frontier towns of Chinese capitalism would, in another context, symbolize the dynamism and hope of a globally integrated, market-driven, and entrepre-neurial China, in contrast with stagnating northern industrial cities such as Daqing and Liaoyang, with all their labour problems. Far from China's communication and cultural industry being able to achieve a 'success of its own' in the global marketplace, its inability to meet the cultural needs of a fractured Chinese society appears even more self-evident as the political economic, cultural, and ecological contradictions of the country's global integration deepen.

NOTES

I would like to thank the editors, as well as Dan Schiller and Rob Duffy for their invaluable comments and editorial suggestions in preparing this article.

1   'Murdoch's Appeal to Chinese Leaders', October 9, 2003. The Associate Press, http://www.afr.com/article s/2003/10/09/1065601040384.thml, accessed October 10, 2003.

2   Cao Peng, 'Twenty Keywords of the Chinese Media Industry in 2003,' http://peopledaily.com.cn/gb/guoji/1031/2304950.html. Accessed January 19, 2004.

3   Dan Schiller, 'Poles of Market Growth? Open Questions About China, Information and the World Economy', paper submitted the Conference on 'Transnational Media Corporations and National Media Systems: China after Entry into the World Trade Organization,' Rockefeller Conference Center at Bellagio, Italy, May 17-21, 2004.

4   Leo Panitch and Sam Gindin, 'Global Capitalism and American Empire,' in *Socialist Register 2004*, London: Merlin Press, 2003, pp. 1-42.

5   Panitch Gindin, 'Global Capitalism,' p. 17.

6   Zhenzhi Guo, *A History of Chinese Television*, Beijing: Zhongguo Renmindaxue Chubanshe, 1991; Yuezhi Zhao and Zhenzhi Guo, 'Television in China: History, Political Economy, and Culture,' in Janet Wasko (ed.), *A Companion to Television*, London: Blackwell, forthcoming.

7   Yuezhi Zhao and Dan Schiller, 'Dances with Wolves? China's Integration

with Digital Capitalism,' *Info* 3:2 (April 2001), pp. 137-151.

8   Yuezhi Zhao, 'Transnational Capital, the State, and China's Semi-Integrated Communication Industries in a Fractured Society,' *The Public/Javnost* 10:4 (2003), pp. 58-74.

9   Wang Hui, *China's New Order: Society, Politics, and Economy*, edited by Theodore Hunters, Cambridge, Mass: Harvard University Press, 2003.

10   Liu Jianming, 'The Radiating Power of Globalized Audio-Visual Products', paper presented at the International Conference on 'Mass Media in the Era of Globalization, Marketization, and High-Tech,' Shanghai University, Shanghai, China, October 2003.

11   Wu Mei, 'Globalization and Language Sovereignty: The Use of English on China's Television and in Public Signs,' paper presented at the conference on 'Asian Culture and Media Studies', Beijing Broadcasting Institute, Beijing, China, December 2003.

12   Herbert I. Schiller, 'Not Yet the Post-Imperialist Era,' *Critical Studies in Mass Communication*, 8 (1991), p. 15.

13   Emad El-Din Aysha, 'The Limits and Contradictions of 'Americanization,' *Socialist Register* 2004, London: Merlin, pp. 245-260.

14   Zhao and Schiller, 'Dances with Wolves?' p. 140.

15   Leslie Sklair, *The Transnational Capitalist Class*, Oxford: Blackwell, 2001, p. 256.

16   Yuezhi Zhao, '"Entering the World": Neo-liberal Globalization, the Dream to be a Strong Nation, and Chinese Press Discourses on the WTO', in C.C. Lee (ed.), *Chinese Media, Global Context*, London: Routledge, 2003, pp. 32-56.

17   Wang, *China's New Order*, p. 102.

18   Guo Zhenzhi, 'A Perspective on the Chinese New Media Based on Their Coverage of the Iraqi War and SARS', *Chuanmei Yanjiu*, http://www.rirt.com.cn/magazine/ml_11.asp, accessed February 5, 2004.

19   James Compton, *The Integrated News Spectacle: A Political Economy of Cultural Performance*, New York: Peter Lang Publishing, 2004.

20   Panitch and Gindin, 'Global Capitalism,' p. 19.

21   Ibid.

22   This section draws on, updates, and develops material presented in Zhao and Schiller, 'Dances with Wolves?'

23   Stanley Rosen, 'China Goes Hollywood,' *Foreign Policy*, January/February 2003, pp. 94-98.

24   Dai Jinhua, 'Chinese Cinema: Sinking in Happiness ...', *Xiandai Chuanbo*, January 1999, p. 21.

25   Liu Xitao, 'China's Film Industry Suffers a Major Blow with WTO Entry,' *Qiaobao*, November 24, 1999, B1.

26   Rosen, 'China Goes Hollywood,' p. 98.

27   The People's Daily, 'Warner Brothers Marches into China's Cinema Market,' http://english.peopledaily.com.cn/200401/18/eng20040118_132895.shtml. I am very grateful to Bingchun Meng for sharing this piece of information with me.

28 Peng Jingfeng, Xuchang, 'An Allover Reshaping of Film Distribution Channels,' *Shenzhou Shibao*, July 20, 2003, C3.

29 Schiller, 'Poles of Market Growth?' pp. 1-2.

30 'China to Promote Own Alternative to DVDs,' Associate Press, November 18, 2003.

31 Dan Schiller, 'Communications and Power: Interpreting China's Emerging Role,' *Media Development* 3/2003, p. 13.

32 This section draws on, updates, and develops material presented in Zhao, 'Transnational Capital,' pp. 53-74.

33 Articulated by Jiang Zemin in 2000, the Party represents 'the development trends of advanced productive forces,' 'the orientations of an advanced culture,' and 'the fundamental interests of the overwhelming majority of the people of China.' This revisionist thesis, which effectively modifies the Party's claim to be the vanguard of the working class, was incorporated into the Constitution of the Chinese Communist Party at the 16th Party Congress in November 2002 amidst considerable opposition within the Party.

34 IDG website, http://www.idg.com/www/idgpubs.nsf/webPubsByCountry View/, accessed February 16, 2004.

35 'Lad Mags Go to China,' p. 12.

36 Kim Chipman, 'Playboy's Interest in China Rises,' *The Vancouver Sun*, October 22, 2002, D11.

37 The New York Times, 'Lad Mags Go to China,' April 18, 20004, Section 4, p. 12.

38 Interview, December 2003, Vancouver, Canada.

39 The American and Chinese difference here underscores the different patterns of domestic and transnational integration between the Fordist and post-Fordist modes of capitalist accumulation. I am very grateful to Dan Schiller for pointing out the significance of this difference to me.

40 China purchased $100 billion worth of dollars in US Treasury bonds in the first ten month of 2003 alone. See Robert Brenner, 'New Boom or New Bubble: The Trajectory of the US Economy', *New Left Review* 25, Jan-Feb 2004, p. 87.

41 Yue Jianyong and Chen Man, 'Why Does China Rely Upon FDI', *Dangdai Zhongguo Yanjiu*, 10:3, 2003, pp. 86-87; see also, 'Chinese Capital Flight Fever,' *Kaifang* (*Open Magazine*, Hong Kong), November 2003, p. 30.

42 'Another Wave of Capital Flight and Fleeing of High-Level Officials in China,'
http://www.wenxuecity.com/BBSview.asp?SubiD=newsdirect&MsgID=18 6665, accessed February 6, 2004.

43 Yue and Chen, 'Why Does China,' pp. 87-88.

44 For an overview of the reconstitution of class power in China, see He Qinglian, 'China's Listing Social Structure,' *New Left Review*, September/October 2000, pp. 69-99.

45 Louis Lim, 'China's Wealth Gap Widens to Gulf,' BBC News, http://news.bbc.co.uk/2/hi/asia-pacific/3488228.stm. February 26, 2004, accessed February 26, 2004.

46   Luigi Tomba, 'Creating an Urban Middle Class: Social Engineering in Beijing,' *The China Journal* 51, January 2004, pp. 1–26.

47   Colin Powell, 'A Strategic Partnerships', *Foreign Affairs*, Jan/Feb 2004, Vol. 83:1. http://www.foreignaffairs.org/20040101faessay83104/colin-l-powell/a-strategy-of-partnerships.html.

48   Ye Zicheng, 'Move Beyond a Polarization Perspective (Part 2)', *Nanfang Zhoumo*, January 15, 2004, http://www.nanfangdaily.com/cn/am/200401150698.asp, accessed January 20, 2004.

49   Brenner, 'New Boom or New Bubble?' Minqi Li, 'After Neoliberalism: Empire, Social Democracy, or Socialism?' *Monthly Review* 55:8, January 2004, pp 1–18. See also, Schiller, 'Communications and Power,' pp. 13–15.

50   For a detailed description of elite ideological struggles during the post-1992 period, see Joseph Fewsmith, *China Since Tiananmen: The Politics of Transition*, Cambridge: Cambridge University Press, 2001.

51   Bruce Gilley, 'The "End of Politics" in Beijing,' *The China Journal* 51, January 2004, pp 115–135.

52   Joseph Kahn, 'Losing Ground: China's Leaders Manage Class Conflict Carefully,' *The New York Times*, January 25, 2004, Internet edition, accessed January 25, 2004.

53   Yu Jianrong, 'Organized Contestation by Farmers and Its Political Risks,' *Zhanlue yu Guanli (Strategy and Management)* 58, 2003: 3, pp. 1–16.

54   In January 2004, for example, a traffic accident in which a rich BMW driver killed a poor peasant woman in Northeast China provoked a covert debate on class power in the national media. See Philip Pan, 'Traffic Death Pits China's BMW Set against Peasants', *The Vancouver Sun*, January 17, 2004, A19.

55   See Wang Hui's *China's New Order* for an example of new leftist analysis on China's reform and global integration.

56   See the Chinese website http://www.minfeng.net for the script of *Che Guevara* and other leftist plays as well as related interviews, news reports, and audience responses.

57   Yuezhi Zhao, 'Falun Gong, Identity, and the Struggle for Meaning Inside and Outside China,' in Nick Couldry and James Curran (eds.), *Contesting Media Power: Alternative Media in a Networked World*. Lanham: Rowman & Littlefield, 2004, pp. 209–224.

58   Jan Wong, 'How China Failed the World,' *The Globe and Mail*, April 5, 2003, F6.

US EMPIRE AND SOUTH AFRICAN SUBIMPERIALISM

PATRICK BOND

Imperialism, subimperialism and anti-imperialism are all settling into durable patterns and alignments in Africa – especially South Africa – even if the continent's notoriously confusing political discourses sometimes conceal the collisions and collusions. 'All Bush wants is Iraqi oil', the highest-profile African, Nelson Mandela, charged in January 2003. 'Their friend Israel has weapons of mass destruction but because it's [the USA's] ally, they won't ask the UN to get rid of it .... Bush, who cannot think properly, is now wanting to plunge the world into a holocaust. If there is a country which has committed unspeakable atrocities, it is the United States of America.'[1] Mandela's remarks were soon echoed at a demonstration of 4,000 people outside the US embassy in Pretoria, by African National Congress (ANC) secretary-general Kgalema Motlanthe: 'Because we are endowed with several rich minerals, if we don't stop this unilateral action against Iraq today, tomorrow they will come for us.'[2] After the fall of Baghdad, Mandela again condemned Bush: 'Since the creation of the United Nations there has not been a World War. Therefore, for anybody, especially the leader of a superstate, to act outside the UN is something that must be condemned by everybody who wants peace. For any country to leave the UN and attack an independent country must be condemned in the strongest terms.'[3]

This was not merely conjunctural anti-war rhetoric. Mandela's successor Thabo Mbeki is just as frank when addressing the broader context of impe-rial power, for example when welcoming dignitaries to the August 2002 Johannesburg World Summit on Sustainable Development: 'We have all converged at the Cradle of Humanity to confront the social behaviour that has pity neither for beautiful nature nor for living human beings. This social behaviour has produced and entrenches a global system of apartheid.'[4] Mbeki's efforts to insert the phrase 'global apartheid' in the summit's final document failed, due to opposition by US secretary of state Colin Powell, who in turn was heckled by NGO activists and Third World leaders in the final plenary session. A year later, in the immediate run-up to the 2003 World Trade Organization (WTO) ministerial meeting in Cancun, Mbeki even hinted that Third World governments should align themselves with radical social movements: 'They may act in ways you and I may not like and break windows in the street but the message they communicate relates.'[5] Moreover, in light of Pretoria's centrality to the new India-Brazil-South Africa bloc and the G20 group often credited with causing the Cancun summit's collapse, the logical impression is that the anti-imperialist movement has an important state ally in Africa.

Unfortunately, these postures can best be understood as 'talking left, walking right', insofar as they veil the underlying dynamics of accumulation, class struggle and geopolitics. To illustrate, in early 2003, at the same time as Mandela's outburst, the ANC government permitted three Iraq-bound warships to dock and refuel in Durban, and the state-owned weapons manufacturer Denel sold $160 million worth of artillery propellants and 326 hand-held laser range finders to the British army, and 125 laser-guidance sights to the US Marines.[6] South Africa's independent left immediately formed a 300-organization Anti-War Coalition which periodically led demonstrations of 5,000-20,000 protesters in Johannesburg, Pretoria and Cape Town. Despite the embarrassment, Pretoria refused the Coalition's demands to halt the sales. George W. Bush rewarded Mbeki with an official visit in July 2003, just as the dust from the Baghdad invasion had settled. 'Let us use this visit to impact as best as possible on the consciences of the American electorate', the South African Communist Party (SACP) secretary-general, Blade Nzimande, remarked. 'It would, we believe, be a mistake to press for a cancellation of the visit. But it would be equally mistaken to present the invasion of Iraq as a 'thing of the past', as 'something we've put behind us', as we now return to bi-national US/SA business as usual.'[7]

But business as usual seemed to prevail. As Johannesburg's Business Day editorialized, the 'abiding impression' left from Bush's Pretoria stopover was 'of a growing, if not intimate trust between himself and president Thabo Mbeki. The amount of public touching, hugging and backpatting they went through was well beyond the call of even friendly diplomatic duty.'[8] Organizing large demonstrations in Pretoria and Cape Town, the Anti-War Coalition countered: 'The ANC and SACP claim to be marching against the war ... while hosting the chief warmonger, George Bush. The ANC's public relations strategy around the war directly contradicts their actions, which are pro-war and which have contributed to the deaths of thousands of Iraqi civilians.'[9] Public relations finally caught up to *realpolitik*, as Mandela, too, recanted his criticism of Bush in May 2004, because 'It is not good to remain in tension with the most powerful state.'[10] A month later, Mbeki joined the G8 summit in Sea Island, Georgia, along with Africa's other main pro-Western rulers: Abdelaziz Bouteflika of Algeria, John Kufuor of Ghana, Olusegun Obasanjo of Nigeria, Abdoulaye Wade of Senegal and Yoweri Museveni of Uganda. Treated only to a lunch meeting which began late and ended early, the Africans promised the G8 to help unblock the multilateral 'logjam' that emerged at the Cancun WTO summit. The next day, Mbeki was in Washington for the funeral of Ronald Reagan – a notorious supporter of the old Pretoria regime, even during the mid-1980s states of emergency – and justified his presence to National Public Radio: 'For those of us who were part of the struggle against apartheid, it was actually during Reagan's presidency [that] the US government started dealing with the ANC.'[11]

How can we understand this political inconsistency? How much does it reflect the requirements of a US-led capitalist empire that uses Africa for surplus extraction and the spreading and deepening of global neoliberalism, and that especially relies on South Africa for legitimacy and subimperial deputy-sheriff support? To answer, consider first the context of modern imperialism, which in Africa combines an accumulation strategy based on neoliberalism and the extraction of ever cheaper minerals and cash crops, with increasing subservience to US-led, indirect, neocolonial rule. The next step is to locate South Africa's position as the regional hegemon, identifying areas where imperialism is facilitated in Africa by the Pretoria-Johannesburg state-capitalist nexus, in part through Mbeki's New Partnership for Africa's Development (NEPAD) and in part through the logic of private capital.

NEOLIBERALISM AND SURPLUS EXTRACTION

What does imperialism 'need' from Sub-Saharan Africa, whose 650 million people generate just 1 per cent of global GDP? During the twentieth century, a great organic tradition of anti-imperialist political economy and radical politics emerged to explain general and specific cases of African subordination and promote revolutionary solutions. More recently, a revival of commentaries concerning imperialism's logic has provided at least three strands of argument that are especially relevant for the purposes of this essay. First, the transition from post-War prosperity to the neoliberal era, beginning around 1980, can be traced to problems experienced in maintaining capital accumulation in the core regions of capitalism. Second, these problems were managed from the core – especially the Bretton Woods Institutions and the US state/military – through techniques that amplified uneven development and threatened Africa's social and economic reproduction. And third, these forms of management left the continent and its main political actors at the beck and call of imperial power, particularly the US state's, notwithstanding a variety of multilateral outlets and regional associations.

Recent analyses of the sustained crisis tendencies in global capitalism's core regions have shown that the current economic conjuncture follows logically from a long structural crisis of capitalism characterized by three decades of lower global GDP growth during a period of persistent 'overaccumulation', untenable speculation and periodic financial collapses, frantic outsourcing of production across the world, hyperactive trade, the emergence of system-threatening ecological problems, soaring inequality, and the near-universal lowering of both labour's remuneration and the social wage.[12] In the last decade, one symptom of global capitalism's desperation is the extraction of surpluses from the Third World at an unprecedented rate. Thus, from a situation of positive net financial flows of more than $40 billion per year to 'developing economies' during the mid-1990s, the East Asian crisis was followed by a $650 billion South-North drain in the four years 1999-2002.[13]

Although Africa is typically given very little attention in contemporary Marxist accounts of imperialism, there is no question that the continent has been drawn deeper into global circuits of crisis management through the irresponsible liberalization of trade and finance that, in turn, cheapened the continent's products for northern consumption.[14] While some commodity prices – for oil, rubber and copper – have risen in recent years, thanks to Chinese demand, the major coffee, tea and cotton exports many countries rely upon continue to stagnate or fall.[15] Debt servicing also grew ever more onerous, notwithstanding the Bank/IMF 'Highly Indebted Poor Countries' (HIPC) relief initiative. From 1980 to 2000, Sub-Saharan Africa's total foreign debt soared from $60 billion to $206 billion, and the ratio of debt to GDP rose from 23 per cent to 66 per cent, leaving Africa repaying $6.2 billion more than it received in new loans in 2000.[16] Meanwhile, donor aid was down 40 per cent from 1990 levels, and capital flight exacerbated the problem of access to hard currency. James Boyce and Léonce Ndikumana established that a core group of thirty Sub-Saharan African countries, with a joint foreign debt of $178 billion, suffered a quarter century of capital flight by elites totalling more than $285 billion, including imputed interest earnings, leaving Sub-Saharan Africa 'a net creditor vis-à-vis the rest of the world.'[17]

Drawing upon Rosa Luxemburg's insights into the interactions between capitalism and non-capitalist aspects of production and social reproduction, David Harvey has provided a nuanced explanation of how the permanent process of primitive accumulation[18] evolves into what he terms a system of 'accumulation by dispossession'.[19] That process is very important for understanding contemporary imperialism in Africa. Accumulation by dispossession intensifies as a result of the onset of capitalist crisis and the widespread adoption of neoliberalism, as the system seeks to mitigate and displace (though never fully resolve) crisis tendencies. Harvey interprets these reactions as 'spatial and temporal fixes' for overaccumulated capital, because they also serve as crisis management tools.[20]

Beyond these processes, the sphere of reproduction – where much primitive accumulation occurs through unequal gender power relations – remains central to capitalism's looting. This is especially evident in areas such as Southern Africa which are characterized by migrant labour flows, largely through the super-exploitation of rural women in childrearing, healthcare and eldercare. More broadly, this is part of what Isabella Bakker and Stephen Gill term 'the reprivatization of social reproduction'.[21] For Africans, the denial of access to food, medicines, energy and even water is the most extreme result; people who are surplus to capitalism's labour requirements find that they must fend for themselves or die. The scrapping of safety nets in structural adjustment programmes worsens the vulnerability of women, children, the elderly and disabled people. They are expected to survive with less social subsidy and greater pressure on the fabric of the family during economic crisis, which makes women more vulnerable to sexual pressures and, therefore, HIV/AIDS.[22] Even in wealthy South Africa an early death for millions was the outcome of state and employer AIDS policy, with cost-benefit analyses demonstrating conclusively that keeping most of the country's five million HIV-positive people alive through patented medicines cost more than these people were 'worth'.[23]

The imposition of neoliberal policies in this spirit has amplified combined and uneven development in Africa. In macroeconomic terms, the 'Washington Consensus' entails trade and financial liberalization, currency devaluation, lower corporate taxation, export-oriented industrial policy, austere fiscal policy aimed especially at cutting social spending, and monetarism in central banking (with high real interest rates). In microdevelopmental terms, neoliberalism implies not only three standard microeconomic strategies – deregulation of business, flexibilized labour markets and privatization (or corporatization and commercialization) of state-owned enterprises – but also the elimination of subsidies, the promotion of cost-recovery and user fees, the disconnection of basic state services to those who do not pay, means-testing for social programmes, and reliance upon market signals as the basis for local development strategies. As Gill has shown, enforcement is crucial, through both a 'disciplinary neoliberalism' entailing constant surveillance, and a 'new constitutionalism' that locks in these policies in over time.[24]

Leo Panitch and Sam Gindin point to US empire's management capacities via the neoconservative petro-military-industrial complex in the Bush

White House and the Pentagon, and the Washington Consensus nexus of the US Treasury, Bretton Woods Institutions and Wall Street.[25] While they do not see this as emanating from the need to displace a structural economic crisis at home, the Sub-Saharan African case seems, in fact, to demonstrate both the structurally-rooted need of global capital to extract surpluses, and the importance of Washington's political-economic power. However, in a recent survey, Robert Biel identified two central contradictions in US imperialism vis-à-vis Africa: 'First, central accumulation always tends to siphon away the value which could form the basis of state-building, bringing with it the risk of "state failure", leading to direct intervention. Second, the international system becomes increasingly complex, characterized by a range of new actors and processes and direct penetration of local societies in a way which bypasses the state-centric dimension.' Because of the complexity of indirect rule, and the difficulty of coopting all relevant actors, Biel continues, 'A reversion to the deployment of pure power is always latent, and the post-September 11th climate has brought it directly to the fore. This is a significant weakness of international capitalism.'[26] Likewise, Panitch and Gindin argue, 'An American imperialism that is so blatantly imperialistic risks losing the very appearance that historically made it plausible and attractive .... This is especially important. Since the American empire can only rule through other states, the greatest danger to it is that the states within its orbit will be rendered illegitimate by virtue of their articulation to the imperium.'[27] Indeed, one critical area of agreement between most political economists today is the ongoing relevance of the national state, not only to accumulation via traditional facilitative functions (securing property rights, the integrity of money, and the monopoly on violence), but also to the 'coauthorship' of the neoliberal project, in turn reflecting a shift in the balance of forces within societies and state bureaucracies. South Africa is an excellent case in point, we shall observe.

In sum, thanks largely to capitalist crisis tendencies and the current orientation to accumulation by dispossession, imperialism can neither deliver the goods nor successfully repress sustained dissent in Africa, not least in Sub-Saharan Africa, rife with 'state failure' and 'undisciplined neoliberalism' (witnessed in repeated IMF riots). The ideological legitimation of 'free markets and free politics' requires renewal, therefore. For this, the US needs a subimperial partner, even one whose politicians are occasionally as cheeky as those in Pretoria – and who have become, hence, just as vital for broader systemic legitimation as Washington's talk-left, walk-right allies in New Delhi and Brasilia. After all, anti-imperial critique continues to emerge throughout Africa, not just rhetorically (as cited at the beginning of this essay) but also in practical form, as when trade ministers from low-income Africa

– *not* the G20 or South Africa, India and Brazil – withdrew their support for a consensus at the WTO's Seattle and Cancun summits. Thus NEPAD becomes an especially important surrogate for imperialism, as argued below. Next, however, we consider the expansion of US geopolitical and military activities.

WASHINGTON'S REACH

What are US planners up to in Africa? As one illustration, an expert at the US Naval War College recently drew up 'The Pentagon's New Map', high-lighting countries now considered danger zones for imperialism. In Africa, these included Angola, Burundi, the Democratic Republic of the Congo (DRC), Rwanda, Somalia and even South Africa, sites which could not only 'incubate the next generation of global terrorists', but also host interminable poverty, disease and routine mass murder.[28] Benign – or malign – neglect would no longer be sufficient. The period during the 1990s after the failed Somali intervention, when Washington's armchair warriors let Africa slide out of view, may have come to an end with September 11. Army General Charles Wald, who controls the Africa Programme of the European Command, told the BBC in early 2004 that he aims to have five brigades with 15,000 men working in cooperation with regional partners including South Africa, Kenya, Nigeria and two others still to be chosen.[29] NATO's Supreme Allied Commander for Europe, General James Jones, confirmed the US geographical strategy in May 2003: 'The carrier battle groups of the future and the expeditionary strike groups of the future may not spend six months in the Mediterranean Sea but I'll bet they'll spend half the time down the West Coast of Africa.'[30] Within weeks, 3,000 US troops had been deployed off the coast of Liberia (and went briefly ashore to stabilize the country after Charles Taylor departed). Potential US bases were suggested for Ghana, Senegal and Mali, as well as the North African countries of Algeria, Morocco and Tunisia.[31] Another base was occupied by 1,500 US troops in the small Horn country of Djibouti. Botswana and Mozambique were also part of the Pentagon's strategy, and South Africa would remain a crucial partner.

Central and eastern Africa remains a problem area, and not merely because of traditional French and Belgian neocolonial competition with British and US interests.[32] President Clinton's refusal to cite Rwanda's situation as formal genocide in 1994 was an infamous failure of nerve in terms of the emerging doctrine of 'humanitarian' imperialism – in contrast to intervention in the (white-populated) Balkans. With an estimated three million dead in Central African wars, partly due to struggles over access to coltan and other mineral riches, conflicts worsened within the Uganda/Rwanda bloc, vis-à-vis the revised alliance of Laurent Kabila's DRC, Zimbabwe, Angola and Namibia. Only with Kabila's assassination in 2001 and Pretoria's management of peace deals in the DRC and Burundi, did matters settle, however briefly, into a fragile peace combining neoliberalism with opportunities for minerals extraction. However, as turmoil resumed in mid-2004, it was clear that coups and outbreaks of strife would be a constant threat, demonstrating how precarious Pretoria's elite deals are when deeper tensions remain unresolved. Another particularly difficult site is Sudan, where US Delta Force troops have been sighted in informal operations (although not to protect Darfur from genocide), perhaps because although China showed some interest in oil exploration there during the country's civil war chaos, US oil firms have subsequently arrived. On the west coast, the major petro prize remains the Gulf of Guinea. With oil shipment from Africa to Louisiana refineries taking many fewer weeks than from the Persian Gulf, the world's shortage of super-tankers is eased by direct sourcing from West Africa's offshore oil fields.

In this context, it is not surprising that of $700 million destined to develop a 75,000-strong UN peace-keeping force in coming years, $480 million is dedicated to African soldiers.[33] But Africa is also a site for the recruitment of private mercenaries, as an estimated 1,500 South Africans – including half of Mbeki's own 100 personal security force – joined firms such as South Africa's Executive Outcomes and British-based Erinys to provide more than 10 per cent of the bodyguard services in occupied Iraq.[34] Some African countries, including Eritrea, Ethiopia and Rwanda, joined the 'Coalition of the Willing' against Iraq in 2003, although temporary UN Security Council members Cameroon, Guinea and the Republic of the Congo opposed the war, in spite of Washington's bullying. The Central African Republic proved reliable during the reconciliation of Jacques Chirac and the Bush regime in March 2004, when Haitian president Jean-Bertrand Aristide was kidnapped and temporarily dumped there, prior to taking up a cautious residence in South Africa. Africa is also an important site for Washington's campaigns against militant Islamic networks, especially in Algeria and Nigeria in the north-west, Tanzania and Kenya in the east, and South Africa. Control of African immigration to the US and Europe is crucial, in part through the expansion of US-style incarceration via private sector firms like Wackenhut, which has invested in South African privatized prison management, along with the notorious Lindela extradition camp for 'illegal immigrants', part of a highly racialized global detention and identification system.

Of course, the US military machine does not roll over Africa entirely unimpeded. Minor roadblocks have included Pretoria's rhetorical opposition to the Iraq war, conflicts within the UN Human Rights Commission (espe-cially over Zimbabwe), and the controversy over US citizens' extradition to the International Criminal Court. On the eve of Bush's 2003 Africa trip, the Pentagon announced that it would withdraw $7.6 million worth of military support to Pretoria because the South African government – along with thirty-four military allies of Washington (and ninety countries in total) – had not agreed to give US citizens immunity from prosecution at The Hague's new International Criminal Court. Botswana, Uganda, Senegal and Nigeria, also on Bush's itinerary, signed blackmail-based immunity deals and retained US aid.[35]

Competition from other neocolonial sponsors has occasionally been a factor limiting US arrogance, for example in the only partially successful attempt by Monsanto to introduce genetically modified (GM) agriculture in Africa. Zambia, Zimbabwe and Angola have rejected World Food Programme and US food relief because of fears of future threats to their citizens, and not coincidentally, to European markets. Linking its relatively centralized aid regime to trade through bilateral regionalism, the European Union aims to win major Africa-Caribbean-Pacific (ACP) country concessions on investment, competition, trade facilitation, government procurement, data protection and services, which along with grievances over agriculture, industry and intellectual property were the basis of ACP withdrawal from Cancun. The EU's 'Economic Partnership Agreements' (EPAs) under the Cotonou Agreement (which replaced the Lome Convention) will signify a new, even harsher regime of 'reciprocal liberalization' to replace the preferential agreements that tied so many African countries to their former colonial masters via cash-crop exports. If the EPAs are agreed upon by late 2005 and implemented from 2008, as presently scheduled, what meagre organic African industry and services remained after two decades of structural adjustment will probably be lost to European scale economies and technological sophistication. An April 2004 meeting of parliamentarians from East Africa expressed concern, 'that the pace of the negotiations has caught our countries without adequate considerations of the options open to us, or understanding of their implications, and that we are becoming hostage to the target dates that have been hastily set without the participation of our respective parliaments.' Even Botswana's neoliberal president Festus Mogae admitted, 'We are somewhat apprehensive towards EPAs despite the EU assurances. We fear that our economies will not be able to withstand the pressures associated with liberalization.'[36] But the EU's substantial aid carrots and sticks will be the final determinant, overriding democratic considerations.

What of Washington's development aid to Africa? During the early 1990s, numerous US Agency for International Development mission offices in Africa were closed by the Clinton Administration. The highest-profile measures now relate to HIV/AIDS treatment, amounting to what the State Department called its 'full-court press' – including threats of further aid cuts – against governments which made provisions for generic medicines production; something which Clinton only backed away from in late 1999 because of sustained activist protest.[37] Bush promised a $15 billion AIDS programme, then whittled it down to a fraction of that, then refused to provide funds to the UN Global Fund to Fight AIDS, TB and Malaria, and then prohibited US government financing of generic medicines. Bush also introduced an innovative vehicle to fuse neoliberal market conditionality with, supposedly, greater social investment: the Millennium Challenge Account (MCA). With USAID budgets still declining in real terms, the delinked MCA funding will rise from $1 billion in 2004 to $5 billion in 2006, a 100 per cent increase on 2004 spending for all US overseas development assistance. But of seventy-four 'low income' countries that are meant to be eligible, of which thirty-nine are in Africa, only sixteen passed the first test of governance and economic freedom in May 2004. Half of these were African: Benin, Cape Verde, Ghana, Lesotho, Madagascar, Mali, Mozambique and Senegal. The criteria for funding these countries' aid programmes have been established by a series of think tanks and quasi-government agencies: Freedom House (civil liberties and political rights), the World Bank Institute (accountability, governance and control of corruption), the IMF and the Heritage Foundation Index of Economic Freedom (credit ratings, inflation rates, business start-up times, trade policies and regulatory regimes), and the World Health Organization and the UN (public expenditure on health and primary education, immunization rates and primary school completion rates).[38] Washington's attempt to disguise and legitimize imperialism through aid that carries 'good governance' and 'social investment' conditionalities dates to the Clinton era, but under Bush's MCA it involves more sophisticated disciplinary neoliberal surveillance, especially in combination with the World Bank.[39]

However, with so few African states receiving MCA funding, and with so much more at stake than can be handled by the expansion of military spending, it is vital for Washington to identify reliable allies in Africa to foster both imperialist geopolitics and neoliberal economics. Does South Africa qualify? There is much to consider in the hectic activities of Mbeki and his two main internationally-oriented colleagues – finance minister Trevor Manuel (chair of the IMF/World Bank Development Committee in 2002-04) and trade/privatization minister Alec Erwin (the leading candidate to replace Supachai Panitchpakdi as WTO director-general in 2005 if his health allows). But the question must be posed: are these men breaking or instead shining the chains of global apartheid?

PRETORIA'S SUBIMPERIAL FUNCTIONS

During an August 2003 talk to business and social elites at Rhodes House in Cape Town, Nelson Mandela offered the single most chilling historical reference possible: 'I am sure that Cecil John Rhodes would have given his approval to this effort to make the South African economy of the early 21st century appropriate and fit for its time.'[40] Indeed, in Rhodes' spirit, Mandela's less honourable foreign policy intentions were difficult to disguise. Although South Africa can claim one intervention worthy of its human rights rhetoric – leadership of the 1997 movement to ban landmines (and hence a major mine-clearing role for South African businesses which had helped lay the mines in the first place) – Mandela's government sold arms to governments which practised mass domestic violence, such as Algeria, Colombia, Peru and Turkey; recognized the Myanmar military junta as a legitimate government in 1994; gave the country's highest official award to Indonesian dictator Suharto three months before his 1998 demise (in the process extracting $25 million in donations for the ANC); and invaded neighbouring Lesotho in 1998, at great social and political cost, mainly so as to secure Johannesburg's water supply. The latter incident was, according to veteran foreign policy scholar Peter Vale, 'rash – a rashness born, perhaps, of the power of mimicry and sanctioned by the new world order discourses, a call to policy action encouraged by an ensemble of new controlling values.'[41]

Once the South African government had shown its willingness to put self-interest above principles, the international political power centres placed increasing trust in Mandela, Mbeki, Manuel and Erwin, giving them insider access to many international elite forums. As global-establishment institutions came under attack and attempted to reinvent themselves with a dose of New South African legitimacy (such as Mandela's 1998 caressing of the IMF during the East Asian crisis, and of Clinton during the Lewinsky scandal), Pretoria's leading politicians were allowed, during the late 1990s, to preside over the UN Security Council, the board of governors of the IMF and Bank, the United Nations Conference on Trade and Development, the Commonwealth, the World Commission on Dams and many other important global and continental bodies. Simultaneously taking Third World leadership, Pretoria also headed the Non-Aligned Movement, the Organization of African Unity and the Southern African Development Community. Then, during a frenetic two-year period beginning in September 2001, Mbeki and his colleagues hosted, led, or played instrumental roles at the following dozen major international conferences or events: the World Conference Against Racism in Durban (September 2001); the launch of NEPAD in Abuja, Nigeria (October 2001); the Doha, Qatar ministerial summit of the World Trade Organization (November 2001); the

UN's Financing for Development conference in Monterrey, Mexico (March 2002); the G8 summits in Genoa, Italy (July 2001) and Kananaskis, Canada (June 2002); the African Union launch in Durban (July 2002); the World Summit on Sustainable Development (WSSD) in Johannesburg (August–September 2002); the Davos World Economic Forum (January 2003); the Evian G8 Summit (June 2003); George W. Bush's first trip to Africa (July 2003); the Cancun WTO ministerial (September 2003); and the World Bank/IMF annual meeting in Dubai (September 2003).

However, virtually nothing was actually accomplished through these opportunities. At the UN racism conference, Mbeki colluded with the EU to reject the demand of NGOs and African leaders for slavery/colonialism/apartheid reparations. By all accounts, NEPAD provided merely a homegrown version of the Washington Consensus. At Doha, Erwin split the African delegation so as to prevent a repeat of the denial of consensus that had foiled the Seattle ministerial in December 1999. In Monterrey, Manuel was summit co-leader (with Michel Camdessus and disgraced Mexican ex-president Ernesto Zedillo), but his role was merely to legitimize ongoing IMF/WB strategies, including debt relief gimmicks. From Kananaskis, Mbeki departed with only an additional $1 billion commitment for Africa (aside from funds already pledged at Monterrey). The African Union supported both NEPAD and the repressive Zimbabwean regime of president Robert Mugabe. At the Johannesburg WSSD, Mbeki undermined UN democratic procedure, facilitated the privatization of nature, and did nothing to address the plight of the world's poor majority. In Davos, global elites ignored Africa and from Evian, Mbeki returned with nothing. For hosting a leg of Bush's Africa trip, Mbeki became the US 'point man' on Zimbabwe (as Bush pronounced), and avoided any conflict over Iraq. In Cancun, the collapse of trade negotiations left Erwin 'disappointed', because he and his G20 colleagues hoped for a deal, no matter how contrary it would be to ACP country interests. At Dubai, with Manuel leading the Development Committee, there was no Bretton Woods democratization, no new debt relief and no 'Post-Washington' policy reform. This was evident in March 2004 when a new IMF managing director was chosen, amidst Third World elite consternation about the job's reserved 'European-only' designation. Nothing else, aside from the peace-keeping funding and a minor extension of the ineffectual HIPC, was provided at Sea Island, while in contrast, Iraq won debt cancellation worth $87 billion.

There is insufficient space to recount here details of Mbeki's consistent defeats.[42] In sum, however, Pretoria's failures left South Africa slotted into place as a subimperial partner of Washington and the EU. Although such a relationship dates to the apartheid era, the ongoing recolonization of Africa

– in political, military and ideological terms – and the reproduction of neoliberalism together require a strategy along the lines of NEPAD.

From the late 1990s, Mbeki had embarked upon an 'African Renaissance' branding exercise, which he endowed with poignant poetics but not much else. By 2001, Mbeki managed to sign on as partners for NEPAD's first draft, the 'Millennium Africa Recovery Plan', two additional rulers from the crucial North and West of the continent: Bouteflika and Obasanjo. Both suffered regular mass protests and various civil, military, religious and ethnic disturbances at home. By early 2001, in Davos, Mbeki made clear whose interests NEPAD would serve: 'It is significant that in a sense the first formal briefing on the progress in developing this programme is taking place at the World Economic Forum meeting. The success of its implementation would require the buy in from members of this exciting and vibrant forum!'[43] International capital would, in theory, benefit from large infrastructure construction opportunities on the public-private partnership model, privatized state services, ongoing structural adjustment, intensified rule of international property law and various NEPAD sectoral plans, all coordinated from a South African office staffed with neoliberals and open to economic and geopolitical gatekeeping. Once Mbeki's plan was merged with an infrastructure-project initiative offered by Wade, it won endorsement at the last meeting of the Organization of African Unity, in June 2001. (In 2002 the OAU was transformed into the African Union, and NEPAD serves as its official development plan.)

In early 2002, global elites celebrated NEPAD in sites ranging from the World Economic Forum meeting in New York City to the summit of self-described 'progressive' national leaders (including Blair) who gathered in Stockholm to forge a global Third Way. Elite eyes were turning to the world's 'scar' (Blair's description of Africa), hoping that NEPAD would serve as a large enough bandaid, for as *Institutional Investor* magazine reported, the G8's 'misleadingly named' Africa Action Plan represented merely 'grudging' support from the main donors with 'only an additional $1 billion for debt relief. (The G8) failed altogether to reduce their domestic agricultural subsidies (which hurt African farm exports) and – most disappointing of all to the Africans – neglected to provide any further aid to the continent.'[44] Mbeki had requested $64 billion in new aid, loans and investments each year, but South Africa's *Sunday Times* reported that 'the leaders of the world's richest nations refused to play ball.'[45]

So on the one hand, within a period of weeks in mid-2002, NEPAD was endorsed by the inaugural African Union summit, by the WSSD, and by the UN heads of state summit in New York. On the other, pro-NEPAD lip-service could not substitute for the missing 'new constitutionalism' (to borrow Gill's phrase) that would translate into long-term, non-retractable leverage over the continent. The main reason for doubt about Mbeki's commitment to disciplinary neoliberalism and the rule of law was his repeated defence of the main violator of liberal norms, Mugabe.[46] Both Mbeki and Obasanjo termed Zimbabwe's stolen March 2002 presidential election 'legitimate', and they repeatedly opposed punishment of the Mugabe regime by the Commonwealth and the UN Human Rights Commission. The NEPAD secretariat's Dave Malcomson, responsible for international liaison and coordination, admitted to a reporter, 'Wherever we go, Zimbabwe is thrown at us as the reason why NEPAD's a joke.'[47] Nevertheless, NEPAD was still, in mid-2003, considered by the Bush regime's main Africa official to be 'philosophically spot-on'.[48] Just prior to the Evian summit, the former International Monetary Fund managing director Michel Camdessus, subsequently France's personal G8 representative to Africa, explained NEPAD's attraction in the following way: 'The African heads of state came to us with the conception that globalization was not a curse for them, as some had said, but rather the opposite, from which something positive could be derived .... You can't believe how much of a difference this makes.'[49]

THE CONTRADICTONS OF SUBIMPERIALISM

There were many observers who, like Manuel Castells, thought that 'the end of apartheid in South Africa, and the potential linkage between a democratic, black majority–ruled South Africa and African countries, at least those in eastern/southern Africa, allows us to examine the hypothesis of the incorporation of Africa into global capitalism under new, more favourable conditions via the South African connection.'[50] In reality, the most important new factor in that incorporation is the exploitative role of Johannesburg businesses, especially in the mining, construction, financial services, retail and tourism sectors.[51] Those quite substantial investments have been, mainly, takeovers, not greenfield projects. Indeed, in spite of a high-profile mid-2002 endorsement of NEPAD by 187 individuals and firms, led by Anglo American, BHP Billiton and Absa, there were no investments made in twenty key infrastructure projects two years later, only vocal corporate complaints that NEPAD's emerging peer-review system had insufficient 'teeth' to discipline errant politicians. According to the (pro-NEPAD) *Sunday Times* after a disappointing World Economic Forum regional summit, 'The private sector's reluctance to get involved threatens to derail NEPAD's ambitions.'[52] Much is made of Johannesburg-based corporations' malevolent attitudes and extractive orientation. The prospect that these firms will be 'new imperialists' was of 'great concern', according to a leading member of Mbeki's cabinet, Jeff Radebe: 'There are strong perceptions that many South African companies working elsewhere in Africa come across as arrogant, disrespectful, aloof and careless in their attitude towards local business communities, work seekers and even governments.'[53]

But who, really, is to blame for this power relationship? Ideological backing for corporate-oriented subimperialism can usually be found within the South African Institute for International Affairs (SAIIA) at Johannesburg's University of the Witwatersrand. Yet because SAIIA heartily supports Pretoria's pro-corporate strategy, its writers have the space to speak a certain kind of *realpolitik* truth to corporate power. In 2001, a SAIIA researcher warned that Erwin's self-serving trade agenda 'might signify to the Africa group of countries that South Africa, a prominent leader of the continent, does not have their best interests at heart.'[54] In 2003, a colleague issued a technical report on trade which conceded that African governments viewed Erwin 'with some degree of suspicion' because of his promotion of the WTO. Indeed, at Seattle and Cancun Erwin stood in direct opposition to the bulk of the lowest-income countries, whose beleaguered trade ministers were responsible for derailing both summits.[55]

A few South African journalists have also picked up hostile vibes from the rest of the continent. In August 2003, the *Sunday Times* remarked on Southern African government delegates' sentiments at a Dar es Salaam regional summit: 'Pretoria was "too defensive and protective" in trade negotiations [and] is being accused of offering too much support for domestic production "such as duty rebates on exports" which is killing off other economies in the region.'[56] More generally, according to the same paper, reporting from the July 2003 African Union meeting in Maputo, Mbeki is 'viewed by other African leaders as too powerful, and they privately accuse him of wanting to impose his will on others. In the corridors they call him the George Bush of Africa, leading the most powerful nation in the neighbourhood and using his financial and military muscle to further his own agenda.'[57]

Mbeki's agenda is not that of the majority of Africans or South Africans. If the largely parasitical – not development-oriented – Johannesburg corporations profit from NEPAD's legitimation of neoliberalism and lubrication of capital flows out of African countries, these flows mainly end up in London, where Anglo American Corporation, DeBeers, Old Mutual insurance, South African Breweries and others of South Africa's largest firms re-listed their financial (though not operational) headquarters during the late 1990s. And if Mbeki and his colleagues are benefiting from the high profile provided by NEPAD and all the other global-managerial functions discussed above, the real winners are those in Washington and other imperial centres who, increasingly, require a South African frontman for the ongoing super-exploitation and militarization of Africa.

The function of Pretoria's anti-imperialist rhetoric, cited at the outset, is evident: disguising subimperial practices during an encouraging recent rise of social movement protest against neoliberalism at home[58] and across the African continent.[59] The African left has expressed deep scepticism about Mbeki's main strategies, for example in a hard-hitting resolution from a conference of the Council for Development and Social Science Research in Africa and Third World Network-Africa in April 2002,[60] and in various independent statements by leading intellectuals and organizations.[61] Not only do the left forces nearly uniformly oppose NEPAD, they also openly call for their finance ministers to default on the illegitimate foreign debt. They advocate not only kicking the World Bank and IMF out of their countries, but also international strategies for defunding and abolishing the Bretton Woods institutions. US groups like the Center for Economic Justice and Global Exchange work with Jubilee South Africa and Brazil's Movement of the Landless, amongst others, to promote the 'World Bank Bonds Boycott', asking of their Northern allies: is it ethical for socially-conscious people to invest in the Bank by buying its bonds (responsible for 80 per cent of the institution's resources), and to receive dividends which represent the fruits of enormous suffering? Other examples of what is being termed 'deglobalization' include the successful efforts to deny Trade-Related Intellectual Property Rights status to AIDS medicines, to keep GMOs out of several Southern African agricultural markets, and to reject French and British water privatizers. To these ends, the African Trade Network and the Gender and Trade Network in Africa put intense pressure on the continent's delegates to reject the WTO's Cancun proposals. And with the US and EU offering no concessions on matters of great importance to Africa, bilateral or regional trade deals are also resisted by both civil society groups and African governments.

On a more local level, inspiring examples of what might be termed 'decommodification' are underway in Africa, especially South Africa. There, independent left movements are struggling to turn basic needs into human rights: free anti-retroviral medicines to fight AIDS and other health services; free water (50 litres/person/day); free electricity (1 kilowatt hour per person per day); thorough-going land reform; prohibition on services disconnections and evictions; free education; and even a 'Basic Income Grant', as advocated by churches and trade unions. The idea is that all basic services should be provided to all as a human right, and to the degree that it is feasible, financed through imposition of much higher prices for luxury consumption.

Because the commodification of everything is still under way in South Africa, this could provide the basis for a unifying agenda for a widescale movement for fundamental social change, if linked to the demand to 'rescale' many political-economic responsibilities that are now handled by embryonic world-state institutions under the influence of neoliberal US administrations. The decommodification principle could become an enormous threat to imperial capitalist interests, in the form of a denial of private intellectual property (such as AIDS medicines), resistance to biopiracy, the exclusion of GM seeds from African agricultural systems, the nationalization of industries and utilities, or the empowerment of African labour forces. To make any progress, delinking from the most destructive circuits of global capital will also be necessary, combining local decommodification strategies and tactics with the call to close the World Bank, the IMF and the WTO. Beyond that, the challenge for Africa's progressive forces, as ever, is to establish the difference between 'reformist reforms' and reforms that advance a 'non-reformist' agenda. The latter would include generous social policies stressing decommodification, and capital controls and more inward-oriented industrial strategies allowing democratic control of finance and ultimately of production itself. These sorts of reforms would strengthen democratic movements, directly empower the producers, and, over time, open the door to the contestation of capitalism itself.

Not only does imperialism stand in the way, however, so do Pretoria's various subimperial barriers. Notwithstanding occasionally leftist rhetoric and the world-historic damage inflicted by US empire, Mbeki and his colleagues are situating South Africa as the continent's leading bourgeois-aspirant country, parallel to what Frantz Fanon so poignantly described as the stunted 'national bourgeoisie' of a post-colonial African state, i.e., the modern equivalent of an old Bantustan, where the coopted elite prosper under conditions of global apartheid:

> Content with the role of the Western bourgeoisie's business agent, it will play its part without any complexes in a most dignified manner. But this same lucrative role, this cheap-Jack's function, this meanness of outlook and this absence of all ambition symbolize the incapability of the middle class to fulfill its historic role of bourgeoisie. Here, the dynamic, pioneer aspect, the characteristics of the inventor and of the discoverer of new worlds which are found in all national bourgeoisies are lamentably absent .... In its beginnings, the national bourgeoisie of the colonial country identifies itself with the decadence of the bourgeoisie of the West. We need not think that it is jumping ahead; it is in fact beginning at the end. It is already senile before it has come to know the petulance, the fearlessness, or the will to succeed of youth.[62]

NOTES

1   South African Press Association (Sapa), 29 January 2003.
2   *Business Day*, 20 February 2003.
3   Reuters, 28 June 2003.
4   Thabo Mbeki, 'Address at the Welcome Ceremony of the WSSD', Johannesburg, 25 August 2002.
5   *The Straits Times*, 3 September 2003.
6   Andy Clarno, 'Denel and the South African Government: Profiting from the War on Iraq', *Khanya Journal*, 3(March), 2003.
7   *Umsebenzi*, 2, 13, 2 July 2003.
8   *Business Day,* 11 July 2003.
9   Anti-War Coalition Press Statement, 1 July 2003.
10   *Mail and Guardian,* 24 May 2004.
11   *Washington File,* 11 June 2004.
12   See, e.g., Robert Brenner, *The Boom and the Bubble*, London: Verso, 2003; Robert Pollin, *Countours of Descent: US Economic Fractures and the Landscape of Global Austerity*, London: Verso, 2003; Ellen Meiksins Wood, *Empire of Capital*, London: Verso, 2003; and Robert Biel, *The New Imperialism*, London: Zed Books, 2000.
13   United Nations Conference on Trade and Development, *Trade and Development Report 2003,* Geneva, 2003, p. 26.
14   Giovanni Arrighi, 'The African Crisis: World Systemic and Regional Aspects', *New Left Review,* 15, 2002; John Saul and Colin Leys, 'Sub-Saharan Africa in Global Capitalism', *Monthly Review,* July 1999.
15   Michael Barratt Brown, 'Africa's Trade Today', Paper for the Review of African Political Economy and CODESRIA 30th Anniversary Conference, Wortley Hall, Sheffield, 27–29 May 2004. See also Michael Barratt Brown and Pauline Tiffen, *Short Changed: Africa and World Trade*, London: Pluto Press, 1992.
16   World Bank, *Global Finance Tables*, Washington, DC, 2002.
17   James Boyce and Leonce Ndikumana, 'Is Africa a Net Creditor? New Estimates of Capital Flight from Severely Indebted Sub-Saharan African Countries, 1970-1996', Occasional Paper, University of Massachusetts/Amherst Political Economy Research Institute, 2002.
18   Michael Perelman, *The Invention of Capitalism: Classical Political Economy and the Secret History of Primitive Accumulation*, Durham: Duke University Press, 2000.
19   David Harvey, *The New Imperialism*, Oxford and New York: Oxford University Press, 2003.
20   David Harvey, *The Limits to Capital,* Second Edition, London: Verso, 1999.
21   Isabella Bakker and Stephen Gill, 'Ontology, Method and Hypotheses', in I. Bakker and S. Gill, eds., *Power, Production and Social Reproduction,* Basingstoke: Palgrave Macmillan, 2003, p. 36.
22   See, e.g., Dianne Elson, 'The Impact of Structural Adjustment on Women: Concepts and Issues', in B. Onimode, ed., *The IMF, the World Bank and the*

African Debt, London: Zed Books, 1991; and Sara Longwe, 'The Evaporation of Policies for Women's Advancement', in N. Heyzer et al., eds., *A Commitment to the World's Women*, New York: UNIFEM, 1991. A comprehensive African literature review by Dzodzi Tsikata and Joanna Kerr shows that 'mainstream economic policymaking fails to recognize the contributions of women's unpaid labour – in the home, in the fields, or in the informal market where the majority of working people in African societies function. It has been argued that these biases have affected the perception of economic activities and have affected economic policies in ways that perpetuate women's subordination.' See Dzodzi Tskikata and Joanna Kerr, eds., *Demanding Dignity: Women Confronting Economic Reforms in Africa*, Ottawa: The North-South Institute and Accra: Third World Network-Africa, 2002.

23   In the case of the vast Johannesburg/London conglomerate Anglo American Corporation, the cut-off for saving workers in 2001 was 12 per cent – the lowest-paid 88 per cent of employees were more cheaply dismissed once unable to work, with replacements found amongst South Africa's 42 per cent unemployed reserve army of labour. For more, see Patrick Bond, *Elite Transition: From Apartheid to Neoliberalism in South Africa*, Foreword to the Second Edition, London: Pluto Press, 2004.

24   Stephen Gill, *Power and Resistance in the New World Order*, Basingstoke: Palgrave Macmillan, 2003.

25   Leo Panitch and Sam Gindin, 'Global Capitalism and American Empire', in *Socialist Register 2004*, London: Merlin Press, 2003.

26   Robert Biel, 'Imperialism and International Governance: The Case of US Policy Towards Africa', *Review of African Political Economy*, 95, 2003, p. 87.

27   Panitch and Gindin, 'Global Capitalism and American Empire', p. 33.

28   Thomas Barnett, 'The Pentagon's New Map', United States Naval War College, http://www.nwc.navy.mil/newrules/ ThePentagonsNewMap.htm, 2003.

29   Martin Plaut, 'US to Increase African Military Presence', http://www.bbc.co.uk, 23 March 2004.

30   http://www.allAfrica.com, 2 May 2003.

31   *Ghana News*, 11 June 2003.

32   Ian Taylor, 'Conflict in Central Africa: Clandestine Networks and Regional/Global Configurations', *Review of African Political Economy*, 95, 2003, p. 49.

33   The major dilemma, here, appears to be the very high level of HIV-positive members of the armed forces in key countries. See Stefan Elbe, *Strategic Implications of HIV/AIDS*, Adelphi Paper 357, International Institute for Strategic Studies, Oxford: Oxford University Press, 2003, pp. 23-44.

34   *Vancouver Sun,* 11 May 2004.

35   Sapa, 2 July 2003. Other African countries where US war criminals are safe from ICC prosecutions thanks to military-aid blackmail are the DRC, Gabon, the Gambia, Ghana, Kenya, Mauritius, Sierra Leone and Zambia.

36   http://www.epawatch.net/general/text.php?itemID=161&menuID=28;

http://www.twnafrica.org/atn.asp.

37 Patrick Bond, 'Globalization, Pharmaceutical Pricing and South African Health Policy: Managing Confrontation with US Firms and Politicians', *International Journal of Health Services*, 29(4) 1999.

38 Cited in *SA Institute for International Affairs e-Africa*, May, 2004. These rating systems follow the examples set in the Africa Growth and Opportunity Act, which by 2003 applied to 39 countries; the remaining 13 African states were vetoed by the White House for various reasons. AGOA conditionalities include adopting neoliberal policies, privatizing state assets, removing subsidies and price controls, ending incentives for local companies, and endorsing US foreign policy.

39 See Nancy Alexander, 'Triage of Low-Income Countries? The Implications of the IFI's Debt Sustainability Proposal', Washington, http://www.servicesforall.org/ html/otherpubs/ judge_jury_ scorecard.pdf, 2004.

40 *Sowetan*, 26 August 2003.

41 Peter Vale, *Security and Politics in South Africa: The Regional Dimension*, Cape Town: University of Cape Town Press, 2003, p. 133.

42 My own documentation can be found in Patrick Bond, *Talk Left, Walk Right: South Africa's Frustrated Global Reforms*, Pietermaritzburg: University of KwaZulu-Natal Press, 2003; Against Global Apartheid: South Africa Meets the World Bank, IMF and International Finance, Second Edition, London: Zed Books, 2003; *Unsustainable South Africa: Environment, Development and Social Protest*, London: Merlin Press, 2003; and ed., Fanon's Warning: A Civil Society Reader on the New Partnership for Africa's Development, Trenton: Africa World Press. See also Ian Taylor, *Stuck in Middle Gear: South Africa's Post-Apartheid Foreign Relations*, Westport: Praeger, 2001.

43 *Business Day*, 5 February 2001.

44 Deepath Gopinath, 'Doubt of Africa', *Institutional Investor Magazine*, May, 2003.

45 *Sunday Times*, 30 June 2002; *Business Day*, 28 June 2002.

46 There is enormous confusion over Mbeki's role in Zimbabwe, which is addressed in Patrick Bond and Masimba Manyanya, *Zimbabwe's Plunge: Exhausted Nationalism, Neoliberalism and the Search for Social Justice*, London: Merlin Press, Pietermaritzburg: University of Natal Press and Harare: Weaver Press, 2003. For an important critique of Mugabe from an Afro-feminist standpoint, see Horace Campbell, *Reclaiming Zimbabwe: The Exhaustion of the Patriarchal Model of Liberation*, Cape Town: David Philip, 2003.

47 *Business Day*, 28 March 2003.

48 Gopinath, 'Doubt of Africa'. A few months later, Walter Kansteiner resigned as assistant secretary of state for Africa, but the sentiment remained.

49 http://www.g7.utoronto.ca/ summit/2003evian/ briefing_apr030601.html.

50 Manuel Castells, *The Information Age, Volume III: End of Millennium*, Oxford: Blackwell Publishers, 1998, p. 88.

51 For documentation, see Darlene Miller, 'South African Multinational Corporations, NEPAD and Competing Claims on Post-Apartheid Southern Africa', Institute for Global Dialogue Occasional Paper 40, Johannesburg,

2004; Darlene Miller, 'SA Multinational Corporations in Africa: Whose African Renaissance?', International Labour Research and Information Group Occasional Paper, Cape Town, 2003; and John Daniel, Vinesha Naidoo and Sanusha Naidu, 'The South Africans have Arrived: Post-Apartheid Corporate Expansion into Africa', in J. Daniel, A. Habib and R. Southall, eds., *State of the Nation: South Africa 2003-04*, Pretoria: Human Sciences Research Council, 2003 (although note that this latter chapter does not subscribe to the argument that Pretoria is subimperialist).

52   *Sunday Times*, 24 May 2004.

53   Sapa, 30 March 2004.

54   *Mail & Guardian*, 16 November 2001.

55   *Business Day*, 2 June 2003.

56   *Sunday Times*, 24 August 2003.

57   *Sunday Times,* 13 July 2003.

58   http://www.ukzn.ac.za/ccs; http://www.red.org.za; http://www.aidc.org.za; http://southafrica.indymedia.org; http://www.khanyacollege.org.za.

59   For more on the African left, see John Fisher, 'Africa', in E. Bircham and J. Charlton, eds., *Anti-Capitalism: A Guide to the Movement*, London: Bookmarks, 2002; Leo Zeilig, ed., *Class Struggle and Resistance in Africa*, Cheltenham: New Clarion, 2002; Bond, *Talk Left, Walk Right,* Chapter Twelve; and Trevor Ngwane, 'Sparks in Soweto', *New Left Review,* 21, 2003.

60   Council for Development and Social Science Research in Africa, Dakar and Third World Network-Africa, 'Declaration on Africa's Development Challenges', Resolution adopted at the 'Joint Conference on Africa's Development Challenges in the Millennium', Accra, 23-26 April 2002, reprinted in Bond, *Fanon's Warning.*

61   See http://www.codesria.org, for Jimi Adesina, 'Development and the Challenge of Poverty: NEPAD, Post-Washington Consensus and Beyond', Paper presented to the Codesria/TWN Conference on Africa and the Challenge of the 21st Century, Accra, 23-26 April 2002; and Dani Nabudere, 'NEPAD: Historical Background and its Prospects', in P. Anyang'Nyong'o, et al., eds., *NEPAD: A New Path?* Nairobi: Heinrich Böll Foundation 2002.

62   Frantz Fanon, *The Wretched of the Earth*, New York: Grove Press, 1963, pp. 152-153.

TERROR, CAPITAL AND CRUDE: US COUNTERINSURGENCY IN COLOMBIA

DOUG STOKES

During the Cold War the US intervened in more states in Latin America than in any other continent, with US-sponsored counterinsurgency as the primary means of US coercive statecraft. US planners argued that this kind of 'support' for allied states was designed to contain the influence of the Soviet Union through the destruction of left-wing armed insurgencies that were portrayed as instances of Soviet expansionism. George Kennan, the architect of the US's Cold War grand strategy of containment, explained that in dealing with communism in Latin America the final answer 'may be an unpleasant one' but the US 'should not hesitate before police repression by the local government'. It was, he continued, 'better to have a strong regime in power than a liberal government if it is indulgent and relaxed and penetrated by Communists'.[1]

Throughout this period Colombia remained one of the largest recipients of US counterinsurgency funding and training aimed at destroying the Revolutionary Armed Forces of Colombia (FARC), an indigenous insurgency movement. The FARC were portrayed as Soviet-backed guerrillas, and a threat to the pro-US Colombian state. During these years the Colombian military carried out widespread human rights abuses. Although these abuses were not publicly approved, they were considered a necessary evil required to prevent the alleged devastating consequences to US security should a potentially pro-Soviet state come to power in Latin America. Since the end of the Cold War the US has not only continued to fund and train the Colombian military for its fight against the FARC, but actually dramatically escalated its support, to the extent that Colombia is now the third largest recipient of US military aid in the world. This is despite the US's publicly declared commitment to post-Cold war democracy promotion and humanitarian intervention to prevent human rights abuses, and the continuing record of gross human rights abuses committed by the Colombian military and their paramilitary allies.

In 2002 there were over 8,000 political assassinations in Colombia, 80 per cent of them carried out by paramilitary groups allied to the Colombian military.[2] While the US has been 'promoting polyarchy' in Latin America generally, relying more on consent than coercion to maintain its domination,[3] in Colombia it steadfastly supports a state that primarily relies on state terror to crush dissent and popular pressures for reform. Insofar as the US continues to underwrite and sponsor this state terror, it may fairly be said – without minimizing the role of the Colombian ruling class in this process – to be 'promoting terrorocracy' in Colombia.

This is not to say that consensual mechanisms are unimportant even in this case. As David Harvey argues, US policy relies upon processes of consent and cooperation in order 'to make the claim that it is acting in the general interest plausible to others, even when, as most people suspect, it is acting out of narrow self-interest. This is what exercising leadership through consent is all about'.[4] In relation to Colombia the principal means for the forging of consent during the post-Cold War era has been the deployment of new discourses on the 'war on drugs', and now the 'war on terror', to secure consent for the use of coercion. The aim of this essay is to show, first, that the US has used counter-insurgency as the principal coercive means for the stabilization and defence of capitalism in Colombia; second, that inherent within this US coercive strategy in Colombia is the promotion of sectoral interests of transnational capital primarily concentrated in oil; and third, that internal to this process has been an attempt to make the coercive forms of US-sponsored terror seems necessary and acceptable.

COUNTERINSURGENCY IN COLOMBIA DURING THE COLD WAR

The mutually supportive relation between US coercive statecraft and the reproduction of capitalism was recognized at the very beginning of the US's counterinsurgency (CI) aid and training for the Colombian military in the late 1950s and early 1960s. Following a decade of civil war in Colombia, there were growing US concerns about armed peasant 'enclaves' throughout Colombia's southern regions. A 1959 US memo from Roy Rubottom, US assistant Secretary of State for Inter-American Affairs, outlined the rationale for the provision of US CI training for Colombia. The memo argued that although 'it would be difficult to make the finding of present Communist danger in the Colombian guerrilla situation', the 'continuance of unsettled conditions in Colombia contributes to Communist objectives' and threatens the 'establishment of a pro-US, free enterprise democracy'.[5] Colombia was one of the largest recipients of US direct foreign investment (FDI) in South America. Of the $399 million of US FDI in Colombia in 1959, most ($225 million) was in oil, followed by manufacturing, public utilities and trade.[6] Colombia's close proximity to the Panama Canal also worried US planners in the early years of CI assistance: instability near the canal zone could potentially damage world trade and US strategic access. In 1960, Colonel Edward Lansdale, US Assistant Secretary of Defence for Special Operations, argued that the US should 'undertake assistance to Colombia to correct the situation of political insurrection' near the Canal Zone, a 'place so vital to our own national security'.[7]

Internal US documentation related to CI reveals the American state's active promotion of the widespread surveillance and policing of progressive elements in civil society so as to prevent the 'subversion' of capitalist socio-economic relations. One manual used to train Colombia CI forces told them to ask: 'Are there any legal political organizations which may be a front for insurgent activities? Is the public education system vulnerable to infiltration by insurgent agents? What is the influence of politics on teachers, textbooks, and students, conversely, what influence does the education system exercise on politics?'[8] They then were told to ask what 'is the nature of the labor organizations; what relationship exists between these organizations, the government, and the insurgents?' In outlining targets for CI intelligence operations the manual identified a number of different occupational categories and generic social identities. These included 'merchants' and 'bar owners and bar girls' and 'Ordinary citizens who are typical members of organizations or associations which … play an important role in the local society'. In particular US-backed CI forces were to concentrate on '[l]eaders of Dissident groups (minorities, religious sects, labor unions, political factions) who may be able to identify insurgent personnel, their methods of operation, and local agencies the insurgents hope to exploit'. In an overt indication of the equation of labour movements with subversion the manual then went on to state that insurgent forces typically try to work with labour unions and union leaders so as to determine 'the principal causes of discontent which can best be exploited to overthrow the established government [and] recruit loyal supporters'. The manual stated that organizations that stress 'immediate social, political, or economic reform may be an indication that the insurgents have gained a significant degree of control', and moved on to detail a series of what it terms 'Insurgent Activity Indicators':

> Refusal of peasants to pay rent, taxes, or loan payments or unusual difficulty in their collection. Increase in the number of entertainers with a political message. Discrediting the judicial system and police

organizations. Characterization of the armed forces as the enemy of the people. Appearance of questionable doctrine in the educational system. Appearance of many new members in established organizations such as labor organizations. Increased unrest among labourers. Increased student activity against the government and its police, or against minority groups, foreigners and the like. An increased number of articles or advertisements in newspapers criticizing the government. Strikes or work stoppages called to protest government actions. Increase of petitions demanding government redress of grievances. Proliferation of slogans pinpointing specific grievances. Initiation of letterwriting campaigns to newspapers and government officials deploring undesirable conditions and blaming individuals in power.[9]

US CI strategy was thus directly at odds with broad swathes of democratic activity and served to entrench a particular kind of political stability in Colombia. Central to this security posture was the secret advocacy of state terrorism and the development of covert paramilitary networks. In 1962, the head of a US Army Special Warfare team that provided the initial blueprint for the reorientation of the Colombian military for CI, General William Yarborough, stated:

> It is the considered opinion of the survey team that a concerted country team effort should be made now to select civilian and military personnel for clandestine training in resistance operations in case they are needed later. This should be done with a view toward development of a civil and military structure for exploitation in the event that the Colombian internal security system deteriorates further. This structure should be used to pressure toward reforms known to be needed, perform counter-agent and counter-propaganda functions and as necessary execute paramilitary, sabotage and/or terrorist activities against known communist proponents. It should be backed by the United States ... The apparatus should be charged with clandestine execution of plans developed by the United States Government toward defined objectives in the political, economic and military fields. This would permit passing to the offensive in all fields of endeavor rather than depending on the Colombians to find their own solution.[10]

Prior to the ending of the Cold War, the Office of Public Diplomacy (OPD) was set up to manage public perceptions of US policy and to sell US intervention in Latin America to both domestic and international audiences.[11] It was particularly concerned with producing consent for the Reagan administration's interventions in Central America against the El Salvadoran insurgents and the Sandinista (FSLN) government in Nicaragua. Importantly, the OPD concluded that anti-communism was becoming an increasingly ineffective pretext to justify US intervention in Latin America prior to the ending of the Cold War. One OPD memo argued that new propaganda themes needed to be developed so as to 'stress and exploit the negative characteristics of our adversaries'.[12] These themes were identified in another OPD memo that yields especially important insights into the evolution of US propaganda themes and their development prior to the ending of the Cold War. The memo outlined a series of 'supporting perceptions' that needed to be stressed so as to ease the Administration's goal of portraying aid to the Nicaraguan contras as a 'vital national interest of the United States'. These supporting perceptions were that the 'FSLN is racist and represses human rights', that the 'FSLN is involved in U.S. drug problem[s]', and that 'the FSLN are linked to worldwide terrorism'. These themes were identified using public opinion surveys 'to see what turns Americans against the Sandinistas' and thus produce consent for US intervention.[13] (In 2002, the Bush administration appointed Otto Reich, the man in charge of the OPD throughout the 1980s, as its Assistant Secretary of State for Western Hemisphere Affairs.)

In 1987, John Waghelstein, a leading US CI specialist, explained the utility of stressing drugs to sell US intervention to appropriate audiences. He argued that it would foster a 'melding in the American public's mind and in Congress of this connection [leading] to the necessary support to counter the guerrilla/narcotics terrorists in this hemisphere'.[14] With the linkage between guerrillas and drugs, 'Congress would find it difficult to stand in the way of supporting our allies with the training, advice and security assistance necessary to do the job' of CI whilst those 'church and academic groups' who have 'slavishly supported insurgency in Latin America' would 'find themselves on the wrong side of the moral issue'. Most importantly the US would 'have the unassailable moral position from which to launch a concerted offensive effort using Department of Defense (DOD) and non-DOD assets'. The forging of consent has thus been crucial in smoothing the way for the US's continued terrorocracy promotion in Colombia.

COUNTERINSURGENCY IN COLOMBIA AFTER THE COLD WAR

The $1.3 billion 'Plan Colombia' initiated under President Clinton was sold to both US domestic and international opinion as an essential component of the US's war on drugs in South America. In the words of Congressman Cass Ballanger, since the end of the Cold War 'US foreign policy toward Colombia has solely focussed on counternarcotics activities.' The US Congress' concern to limit US 'efforts to [a] counterdrug strategy in an attempt to avoid getting tangled in what seems to be an endless internal struggle' ensured that Plan Colombia was presented as a 'counternarcotics operations only'.[15] A central component of Plan Colombia's implementation was the formation and retraining of a series of new Colombian 'counter-narcotic' brigades to ultimately destroy the FARC. The latter were now characterised as 'narco-guerrillas', and as the principal agents in Colombia allegedly responsible for drug trafficking to the US.

The designation of the FARC as 'narco-guerrillas' is grossly disingenuous. In Colombia's southern region there is a long-standing pattern of small-scale coca cultivation by peasants displaced through the decades of civil war and unequal landholding, but by the late 1990s cultivation had spread quite widely throughout the country, with coca concentrations in eastern and western Colombia, as well as in the paramilitary strongholds in Colombia's northern departments.[16] More important than the geographical areas where coca is grown, however, are the trafficking networks that are concentrated in the north of Colombia. These are operated, protected and sustained by Colombia's narco-mafia and their paramilitary armies. It is these trafficking networks that are responsible for transhipment into US markets and laundering the proceeds into both Colombian and international financial networks. The US has completely ignored these in Plan Colombia.

The former Deputy Administrator with the US Drug Enforcement Administration (DEA), James Milford, has acknowledged that, while the FARC 'generate revenue by "taxing" local drug related activities' in those regions it controls, 'there is little to indicate the insurgent groups are trafficking in cocaine themselves, either by producing cocaine … and selling it to Mexican syndicates, or by establishing their own distribution networks in the United States.'[17] On the other hand, he pointed out that Carlos Castano, who heads the paramilitary umbrella group, the AUC (United Self-Defence Forces of Colombia), is a 'major cocaine trafficker in his own right' and has close links to the North Valley drug syndicate which is 'among the most powerful drug trafficking groups in Colombia'. Donnie Marshall, the former Administrator of the DEA, also confirmed that right-wing paramilitary groups 'raise funds through extortion, or by protecting laboratory operations in northern and central Colombia. The Carlos Castano organization and possibly other paramilitary groups appear to be directly involved in processing cocaine. At least one of these paramilitary groups appears to be involved in exporting cocaine from Colombia.'[18] Marshall concluded that 'at present, there is no corroborated information that the FARC is involved directly in the shipment of drugs from Colombia to international markets'.

Klaus Nyholm, the Director of the United Nations Drug Control Programme (UNDCP), has pointed out that the 'guerrillas are something different than the traffickers, the local fronts are quite autonomous. But in some areas, they're not involved at all. And in others, they actively tell the farmers not to grow coca'.[19] In the rebels' former Demilitarised Zone, Nyholm stated, 'drug cultivation has not increased or decreased' once the 'FARC took control'. Indeed, Nyholm noted in 1999 that the FARC were cooperating with a $6 million UN project to replace coca crops with new forms of legal alternative development.[20] And he recently went so far as to say that

> the paramilitary relation with drug trafficking undoubtedly is much more intimate [than the FARC's].... Many of the paramilitary bands started as the drug traffickers' hired guns. They are more autonomous now, but have maintained their close relations with the drug traffickers. In some of the coastal towns it can, in fact, sometimes be hard to tell whether a man is a paramilitary chief, a big coca planter, a cocaine lab owner, a rancher, or a local politician. He may be all five things at a time'.[21]

Clearly, the FARC are bit players in comparison to the paramilitary networks and the cocaine barons that these paramilitaries protect. So why, with the both the US and the UN anti-drug agencies consistently reporting over a number of years that the paramilitaries are far more heavily involved than the FARC in drug cultivation, refinement and transhipment to the US, has Plan Colombia emphasized the FARC's alleged links to international drug trafficking? The reason is quite simply that paramilitaries have long been central to the operation of US-backed Colombian counterinsurgency and terrorocracy. Going all the way back to William Yarborough's call in 1962 for an integrated paramilitary network, the US has been instrumental in setting up and perpetuating the paramilitary networks that are responsible for the vast majority of human rights abuses committed in Colombia today, the victims primarily being trade unionists, journalists, teachers, human rights workers and the poor.[22]

Crucial to this was a US-led reorganization of Colombia's military intelligence in 1991, with the help of US Department of Defence and CIA advisers in Colombia. Human Rights Watch obtained a copy of the official Colombian government order authorizing this secret reorganisation, and it was confirmed as authentic by the then Colombian Defense Minister, Rafael Pardo.[23] The order said nothing about aiding the Colombian military in counter-narcotics efforts. Instead it focused solely on combating what was called 'escalating terrorism by armed subversion' through the creation of what Human Rights Watch characterised as a 'secret network that relied on paramilitaries not only for intelligence, but to carry out murder'.[24] The reorganisation further incorporated the paramilitary networks within Colombia's military whilst making this relationship harder to track. For example, the order stated that all 'written material' was to be 'removed' and any 'open contacts and interaction with military installations' was to be avoided by paramilitaries. The handling of the networks was to be conducted covertly which allowed for the 'necessary flexibility to cover targets of interest'. Human Rights Watch noted that once this secret reorganisation of Colombian military intelligence was complete, paramilitary violence 'dramatically increased'.

By thus facilitating the incorporation of the principal paramilitary terrorist networks into the prevailing Colombian CI strategy, the US sought to obscure the linkages further by making the relationship more covert – this despite the US State Department's admission that the paramilitaries are essentially 'a mercenary vigilante force, financed by criminal activities' and the paid private army of 'narcotics traffickers or large landowners'.[25] Paramilitary involvement in narcotics quite clearly takes a back-seat in relation to the overriding priority of the US: the destruction of the FARC and the maintenance of terrorocracy so as to insulate the Colombian political system from democratic pressures. In a moment of candour, Carlos Castano, the head of the paramilitary AUC already mentioned above, not only conceded that drug trafficking and drug traffickers financed 70 per cent of his organization's operations, but boasted that his paramilitaries 'have always proclaimed that we are the defenders of business freedom and of the national and international industrial sectors.'[26]

The explicit counter-terror orientation of US policy in the aftermath of September 11th has led to a shift from the language of counter-narcotics to counter-terrorism to justify US CI operations in Colombia. US Attorney General John Ashcroft now designated the FARC the 'most dangerous international terrorist group based in the Western Hemisphere'.[27] And US Senator John McCain argued that 'American policy has dispensed with the illusion that the Colombian government is fighting two separate wars, one against drug trafficking and another against domestic terrorists.' The US, he said, had abandoned 'any fictional distinctions between counter-narcotic and counter-insurgency operations'.[28] The Bush administration's 2003 aid package for the Colombian military, the Andean Regional Initiative (ARI), allocated approximately $538 million for 2003. Tellingly, the ARI also contains a component that will send $98 million to a new 4,000 strong Colombian military unit trained to protect the Caño Limón pipeline owned by the US multinational oil corporation, Occidental Petroleum.

Both the new US discourse and increased military aid, despite the ongoing and widespread collaboration between the Colombian military and their paramilitary allies, flies brazenly in the face of Amnesty International's compelling documentation of the long-standing collusion between paramilitary forces and the Colombian military whereby in 'areas of long-standing paramilitary activity, reliable and abundant information shows that the security forces continued to allow paramilitary operations with little or no evidence of actions taken to curtail such activity'. One Colombian military unit set up specifically to deal with paramilitarism was no more than a 'paper tiger', Amnesty noted, and called the official Colombian government office that allegedly monitors paramilitary massacres 'a public relations mouthpiece for the government'.[29]

Colombia's new hard-line President, Alvaro Uribe, has begun to negotiate with the paramilitaries so as to grant them a general amnesty and incorporate them more overtly into the Colombian military. Uribe's negotiations with the AUC are ongoing, and he has put a bill before the Colombian Congress that will allow paramilitary leaders to buy themselves immunity from punishment for human rights abuses. According to Human Rights Watch, this 'amnesty bill' essentially amounts to 'checkbook impunity'.[30] The UN High Commissioner for Human Rights has also condemned the bill and argued that it 'opens the door to impunity' as it 'voids prison sentences by allowing responsible parties to avoid spending a single day in jail'.[31] Yet Uribe's policies have been endorsed by the US. Secretary of State Colin Powell has declared that the US is 'firmly committed to President Uribe and his new national security strategy,' pledging that the Bush administration would work 'with our Congress to provide additional funding for Colombia.'[32] Gordon Sumner, who was formerly President Reagan's special envoy to Latin America, stated bluntly the best way to get around the public relations problem presented by Uribe's amnesty bill: 'First, have them answer the law, cut out the drugs, and embrace human rights', then try to 'bring them under the tent, to fight against the guerrillas, who are the biggest threat'. In Colombia, he said, the 'battle is never too crowded with friends'.[33]

THE POLITICAL ECONOMY OF
COUNTERINSURGENCY IN COLOMBIA

The US CI intervention in Colombia cannot be separated from a wider set of regional US economic, strategic and political considerations that transcend conventional juridical definitions of sovereignty. The interlocking ties between US and Colombian capital have depended on the maintenance of a favourable investment climate, unhindered market access and the repatriation of profit by US-transnationals. This interwoven nature of the political economy of US and Latin American markets figures prominently in the thinking of US military planners. For example, General Peter Pace, the Commander in Chief of the US's Southern Command (USSOUTHCOM) under the Clinton Administration, and thus responsible for implementing US security assistance programs throughout Latin America, argued that vital US national interests, which he defined as 'those of broad, over-riding importance to the survival, safety and vitality of our nation,' included the maintenance of stability and unhindered access to Latin American markets by US transnationals in the post-Cold War period. Noting that 'our trade within the Americas represents approximately 46 per cent of all US exports, and we expect this percentage to increase in the future', Pace went on to explain that underlying the US military's role in Colombia was the need to maintain a 'continued stability required for access to markets ... which is critical to the continued economic expansion and prosperity of the United States'. US security assistance to the Colombian military was necessary because any 'loss of our Caribbean and Latin American markets would seriously damage the health of the US economy'.[34]

The current Commander in Chief of USSOUTHCOM, General James T. Hill, has taken the same position. He has stated that the 'US conducts more than 360 billion dollars of annual trade with Latin America and the Caribbean, nearly as much as with the entire European Community,' and added that by the year 2010 'trade with Latin America is expected to exceed that with the European Economic Community and Japan combined ... these links will only grow as we progress toward the President's vision of a Free Trade Agreement of the Americas'.[35] In this context, General Hill outlined the utility of the Southern Command's 'security cooperation activities' which were designed to expand US 'influence, assure friends, and dissuade potential adversaries' whilst promoting stability 'through training, equipping, and developing allied security force capabilities'. Notably, Hill argued that 'Southern Command will play a crucial role in developing the kinds of security forces that help provide the ability to govern throughout the region, and particularly in Colombia'.

All this makes it abundantly clear that US security assistance to Colombia serves a broader agenda for capitalist stability in South America. The principal non-state threat to this is the Colombian insurgency. Stability therefore requires the eradication of this threat. Marc Grossman, US Undersecretary of State for Political Affairs, underscored the crucial role that economic interests play in driving US intervention in Colombia, when he stated that the Colombian insurgents

> represent a danger to the $4.3 billion in direct U.S. investment in Colombia. They regularly attack U.S. interests, including the railway used by the Drummond Coal Mining facility and Occidental Petroleum's stake in the Caño Limón oil pipeline. Terrorist attacks on the Caño Limón pipeline also pose a threat to U.S. energy security.

Colombia supplied 3% of U.S. oil imports in 2001, and possesses substantial potential oil and natural gas reserves.[36]

Colombia is now the US's seventh largest oil supplier and has discovered vast oil reserves within its territory.[37] Brent Scowcroft, a former US National Security Adviser, has argued that 'Colombia's oil reserves of 2.6 billion barrels – only slightly less than OPEC members Qatar, Indonesia and Algeria – could serve as a major energy source, but will remain untapped unless stability is restored'.[38] Perhaps even more important is the fear that instability in Colombia threatens regional stability, and in particular Colombia's neighbour Venezuela. Republican Senator Paul D. Coverdell explicitly explains the regional focus of US intervention in Colombia in terms of the possibility that the 'destabilization of Colombia' could directly affect

> bordering Venezuela, now generally regarded as our largest oil supplier. In fact, the oil picture in Latin America is strikingly similar to that of the Middle East, except that Colombia provides us more oil today than Kuwait did then. This crisis, like the one in Kuwait, threatens to spill over into many nations, all of which are allies.[39]

The wider strategic considerations that link counterinsurgency in Colombia to US access to South American oil grow out of fears of regional instability generated by the FARC. General Pace had already made this clear before the election of George W. Bush, let alone September 11. He started by explaining how important South American oil is to the US, arguing that there is a 'common misperception' that the US 'is completely dependent on the Middle East' for oil, when in fact Venezuela provides '15%–19% of our imported oil in any given month'. Pace then went on to note that the 'internal conflict in Colombia poses a direct threat to regional stability' and US oil interests, with 'Venezuela, Ecuador, and Panama' the 'most vulnerable to destabilization due to Colombian insurgent activity along their borders'.[40] Of course, unhindered access to South American oil became an even more pressing concern for US planners after the September 11th attacks, and this concern can only increase in the context of the continuing instability generated by the Anglo-American occupation of Iraq. The US Ambassador to Colombia, Anne Patterson, explained that 'after September 11, the issue of oil security has become a priority for the United States', especially as the 'traditional oil sources for the United States' in the Middle East have become even 'less secure'. By sourcing US energy needs from Colombia, which 'after Mexico and Venezuela' is 'the most important oil country in the region', the US would have 'a small margin to work with' in the face of a crisis and could 'avoid [oil] price speculation'.[41]

The centrality of US oil concerns in Colombia has been illustrated clearly by the Bush administration's request for $98 million for the specially trained Colombian military CI brigade, mentioned before, as part of the Andean Regional Initiative. Unlike the more generic Colombian CI brigades, this brigade will be devoted solely to protecting the US multinational Occidental Petroleum's 500-mile long Cano Limon oil pipeline in Colombia.[42] US Secretary of State Colin Powell explained that the money will be used to 'train and equip two brigades of the Colombian armed forces to protect the pipeline' to prevent rebel attacks which are 'depriving us of a source of petroleum'.[43] Acknowledging that the money involved had nothing to do with the war on drugs, Ambassador Patterson said bluntly: 'it is something that we must do' because it is 'important for the future of the country, for our oil sources and for the confidence of our investors'.[44]

This new security arrangement between the US, Colombian CI brigades and US oil transnationals essentially makes official what has been a long-standing relationship. In December 1998, for example, US mercenaries working for the US security company Airscan (which has managed the protection of Occidental Petroleum's pipelines in Colombia since 1997) were involved in planning a Colombian military attack on an alleged FARC column near the community of Santa Domingo in Colombia's Arauca region. During the attack a Colombian air force helicopter dropped a bomb on the community; it killed eighteen civilians, including nine children (no FARC rebels were killed).[45] In their testimony to Colombian investigators of the incident, the helicopter pilots stated that the operations were planned at Occidental's facilities.[46] (British Petroleum also financed paramilitaries in Colombia to protect its oil pipelines, and was condemned for this by the European Parliament in 1998.)[47] The special pipeline CI brigade will thus formalise this longstanding and intimate relationship, and will use the so-called 'counter-narcotics' brigades for the protection of the sectoral interests of the transnational oil companies. Bush himself made this clear when he stated in 2003 that 'the budget will extend the reach of counter-narcotics brigades in southern Colombia while beginning training of new units to protect the country's economic lifeline, an oil pipeline. In 2001, Colombia was the source of about two percent of US oil imports, creating a mutual interest in protecting this economic asset'.[48] In sum, the destabilising presence of the FARC and the ELN combined with their bombings of the pipelines of the large oil transnationals has necessitated the elimination of these groups so as to guarantee a relatively unhindered source of non-Middle Eastern oil.

THE CURRENT SITUATION

The Colombian state remains firmly wedded to the implementation of neo-liberal reforms, and the increasing militarization of social life under the pretext of a 'war on terror'. The reforms are pushing more of Colombia's people into poverty. In 1999, at the inception of Plan Colombia, the World Bank noted that 'more than half of Colombians [were] living in poverty … the proportion of poor [has] returned to its 1988 level, after having declined by 20 percentage points between 1978 and 1995.' The recession of the mid-1990s added to Colombia's woes and contributed to 'a rise in inequality, a decline in macroeconomic performance, and a doubling in unemployment'.[49] The picture is less bleak for Colombia's elites. In 1990 the ratio of income between the poorest and richest 10 per cent was 40:1. After a decade of economic restructuring this reached 80:1 in 2000.[50]

Under Uribe Colombia is undergoing further IMF structural adjustment in the interests of transnational corporations. In the oil industry, for example, Uribe is lowering the royalties paid to Colombia by foreign oil companies and has effectively privatized the state-owned oil company, Ecopetrol. Uribe argued that this was necessary in order to make Colombia internationally 'competitive' and to prevent it becoming a net importer of oil. Meanwhile, Colombia's oil regions are becoming fully militarized, with the paramilitaries effectively running a number of towns. This model of what Uribe euphemistically terms 'Democratic Security' is being rolled out across Colombia as an integral part of the joint US-Colombia militarization program.[51]

Given the ongoing difficulties in maintaining the occupation of Iraq, there is every reason to assume that Colombia and Venezuela will become increasingly important to US oil needs, leading to further militarization, with Uribe's Colombia increasingly acting as a base for destabilization directed against Hugo Chavez's government in Venezuela.[52] Amidst these developments the Bush Administration is looking to increase its support for the Colombian state by seeking to raise the number of US troops stationed there whilst maintaining the very high levels of military assistance.[53] There is no reason to assume that a Democratic administration under John Kerry would follow a different path, given his wholehearted endorsement of Bush's 'war on terror' and his hard-line condemnation of Chavez as a dictator.[54]

On the other hand the FARC remain a formidable military force in Colombia, Uribe's security reforms having failed to deal the guerrillas any significant military blow. The FARC has not yet been weakened to the point where they can be drawn in to a peace process which ends the war but leaves intact the existing unequal economic and social structures. In short, there is a deadlock between the CI strategy of the US-backed Colombian state and the guerrillas, which in the absence of any political process or redistributive economic reforms continues to contribute to the suffering of Colombia's civilian population.

NOTES

This essay draws on my research for my forthcoming book, *America's Other War: Terrorizing Colombia*, London: Zed Books, 2004.

1   George Kennan, quoted in David F. Schmitz, *Thank God They're On Our Side. The United States & Right-Wing Dictatorships 1921-1965*, Chapel Hill: The University of North Carolina Press, 1999, p. 149. The same tone was sounded in the closing years of the Cold War, as in Alexander M. Haig, Jr., *Caveat: Realism, Reagan, and Foreign Policy*, New York: Macmillan, 1984. For a good general picture, see Lars Schoultz, *Beneath the United States: A History of US Policy Toward Latin America*, London: Harvard University Press, 1998.

2   Human Rights Watch, *Colombia*, undated http://www.hrw.org/americas/colombia.php. On the extent of current US military aid, see Frances Robles, 'US Restates Its Support of Colombia: Rumsfeld Sees Progress by the Military', *Miami Herald*, 20 August 2003, http://www.miami.com/mld/miamiherald/6572125.htm.

3   See William Robinson's excellent *Promoting Polyarchy: Globalization, US Intervention, and Hegemony*, Cambridge: Cambridge University Press, 1996.

4   David Harvey, *The New Imperialism*, Oxford: Oxford University Press, 2003, p. 39.

5   Mr Roy Rubottom, 'Subject: President Lleras' Appeal For Aid In Suppressing Colombian Guerrilla Warfare Activities', 21 July 1959, http://www.icdc.com/~paulwolf/colombia/rubottom21jul1959a.jpg.

6   Stephen J. Randall, *Colombia and the United States: Hegemony and Interdependence*, Georgia: University of Georgia Press, 1992, p. 241.

7   US Department of State, 'Preliminary Report, Colombia Survey Team, Colonel Lansdale', 23 February 1960, http://www.icdc.com/~paulwolf/colombia/ lansdale23feb1960a.jpg.

8   US Department of the Army, 'Stability Operations-Intelligence', FM 30-21, 1970, pp. 73-78.

9   US Department of the Army, 'Stability Operations-Intelligence: Appendix E', FM 30-21, 1970, pp. E1-E7.

10   William Yarborough, Headquarters United States Army Special Warfare Center, 'Subject: Visit to Colombia, South America, by a Team From Special Warfare Center, Fort Bragg. Supplement, Colombian Survey Report', February 26, 1962, http://www.icdc.com/~paulwolf/colombia/surveyteam26feb1962.htm.

11   My detailed analysis of the OPD will be forthcoming in 2005 as 'Gluing the Hats On: Power, Agency and Reagan's Office of Public Diplomacy' in *International Relations*.

12   'Public Diplomacy Strategy Paper', May, 1983, p. 11, located in the National Security Archive, 'Public Diplomacy and Covert Propaganda: the Declassified

Record of Ambassador Otto Reich', http://www.gwu.edu/~nsarchiv/NSAEBB/NSAEBB40/.

13   *Public Diplomacy Action Plan: Support for the White House Educational Campaign*,12 March 1985, pp. 1-4.

14   John Waghelstein, 'A Latin-American Insurgency Status Report', *Military Review,* LXVII(2), February, 1987, available at http://www.leavenworth.army.mil/milrev/.

15   Cass Ballanger, *US Policy Toward Colombia*, House of Representatives, Subcommittee on the Western Hemisphere, Washington DC., 11 April 2002, p. 5.

16   Center for International Policy, *The 'War on Drugs' Meets the 'War on Terror'*, February, 2003, http://ciponline.org/colombia/0302ipr.htm.

17   James Milford, DEA Congressional Testimony, House International Relations Committee, Subcommittee on the Western Hemisphere, July 16, 1997, http://www.usdoj.gov/dea/pubs/cngrtest/ct970716.htm.

18   DEA Congressional Testimony, *Statement of Donnie R. Marshall*, Senate Caucus on International Narcotics Control, February 28, 2001, http://www.usdoj.gov/dea/pubs/cngrtest/ct022801.htm.

19   *The Washington Post*, 10 April 2000.

20   *Associated Press*, 6 August 1999.

21   Correspondence conducted by author with Klaus Nyholm, 23 January 2003.

22   Human Rights Watch, *The 'Sixth Division': Military-paramilitary Ties and US Policy in Colombia*, Washington: Human Rights Watch, 2001. There are numerous human rights reports that confirm the role of paramilitaries in Colombia's ongoing war against dissent.

23   See Human Rights Watch/Americas Human Rights Watch Arms Project, *Colombia's Killer Networks: the Military-Paramilitary Partnership and the United States,* London: Human Rights Watch, 1996, pp. 28-30. The original documents of the order are presented in both Spanish and English at pp. 105-150.

24   Human Rights Watch, *Colombia's Killer Networks*, p. 38-39.

25   State Department Human Rights Report, *Colombia: Country Reports on Human Rights Practices*, 2001, http://www.state.gov/g/drl/rls/hrrpt/2001/wha/8326.htm.

26   This was reported on 6 September 2000 by *Reuters* and *CNN*, http://www.cnn.com/2000/WORLD/americas/09/06/colombia.paramilitary.reut/.

27   John Ashcroft, *Prepared Remarks of Attorney General John Ashcroft*, Drug Enforcement Administration, 19 March 2002, http://www.ciponline.org/colombia/02031903.htm.

28   John McCain, *Speech by Senator John McCain (R-Arizona)*, 6 June 2002, http://www.ciponline.org/colombia/02060604.htm.

29   Amnesty International USA, *Human Rights and USA Military Aid to Colombia* II, January, 2001, http://web.amnesty.org/ai.nsf/Recent/ AMR230042001!Open.

30   Human Rights Watch, *Colombia's Checkbook Impunity*, 22 September 2003, http://hrw.org/backgrounder/americas/checkbook-impunity.htm.

31   UN High Commissioner for Human Rights Bogotá Field Office, *Observaciones al Proyecto de Ley Estatutaria que trata sobre la reincorporacion de miembros de grupos armados*, Bogotá: UNHCHR, 2003.

32   Powell quote taken from Steven R. Weisman, 'Powell Says US Will Increase Military Aid For Colombia', *The New York Times*, 5 Dec 2002.

33   Gordon Sumner quote from Steve Salisbury, 'Colombia War Takes Right Turn', *Washington Times*, 28 Jan 2003.

34   Peter Pace, *Advance Questions for Lieutenant General Peter Pace. Defense Reforms*, United States Senate Committee on Armed Services, 2000, http://www.senate.gov/~armed_services/statemnt/2000/000906pp. pdf.

35   James T. Hill, *Posture Statement*, US Southern Command, House Armed Services Committee, 12 March 2003, http://www.house.gov/hasc/openingstatementsandpressreleases/108thcongress/03-03-12hill.html.

36   Marc Grossman, *Testimony of Ambassador Marc Grossman before the House Appropriations Committee's Subcommittee on Foreign Operations*, 10 April 2002, http://www.ciponline.org/colombia/02041001.htm.

37   Donald E, Schulz, *The United States and Latin America: Shaping an Elusive Future*, Carlisle PA: Strategic Studies Institute, 2000, p. 3.

38   Brent Scowcroft and Bob Graham, 'Quick Aid to Colombia – For Our Sake', *Los Angeles Times*, 26 April 2000.

39   *Washington Post*, 10 April 2000.

40   Peter Pace, *Advance Questions for Lieutenant General Peter Pace. Defense Reforms*, United States Senate Committee on Armed Services, 2000, http://www.senate.gov/~armed_services/statemnt/2000/000906pp. pdf.

41   *El Tiempo*, 10 February 2002, http://www.amazonwatch.org/newsroom/mediaclips02/col/020210_col_et.html.

42   *Christian Science Monitor*, 5 March 2002.

43   House Appropriations Committee, *Secretary of State Colin Powell before the Foreign Operations Subcommittee*, 12 February 2002.

44   *El Tiempo*, 10 February, 2002.

45   Rainforest Action Network, 'Oxy's Cozy Relationship with Colombian Military Turns Fatal', 25 June 2001, http://www.amazonwatch.org/newsroom/newsreleases01/june2501_oxy.html.

46   Stratfor, 'U.S. Pressures Colombia Over Human Rights Violations', 15 January 2003, http://www.stratfor.biz/Story.neo?storyId=209166.

47   Human Rights Watch, *Corporations and Human Rights*, undated, http://www.hrw.org/about/initiatives/corp.html.

48   George Bush, *President's Budget Message on Andean Counterdrug Initiative*, Washington, US Department of State, 4 February 2002, http://usinfo.state.gov/regional/ar/colombia/andean04.htm.

49   Carlos Velez, *Colombia Poverty Report, Volume 1,* Washington: The World Bank, March, 2002.

50   Mario Novelli, 'Globalisations, Social Movement Unionism and New Internationalisms: The Role of Strategic Learning in the Transformation of the Municipal Workers Union of EMCALI', forthcoming in *Globalization, Education, Societies*.

51   *Colombia Journal*, 10 May 2004; See also BBC Website, 6 May 2002, http://news.bbc.co.uk/2/hi/americas/3683851.stm.

52   *Bloomberg*, 12 May 2004; See also *BBC*, 13 May 2004, http://news.bbc.co.uk/2/hi/americas/3709609.stm.

53   Transcript, hearing of the Senate Armed Services Committee: 'Fiscal Year 2005 National Defense Authorization budget request', 1 April 2004.

54   *Business Wire*, 5 May 2004.

'SIGNS OF THE TIMES': CAPITALISM, COMPETITIVENESS, AND THE NEW FACE OF EMPIRE IN LATIN AMERICA

PAUL CAMMACK

Signs of the times: over lunch on 11 June 2004, Anoop Singh, Director of the IMF's Western Hemisphere Department, urged those present at an international seminar in Port-of-Spain, Trinidad and Tobago on 'Developmental Challenges Facing the Caribbean' to build local institutions 'to unleash the innovation and entrepreneurship that is so crucial to growth'.[1] His advocacy of strong domestic institutions to complement sound macroeconomic policy and flexible labour markets reflected the IMF's shift of focus in the late 1990s, under pressure from the World Bank, from 'adjustment' to competitiveness; and it prefaced a discussion, led by his colleague Sanjay Kathuria, of sources of growth and competitiveness in the region.[2] Just three days later, on 14 June, the second Latin American Competition Forum, sponsored jointly by the OECD and the Inter-American Development Bank (IDB), opened in Washington, DC. Over lunch there, the Keynote Speaker was former Mexican Minister of Foreign Affairs and Minister of Finance José Angel Gurria, of whom more below. In the afternoon, Frédéric Jenny, Chair of the OECD Competition Committee and former head of the French *Conseil de la Concurrence*, acted as an examiner in a peer review of Peru's competition law and policy. A private jet could have taken you on to the Eleventh UNCTAD meeting in Sao Paulo for the same evening – maybe in time to catch the UNCTAD/WTO International Trade Centre 'Competition Tools Fair' before it closed at six. The theme of the conference, designated by secretary-general Rubens Ricupero, was 'improving competitiveness and building capacity in the productive sector'.[3] The 'Sao Paulo Consensus', published in draft on 16 June, showed how far UNCTAD had moved over forty years from its roots in support for a New International Economic Order:

Improving competitiveness requires deliberate specific and transparent national policies to foster a systematic upgrading of domestic productive capabilities. Such policies cover a range of areas, including investment, enterprise development, technology, competition policy, skill formation, infrastructure development, the institutional aspects of building productive capacity, and policies that can contribute to the facilitation of sustained investment inflows, such as investment guarantee schemes and measures related to investment promotion and protection.[4]

Signs of the times, then: a chorus of voices across Latin America, crying 'Compete! Compete!'

The period between 11 March 1990, when Patricio Aylwin assumed office as President of Chile, and 1 January 2003, when Luis Inacio da Silva (Lula) became President of Brazil, witnessed a political revolution in Latin America, opening a new phase of class struggle in the region. It had its origins in the series of defeats inflicted on the left and the working class in the 1970s and 1980s, among which the crushing of Allende's socialist project in Chile and the subsequent foundation of a neoliberal regime under Pinochet was decisive. This critical defeat for the left was a crucial turning point, paving the way for bourgeois hegemony in Chile, and impacting negatively on the balance of class forces across the rest of the region. The wave of struggles to which it gave rise is continuing, with the outcome in the balance. In order to address the novel conjuncture depicted above, this essay steps aside from debates about US empire to explore aspects of the 'internal reorganization' of Latin American states between 1990 and the present. It detects a change in the relationship between 'imperialist' and 'dominated' countries precisely as a consequence of the internalization of the imperatives of international competition, and the emergence of a new bourgeois project. Empire has a new face in the region: it systematically promotes competitiveness, and directly supports the creation of conditions for local accumulation. This agenda is driven as much by the US as by other imperialist powers, but it brings specific contradictions in US relations with the region to the fore and subjects it to challenge, making American leadership of the imperialist bloc problematic.

To address these issues, the principal focus here shifts away from the debate over inter-imperialist rivalry versus joint imperialist control to the ruling-class projects emerging in the dominated countries themselves, seen in the light of Marx's 1867 preface to the first edition of *Capital*. To return to the suggestion there that 'the country that is more developed industrially only shows, to the less developed, the image of its own future' may seem perverse. But to do so is not to negate either the subsequent history of uneven and combined development, or the historical and contemporary significance of imperialism as part of it. Rather, it is to read Marx's observation in its proper context as envisaging the reproduction across the world not of one industrial capitalism after another on the English model, but rather of the 'social antagonisms that spring from the natural laws of capitalist production' – this being the phrase immediately preceding it. Read in this way, the thought connects immediately with the idea of uneven and combined development outlined in the remaining few paragraphs of the preface. First, Marx asserts, Germany suffers 'not only from the development of capitalist production, but also from the incompleteness of that development';

> Alongside the modern evils, we are oppressed by a whole series of inherited evils, arising from the passive survival of archaic and outmoded modes of production, with their accompanying train of anachronistic social and political relations. We suffer not only from the living, but from the dead. Le mort saisit le vif!'[5]

Second, he suggests, once the 'palpably evident' process of transformation in England has reached a certain point, 'it must react on the Continent':

> There it will take a form more brutal or more humane, according to the degree of development of the working class itself. Apart from any higher motives, then, the most basic interests of the present ruling classes dictate to them that they clear out of the way all the legally removable obstacles to the development of the working class.[6]

Third, Marx notes reports that 'in Germany, in France, in short in all the civilized states of the European continent, a radical change in the existing relations between capital and labour is as evident and inevitable as in England', and he quotes US Vice-President Wade as declaring that 'after the abolition of slavery, a radical transformation in the existing relations of capital and landed property is on the agenda':

> These are signs of the times, not to be hidden by purple mantles or black cassocks. They do not signify that tomorrow a miracle will occur. They do show that, within the ruling classes themselves, the foreboding is emerging that the present society is no solid crystal, but an organism capable of change, and constantly engaged in the process of change.[7]

In this spirit, my focus is on some 'signs of the times' in Latin America and further afield. I shall not dwell on the long history of the 'inherited evils' of incomplete capitalist development in the region, except to note their impact on the capacity of the 'ruling class' either to exercise authority over local and foreign capitalists, or to build legitimacy in the eyes of the majority of the population. These twin indicators of the absence of bourgeois hegemony in the region have been much remarked upon, notably in Atilio Boron's dissection of the incapacity of contemporary rulers either to collect taxes from the wealthy or to 'provide the collective goods needed for the bare reproduction of civilized life'.[8] Taking as the starting-point the conclusion that this situation is problematic for Latin American ruling classes themselves, I point to evidence of an emphatic turn across the region to the systematic pursuit of international competitiveness as a response, and the opening up as a consequence of a new phase of class struggle. Taking a cue from Gregory Albo, I explore three aspects of the internal reorganization of the state in Latin America – the internalization of international competitiveness 'as a central objective to mediate between the territorialization of value production and increased dependence upon international circulation'; the pursuit of a 'redistributive strategy of competitive austerity'; and the 'internationalization of state apparatuses to mediate the extension and intensification of the world market' through regionalization and the liberal reform of global regulation.[9]

THE INTERNALIZATION OF INTERNATIONAL COMPETITIVENESS

Competition authorities have proliferated across the region over the last decade or so, as existing agencies have been revamped, and new ones created. As in other policy areas, the precursor was Pinochet's regime in Chile, with the December 1973 'Law for the Defence of Free Competition'. Argentina under Videla followed with the National Commission for the Defence of Competition in 1980, but the major wave has come in the context of democratic regimes in the 1990s. In 1992 the 'Law to Promote and Protect Free Competition' established the agency *Pro-Competencia* in Venezuela, and Indecopi (the Institute for the Defence of Competition and Intellectual Property) was founded in Peru; in 1993 the Federal Competition Commission was created in Mexico, and in the following year Brazil's 'Law for the Defence of Economic Order' restructured the 1962 Administrative Council for the Defence of the Economy, with the aim of 'protecting freedom of initiative and free competition in a special period of market opening, deregulation and privatisation'. Similar agencies were created across Central America from the mid-1990s, as a consequence of the 1994 Alliance for the Sustainable Development of Central America (ALIDES) – the most notable being the National Competitiveness Programme and the Presidential Competitiveness Commission created by President Bolaños in Nicaragua. The introduction of a new law in Argentina in 1999, to replace the existing National Commission with a National Tribunal for the Defence of Competition, completed a cycle of institutional innovation.

These innovations reflect a fundamental reorientation in the political economy of the region. In the wording of an official note in English from the government of Argentina:

> The new Competition Act was passed after the consolidation of the process of economic reforms intended to yield inflation control through the functioning of free market forces, gradual opening of the economy and privatization of state owned assets, in opposition to the 80's decade scenario of price control, trade barriers, and government enterprises, which made competition enforcement useless.[10]

The 1994 law in Brazil similarly reflected and extended the changed climate associated with the Real Plan, as noted in the Brazilian submission to the International Competition Network in 2003:

> Although Brazil has had an antitrust system for more than 30 years, it was only after all the necessary structural reforms had been implemented that it did in fact become operational. The reforms included trade liberalisation, privatisation and the creation of sectoral regulatory agencies, which made it possible to enforce competition rules.[11]

Along with the move away from the system of price controls in force under the previous military regime this new posture reflected Cardoso's identification of social democracy with 'knowing how to increase economic competitiveness, leading to increases in productivity and the rationalisation of the economy'.[12]

The same can be said for Mexico. A 2004 review of Mexico's legislation by the OECD Competition Committee hailed it as 'a product of technical expertise, rather than populist adventurism or political compromise', noting that in the past 'the traditional goal of Mexican competition policy was to eliminate the evils of private monopoly by instituting price control and state ownership'.[13] A parallel review for Chile paid homage to Pinochet, celebrating the country as 'a pioneer in the field of competition law and policy in South America since 1973 when the current law was adopted'. But it also recorded the alacrity with which Chile offered itself for peer review at the first Latin American Competition Forum in Paris in 2003, and detailed the incorporation into law in November 2003 of the review's recommendations. The strengthening of the National Economic Prosecutor's Office and of Anti-Trust provisions under President Lagos reflects the continuing consolidation of competition law under the socialist-led Concertación government, and the consolidated hegemony of 'competitive capitalism' across the political spectrum.[14]

How should we understand these developments? They clearly reflect the reform programme pressed on Latin American countries from Washington and elsewhere since the early 1990s. But they equally suggest the emergence of a new regional programme of capitalist modernization, intended to sweep away 'a whole series of inherited evils, arising from the passive survival of archaic and outmoded modes of production, with their accompanying train of anachronistic social and political relations'.

THE PURSUIT OF COMPETITIVE AUSTERITY

Current hyperactivity around the issue of competitiveness is demonstrably a reaction to the 'palpable evidence' of rapid development in East Asia and elsewhere, and the poor performance of the region in attracting and bene-fiting from foreign direct investment. The tone is set by Jeffrey Sachs and Joaquín Vial, who compare trajectories of economic progress and offer the judgement that 'Only Africa and some less-developed regions in Asia have performed as poorly as Latin America in the twentieth century'.[15] To judge by the IDB 2001 annual report on Economic and Social Progress in Latin America, entitled *Competitiveness: The Business of Growth*, competition fever is endemic across the whole region.[16] The report sounded the general alarm, in response to the recently emphasized low ranking of Latin American economies in the World Economic Forum's *Global Competitiveness Report*:

> In the 2001 edition, which includes 20 Latin American economies, nine of them for the first time, competitiveness is evaluated on the basis of the quality of the macroeconomic environment, the quality of public institutions, and technological capability. According to these indicators, most Latin American economies rank very low by inter-national comparison. Only Chile and Costa Rica are in positions above the median, while Latin American countries occupy seven of the lowest 11 positions worldwide.[17]

Even Chile, it should be noted, stood in 27th place, with Costa Rica 35th. In the light of these findings, IDB President Francisco Iglesias commissioned the chair of the Bank's External Advisory Group (EAG), none other than José Angel Gurria, to report on the future role of the IDB. The response was explicit:

> The EAG noted that when the IDB was founded forty-two years ago, the individual country's public sector was the dominant engine of growth and investment. Today the reverse is true: Private capital flows represent a large multiple of those which all public institutions combined can provide. Thus, the EAG recommends to significantly expand and augment the Bank's activities in support of the private sector. A second major theme is the EAG's urging of the Bank to help enhance national competitiveness and create a truly enabling envi-ronment for private and public investment in each individual country.

> A third theme is the very strong conclusion that the Bank should intensify its leadership and support of the process of integration and trade liberalization in Latin America and the Caribbean.[18]

The background document for the June 2004 UNCTAD XI session on economic development and capital accumulation similarly highlighted the success of a small number of developing countries, principally in East Asia, in integrating themselves into the global economy as exporters of manufactured goods, and the failure of Latin American countries to do likewise. The verdict was that adjustment policies had been detrimental to 'market-led development based on international competition' and that the record of investment and growth had consequently been 'dismal'. 'Economic policy in Latin America', it concluded, 'has been focusing on international investors rather than on domestic entrepreneurs, whereas the opposite was the case in East Asia'. The upshot was a 'second-generation' focus on the micro-economics as well as the macro-economics of reform, a plea for sequencing and relief from external debt, and a central focus on competitiveness:

> If it is true that labour and – to a very large extent – capital remain in the realm of national Governments, it is obvious that globalization has not reduced at all the need to act at the national level; it may even have increased that need. The smoothing of the adjustment process to more open markets has to be managed by the State, and the maintenance of overall competitiveness of an economy is more than ever before the responsibility of national Governments. By managing competitiveness, national Governments, through the adjustment of nominal wages to productivity or by influencing the movements of the exchange rate, create the conditions for national policy space because they reduce the dependence on foreign capital. If Governments can avoid a dramatic deterioration in the international competitiveness of a large number of domestic companies, the gains resulting from a favourable investment climate in terms of lower interest rates and higher profits may outweigh by far the losses resulting from lower inflows of foreign capital and higher imports.[19]

Labour market reform is an essential element of this strategy, and its principal objective, as elsewhere, is the creation of a 'flexible' labour force. The distinctive feature of the policy now propagated in the region is the switch it advocates from the extraction of absolute surplus value to relative surplus value. The IDB *Competitiveness* report is explicit on this point:

> No productive sector can expect its competitiveness to be based on diminishing the well being of its workers. Even in the most labor-intensive sectors, the possibility of competing and expanding depends not on workers' salaries but on unit labor costs; that is to say, on the

combination of the effective cost per worker and the productivity of labor. In many countries of Latin America, the effective cost per worker could be reduced without sacrificing the well being of workers because legislation provides for excessive mandatory benefits that are costly for firms but of little utility to the workers they supposedly aim to help. Legislation also imposes high firing costs that reduce employment, especially for the youngest workers, and minimum wages that in some countries are excessive for the productivity of the least-skilled workers, thus limiting their possibilities for employment.[20]

A decade ago, such an argument might have appeared a cynical cover for a policy of exploitation of low-cost unskilled labour. But the terms in which ECLAC currently makes the same argument suggest that this is not the case today. Its annual survey, *Foreign Investment in Latin America and the Caribbean, 2003*, describes the steady decline of net FDI inflows from a peak of US$78bn in 2000 to an estimated US$36bn by 2003 as 'the worst performance of any world region'. It then sharply questions the supposed benefits of current patterns of foreign investment: in natural resources it tends not to generate spillover effects throughout the economy; in markets for services it is not internationally competitive and is in sharp decline; in the automobile industry it is failing to generate thriving local supply chains; and in low-cost export platforms comparative advantage is being lost as the US market opens up to new competitors:

> most countries have found that this model is based on unsustainable incentives and that it locks them into a low-value-added trap that has not permitted any significant kind of industrial or technological upgrading. The result has been illusory rather than authentic competitiveness.[21]

The resulting call for proactive productive development strategies is expanded upon in ECLAC's proposal, published ahead of its 30th session of meetings in San Juan, Puerto Rico, in June-July 2004, for 'productive development in open economies'. The volume, launched in advance of the meeting to form the centrepiece of discussions, acknowledges the centrality of the productivity and competition agendas, and the concomitant call for flexible labour markets. But it calls for a switch from the 'flexinsecurity' associated with the combination of limited security in the formal sector and large-scale, unregulated insecurity in the informal sector to a modernized policy of 'flexsecurity'. The 'positive and reasonable flexibilisation with social protection' that ECLAC recommends is supported by an analysis that is entirely consistent with the 'sustainable neoliberalism' of the post-Washington consensus – the inevitability and desirability of risk in a modern competitive economy, and hence the need to provide rational frameworks for its management in ways that nurture long-term efficiency and productivity. To back it up, it offers a programme of productive transformation and formalization of the informal sector, allied to education and training (in other words the transition from informality to flexibility).[22] IDB endorsement of this agenda is to be expected. But on this evidence, UNCTAD and ECLAC are just as convinced that 'the most basic interests of the present ruling classes dictate to them that they clear out of the way all the legally removable obstacles to the development of the working class'.

THE INTERNATIONALIZATION OF STATE APPARATUSES

The international organizations profiled above – from the IMF, the World Bank, the OECD and the EU to UNCTAD, the IDB and ECLAC – are engaged in a shared project, the core of which is the aspiration to build 'competition cultures' at global and regional levels. The striking features of the process are its universality and synchronicity, and the extent to which it reflects a commitment on the part of organizations dominated by or representative of advanced capitalist states to building such cultures *throughout* the global system of states. The European Union adopted the 'Lisbon strategy' in 2000, committing it to make the EU 'the world's most dynamic and competitive economy' by 2010.[23] The promotion of competitiveness within current member states and enlargement towards Eastern Europe were key components of the strategy. It is just as committed to the promotion of competitiveness elsewhere. In April 2002 the Commission's regional strategy document for Latin America was presented by EU Commissioner for External Affairs Chris Patten as 'helping the Latin American countries to face up to the double challenge of economic transformation which will make their economies more competitive while at the same time ensuring the stability of the democratic institutions and the modernisation of government administration'.[24] Successive EU-LAC summits, the third and most recent in Guadalajara, Mexico, in May 2004, have driven this agenda forward. Building competitiveness and competition cultures has become a global enterprise, as the Latin American Competition Forums – an initiative supported by the EU, the OECD and the IDB – demonstrate.

This is not reckoned to be an easy task. Brazil's competition authorities report 'the strong belief shared by Brazilian consumers, that controlled prices were fair prices and, thus, better than those that result from a competitive environment', and detail their efforts at 'disseminating the value of competition within the government and throughout the Brazilian civil society'.[25] On similar lines, the OECD review of competition law and policy in Mexico recalls that in 1998 the Federal Commission 'had no program to explain the benefits of competition and competition law enforcement to consumers', and recommends the development of a base of support for competition policy.[26] Even in the Chilean case, the OECD finds the advocacy of competition across different policy areas and in the public arena deficient:

> Although the Prosecutor's Office must of course take into account the likely costs of competition advocacy, the lack of a more active programme could also be costly. The competition institutions are not well known in Chile, and although market liberalism seems more firmly established in Chile than in many Latin American countries, it faces continuing challenges in that many consumers are not aware of the benefits of competition and of avoiding unnecessary regulatory restrictions on competition, while some academics and business representatives seem to prefer a more laissez-faire approach.[27]

Competition advocacy was a central theme at the first three annual conferences of the International Competition Network (held in Naples in 2002, in Mérida, Mexico in 2003, and Seoul in 2004). The second Latin American Competition Forum also took 'competition advocacy' as its theme, and experts assembled from Europe and Latin America to address the issue of embedding the competition culture across the region. The OECD Secretariat dwelt on the need for an independent and adequately resourced agency well embedded in the overall structure of government, and argued that the factors feeding into effective action were 'fundamentally linked to the competition culture in the country and whether the competition institutions, the competition rules and competition as such have backing from the political level and from the society as a whole'. It urged participants to explore ways in which private actors could be encouraged to pursue remedies to competition law violations and to strengthen competition agencies in relation to investigating possible infringements, sanctioning and remedying anti-competitive behaviour, and advocating for pro-competitive reform.[28] On the following day, OECD Consultant John Clark stressed the need for competition authorities to assume the role of competition advocate, 'acting proactively to bring about government policies that lower barriers to entry, promote deregulation and trade liberalization, and otherwise minimize unnecessary government intervention in the marketplace', and recommended the International Competition Network's 'Toolkit for Competition Advocacy' for the purpose. He then turned to 'building a competition culture', defined as 'an understanding by the public of the benefits of competition and broad-based support for a strong competition policy':

> Building a competition culture is important in every country, but once again it seems that it is especially critical for developing countries.

> There is more education to be done in these countries because, in most cases, the public has not been heavily exposed to competition and competitive markets.[29]

Here, then, were competition experts from Europe coaching their Latin American counterparts not only in the promotion of competition, but also in the construction of hegemonic strategies around it − and in the process creating new competitors for themselves. Another sign of the times, suggesting that 'within the ruling classes themselves, the foreboding is emerging that the present society is no solid crystal, but an organism capable of change, and constantly engaged in the process of change' − and even that a radical transformation in relations between dominant and subordinated states, in the interest of promoting universal capitalist development and bourgeois hegemony, is on the agenda.

THE NEW FACE OF EMPIRE IN LATIN AMERICA

The preceding sections document the emergence across Latin America of a series of national, regional and international projects aimed at 'market-led development based on international competition', going beyond the adjustment-oriented strategies promoted by the IMF in the early 1990s and seeking unequivocally to internalize at a national level the logic of capitalist reproduction and bourgeois hegemony. Among other things, of course, they emphatically confirm the centrality of the state to the reproduction of contemporary capitalism. At the same time they are supported and promoted by a range of international institutions, with the European Union playing a significant role. The striking feature of the overarching project they reflect is that it is aimed at generalising capitalist social relations across the whole of the world market, and at the same time containing the antagonisms inherent in them.[30]

Such a project does not obliterate the history or contemporary reality of imperialism. But it suggests that as the world market nears completion, the global dynamics of competitive capitalism drive the imperialist powers to support the creation of bourgeoisies around the world capable of exercising hegemony, rather than maintain pre-capitalist ruling elites − in effect, to create competitors for themselves. I have argued elsewhere that it is precisely this that is the logic of 'global governance'.[31] In particular, the 'Wolfensohn-Stiglitz project' spear-headed by the World Bank and the partially-reformed IMF is focused explicitly on building institutions that will sustain local accumulation, competitiveness, and bourgeois hegemony.[32] In Latin America in particular this clearly reflects an imperialist strategy on the part of the EU, which recently overtook the US as the largest source of FDI in Latin America; the 'periodic note' released by the IDB to mark the 2004 EU-LAC summit draws particular attention to the EU's role as 'the world's leading outward investor', and spells out clearly the logic of EU engagement.[33] But at the same time EU interest in Latin America reflects a new phase of 'inter-imperialist rivalry', which takes the form of promoting competitiveness in the region, while simultaneously using the threat of competition from the region to push its member governments to deepen the competition agenda in their own economies.[34]

What, then, of US Empire in the region? Even (perhaps especially) the world's leading capitalist power can scarcely abolish the laws of capitalist development. Nor can it wish away the contradictions inevitably generated as its advocacy of global capitalist competition runs up against its imperialist defence of its own primacy. In the present conjuncture, this makes its ability to exercise global leadership problematic. Among relevant signs of the times are the increasingly insistent denunciation of US *and* EU protectionism by the leaders of the IMF and the World Bank as well as by various emerging groupings of the developing countries themselves; the combination of reluctant recognition of the International Criminal Court by the US, and its insistence upon bilateral agreements to rule out appeals to it; the grotesque combination of its advocacy of liberal reform and its unilateral seizure of resources and market opportunities in Iraq; and its defeat by Brazil at the WTO over subsidy payments. At the regional level such contradictions are particularly acute – after all, whatever may be said regarding the benevolent impact of US hegemony for Europe and the advanced capitalist states generally in the post-war period, in Latin America it has supported the most reactionary forces and obsessively opposed reforms that might have allowed more competent local bourgeoisies to emerge.

Left to its own devices, the United States was never likely to be the architect of the 'Latin American rescue of the nation state', as it had been in Europe.[35] As noted above, its claim to contribute positively to Latin American development is currently called into question by evidence both that the forms of investment it has favoured do not contribute to local competitiveness, and that it is switching investment away to cheaper export platforms (notably, China displaced Mexico in 2003 as the second largest source of US inward investment). The strongest US voices in favour of the promotion of competition in Latin America come from centres of post-Washington Consensus fervour such as the Harvard Centre for International Development, while the US authorities predictably focus their energies on the European Union's back yard in former Eastern Europe. In Latin America, in contrast, the European Union appears to be playing a leading role.

The US is among the 'coalition of the willing' in the promotion of the new global project of 'bourgeois hegemony through competitiveness', but it is not calling all the shots, nor can it escape the contradictions inherent in the project. Overall, rivalry between the advanced capitalist countries is extending the social relations of capitalism across the multiplicity of nation states, on a genuinely global scale. Imperialism, it turns out, is the pioneer of capitalism after all.[36]

NOTES

1   Anoop Singh, 'The Caribbean Economies: Adjusting to the Global Economy', Port-of-Spain, Trinidad, 11 June 2004, at http://www.imf.org/external/np/speeches/2004/061104a.htm.

2   For the switch from 'adjustment' to 'competitiveness' during the 1990s, see Paul Cammack, 'What the World Bank Means by Poverty Reduction and Why it Matters', *New Political Economy*, 9(2), 2004. Regarding the individuals identified here, note that Singh, an adviser to the Governor of the Reserve Bank of India in the early 1980s, has previously worked in the IMF's Asia and Pacific Department; and that Kathuria is author of *Competing through Technology and Manufacturing – A Study of the Indian Commercial Vehicles Industry*, New Delhi: OUP, 1996; and also, with James Hansen, of *India: A Financial Sector for the Twenty-first Century*, New Delhi: OUP, 1999.

3   See UNCTAD, 'Preparations for UNCTAD XI: Submission by the Secretary-General of UNCTAD', TD (XI) PC/1, 6 August, 2003.

4   UNCTAD, 'Draft São Paulo Consensus', TD/L.380, Sao Paulo, 16 June 2004, para. 43, p. 10.

5   Karl Marx, 'Preface to the First Edition', *Capital*, Volume 1, Harmondsworth: Penguin, 1976, p. 91.

6   Ibid., p. 92.

7   Ibid., pp. 92-3.

8   Atilio A. Boron, 'State Decay and Democratic Decadence in Latin America', in *Socialist Register 1999*, London: Merlin Press, 1999, pp. 217 et seq.

9   Gregory Albo, 'The Old and New Economics of Imperialism', in *Socialist Register 2004*, London: Merlin Press, 2003, pp. 104-5.

10   Comisión Nacional de Defensa de la Competencia, 'Argentinian Report on Competition Policy, 2002', at http://www.mecon.gov.ar/cndc/memoria02/memoria02_english.pdf.

11   Cited in European Commission, *Capacity Building and Technical Assistance: building credible competition authorities in developing and transition economies*, Report prepared for the International Competition Network, 2003, p. 29.

12   Cited in Paul Cammack, 'Cardoso's Political Project in Brazil: The Limits of Social Democracy', in *Socialist Register 1997*, London: Merlin Press, 1997, p. 236. Cf. Claudio Monteiro Considera and Mariana Tavares de Araujo, 'Competition Advocacy in Brazil – Recent Developments', SEAE Working Paper, November, 2002, pp. 4-5: 'In June 1994, Brazil moved definitively from price control to competition policy with the enactment of Law no.

8.884'.

13   OECD, *Competition Law and Policy in Mexico: An OECD Peer Review*, Paris: OECD, 2004, pp. 11-12.

14   OECD/IDB, *Competition Law and Policy in Chile: A Peer Review*, Paris: OECD, January, 2004. The phrase cited appears on the back cover, and on the OECD website.

15   Jeffrey Sachs and Joaquín Vial, 'Can Latin America Compete?', in Joaquín Vial and Peter Cornelius, eds., *The Latin American Competitiveness Report 2001-2002*, New York: World Economic Forum/OUP, 2002, p. 10.

16   The Central American republics have adopted Korea and Ireland respectively as target reference points for 2010 and 2020 respectively for improvements in their competitiveness: Programa Nacional de Competitividad Nicaragua/CLACDS, 'Agenda para la Competitividad de Centroamerica hacia el Siglo XXI', June, 1999, p. 11.

17   IDB, *Competitiveness: the Business of Growth*, Washington DC: IDB, 2001, p. 1.

18   IDB, *The Challenge of Being Relevant: The Future Role of the IDB*, Report of the External Advisory Group (EAG), February, 2002, p. 2. For the IDB response, see IDB, 'Competitiveness and Building Consensus: Strategic Options for IDB Operations', *Seminar Paper*, November, 2002, at http://www.iadb.org/res/publications/pubfiles/pubS-150.pdf. Gurria, a long-time member of the US-based Centre for International Private Enterprise, is author with Paul Volcker of a 2001 report which advocated the systematic reorientation of the multilateral development banks to make them regional agents of the World Bank's strategy for the promotion and regulation of global capitalism: see Carnegie Endowment for International Peace/Inter-American Dialogue, *The Role of the Multilateral Development Banks in Emerging Market Economies*, Findings of the Commission on the Role of the MDBs in Emerging Markets (chaired by José Angel Gurria and Paul Volcker), 2001 at http://www.thedialogue.org/publications/program_reports/MDB_report.pdf.

19   UNCTAD, 'Economic Development and Capital Accumulation: Recent Experience and Policy Implications', Background paper prepared by the Division on Globalization and Development Strategies, June, 2004, p. 12, at http://www.unctad.org/en/docs/2_63_PolicyPaper_en.pdf.

20   IDB, *Competitiveness*, p. 4.

21   ECLAC, *Foreign Investment in Latin America and the Caribbean, 2003*, pp. 9-18; passage quoted is from p. 17.

22   ECLAC, *Desarrollo productivo en economías abiertas*, Santiago: ECLAC, June, 2004, ch. 9, esp. pp. 305-306.

23   European Commission, 'An Agenda of Social and Economic Renewal for Europe', Doc, 00/7, Brussels, 24 February 2000.

24   Comment at the time of the launching of the European Commission's 'Latin American Regional Strategy Document: 2002-2006 Programming', European Commission, April, 2002, at http://europa.eu.int/comm/external_relations/la/rsp/index_en.htm.

25   Monteiro Considera and Tavares de Araujo, 'Competition Advocacy in Brazil', p. 10.

26 OECD, *Competition Law and Policy in Mexico*, p. 61 and para 6.2.9 pp. 71-72.

27 OECD, *Competition Law and Policy in Chile*, p. 61.

28 OECD/IDB, 'Institutional Challenges to Promoting Competition', Note by the OECD Secretariat, Second Meeting of the Latin American Competition Forum, Washington DC, 14 June 2004, pp. 6, 8.

29 OECD/IDB, 'Competition Advocacy: Challenges for Developing Countries', at http://www.iadb.org/europe/PDFs/LAFC2004/competition%20advocacy-Clark.pdf.

30 Paul Cammack, 'Making Poverty Work', in *Socialist Register 2002*, London: Merlin Press, 2001.

31 Paul Cammack, 'The Governance of Global Capitalism', *Historical Materialism*, 11(2), 2003, pp. 37-59.

32 Paul Cammack, 'What the World Bank Means by Poverty Reduction, and Why it Matters', *New Political Economy*, 9(2), 2004, pp. 189-211.

33 IDB, Special Office in Europe, 'Periodic Note on Integration and Trade in the Americas', May, 2004, p. 25.

34 See European Commission, 'Some Key Issues in Europe's Competitiveness – Towards an Integrated Approach', COM (2003) 704 final, Brussels, 21 November 2003. The document opens with the declaration that 'Europe must become more competitive', and later warns of 'strong new competitors' (p. 5) in South East Asia and Latin America.

35 See Leo Panitch and Sam Gindin, 'Global Capitalism and American Empire', in *Socialist Register 2004*, London: Merlin Press, 2003, p. 17, referring to the title of Alan S. Milward's *The European Rescue of the Nation State*, London: Routledge, 2000.

36 The reference is to Bill Warren's *Imperialism, Pioneer of Capitalism*, London: Verso, 1980. I do not endorse Warren's argument in the terms in which it was made. But a glance at the theses that would have informed the development of his work had he lived (pp. xi-xii) suggests its relevance to the situation outlined here.

THE RUSSIAN STATE IN THE AGE OF AMERICAN EMPIRE

BORIS KAGARLITSKY

There is a debate going on in Russia. One school of thought sees president Vladimir Putin as a great Russian patriot defending the country from the imperialist ambitions of America. Another school of thought sees him merely as an American puppet.

Naturally, Putin's patriotism is no more (and no less) honest than his proclaimed desire to keep Russia democratic. His claims to defend national interests can be taken seriously only by those who accept any government propaganda at face value. Despite its patriotic rhetoric, the Putin administration has made a whole series of valuable gifts to the leadership of the US. Russian military bases in Vietnam and Cuba were closed, the latter move looking like a direct invitation to the US to invade the island, while with Moscow's agreement US military bases were established in Central Asia. The Republican administration of George W. Bush is viewed in the Kremlin as an optimal partner, unlike the Democrats with their tedious queries about human rights.

What is more important, the Russian government is helping G.W. Bush's administration economically. As an oil-producing economy in a period of high oil prices, Russia enjoys a massive inflow of petrodollars. In May 2003, currency reserves at the nation's Central Bank hit record levels, exceeding 60 billion US dollars, and have kept on rising rapidly. But this huge sum of money isn't invested in the domestic economy or used to solve the country's dramatic social problems. On the contrary, in 2004 the Moscow government was cutting social spending and launching a new attack on the remaining elements of the welfare state, claiming that there weren't enough resources. All the extra money is withdrawn from the economy and goes into a Stabilization Fund, theoretically designed to be used when oil prices decline. In fact, much of this money is invested in US government bonds. Instead of solving Russia's own problems the Moscow government is busy supporting the dollar and pulling the US economy out of recession.

THE RUSSIAN ENIGMA

If attempts to present Putin as a great national leader resisting US domination can hardly withstand any encounter with the facts, this doesn't mean that the opposite view is right. Those who see Putin merely as an American puppet are not very convincing either. Putin's tough declarations concerning the US invasion of Iraq brought an outburst of nostalgic joy among the patriotic community; for several minutes, in fact, it seemed as if Russia was opposing the US. But strangely enough, the threatening speeches that resounded in Moscow made no impact whatever on Washington, and were not even reflected in US-Russian relations. The members of the Bush administration understood not only how weak Putin's Russia really was, but also how dependent it was. The source of the USA's problems was quite justifiably seen as lying in France and Germany, which might have been suspected of advancing their own ambitious project as an alternative to US hegemony. What at first glance might have seemed like a struggle between Russia and the US was in fact a struggle over Russia, waged between the US and Western Europe. For precisely this reason Washington, which reacted with extreme irritation to the position taken in Paris, displayed only condescension with regard to Moscow.

The contradictory images of Putin's administration, which can thus be labelled 'nationalist' and 'comprador' at the same time, reflect the objective contradictions of today's Russian political economy, and – partly as a result of this – a total lack of coherence in Moscow's foreign policy. Not only are Russian elites divided into pro-European and pro-American currents, but also, to make things even more confusing, neither current has a clear view or a consistent political line. Both sides base their perspectives on wishful thinking, believing either in American invincibility or in the unstoppable rise of a United Europe. Both sides are wavering.

Ideology is also confused. Political liberals are protesting against the growing repressiveness of Russia's political system and they worry about the xenophobia that is becoming fashionable among larger and larger sections of society. But they also are in love with Israel, support G.W. Bush in his war on terrorism, and see America as the ideal democracy. Many of them hate Western Europe for its 'liberal irresponsibility', its 'multicultural permissiveness' and its 'support for Palestinian terrorists'. Some pin their hopes on the US Democrats, expecting them to fix what G.W. Bush has damaged 'in a moment of craziness'. But never do they see any problem with American imperialism as such. To make things worse, economic liberals see no problem in either repression or xenophobia, and remind everyone that the Russian economy never did so well in twenty years as it is doing under Putin. They are also happy with US policies because these policies, for good or bad reasons, help to keep oil expensive. And the nationalists, of course, hate America, but share President Bush's concern with terrorism and the 'Islamic threat'. Funnily enough, the most anti-Semitic politicians in Russia are also the greatest admirers of the 'Israeli security model'.

This confusion isn't a cultural or political phenomenon. In fact, the weakness of Russia's elite in international affairs is just a function of its economic and social weakness, which can't be compensated for even by the highest oil prices on the world market. Russia isn't a global player, nor even a self-defined minor actor (like, say, Finland or Japan). It is simply a battlefield for the global conflicts which are emerging – not a subject but an object of international relations. This object is alive and has senses. It is even aware of some (though not all) of its interests. But it is unable to act consistently.

Putin proclaimed a new national idea: competitiveness. Patriotism was finally placed at the service of capitalism. This totally bourgeois view of life contrasted with the orgiastic embezzlement of the naive Yeltsin epoch, which perceived capitalism exclusively as a consumer society. The people who made up the Putin draft were denied the scope of their predecessors; pragmatic through and through, they were thus completely anonymous. The triumph of greyness and pettiness that is evident at all levels of the Russian state and business is also clear proof that the country's elite has finally learnt the rules of bourgeois behaviour. Taking the place of the oligarchs was the bureaucratic bourgeoisie, collaborating closely with Western capital. This collaboration, moreover, has become much more fundamental and long-term, just as Russian capitalism has also become more mature. The problem, however, is that ruling elites in Russia remain deeply dependent on oil exports, and on Western financial markets. At the same time they feel much less dependent on the population of their own country, which seems to be obedient, passive and demoralized. As long as local markets and the local population are of very little interest to the rulers, the country is doomed to remain dependent, no matter what is proclaimed in official declarations.

THE GREAT FRIENDSHIP

The war on Iraq revealed hidden animosities, made contradictions visible and provoked open conflicts in Euro-American relations. However no such moment of truth occurred in Russian-American relations. After a period of cooling in their relationship, Russia and the US are experiencing an acute bout of mutual sympathy. This seems a little strange against the background of the nationalist declarations uttered by President Putin during the first months of his rule. Journalists and political analysts are perplexed by such an abrupt change of course. What is going on? With the general situation since September 11 leaving Moscow without room for manoeuvre, is this move designed to serve the interests of the oil magnates, who are trying to cement friendships with their US colleagues in the hope of making money out of military collaboration with Washington? No explanation seems really convincing.

To the outside observer, the Kremlin's actions might have seemed like a sharp about-face. In fact, the actions were thoroughly premeditated, and preparations for them had been made long before. All that had been lacking was a pretext, and the formation of the anti-terrorist coalition supplied this. The puzzle does not lend itself to solution for the simple reason that it is not a puzzle at all. Russian policy has been consistently pro-American. Russian rhetoric, meant for internal consumption, is something quite different.

Throughout most of the 1990s Washington had few allies more consistent or devoted than Russia under Yeltsin. In their anxiety to please Washington, the Russian authorities were not deterred even by the fact that their actions contravened all the normally accepted concepts of national interest. While the other side was expanding its weaponry, the Russian authorities single-mindedly reduced their armaments. One by one the limitations on American exporters and entrepreneurs operating in Russia were dropped, while the US retained its own protectionist measures, introduced as far back as the 1970s, when they were designed to secure permission for Soviet Jews to leave the USSR. Since then all barriers to emigration have been removed, more than a million people have left Russia, and for many years Western embassies have had to try to stem the flood of Russian citizens seeking entry. Nevertheless, the US restrictions remain in place.

In fact, the Russian leadership could hardly have done more to carry out the tasks posed in Washington if it had consisted entirely of officers of the US intelligence services. The politicians in power in Russia were not traitors, still less CIA agents; it was just that their strategies were based on clear, simple principles that they had assimilated during the years that saw the collapse of the Soviet Union. There is only one boss in the world, the USA, and this boss has to be pleased. Winning the sympathy of the boss constitutes the highest national interest.

Their loyalty has been rewarded, if not for Russia as a whole, then at any rate for its elites. Moscow's strategic goal has been to win recognition from the Western elites for the new ruling class that arose out of the plunder of state property. The Russian president's participation in the G7 summit of the industrially developed countries was a sign that the chosen strategy was working. The transforming of the 'seven' into the 'eight', with equal formal status for the Russian leader, was a fundamental foreign policy success.

This approach broke down only in the late 1990s, when in a context marked by continually falling living standards and the destruction of industry, the anti-Western mood in Russia reached a critical limit. The economic crisis was developing in parallel with the disillusionment of the population with neoliberalism, the free market and 'Western values'. The crash of the ruble in August 1998 was perceived by the public as final proof of the bankruptcy of the course Russia had followed throughout the 1990s.

PUTIN'S REGIME

When Vladimir Putin came to power in 1999, first as prime minister, later to become president, it was almost impossible for a politician looking for public support to openly proclaim neoliberal economic goals and pro-American foreign policies. However, the same oligarchic group remained in power with the same, not-so-hidden, agenda. A veteran of the state security organs, Putin was used to uttering ritual patriotic phrases whose function was not so much to mask different views as to conceal an absence of any views whatever. A petty bureaucrat from St. Petersburg, without political experience or even particular ambitions, Putin was raised in an instant to the summit of the political Olympus precisely because he had no record to be measured against. A complete dilettante in virtually all fields of state administration, Putin was the ideal partner for the oligarchy. As befitted a state security officer, the new president valued power very highly, but had absolutely no idea of what to do with it. His first two years were spent mainly in reshuffling his officials.

During the great crash of 1999 many Moscow-based banks were bankrupted, and even some oil oligarchs suffered heavy losses. Their smaller rivals in St. Petersburg, however, became stronger. A whole new team of aggressively pro-Western business people from 'the Northern capital' rushed to Moscow as part of Putin's entourage to take key positions in big privatized companies, as well as public office. The president was interested solely in the personal loyalty of his appointees. Meanwhile, the oligarchic groups were restoring their lost control. Capital flight resumed, the wages of most of the population again stagnated, and Western corporations gradually began rebuilding their positions in Russia, positions that had been shaken at the time of the crash.

The War on Terrorism was proclaimed as Russia's top priority long before September 11. It became the public justification for the increasingly authoritarian tendencies of the new administration. But it was also a message to the West. Long before September 11 Putin and his team had tried to attract

Western support and discourage criticism of human rights violations, explaining that the war they were fighting in Chechnya was not an attempt to preserve the position of Russian oil companies in the Caucasus, but a struggle to save Western civilization from the Islamic threat. In their public rhetoric Chechnya became the heart of a global Islamic conspiracy aimed not so much against Russia as against the new global order. Initially the Western powers listened to this sceptically, and kept reminding the Kremlin that the massive atrocities of the military in Chechnya didn't look like entirely civilized behaviour. After September 11, however, the mood changed and Moscow was recognized as a partner in anti-terrorist coalitions, alongside other great defenders of human rights such as the governments of Pakistan, Kazakhstan, Uzbekistan and Georgia.

Another major political accomplishment was the Law on Extremism passed by the Russian Duma as its contribution to the international anti-terrorist effort. This law follows the same lines as similar legislation passed in Kazakhstan, Uzbekistan, Pakistan and other allies of G.W. Bush's new crusade. Defining 'extremism' in the broadest sense, this law gives the police the right to attack legal rallies and demonstrations if they spot 'one single extremist present in the crowd'. The law also gives authorities the right to 'de-register' (i.e. ban) political parties and non-governmental organizations suspected of being involved in extremism. That the theory of class struggle is included in the list of extremist ideas which should be prevented from spreading speaks volumes about the ideological transformation of the Russian state from Soviet times.

Under Yeltsin the authorities had spoken openly of what they were doing, and even taken pride in it. Under Putin they preferred to remain silent, or to lie. This was the new political element which the state security veterans who filled the corridors of the Kremlin had introduced. The state pursued an even harsher line with regard to housing subsidies and education, preparing to dismantle the last remnants of the Soviet 'safety net', but at the same time talked unceasingly of its 'concern for the poor'. The income tax for the rich was drastically cut, with the explanation that this was better for social justice. Now Russia has a 13 per cent flat income tax, which the authorities proudly advertise as the lowest income tax in Europe. For the poor, however, the tax, rose by 1 per cent. A New Labor Code was introduced in 2001 limiting the right to strike and form trade unions. Oligarchs looked at this with increasing satisfaction while 'patriotic' intellectuals who had initially welcomed Putin's arrival in the Kremlin became increasingly confused.

While expounding on the greatness of Russia and promising new technological breakthroughs, the country's leadership took the decision to abandon the unique *Mir* space station. In principle, it would have been thoroughly advantageous to use the station jointly with the Chinese, who promised to pay for everything. But such a turn of events would not have been to the liking of the US, and *Mir* was allowed to crash into the ocean.

Russian business entrepreneurs who were close to the government sought to win contracts within the framework of the American anti-missile defence programme, which the Kremlin at the same time was publicly condemning. Unfortunately for Russian arms-makers, very little was offered from the American side. In spite of all declarations of friendship, the Russian arms industry sells much more to China than to the West. More successful are the oil oligarchs. During his visit to Moscow President Bush promised that America would buy oil from Russian companies, and some had already been delivered. But this hardly looked like a great commercial success capable of inspiring the citizenry.

Not only has Russia received nothing in return for its services, but it has also fallen victim to the restrictions imposed by the US on imports of steel. These restrictions were aimed primarily at Germany, but they hit Russian steelmakers hard. It was at this point that the Russian government, for the first time in years, decided to show toughness, and limited imports of American chicken products 'on medical grounds'. To everyone's surprise, this was enough to induce Washington to make matching concessions. Finally, the long-awaited understanding was reached between the Putin administration and George Bush. The Americans recognized Russia as having a market economy, and provided slightly enhanced access for Russian goods to US markets. Moscow ceased to regard American chickens as harmful to health. The government is preparing to join the World Trade Organization.

NATIONALISM AND THE CHECHEN WAR

Within the Kremlin, people thought they had found a magical device for 'selling' the population anything whatever. This device was nationalism. With the help of patriotic rhetoric, lightly spiced with racist demagogy and clericalism, any political course could be rendered 'truly national', regardless of its content. At first the declarations by the authorities aroused hysteria in the liberal-minded intelligentsia of Moscow and St Petersburg, but after a certain time, when it became clear there was nothing behind the demagogy, the public started to calm down.

In practice, the sole manifestation of the 'national course' was the repression in Chechnya, which did not let up for a single day. The war in Chechnya, which had been launched as part of Putin's election campaign in 1999, continued through sheer inertia. Russian society had grown used to the deaths each week of dozens of soldiers, and had ceased to react to reports of reprisals against peaceful civilians. Since racism had to some degree become part of official consciousness, the accounts of murder, rape and plunder in the Caucasus republic were perceived rather as good news, as proof that the authorities were taking an honest and serious attitude to the Chechen problem.

When certain Western commentators after 11 September 2001 predicted a 'toughening of Russian policy in Chechnya', they showed appalling naivety. To 'toughen' this policy was by then simply impossible. Everything that could be done to a peaceful population had already been done, beginning with the setting up of 'filtration' camps, and ending in the disappearance of people without trace. The only thing that had not been tried was the extermination of the entire population down to the last individual, or total deportation. But such things did not enter into the plans of the Russian specialists on 'solving the Chechen problem'. If the Chechens had all been swiftly wiped out, there would have been no one to rob and humiliate. In any case, constant warfare was needed as proof of the 'national orientation' of the regime, which did not show such concern for national interests in any other field.

The ideological question, however, remained unresolved. It is very hard to depict unilateral concessions to a foreign power as a supreme manifestation of patriotism. The events of 11 September helped solve the problem. In the immediate aftermath of these events, Moscow declared its solidarity with the US in the struggle against international terrorism, set about closing down its last military installations in Vietnam and Cuba, backed the stationing of US troops in the former republics of Central Asia and, later, supported the sending of American units to Georgia, right on the Russian border. Even before this, Moscow's opposition to the expansion of NATO to the east and to the anti-missile defence program had been merely rhetorical. General statements had not been followed by any serious diplomatic initiatives. Now, even the statements were discarded.

Neither the aims of the US and its allies, nor the methods they employed, were ever called into question by the Kremlin. Or rather, Putin criticized the West for being too soft on terrorism. During his visit to Brussels immediately after the American bombing of Afghanistan he explained to Western leaders that the concept of collateral damage must be extended to any civilian casualties. According to Putin, terrorists must be seen as responsible for any civilian deaths, no matter how these deaths happened and who actually killed people. It is impossible to fight terrorism without attacking civilians, and we must blame the terrorists for everything. If there were no need to fight terrorism, the war wouldn't have started at all, and these deaths wouldn't happen.

Russian diplomats and politicians speaking at international forums became very close to their Israeli colleagues when defending the actions of their respective armed forces in the occupied territories. The irony of the situation, however, is that the 'Israeli model' was most praised by some hard-line Russian nationalists. A good example is Dmitry Rogozin, the leader of the 'Rodina' faction in the State Duma, who was never before heard saying anything positive about Jews.

As before, Moscow's main concern was to have its status formally recognized by its partners. Desperate pleas were made to Washington to have it officially call the Chechen fighters 'terrorists', and to equate them with the evil-doers who had blown up the World Trade Center in New York. This could not have any effect on the real development of the Chechnya campaign, but Moscow's concerns lay elsewhere. What the Kremlin needed was not a resolution of the Chechen problem, but moral vindication. The Russian bureaucrats wanted to feel comfortable at international forums; they were tired of having to justify themselves with regard to murdered women and children.

The attitude adopted by the Russian elite is not hard to understand. After all, Western politicians and military leaders often do the same, without having to accept criminal or even moral responsibility. While Washington claims the right to bomb anyone it likes, regional rulers who kill a few thousand of their subjects have hanging over them the spectre of the Hague international tribunal. Moscow has therefore demanded equal rights, in the sense of being freed from all moral responsibility. But Washington, in its arrogance, has not conceded even this. For Putin, the lack of even minimal benefits from his military-political collaboration with the US has begun turning into a domestic political problem. Dissatisfied military officers, and nationalists who honestly believed the official rhetoric, feel themselves betrayed.

The nationalist media are getting angry. Open letters are sent to Putin by retired officers who call him a traitor for surrendering Russian military bases in Central Asia to the Americans, and for abandoning Russian positions in Vietnam and Cuba. Whole police battalions refuse to serve in Chechnya because they see no meaning in continuing this war. Vlad Shurygin, a 'patriotic' journalist known to be very close to the military, recently called Putin 'a new Gorbachev'. Contrary to what people might think in the West, in Russia this is the worst accusation one can make. With 80 per cent of the population considering the last Soviet president to be a 'traitor', personally responsible for the disasters that followed the disintegration of the Union, the comparison doesn't look very attractive. For a military man and a nationalist like Shurygin to compare Putin with Gorbachev is the most extreme expression of hatred.

Anti-American feelings not only remain strong in Russia, but have become even more visible since US troops entered Central Asia. Opinion polls show that about 60 per cent of Russian population see the US as a hostile government. And the more Putin does to please Bush, the less support he has at home. Sooner or later, the growing dissatisfaction will become a serious problem for the Kremlin. The political police veterans who are running the country will react in their accustomed fashion, seeking to 'tighten the screws'. In doing this, Moscow will find support from the West essential, and there is no doubt that the Bush administration will supply it. For compared to Kazakhstan, Georgia or Uzbekistan, Russia is a bastion of human rights. If Washington has no problems with the openly dictatorial regimes in these other republics, it means that the way is open for the Kremlin.

How far can the clamp-down in Russia go without risk of an outcry from 'Big Brother'? Experience from the 1990s shows that neither the shelling of the parliament, nor 'temporary censorship', nor the banning of 'extremist political parties' is considered a violation of freedom where 'friends of America' are concerned. Consequently, the Kremlin needs to make friends with the US simply for reasons of domestic politics. Putin and his associates have no other way out.

THE STRUGGLE OVER IRAQ

Russia's role in the diplomatic struggle over Iraq was very important. No longer a superpower, Russia inherited a permanent membership on the United Nations Security Council and a right to veto its decisions, but also a huge debt which Iraq owed the Soviet Union. This is why the diplomatic struggle around the war in Iraq was very much a struggle between Washington and Berlin for Russia's vote at the UN. The global crisis that came to a head over the weekend of 14-15 February 2003 resulted in defeat and unprecedented humiliation for the administration of President Bush. Washington had been sure that France would not veto its proposed UN resolution on launching military action against Iraq. But it finally became clear that the US proposal was dead in the water even without a French veto. The weapons inspectors did not follow the script that Washington had expected, and Security Council members took the floor one after the other to state their opposition to war.

An even bigger humiliation for Bush followed in the form of huge anti-war marches around the world, including the United States. The few West European governments that still supported Washington came in for massive street pressure. A consensus was and is building around the world that Bush is a dangerous man. The leadership in Washington kept stubbornly repeating that Saddam Hussein posed a threat to humanity, but their exhortations had the opposite effect. Hussein clearly posed a threat to his own people, but millions of people around the world reached the conclusion that Bush, not Hussein, poses a threat to the planet.

While the US leadership came under attack, Russia once more demonstrated its impotence and insignificance. Over the past decade Russia has been politically dependent on the United States, and economically dependent on Germany. The United States dictated Russia's political agenda, while Germany gradually became its most important business partner and source of foreign investment. This system worked quite well so long as Germany kept a low profile in international affairs and at least made a show of solidarity with the United States. When disagreements between the United States and Germany came to the surface, however, the Russian leadership was at a loss.

Moscow behaved like one of Ivan Pavlov's dogs. So long as the signals come one at a time, the dog's conditioned reflexes respond properly – it salivates at the sound of the bell. Then the scientist gives it two contradictory signals. The poor beast goes into a panic, spinning around in its cage. Something similar happened with the Russian leadership during the winter of 2003. Only when it became clear that France and Germany would secure a majority in the Security Council, and that no veto would be required, did Russian President Vladimir Putin demonstratively side with the victors. For ten years Kremlin ideologues have led the public to believe that Russia must support the United States or risk condemnation from the 'entire civilized world'. The events of February 2003 revealed, however, that Washington is now isolated. Russian policymakers drew the right conclusion in the end. As was immediately obvious, however, their actions were driven not by firm principles or concern for the national interest, but sheer opportunism. The sight of Russian leaders mouthing words dictated in Berlin while never taking their eyes off of Washington was nothing short of embarrassing. During the war in Iraq the Russian government-controlled television resembled the TV of Soviet times, using every opportunity to condemn American aggression. However, when the military operation finished and US troops successfully took over most of Iraqi territory, the Russian elite started panicking again. The tone of propaganda changed and reconciliation with Washington was seen as an absolute necessity.

Unfortunately for Putin and his team, Russia's 'euro-core' patrons saw things very differently. Contrary to most expectations, full-scale reconciliation between the 'euro-core' countries and the US-led 'coalition of the willing' didn't happen very quickly. In this kind of situation Russia's importance in the global struggle is enhanced. The US acquired not only control of Iraqi oil but also the possibility of influencing OPEC, on which the Iraqi puppet administration has a seat. In the 'euro-core' countries only France has its own oil companies and these are much smaller than their American or even British counterparts. This means that it becomes strategically important for the 'euro-core' countries to secure Russian resources for themselves. On the other hand, Washington doesn't really need Russian resources. But the logic of competition means that the US-led fraction of transnational capital has no interest in seeing Russian oil and gas secured by the 'euro-core' economies. This turns Russia into a real battlefield. The 'euro-core' is interested in stabilizing Russia. In fact, that becomes a necessary condition of the success of the 'euro-core' project as such. While relations within the EU become less predictable, stable and tolerant, it becomes a matter of strategic importance for the 'euro-core' to keep Russia on its side. And this is not just for its oil and other resources. Whilst America can play Eastern Europe against the 'euro-core', Germany in its turn can play Russia against the Poles, Czechs and Ukrainians.

RUSSIA AND THE NEW IMPERIALIST GAME

Summing up, the 'euro-core' project needs Russia to be stable and secure, and needs Iraq, occupied by the Anglo-American forces, to remain an unstable and insecure place. The success of the US global project, on the contrary, depends on the ability to keep Iraq stable and destabilize Russia. This is a classical imperialist game, not very different from that of the early twentieth century. The difference, however, is that imperialist blocs today can't be seen as simply national capitalist elites, but rather as supra-national formations, using nation-states in the absence of any better instrument. All the supra-national political instruments designed after the Second World War failed to perform in the new situation and, ironically, instead of being strengthened by market-driven globalization, were undermined by it. Not only are the UN in a shambles and the EU seriously weakened, but even the WTO and the IMF face problems because of the USA's gradual disengagement.

This disengagement is more than just a result of the neoconservative unilateralist approach of the Bush administration. Contrary to liberal theory, market integration doesn't lead to economic homogenization, and if this is true for the European region, it is even truer for the global economy. After twenty years of globalization, global contradictions have increased. Inequality between states and regions is increasing exactly the same way as social polarization. These are just two sides of the same phenomenon. Market polarization globally is accompanied by combined and uneven development and increasing competition. Transnational corporations in their rivalry simply can't avoid forming alliances with states, which remain strategic instruments of capitalist expansion and domination.

The struggle between imperialist powers was always much more than a rivalry of states for territory or even markets. Capitalism is a system which subordinates all human activities to the accumulation of capital. Oppressing people, gaining profits, market competition and even the exploitation of free labour were practised by human societies long before the bourgeois revolutions. But only the bourgeois system organized all these activities for the single purpose of capital accumulation. So the highest form of capitalist competition is the struggle between different centers of accumulation. This was exactly what predetermined so many wars, from the Anglo-Dutch conflicts of the 17th century to the First World War. And this conflict is very much at work now.

In the struggle for influence over official Russia, the conservative leadership of the US had one big advantage over the liberal Europeans. American public opinion showed far less interest in the subtleties of the country's foreign policy than was the case in Western Europe. Support for dictators abroad never became an internal political issue in the US, so long as it did not lead to the death of American citizens. In European countries, by contrast, governments were forced by the post-imperial syndrome to recognize that public opinion is conscious of the human rights position in friendly states. The greater the problems with human rights in Russia, the more freedom of speech was restricted, and the more crude was the rigging of elections, the more the Putin administration created difficulties for itself in Europe, and ended up a hostage to Washington.

What is the meaning of this new situation? EU leaders are not ready for a direct battle with the US, but Eastern Europe and the Middle East will be the areas of greatest contention in the near future. Domestic contradictions will be increased by outside interference. And since it is clearly easier to destabilize than to achieve stability, it is not difficult to predict that in both regions destabilization strategies will be more prevalent than attempts to bring order to these regions. The same may be true for Russia where the Russian elite is already visibly divided into pro-American and pro-German factions, and where we will likely see an escalation of related tensions. But is this necessarily bad news? Although the contradictions between 'core Europe' and the US are nothing like as intense as inter-imperialist contradictions were in the first decades of the last century (and mechanical comparison with the First World War don't work in any case), it is not irrelevant to recall that the contradictions at that time opened up new opportunities for the Left because ruling elites were disunited and confused. Once again, the Left in Russia will have to learn how to develop a revolutionary politics that can make its way through such contradictions.

THE EUROPEAN UNION AND
AMERICAN POWER

JOHN GRAHL

In last year's issue of this *Register* Leo Panitch and Sam Gindin argued that deep economic integration of the most advanced economies had led to an unprecedented concentration of geopolitical power under US hegemony.[1] The present contribution examines the possibility of a European counterweight to this power. Current discussions suggest two ways in which the European Union might represent a challenge to the concentration of power on the US: on the one hand, some member countries could be seen as exemplifying more efficient, more stable or more socially developed economic systems; on the other, the relations among member countries could constitute a superior model of international economic and political organization to that which is today promoted under US leadership.

The first of these issues relate to debates on 'varieties of capitalism': can economic systems which diverge from the 'liberal market economy' of the US and the UK survive in an increasingly interdependent world economy? The claim that this is so is associated with the work of Hall and Soskice, who characterize alternatives as 'coordinated market economies'.[2] The most studied case in question is that of Germany, central to the EU. Other commentators suggest a general convergence on the US model, or put forward various notions of 'hybridization'.[3] The second issue concerns international relations rather than socio-economic systems. It is sometimes argued that the evolution of the European Union has led to law-governed relations among member states, and that this could be an important precedent in the construction of a world international order protecting states against the simple rule of the strong, whether in the economic or the military sphere.

It will be suggested that the European Union could realize both these possibilities: that it could offer a path both towards more social control over economic life and towards a more pluralist and constructive international system. The present direction of change in the EU, however, is away from these possibilities, towards the 'Canadianization' which Panitch and Gindin suggest could be the fate of most countries with advanced economic systems.

THE US AND THE ORIGINS OF THE EU

It is certainly the case that the process of European construction has been sponsored, from the very beginning, by the US. In the autumn of 1949, Secretary of State Dean Acheson wrote to Robert Schuman, the French Minister of Foreign Affairs, to encourage a French initiative towards integration: 'the development of a German Government which can take its place in Western Europe, depends on the assumption by your country of leadership in Europe on these questions'.[4] This can be seen as the green light for the Schuman Plan of the following year, which launched what has become today's European Union. The US saw European integration as helping to promote political and economic stability in Western Europe, and thus as a basis both for a more effective response to the Soviet challenge and for moves towards the liberal international economic order required by American interests.

Of course, the US could not simply impose its desired solution on the Europeans. The very choice of France as leader of the integration drive demonstrates this. The Americans would much have preferred Britain to have played this role because it was a stronger power, one closer to the US on trade and other issues and one with a longer history of Atlantic cooperation. It was only Britain's repeated rejection of a merely European status which made the turn to France necessary. One danger of this switch was that European economic institutions would be less compatible with US designs for the international economy. The perception of this danger has recurred from time to time. But in practice economic conflicts between the US and the EU have been minimal, confined to a few sectoral issues. One reason for this is that although France has always had great political influence on the evolution of the EU, the growth and expansion of the EU itself has limited France's ability to determine the nature of EU institutions. A key example relates to the ambitious market completion programme undertaken by the Europeans in the eighties and which can be seen as giving their present shape to European structures. The US feared the emergence of a 'Fortress Europe' which would have compromised American investment interests by giving inside players key advantages in the big market which was emerging. The French themselves might have gone in this direction: they argued that internal negotiations (on market completion) and external ones (on the Uruguay Round and the WTO) should be synchronized in order not to confer advantages on US corporations active in Western Europe without compensating concessions for European companies from the US. This strategy was not adopted because Britain and West Germany refused it: one aspect of US control over European developments has always been the ability to use other countries (in particular, Germany from the start and, after its accession in 1973, Britain) to dilute French influence, when this was seen as desirable.

Another aspect of US control over developments in Europe turned out to be the separation of economic issues (handled by the EU and its predecessors) from military and related questions (dealt with by NATO). This separation of functions itself seems to have been contingent in its origins – had the French National Assembly not rejected the Pleven Plan in 1954, a much closer relationship between economic and military policies would have been established in Europe. It is unlikely, however, that this would have taken the form of a challenge to US leadership in military matters: the point of the Pleven Plan was to contain a rearmed Germany, not to call US command into question. In any case, the failure of the Pleven Plan, making NATO the exclusive forum for security questions, dissociated economic and military policies in a way which increased US influence over the latter. Here too, concessions were sometimes necessary: the US wanted maximum control over European military policies but at the same time maximum 'burden-sharing' over their costs – some trade-off between these goals was inevitable. But, given the particular position of Germany, whose governments saw NATO as the indispensable guarantor of national survival, it proved possible to extract big European contributions to a military posture essentially defined by the US.

Thus, although US support for the Schuman Plan represented a certain gamble, it was one which paid off – achieving a strong European economy without creating major problems for the US either in economic or in geopolitical terms.

THE GAULLIST INTERLUDE

Between 1958 and 1969, there were continuous frictions between the US and the French-led European order because of the political priorities of one man – Charles de Gaulle. The issues were legion: the organization of NATO, French nuclear armament, French policy in Algeria, the conduct of negotiations with the Soviet Union, the role of the dollar in the international monetary system, the Vietnam war, Britain's application for membership of the EEC.[5] What unified all these disputes was that French policy was aimed at European leadership in ways which directly challenged American power – it was US hegemony itself, rather than the way it was exercised in any particular case, which de Gaulle wanted to reject. It is significant, however, that the French move which provoked the most anguish in Washington was the challenge to the role of the dollar, the key to US economic supremacy and thus to the very basis of its whole geopolitical stance.

The episode closed with French defeat. The *événements* of 1968 led to a huge inflation of the franc which was quite incompatible with de Gaulle's dream of a return to the gold standard. After de Gaulle himself left the scene the following year, his successors were disinclined to maintain his intransigence on such issues as British entry; the 'Trojan horse' was soon admitted into the European citadel.[6] But there were also structural limitations to the Gaullist drive for independence. One of these was obviously the reluctance of West Germany to push its support for European construction past the point at which it might offend the Americans. More fundamentally, the decade of de Gaulle's reign coincided with a huge flow of US investment into the European economy; in many ways it was the US corporations which pioneered the process of European integration. The European commission always sought the emergence of 'European enterprises', rather than French, Dutch or German enterprises, to consolidate the integrated economy; in practice the US multinationals came closest to this idea of Europeanization since they operated freely throughout the old continent.[7] In the early eighties the ill-fated Mitterrand experiment involved a brief attempt to reduce the US economic presence in France; these buy-outs proved as unsustainable as the other aspects of this exercise in economic voluntarism.

After this interlude, US-European relations, at least at an official level, were never again subject to such a fundamental challenge. One can mention the *Ostpolitik* of Willy Brandt in the 1970s,[8] which constituted a certain challenge to the US approach to the Soviet bloc, but Brandt's departure, like that of de Gaulle, was followed by a normalization. Subsequent West German governments continued to develop relations with the East Germans but not in ways which challenged US leadership in East-West relations as a whole. There have since been major movements directed against US policies; massive popular opposition to the Vietnamese war was followed by opposition to the deployment of short-range nuclear weapons in the 1980s. Some European states, notably Sweden, have maintained foreign policy positions in marked opposition to those of the US. Indeed, the most impressive popular rejection of US policies is perhaps the most recent – the massive rejection by peoples and by some governments of the second war against Iraq – but such movements have never called into question the consistent Atlanticism of the EU and its political leaderships. Successive expansions of the EU have probably reduced the possibility of any fundamental rupture – especially the latest admission of a whole string of Trojan horses in the shape of the ex-communist states.[9]

THE NADIR OF AMERICAN POWER – AND ITS
FINANCE-BASED RESURGENCE

The end of the seventies perhaps marks the lowest point of US prestige and influence. The defeat in Vietnam seemed to set limits to the direct exercise of military power. In the economic sphere, the US had great difficulties in responding to the industrial renaissance of Germany and Japan, while continuous inflation of the dollar threatened the centrality of its financial system to adjustment and restructuring processes in the world economy as a whole. Symbolic of this decline was the failed attempt by the Federal reserve to enlist German support for the dollar in the autumn of 1979. Bundesbank leader Emminger boasted of having convinced Paul Volcker that foreign exchange intervention was pointless: 'the real decisive factor was the money supply'.[10] The Americans themselves were readier than at any other time since World War II to consider a more collective approach to the economic problems of the West; this was the era of 'trilateralism', a proposed reshaping of Western hegemony which traded significant increases in Japanese and European political influence against the assumption of heavier international burdens.[11]

As Panitch and Gindin show, the actual outcome of this crisis, hardly anticipated by any of the agents involved, was a decisive restoration of US economic dominance, based on a dramatic assertion of financial power through a complete reversal of economic strategies. The restrictive monetary policies which restored the key place of the dollar and of dollar-based financial markets in world economic relations were immensely damaging in their social consequences, both in the US and around the world, but the 'Volcker shock' represents a key turning point. Since 1980, the relative position of the US economy has continuously strengthened while the German and Japanese challenges, at the time so ominous, have faded virtually into insignificance. The excellence of their industrial systems was no match for the range and scale of the dollar-based financial system.

European Keynesianism, and to a large extent European social democracy as well, were early victims of the turn to neoliberal policies: the kind of Keynesian intervention attempted by most European countries in the late seventies and early eighties simply could not be financed in a world of depreciating European currencies and sky-high American interest rates. One can speculate on whether a common European macroeconomic strategy might have produced a different outcome; the cohesion required for such a strategy did not exist. In particular, German and French macroeconomic policies in the early 1980s were diametrically opposed.

The actual response of the Europeans to the new, extremely adverse, environment arising from the change in US policies was heavily influenced by the neoliberal zeitgeist. National interventionism largely gave way to a drive for more complete integration, focused entirely on market processes. While projects for more developed political integration were abandoned or reduced to token status, an extremely ambitious programme of economic reforms brought down a multitude of non-tariff barriers and in practice extended the integration process for the first time beyond the field of manufactures to cover markets for service outputs and labour and capital inputs. Since this programme, embodied in the Single European Act of 1986, gave rise to the EU in its present form it is worth looking at in a little more detail.

THE FOUR FREEDOMS

The Single Act led, in the first place, to an extensive legislative programme removing specific 'non-tariff barriers' to exchange across member state boundaries. For example, public procurement was opened up to EU-wide competition. But, more fundamentally, basic legal principles were enforced which made any future use of such barriers by member states illegitimate. The principles are usually summed up as the four freedoms: the freedom to move goods, services, labour and capital without hindrance anywhere in the EU. These freedoms are justiciable rights – if national authorities impair them, there are effective legal remedies which can be obtained not only in the European Court of Justice but usually in national courts themselves, since these accept the supremacy of European law on economic questions.[12]

The EU thus involves a system of supranational law limiting, indeed in many ways eliminating, member state sovereignty over economic issues. The EU, and its predecessors, had always been centred on a supranational and law-based structure – this was the case since the Schuman Plan itself. But, until the eighties and the Single Act, the actual functioning of this legal structure had been limited by formal and informal arrangements which left enormous scope for national economic intervention. For example, the requirement to permit the free movement of capital was subject to a host of 'safeguard' clauses which in fact allowed for effective exchange controls. Similarly, although, in principle, legal competence on certain issues might have been transferred from member states to EU institutions, the 'Luxembourg compromise'[13] allowed an individual member state to invoke its own vital interests to refuse a majority decision of the other members. The lack of political legitimacy often inhibited the Commission from litigation against member states which broke the rules by, for instance, subsidising a domestic industry.

In the eighties, most of these exceptions and derogations were swept away. The economic laws of the EU became increasingly hard to ignore or transgress as the Luxembourg compromise was abandoned, exchange rate controls were abolished and the Commission, supported by a general consensus among member states, became much readier to challenge breaches of the rules in the courts. The result was that economic and political practice came into much closer accord with the formal supranational legal system – the EU became a unique example of law-governed international interactions.

From the point of view of European populations, there is no basis for this effective legalization of EU relations. The commitment of European citizens to the institutions of the EU varies from country to country but nowhere does it compare to the deep political allegiance which sustains the institutions of individual member states. Yet such allegiance is not necessary: the EU as an economic structure is strong in spite of a chronic lack of popular support, in spite of the famous 'democratic deficit' and so on. The paradox is explained by the nature of the four freedoms; these are freedoms used above all by the corporations, especially the larger ones which are most likely to operate on a Europe-wide basis (and including, of course, US multinationals and other 'outsiders' who enjoy the same rights as indigenous corporations). The actual structure of the EU, according solid guarantees of market access – embracing output, labour and capital markets – and enforceable against the authorities of all states concerned, represents a uniquely advantageous regime for capital. While such a regime continues, European citizens do not have to love the EU – their employers will do so on their behalf.[14]

For three decades or more commentators have lamented the unbalanced nature of European construction: negative integration outpaces positive integration; social Europe lags behind economic Europe; 'market creation' runs ahead of 'market correction'; and so on.[15] These imbalances are very real, and they help to explain the indifference or hostility of most EU citizens towards European structures which fail to defend them against tightening external constraints. But they also help to account for the political solidity of the structure. The very underdevelopment of a market-correcting social Europe makes for a deep commitment of the dominant economic interests – US as well as European interests – to the institutions which have emerged.

THE REIGN OF FINANCE

Incorrect assessments of financial developments constitute the most important weakness of critical political economy today. The growing role of financial markets is certainly recognized, but the interpretation of this role is usually in terms of dysfunction, speculation, parasitism, even decadence. Industry and production are being sacrificed to rentier interests; the tribute exacted by a hypertrophied financial sector distorts and impedes the restructuring of economic relations.

One reason for this kind of perspective is a very justified concern with the impact of financial liberalization on developing countries. The outcome of the deregulations, privatizations and liberalizations promoted by the Washington consensus in the South has been both socially and economically disastrous; one can see that certain Western interests have been served but not that any developmental process has been advanced. North–South relations, however, represent only a small part, and not a representative part, of the vast global financial system which has emerged over the past three decades and within which the issuance of securities, capitalization and transactions are overwhelmingly concentrated on the OECD countries. This system is far from being the speculative 'casino' as which it is often portrayed.[16] It represents, in fact, a profound innovation in the productive system. It is by no means necessary to accept idealized theories of efficient markets and rational security pricing to arrive at this conclusion. In an economy where markets typically fail to clear, finance is not simply a mechanism for reallocating monetary resources; it becomes a condition of existence of the market economy itself.[17] The power of today's global financial markets derives not from the accuracy of their asset evaluations but from the scale and density of the financial interactions which they establish, from the range over which they deploy monetary resources and from the standards of practice and procedure which they enforce on all the economic agents involved.

The centrality of the dollar today, and the various advantages which the US derives from this centrality, are largely a function of the scale of dollar-based financial markets. In the period immediately following World War II, the primacy of the dollar was to a large extent an industrial phenomenon: the 'dollar shortage' represented a universal hunger for US exports. (Similarly with the key position of the D-mark within the European Monetary System.) Today, the primacy of the dollar rests on the scale and liquidity of North American financial markets and, measured by this yardstick, the preponderance of the US economy, far from giving way to competitive challenge, is greater than ever before. The capitalization of the two largest stock markets, NYSE and NASDAQ, for example, is some $11 trillion – half the world total. Similarly, dollar-denominated securities constitute nearly half of the outstanding issues on world debt markets. Some 90 per cent of recorded foreign exchange transactions involve the dollar. From the point of view of macroeconomic policy, this kind of scale does not so much limit as practically eliminate external financial constraints on the US – there is no external financial domain to which investors or issuers could transfer even a small fraction of this financial activity. (This is the basis for the US practice of 'benign neglect' of the dollar exchange rate.) But the impact of dollar predominance increasingly goes beyond macroeconomic policy formulation – as private sector finance is globalized, the dollar-denominated markets increasingly determine the terms and conditions for corporate finance, and the resulting pressures tend to create a corporate world in the image of the US itself.

In comparison to this worldwide system, the historically established financial systems of Europe are merely a cluster of particularisms. Each depended heavily on longstanding relationships between the users of finance and a small number of inside investors; in each, financial relations were deeply embedded in other social ties – of language, nationality, religious/political affiliation and so on. This embeddedness, as has often been pointed out, can result in a very efficient transfer of information from issuer to investor and a very precise adjustment of the interests of both parties. But it limits financial relations to a specific social and geographical context, and in consequence such systems cannot match the dynamic expansion of the disembedded dollar-based system. With the emergence of the latter the 'inside investor' systems of Western Europe, notably that of Germany, came under immense pressure, as did their socio-economic systems in general.[18]

THE EUROPEAN RESPONSE

The current, very determined, efforts of the European Union to integrate member state financial systems, and to build huge, liquid markets in euro-denominated securities, should be seen in the context of this growing challenge. Certainly, many aspects of the financial integration programme are influenced by the neoliberal thinking which still grips European leaderships. But the essence of the undertaking arises from a material necessity: if the Europeans do not develop their financial markets they will drive every borrower and lender on the planet into the North American ones. This would only tighten external constraints and handicap European enterprises.

Several factors hinder and distort this policy drive. Most important is the inefficient, backward-looking and restrictive macroeconomic regime. The two main elements of this regime are the monetary policy of the European Central Bank and the Stability and Growth Pact which constrains member state budgetary policies. Both are heavily influenced by German models; both put a high premium on 'stability' as against employment and growth. And both can be regarded as a futile attempt to perpetuate the methods of the Bundesbank in the context of a continent-wide monetary union which simply cannot be managed as if it were the highly coordinated German economy of the past. The consequent tendency to lower levels of activity and higher levels of unemployment aggravates the malaise of the German and other key European economies in the difficult adjustment of their socio-economic systems to changing external conditions.

The actual way in which EU elites conceived the financial integration project represented a slavish acceptance of American models: Europe was to become 'the cheapest and easiest place to do business in the world'.[19] Not only financial reforms, but also labour market and social protection policies, liberalization and privatization of public services, the promotion of venture capital and other such measures were all put forward in a completely uncritical attempt to mimic the growth process of the US in the late '90s. Only with the stock market crash and the corporate scandals which followed did signs of a certain reflection on the weaknesses of the US model appear.

THE ABSENCE OF SOCIAL EUROPE

Of course, social Europe does have a certain reality: there are policy communities, declarations and many other documents, a host of comparative and statistical studies and so on. But social policy remains essentially within the competence of the member states. Two reasons can be found for this. On the one hand, the dominant economic interests of the EU prefer things this way – social regime competition allows the corporations to 'regime shop', and in so doing put continuous downward pressure on the redistributive and market-correcting capacities of individual member states. On the other hand, it may be that the member state governments themselves tend to guard their autonomy in social policies all the more fiercely for having abandoned all the key instruments of economic intervention: only social policy initiatives – in the fields of social protection, education and so on – allow them to respond effectively to the political pressures which are still, almost exclusively, determined by national developments.

Labour market policy (where a significant EU competence has emerged) is the exception which proves the rule. Employment strategy is the paradigmatic example of the 'open coordination' used by European institutions outside the key sphere of market integration. It can be regarded as the intersection of the Europeanized domain of economic policy and that of social policy where member states retain autonomy. To leave all employment issues to the member states would be to risk the unravelling of the economic integration which has been achieved, since labour-market or employment measures could then be used as surrogate forms of economic intervention. On the other hand, a full integration and harmonization of labour market regimes would itself be a big step towards an active social Europe which could undermine the clarity of the four freedoms in the economic sphere. What can be observed is a battleground: legislation, in the form of labour market directives or the 'soft' integration of labour market policies, are functional necessities for the big market, but each such initiative becomes a focus for trade union and popular pressure contesting the economic priorities of the EU system.

THE IMPORTANCE OF LAW

It might seem that the account given here of the origin and nature of the EU only confirms its subordination to US interests. Fostered, if not actually initiated, by the US, the process of European construction from the start fitted the geopolitical and economic priorities of the Americans; the sharp separation of military and economic issues, of EU and NATO, although not designed to do so, worked to limit the political ambitions of the project. Struggles for independence and against US hegemony were weakened both by divisions among European countries and by the increasing penetration of their economic space by US investors. The central European response to the Volcker shock, focused on supply-side, market-creating, reforms and without a coherent macroeconomic strategy, weakened control over the European economies while creating a unified space open to further penetration.

However, it is sometimes suggested that the legal form of intra-European integration, governed by a supranational judiciary, makes for a different approach to global interactions to that which tends to prevail in the US. This legal form, present from the origins of the European project, was, as has been seen, powerfully reinforced by the reforms of the 1980s. Member states, and the strongest economic interests within them, recognize that the functioning of EU institutions depends on the primacy of EU law and on corresponding constraints on national policies. The very weakness of the EU in the military and political fields may also dictate a rather different approach to the globalization process. The big European corporations share with US ones the objective of full access to developing economies around the world. Unable, however, to deploy direct political or economic pressure in the same way as the US, the Europeans may be readier to rely on the construction of general legal frameworks and less inclined to resort to unilateral tactics. Peter Gowan argues that, after the Soviet collapse reduced European military dependence on the US, this legalistic internationalism took three forms: the promotion of global human rights and democracy; substantial contributions to development in the South; and 'the theme of the capacity of the EU to promote the peaceful solution of international problems and conflicts'.[20] The refusal of the key EU states, France and Germany, to accept US intervention in Iraq could then be seen as evidence of this kind of transatlantic divergence.

Alongside the structures of economic law − above all competition law − of the EU, there is an important body of law on human and civil rights. This derives not from the EU but from a different structure, the Council of Europe, whose main achievement has been the establishment of a European Court of Human Rights. This gives European citizens a remedy if their basic rights are violated by their own governments. The EU recognizes the

European Charter of Human Rights and thus both supranational judiciaries in Europe will uphold its provisions. But the rights in question are analogous to those promulgated in the US Bill of Rights – they concern individual, civil, freedoms, not social rights. This is a most important development in relations between states but not one which is in contradiction to the rule of markets in economic life.

In spite of the inadequacies of the EU structure from the social point of view – the hard enforcement of the four freedoms against the soft law and open coordination which govern employment and social policies – this commitment to legality must be considered an important aspect of the EU's position in the global system. Clearly it should not be idealized – time was when US intervention was needed to pull Britain and France back from their illegal invasion of an Arab country.[21] But to the extent that the EU and its members are highly committed to a law-bound, institutionalized approach to international affairs, including for instance respect for United Nations decisions, this is in itself a challenge to certain aspects of American power. On the Iraq question, the US successfully divided member states, but it might not always be able to do this.

THE SOCIO-ECONOMIC MODELS OF EUROPE

A more ambitious hope for European influence derives from a variety of socio-economic systems which have introduced more comprehensive constraints on market forces than are found in the US, in short from the European social models. These cannot be discussed in any detail here but some of the problems confronting their present development can be brought out. A first difficulty has already been referred to – the fact that, unlike market transactions and processes, the social protection systems, social services and employment regimes have not been Europeanized. They remain national structures, embedded in very different social contexts.

Compounding this problem is the fact that the economic performance of EU countries with developed social models – most significantly the performance of Germany – has been very weak for over a decade. At the time when Germany's industrial competitiveness seemed to be undermining US economic dominance, the associated social institutions – such as employees' codetermination within the enterprise, the German vocational training system, the highly developed social protection system and so on – enjoyed very great prestige. Today, that relationship is reversed and persistently high unemployment calls into question the continuation of the social model. However much it may be true that rapid growth, at least in a material sense, is hardly desirable for a country like Germany, the current German government seems persuaded that the old social model is obsolete, accepting the view that it gets in the way of rapid growth. It has launched a whole series of reforms designed to limit welfare entitlements and social expenditures, and to reduce employment regulation.[22]

The issue involves recent debates on the 'varieties of capitalism', where the future of the German socio-economic model is the key question in dispute. An influential position, at least until very recently, has been that the German economy derived significant productive advantages from forms of non-market coordination (for example, in the process of wage bargaining). In general, the 'coordinated market economies' of Western Europe were seen as at least holding their own in competition with the 'liberal market economies' of Britain and the US.[23] It was further argued that historical factors – characterized in terms of 'path dependency' and 'institutional complementarity', that is in terms of the way in which specific national institutions reinforced each other – would prevent a convergence of the coordinated systems onto the liberal model, in spite of more intense interactions within the global economy.

Although the institutional *forms* of the European economies are indeed remarkably stable, these views underestimate the deep changes in the priorities and objectives which determine the functioning of institutions. Not only are global market forces promoting deep changes in German economic structures (for example, in corporate finance and in corporate strategies)[24] but elites, both economic and political, are thoroughly committed to such change and seek to accelerate it. The previously vaunted advantages of Germany's strong institutions are often now seen, in neoliberal terms, as the source of damaging 'rigidities'. US practices and institutions are themselves frequently seen, in Germany and elsewhere, as providing a model for European reform. The key forces behind these pressures, as we have seen, are financial.

CONCLUSION

It has been suggested here that in two ways the EU offers a different perspective on international relations and the emergence of a global economy. On the one hand, its internal relations have evolved in a way which constrains national governments to respect supranational law, and this state of affairs is seen as central to the economic performance of both member states and the EU as a whole. This has already promoted a somewhat different attitude to rules and power in the international sphere. Secondly, many European states – although not the EU – have developed social models which in the past have combined very impressive rates of economic development with significantly higher levels of social provision and substantially less inequality than is found in the US.

The two achievements are to a great extent in contradiction with each other since what has worked to cement the legal institutions of the EU has been the limited scope of EU law – which is centred on bourgeois right, on market freedoms and on property rights, with an obvious functionality for the large corporations – while it leaves employment and social rights to the member states. Thus advance in the legal sphere rests on the absence of social Europe, on the failure to include ambitious social policies in the integration project. One result of this is that the achievement of greater equality than in the US still only applies to each European country in turn. Inequalities across EU member states are enormous and dwarf those among regions of the US.

The key policy of European leaderships today, the drive for financial integration, is marked by the same contradiction. The EU's financial integration strategy, although essential to any prospect of European autonomy in economic and social development, threatens, in its existing form, to widen the existing gulf between the market-creating and market-correcting capacities of the EU. The rejection, by the European Parliament, of the Commission's proposed Takeover Directive indicates the degree to which the present strategy for financial integration calls into question social policy objectives in the member states. A unified market in corporate control was seen as central to the integration of corporate financial systems; but Commission proposals completely failed to acknowledge the social issues of such a market. Only a completely diluted directive was accepted by the Parliament. The absence of any European ambition in the social sphere leaves employment regulation, social protection and social service provision to the individual member states where, at best, only defensive measures are to be expected. But so long as continuing economic integration is (correctly) perceived by European populations as working to dissolve existing structures of social control, the integration project will not only lack legitimacy in itself; it will tend to undermine the legitimacy of political institutions in the member states.

Present developments in the world economy also threaten to destabilize the entire structure of the EU. The European systems have to adapt to deep changes, above all in the financial sphere, which call into question the functionality of their institutional structures and the validity of corporate strategies. The European response to this challenge, a drive to integrate its financial markets, is rational as far as it goes; but the efforts being made are weakened by an anachronistic macroeconomic regime and by a continuing neglect of the social dimension in the integration process. The power of attraction of the US model itself helps to explain these weaknesses. European leaderships have increasingly seen Americanization as the only solution to the problems of the old continent; they have not, in recent years, envisaged divergent paths of development.

To overcome these contradictions would require two conditions which are not easily compatible: on the one hand, a rejection of the purely market-creating focus of the present EU and the insertion of a substantive social policy into European strategies; on the other, a determination to preserve and develop the deep integration achieved over the last half century. There is a great deal of opposition to the EU today, but it usually takes the form of protecting the national space from it – with 'disintegrating' effects on the 'common European home'. Only if the progressive forces of opposition find enough common ground to redirect rather than dismantle the European Union could a significant challenge to US hegemony emerge on the old continent.

NOTES

My thanks to Peter Gowan for critical comments on a first draft.

1   Leo Panitch and Sam Gindin, 'Global Capitalism and American Empire', *Socialist Register 2004*, London: Merlin Press, 2003.
2   Peter Hall and David Soskice, eds., *Varieties Of Capitalism: The Institutional Foundations of Comparative Advantage*, Oxford: OUP, 2001.
3   For hybridization see for example S. Casper and H. Kettler, 'National Institutional Frameworks and the Hybridization of Entrepreneurial Business Models: The German and UK Biotechnology Sectors', *Industry and Innovation*, 8(1), 2001, pp. 5-30; Sigurt Vitols, 'Negotiated Shareholder Value: The German Version of an Anglo-American Practice', WZB working paper SP II 2003-25; or Dominique Plihon, Jean-Pierre Ponssard and Philippe Zarlowski, 'Towards a Convergence of the Shareholder and Stakeholder Models', Chaire Développement Durable, École Polytechnique – EDF, cahier 2003-011. For the debate as a whole see Jonathon Perraton and Ben Clift, eds., *Where Are National Capitalisms Now?*, Basingstoke: Macmillan, 2003.
4   Alan S. Milward, *The Reconstruction of Western Europe, 1945-51*, London: Methuen, 1984.
5   Jean Lacouture, 'Nos Cousins Américains', in *De Gaulle, Volume Three, Le Souverain, 1959-70*, Paris: Seuil, 1986.
6   Keith Dixon examines Britain's present position as unofficial spokesman for US interests within the EU: *La mule de Troie: Blair, l'Europe et le nouvel ordre américain*, Paris: Raisons d'Agir, 2003.
7   This was the development famously lamented by J.-J. Servan-Schreiber, *Le Défi Américain*, Paris: Denoël, 1967.
8   Timothy Garton Ash, *In Europe's Name: Germany and the Divided Continent*, New York: Vintage, 1994.
9   On US relations with the new member states see Thomas Schreiber, 'le rêve américain de la "nouvelle Europe"', *Le Monde Diplomatique*, May, 2004.
10   O. Emminger, *D-Mark, Dollar, Währungskrisen*, Stuttgart: Deutsche Verlags-Anstalt, 1986, pp. 390-8.

11   Robert Brenner, *The Boom and the Bubble: The US Economy Today*, London: Verso, 2001.

12   On the unique, and in some ways astonishing, role of law in the EU see J.J. Weiler, *The Constitution of Europe: 'Do the New Clothes have an Emperor?' and other essays on European integration,* Cambridge: CUP, 1999.

13   The compromise originated in a dispute between de Gaulle's France, on the one hand, and other members and European institutions on the other.

14   For the nature of the European polity see Phillipe Schmitter, *How to Democratize the European Union ... And Why Bother?*, Lanham, MD: Rowman and Littlefield, 2000.

15   Fritz Scharf, *Governing in Europe: Effective and Democratic?*, Oxford: OUP, 1999.

16   Widespread views of the foreign exchange market, for example, which portray it as essentially speculative, are based on quite erroneous interpretations. See Grahl and Lysandrou, 'Sand in the Wheels or Spanner in the Works? The Tobin Tax and Global Finance', *Cambridge Journal of Economics*, 27(4), 2003, pp. 597-621.

17   Mainstream economic theory, with its emphasis on market equilibration, may even understate the importance of financial systems, and in fact the efficient markets position has been effectively challenged within mainstream economics by the 'behavioural finance' school. This is because the strong assumptions which are made about market equilibrium suggest that agents can typically cover their purchases from the proceeds of their sales (this is the implication of 'Walras' Law' – every agent in an equilibrated market economy observes the necessary budget constraint). From this point of view, financial relations may certainly increase the efficiency of the market economy but one can conceive the latter without the former. If one rejects this idealized account of markets, and sees that realized sales volumes and realized prices rarely correspond to the plans of the agents concerned, then it follows that over any time period, no matter how short, every agent will incur either a monetary surplus or a deficit. Only effective and comprehensive recycling from surplus to deficit agents, that is to say, only finance, permits the market economy to endure. Likewise, the adjustments necessary to the market economy are essentially financial: they are brought about not in response to 'market signals' but in function of the pressures arising from the need to cover deficit positions. (Clearly, as economic relations become increasingly internationalized so also must financial processes.) The classic account of this reasoning is an article by Jean Cartelier, 'Théorie de la valeur ou hétérodoxie monétaire: les termes d'un choix', *Économie appliquée*, XXXVIII(1), 1985, pp. 63-82.

18   See John Grahl, 'Globalised Finance and the Challenge to the Euro', *New Left Review*, 8, 2001.

19   This objective was proposed by the European Commission in its report to the European Council, Stockholm, March, 2001 (see Corporate European Observer, issue 9, June, 2001, www.corporateeurope.org). To be fair to the Council, the expression was not used in its declaration, although its

deregulatory substance was endorsed.

20   Peter Gowan, 'Cooperation and Conflict in Transatlantic Relations after the Cold War', *Interventions*, 5(2), 2003, pp. 218-232.

21   Apropos of Suez, John Foster Dulles said to the British Prime Minister, 'Anthony, you must be out of your mind'.

22   See John Grahl and Paul Teague, 'The German Model in Danger', *Industrial Relations Journal*, forthcoming.

23   See Hall and Soskice, *Varieties*.

24   For a thorough account of changing strategies, see Wolfgang Streeck and Martin Höpner, *Alle Macht dem Markt?*, Frankfurt am Main: Campus Verlag, 2003.

THE EU AND EASTERN EUROPE: FAILING THE TEST AS A BETTER WORLD POWER

DOROTHEE BOHLE

The invasion of Iraq has deepened a sense of exasperation among many left-leaning West European intellectuals. It has led to intensified calls for a multipolar world order, in which a self-confident European Union (EU) acts as a civilized counterbalance to an openly imperialist America. This political vision rests upon the assumption that European civilization is distinct from American. In socio-economic terms, continental Europe's persisting welfare states are seen as providing an alternative to America's embrace of market fundamentalism. In terms of international politics, Europe is perceived as projecting a multilateral world order based on international law and cosmopolitan human rights, marking a clear difference to the current US agenda.

This essay takes issue with this political vision and its underlying assumptions. If Europe indeed represents a distinctive, and better, civilization than the US, this should be reflected in how the EU has reshaped Eastern Europe after the breakdown of socialism. After all, this was the first historical opportunity for the EU to live up to its own ambitions in world politics. However, instead of exporting welfare capitalism and a security order based on multilateralism and human rights, EU expansion has entailed the re-emergence of economic center-periphery relations within the new Europe. Moreover, Western European states bear a heavy dose of responsibility for the violent break-up of Yugoslavia. The left-liberal vision of Europe as the better world power is based on an unwillingness to critically engage with the EU's conduct of its external relations, and wishful thinking concerning Europe's autonomy vis-à-vis the US.

I. ENLARGING THE EU: THE RE-EMERGENCE OF CENTER-PERIPHERY RELATIONS IN EUROPE

With the breakdown of Communism the EU gained tremendous influence in its immediate neighbourhood and thus a unique chance of promoting its own vision of international politics. Eastern Europe's opening coincided, at least initially, with a relatively conservative American approach to European affairs, which gave the EU a broader room for manoeuvre. Given that Western Europe was just preparing to form a closer political, economic and social union, as codified in the Maastricht Treaty, it seemed well prepared to use this room for manoeuvre.[1]

Holding open the prospect of EU membership has constituted the central policy instrument through which West European states tried to shape the post-socialist development paths of their East European neighbours in the last decade.[2] If we are to believe European politicians, the process of rapprochement has brought economic, social and democratic progress and stability to the region. This view of enlargement is widely shared in the academic world. Most scholars, whether they adhere to the constructivist or rationalist approach to integration, easily agree on one idea, namely that the East European countries gain from enlargement in economic, social and political terms.[3] Politicians and academics are also in agreement that the EU's eastward expansion manifests a successful break with the past by replacing hierarchical relations with a more equal partnership, and a commitment to solidarity. Günter Verheugen, the Enlargement Commissioner of the EU summarizes this view in an exemplary way:

> Peace through integration – This was the idea that guided the beginnings of European integration and it is also the idea that underlies the enlargement that now stands before us. … The impending enlargement will not make Europe weaker but stronger. … No-one will be entering the EU through the back door on 1 May 2004. … And neither will there be any two-class society, because nowhere is it written that a country can only enter the EU when it has reached a level of prosperity at least equivalent to that of Luxembourg. What is written is that any member which has to catch up in development can rely on the solidarity of others.[4]

A careful analysis of the EU agenda in Eastern Europe, including the means used to realize this agenda and the results of Eastern Europe's westward integration so far, reveals a rather different picture than that suggested by European politicians and the academic world.

The aftermath of the breakdown of Communism has been called 'the most dramatic episode of economic liberalisation in economic history'.[5] Virtually all the former socialist countries adopted radical neoliberal reform programs, with almost identical templates for fiscal and monetary stabilization, liberalization of domestic markets and foreign trade, and privatization of the state owned enterprises. Obviously, there were strong endogenous reasons why the neoliberal project could score such an overwhelming victory in Eastern Europe. Economic liberalism as an ideology was very attractive for these societies, in large part because it constituted the most radical alternative to the old system.[6] However, as has often been said, the revolutions in Eastern Europe were bourgeois without a bourgeoisie. Neoliberalism could neither be based on established societal groups, nor cast in terms of a specific national hegemonic project. In this context, Western states, firms, and advisors as well as international financial institutions like the IMF and World Bank became the anchors of the East European reforms.[7]

For the first ten countries that applied for membership, the EU was soon to take over the central role in the reform process. Although its agenda in Eastern Europe was more encompassing than that of the IMF and the World Bank, it was far from providing an alternative economic model. Initially, the EU's main thrust was to secure agreement to the 'market opening' deregulation of the East European economies in accordance with its own internal market program. In the next step, the EU reinforced its influence over East European policy-making by prescribing detailed reforms, including the restructuring and privatization of the industrial and financial sectors and the social security system. In contrast to the other members, moreover, the newcomers had no choice but to adhere to the Economic and Monetary Union. Thus, through the accession process, the EU could establish a far-reaching influence on the emerging capitalist political economies of Eastern Europe. These do not have much in common with the continental European ideal of tamed markets, but are established on clear-cut neoliberal principles.[8]

Rather than exporting a solidaristic model of capitalism to Eastern Europe, the EU has preferred to protect its own political economies as far as possible against disruptive influences of enlargement. The concrete terms of membership indicate that currently the EU is not ready to grant the new members equal social and economic rights. It has allowed for 'transition periods' before the free movement of labour from the East is permitted by Western European states, although this constitutes both an economic and a citizenship right in the EU. In financial terms, the per capita transfer payments for the East European newcomers are significantly lower than those for the older member states.[9] As a consequence, the costs of adaptation and enlargement are largely put on the poorer East European states.

The EU could afford to impose these restrictive conditions because of a fundamental power asymmetry reinforced through insisting on bilateral and differential treatment of each of the applicants. Economically the result was that the basis for a regional 'hub and spoke structure' was created, with each state in the Eastern region relating to the others via its relationship with the western hub.[10] Politically the result was a competitive race for membership among the applicants, a race that has been reinforced through the high level of conditionality the EU has applied.[11]

All in all, rather than exporting the institutional and regulatory foundations for a 'European way of life' to the Eastern countries, the EU has pushed them towards neoliberal reforms. These reforms were the foundation for Western economic actors to gain a maximum degree of influence over the East European economic space. Under their influence, Eastern Europe has been transformed over the last decade into Europe's new semi-periphery. Their economies are characterized by a high degree of penetration by foreign capital, especially in the most strategic sectors. Finance, telecommunication, transport and manufacturing export sectors are dominated by foreign ownership, mostly European, but with US capital close behind.[12] Low labour costs provide one of the main East European competitive advantages. In the industrial sectors, foreign corporations have restructured their production chains to take advantage of this and thus increase their global competitiveness. As a consequence, we see a major eastward expansion and relocation of labour-intensive activities. Foreign investors also contribute to a persistent social gap between East and Western Europe, and local governments often collaborate to preserve Eastern Europe's specific competitive advantage. In terms of work conditions and remuneration, trade union density and collective bargaining capacity as well as social welfare arrangements, East European workers have persistently faced much worse standards than their Western counterparts. Eastern Europe is becoming locked in at the lower end of the pan-European division of labour.[13]

Taken together, the concrete terms and the result of the EU's eastwards expansion do not speak for its capacity to promote a distinct, more socially just variant of capitalism in its neighbourhood. Rather, the EU's agenda in Eastern Europe is heavily influenced by the priorities of the West's capitalist classes, who – far from being committed to the economic, social and political progress of the region as a whole – are mainly interested in the possibility of incorporating Eastern Europe as a new basis for accumulation. The result for Eastern Europe is not vastly different from Mexico's experience in the NAFTA.

II. THE 'HOUR OF EUROPE' AND THE BREAK-UP OF YUGOSLAVIA

If, in economic terms, the EU does not really provide for an alternative to US-led neoliberal globalization, how about its ambitions as a geopolitical power which distinctively adheres to a security order based on human rights and international law? Here again, the East European case, in particular the violent break-up of Yugoslavia, provides a good testing ground. The collapse of Yugoslavia coincided with the attempt of the EU to achieve more regional autonomy in the post-cold war order. The Maastricht Treaty not only gave birth to the Economic and Monetary Union, but also codified plans for a common foreign and security policy. At the same time, the US pursued a relatively conservative European policy, indeed pushing Europe to take over some responsibility for Eastern Europe.[14] Thus, from the beginning, the EU viewed the collapse of Yugoslavia 'as an opportunity for the assertion of European power and independence'. The Yugoslav crisis was to be 'the hour of Europe', not the 'hour of the Americans'.[15]

The unfolding of the Yugoslav crisis demonstrated, however, the incapacity of European powers to promote a stable security order even in the European space. National rivalries repeatedly undermined such attempts, and were skilfully exploited by the US once it decided to give up its conservative stance in the region. In early 1991, as the relations between the Yugoslav republics seriously deteriorated, both the EC and the US sought to support and stabilize a federal Yugoslavia. The same position still guided a peace conference of September 1991, where the EC envoy, Lord Carrington, 'sought to secure agreement on a loose confederation of all the republics along with the protection of minorities and the principle of the inviolability of borders.'[16] The same conference established an Arbitration Commission, which was to make recommendations on the recognition of sovereignty of the republics. But the goals of the peace conference were soon torpedoed by Germany's unilateral recognition of Slovenia and Croatia. This aggravated the Serbo-Croatian war and encouraged its spread to Bosnia.[17] It also intensified inter-European rivalry, with France and Britain adopting a pro-Serbian policy.

The war in Bosnia most clearly reflects the failure of the West European powers to promote stability and security. As Susan Woodward has shown, Bosnia was not considered significant to global security, and no Western state had any vital national interest in Bosnia.[18] The approach of the European powers – no less than that of the US – to the unfolding war therefore lacked commitment and coherence. The German rush towards recognizing Croatia and Slovenia had left Bosnia vulnerable, as it increased the tensions within it. Despite early warnings of the dangers, the European powers were not prepared to provide any security guarantees. Predictably, once Bosnia declared its independence in 1992 and received EC recognition, this step fuelled the conflicts rather than resolving them.[19] The recognition of the new republic, within which different forces had started to struggle for national influence and independence themselves, was not helpful. Recognition came too early: Bosnia's ties with Croatia and Serbia were not yet clarified, nor had any arrangement been reached between the three national political parties.[20] No European power was willing to undertake any military intervention operation to put a stop to the ensuing war. Rather they increasingly relied on UN involvement, whose task was strictly confined to humanitarian aid, and who failed disastrously in the face of ethnic cleansing, which was partly the result of European support for a strategy of ethnic partition in Bosnia. The historical opportunity for Europe to demonstrate that it had the capacity to provide a security order based on human rights and international law came during the first years of the break-up of Yugoslavia. The actual outcome does not speak well for such a European capacity.

From 1994 on, the US forcefully re-entered the European scene. At the centre of its new offensive strategy stood the transformation of the role of NATO. Zbigniev Brzezinski called the transformation one of a 'double enlargement', i.e. the expansion of NATO into Central and Eastern Europe, and the transformation of its military tasks from that of defence against Communism to out-of-area strikes in the name of humanitarian intervention.[21] NATO expansion moreover went hand in hand with freeing military operations from UN control. In 1995, only a few months after the US outlined its new conception for NATO, the bombing of Bosnian Serb targets started under its auspices. The American-staged Dayton Agreement, which was concluded soon afterwards, demonstrated that the 'European hour' in bringing stability to Yugoslavia was definitely over.

The war on Yugoslavia over Kosovo (coming immediately after Poland, Hungary and the Czech Republic were admitted to NATO membership) was the most important instance in the new offensive strategy in the 1990s. Officially the war was launched as a humanitarian effort on behalf of the Kosovar Albanians, but the military annex presented at the Rambouillet conference, held a few days before bombing began, hardly spoke to noble humanitarian aims. Rather, this text foresaw complete control of Kosovo by NATO, including its right to alter the infrastructure of Yugoslavia, and free access to public facilities such as telecommunication, broadcast, roads or ports. This annex was a clear provocation to Yugoslavia, which accordingly did not sign it. What further made incredible the stated goal of going to war to protect the Kosovar Albanians was NATO's exclusive reliance on an air campaign, which left the forces on the ground free to do whatever they wished to with the Albanians. And indeed, the war had the 'predicted result of a massive displacement of Kosovo Albanians'.[22]

According to Peter Gowan the US was pursuing altogether different aims than humanitarian ones. He interprets the war as a means of the US reassuming leadership in Europe, by subordinating West European states and multilateral institutions to NATO, and effectively undermining European attempts of regional autonomy.[23] Indeed, this strategy worked; although the war was an American one from beginning to end, and European leaders had to be cajoled into it, this was not too difficult to achieve, not least because of intra-European rivalries. As a reaction to Germany's perceived new assertiveness, France had begun to reposition itself closer to Britain and the US, and the Kosovo war gave France the option of putting Germany in its place. It was even less difficult to convince British forces of the necessity of the war. And while Germany was excluded from the Rambouillet negotiations, the US put big pressure on Germany to participate in the war proper. The US success in subordinating Germany was absolute: a Red-Green government led Germany into its first military operation since the Second World War, despite the fact that the UN did not sanction the intervention.

The war demonstrated to Western Europe it's own military weakness. The overwhelming imbalance between the American and European military capacities was made evident. Notably, the ensuing 'European Security and Defence Policy' has evolved firmly under the umbrella of the US; 'it serves', as Alan Calfruny has put it, 'to institutionalize Europe's subordinate position in the transatlantic relationship.'[24]

III. RE-EVALUATING THE EUROPEAN PROJECT

There is clearly little to celebrate in terms of Europe providing a distinct and better alternative to the American imperial order. The exasperation with America's aggressive stance in world politics that worries many European left-liberal intellectuals is certainly understandable, but their alternative political vision is marred by serious analytical and ideological shortcomings.

The first question to arise in this context is why left-leaning intellectuals so rarely reflect critically on EU expansion to the East, although it is here, in its immediate neighbourhood, that its political and economic strategies can be best assessed. A good many Western left intellectuals have seen Western Europe – because it so successfully resolved territorial, national and welfare questions – as a role model for Eastern Europe; and yet at the same time they have not seemed to believe that Eastern Europe would ever attain such achievements. Authoritarian temptations, a waning acceptance of democracy, the outburst of ethnic violence, racism and xenophobia were often seen as the almost inevitable consequences of the transformation process.

Claus Offe, one of the most ardent representatives of this view, argues that Eastern Europe's extrication from Communism opens a 'Pandora's Box full of paradoxes' that threatens to obstruct advancement towards the market economy and liberal democracy.[25] Consequently, he makes the case for an international system that rewards progress on this road, and sanctions misbehaviour, as one possible solution for controlling the almost inevitable authoritarian or populist reactions. And Jürgen Habermas, in his famous open letter reacting to the war on Iraq, shows a similar distrust of Eastern Europe.

Referring positively to US Secretary of Defense Donald Rumsfeld's infamous differentiation, Habermas sees an increasing gap between 'old Europe' and the Central East European Countries that 'strive to join the European Union, without being ready yet to limit their only recently won sovereignty again'. In this context, Habermas advocates a European integration at different speeds, which will allow (old) core Europe to advance its own particular vision of Europe. Due to core Europe's 'soft' power, the new members then will be pulled along.[26]

Such a patronizing attitude towards Eastern Europe is shared by conservatives. Indeed, Wolfgang Schäuble, the German conservative party's foreign policy mastermind, first articulated the idea of 'core Europe' organizing an enlarged EU. And while Habermas's outrage at the letter from eight West and East European countries expressing loyalty to Bush's war on Iraq was intellectually more challenging than Jacques Chirac's reaction that Eastern Europeans acted like misbehaving children, the sentiments of the two were not dissimilar. The specifically left-wing tune to patronizing Eastern Europe is the one that accuses East European societies of embracing market radicalism rather than adhering to the welfare state model of continental Europe. Already in the early 1990s, Claus Offe said he would find it not surprising at all if in 'Central and Eastern Europe those shrill voices of a ruthless individualistic, chauvinistic and particularistic reaction – an East European variety of Thatcherism – would take hold'.[27] Such voices, he claimed, had been to a large extent silenced in continental Europe for forty years, and the only solution he could see to the threat of the re-emergence of such reactionary forces was the strengthening of the Western Left, which would both allow for the construction of a new social contract, and for the defence of welfare achievement in the West.

There are several problems with this not uncommon view. First, it ignores the role of the West in exporting market-radicalism to the East, and conveniently locates the responsibility for this socio-economic choice solely in the East. Second, and more troublesome, it ignores the responsibility of the Western left in denying Eastern Europe equal access to European resources and citizenship rights. After all, trade unions, Social Democratic parties and left-wing intellectuals called for protecting domestic labour markets from the inflow of Eastern workers. While this position reflects the weakness of the Western left, which makes it take defensive steps, it has yet to prove that it is able to develop forms of transnational solidarity. The defence of the welfare state is by no means enough, as solidarity is thereby confined to boundaries of the nation state.

Moreover, the proponents of the idea of Europe as a civilized counterbalance to the US tend to conflate the internal achievements of European integration with the EU's external policy. While it is indeed true that European integration successfully contributed to taming Germany and provided one of the institutional pillars for peaceful coexistence of the West European powers, it does not follow from this that the EU is peaceful and norm-abiding in its external relations. The early years of European integration certainly did not tame France or Belgium in their colonial wars. It requires an unwarranted intellectual shortcut to assume that the EU does not bear the imprint of this legacy from its leading member states. The colonial history, and even more the history of Nazi Germany, should remind us that for European states imperialism and violence are far from alien. That imperialist reflexes have been more dormant in Europe's recent history might have to do with some historical learning. Equally or even more important, however, was the relative weakness of all major European powers after the Second World War. The lack of capabilities and opportunities to sustain the old European imperialism should not be confounded with an achievement of European civilization. Given the not so distant violent and imperial past of Europe, and its recent failures in living up to its newer, more enlightened values, there is a certain degree of rather unsettling self-righteousness in a position that claims that Europe 'can offer this world a great potential for civilisation. We have our peace model, integration. No one else has as much experience as we have of the solution of conflicts by civil means or of the successful transformation of systems.'[28]

The position that Europe needs more self-assertive politics can certainly be advanced without these unsettling moral undertones. It may be put in terms of the necessity to build up a counterbalance to the US, simply because 'overwhelming power is always a threat, regardless of who possesses it. Prudence dictates that states that face overwhelming power ought to form a balancing coalition against the overwhelmingly powerful.'[29] Yet, the fallacy of this less value-laden position is the assumption of an autonomous European capitalism. This assumption was already refuted in the 1970s by Nicos Poulantzas, who argued that at the core of the new phase of imperialism was the relationship between American capital and the rest of the developed world, rather than the capitalist peripheries. Through foreign direct investment, American capital has penetrated the European social formations. Acting as a powerful social force within these societies, it led to a transatlantic realignment of European bourgeoisies and states.[30] In their recent work, Sam Gindin and Leo Panitch have revived this chain of argument, and demonstrated the increased penetrative capacity of American power after the crisis of the 1970s.[31]

European capitalism needs to be understood *within* the framework of American neoimperialism, not as distinct or separate. This has strategic political consequences for the Left. If the idea of a distinct European political identity is based on wrong premises, then the struggle against neoliberalism and military chauvinism is not one of Europe against America, but one that has to be fought *within* both the American and European societies.

NOTES

1   The European Union was created in 1992 with the signature of the Treaty of Maastricht. I will use the term European Community (EC) if I refer to events before the Treaty of Maastricht.

2   As of May 2004, eight East European states became members of the EU: Poland, Hungary, Czech Republic, Slovak Republic, Slovenia, Latvia, Estonia and Lithuania. Bulgaria and Romania are hoping to join in 2007, and Croatia has recently started the accession negotiations.

3   See e.g. Ulrich Sedelmeier, 'Accommodation Beyond Self-Interest? Identity, Policy Paradigms, and the Limits of a Rationalist Approach to EU Policy towards Central Europe', *Politique Européenne*, 3(January), 2001; Frank Schimmelfennig, 'The Community Trap: Liberal Norms, Rhetorical Action, and the Eastern Enlargement of the European Union', *International Organization*, 55(1), 2001, pp. 47-80; Andrew Moravcsik and Milada A. Vachudova, 'National Interests, State Power and EU Enlargement', *East European Politics and Society*, 17(1), 2003, pp. 42-57.

4   Günter Verheugen: 'Enlargement of the European Union. Expectations, Achievements and Prospects', Speech, Szczecin, March 4, 2004. At http://europa.eu.int/comm/commissioners/verheugen/pdf/04032004en.pdf, pp. 6, 22-23.

5   Peter Murrell, 'How Far has the Transition Progressed?', *Journal of Economic Perspectives*, 10(2), pp. 25-44, here p. 31.

6   Jerzy Szacki, *Liberalism after Communism,* Budapest: Central University Press, 1995.

7   Dorothee Bohle, *Europas neue Peripherie. Polens Transformation und transnationale Integration*, Münster: Westfälisches Dampfboot, 2002; Peter Gowan, 'Neo-Liberal Theory and Practice for Eastern Europe', *New Left Review*, 213, pp. 3-60; Béla Greskovits, *The Political Economy of Protest and Patience. East European and Latin American Transformations Compared,* Budapest: Central European University Press, 1998.

8   Heather Grabbe, 'A Partnership *for* Accession? The Implications of EU Conditionality for the Central and East European Applicants', EUI Working Paper 99/12, San Domenico di Fiesole (FI): European University Institute, 1998.

9   In the first year after accession Poland will receive 67 Euros per capita, Hungary 49, Slovenia 41 and the Czech Republic 29. By contrast, Greece, Ireland, Portugal and Spain currently receive respectively 437, 418, 211, and 216 Euros per capita. See Karl Debbaut, 'EU Enlargement after Copenhagen', at http://www.worldsocialist-cwi.org/eng/2003/01/25eu.html. For a thorough discussion of the financial terms of enlargement see Andrew

Mayhew, 'The Financial and Budgetary Impact of Enlargement after Accession'. SEI Working Paper No. 65. 2003, at: http://www.sussex.ac.uk/sei/documents/wp65.pdf.

10 Peter Gowan, 'Eastern Europe, Western Power and Neo-Liberalism', *New Left Review*, 216, 1996, pp. 129–140.

11 Grabbe, 'Partnership'.

12 See Daniel C. Vaughan-Whitehead, *EU Enlargement versus Social Europe?*, Cheltenham: Edward Elgar, 2003, pp. 361–411; and Otto Holman, 'The Enlargement of the European Union towards Central and Eastern Europe: The Role of Supranational and Transnational Actors', in A. Bieler and A. D. Morton, eds., *Social Forces in the Making of the New Europe. The Restructuring of European Social Relations in the Global Political Economy*, Basingstoke: Palgrave, 2001, p. 177.

13 Dorothee Bohle and Bela Greskovits, 'Capital, Labor and the Prospects of the European Social Model in the East', Harvard University, Center for European Studies, Central and Eastern European Working Paper, 58, 2004.

14 Kees van der Pijl, 'From Gorbachev to Kosovo: Atlantic Rivalries and the Re-incorporation of Eastern Europe', *Review of International Political Economy*, 8(2), 2001, pp. 275–310.

15 Alan W. Cafruny, 'The Geopolitics of US Hegemony in Europe, 1989–2002', in A. W. Cafruny and M. Ryner, eds., *A Ruined Fortress? Neoliberal Hegemony and Transformation in Europe*, Lanham etc: Rowman and Littlefield, 2003, p. 98.

16 Cafruny, 'Geopolitics', p. 99.

17 Susan L. Woodward, *Balkan Tragedy. Chaos and Dissolution after the Cold War*, Washington: The Brookings Institution, 1995, pp. 146–199.

18 Ibid., pp. 273–333.

19 Germany, this time in line with the EC, hesitated to recognize Bosnia. It was the US who insisted on recognition.

20 Woodward, 'Balkan Tragedy', p. 273.

21 Brzezinski, quoted in Peter Gowan, 'Making Sense of NATO's War on Yugoslavia', in *Socialist Register 2000*, London: Merlin Press, 2000, pp. 257–281, here p. 275.

22 van der Pijl, 'Gorbachev', p. 301.

23 Gowan, 'NATO's war', p. 270.

24 Cafruny, 'Geopolitics', p. 100.

25 Claus Offe, 'Das Dilemma der Gleichzeitigkeit. Demokratisierung, Marktwirtschaft und Territorialpolitik in Osteuropa', in C. Offe, ed., *Der Tunnel am Ende des Lichts. Erkundungen der politischen Transformation im Neuen Osten*, Frankfurt Main: Campus, 1994, pp. 57–80.

26 Jürgen Habermas, Jacques Derrida, 'Unsere Erneuerung. Nach dem Krieg: Die Wiedergeburt Europas', *Frankfurter Allgemeine Zeitung*, May 31, 2003, pp. 33–4. As the letter was composed by Habermas, with Derrida merely signing it, I refer to it as the Habermas letter.

27 Claus Offe, 'Wohlstand, Nation, Republik. Aspekte des deutschen Sonderweges vom Sozialismus zum Kapitalismus', in C. Offe, *Tunnel*, p. 42.

28   Verheugen, 'Enlargement', p. 32.
29   Glyn Morgan, 'Hayek, Habermas, and European Integration', 2003, http://www.courses.fas.harvard.edu/~ss10/Downloads/Glyn_Morgan_on_H abermas_article.pdf, p. 26.
30   Nicos Poulantzas, *Classes in Contemporary Capitalism*, London: Verso, 1975.
31   Leo Panitch and Sam Gindin, 'American Imperialism and Eurocapitalism: The Making of Neoliberal Globalization', *Studies in Political Economy*, 71/72(Autumn/Winter), 2003/2004, pp. 7–38.

HABERMAS'S MANIFESTO FOR A EUROPEAN RENAISSANCE: A CRITIQUE

FRANK DEPPE

I

On May 31, 2003 leading European newspapers published a 'Manifesto' calling for a 'Renaissance of Europe'. The text was written by Jürgen Habermas, and supported by Jacques Derrida, Umberto Eco, Richard Rorty and other intellectuals.[1] In February of that year millions of people had protested in the capitals of Europe, as elsewhere around the world, against the preparation of war against Iraq by the Bush administration. While these protests had not prevented the 'violation of international law' that the invasion of Iraq in April represented, what was especially significant about these protests, the Manifesto suggested, was that they nevertheless contributed to the 'birth of a European public'. Above all, they raised anew the issue of a 'European identity', and of a 'vision for the future of Europe' that might represent an alternative to the global strategies of US imperialism.

Habermas was well aware of the fact that the war against Iraq intensified – like a 'catalyst' – contradictions and tensions not only in the transatlantic relationship, but also within the European Union itself. The gap between those European states who joined the 'coalition of the willing' – Great Britain, Spain, Italy, along with Poland and the other states of Donald Rumsfeld's 'New Europe' – and those from 'Old Europe' who refused to join Bush's alliance for this war (France, Germany, Belgium, Luxemburg) only reflected the existence of deeper conflicts in the field of European politics which had intensified since the Nizza Summit of December 2000: conflicts on institutional and financial issues, on eastward enlargement, on the New Constitution of Europe and especially on its Common Security and Defense Policy. The war further widened the gap between the Anglo-Saxon and the continental countries of Western Europe as well as the gap between Western Europe and the new members in Middle and Eastern Europe. It could be surmised that American neo-conservatives calculated the US could achieve at least two goals by attacking Iraq: winning the war and acquiring direct American control over the Middle East, and weakening the European Union which is regarded as a partner, but also as a potential rival – especially in respect to the restructuring of 'Eurasia', the area of the world Brzezinski has called the 'Grand Chessboard' of geopolitical strategy in the post-Communist era.[2]

The message of the Manifesto was that the citizens of Europe needed to become aware of their common political fate. The need to enlarge their 'national identities' with a European dimension was related to the importance of ensuring that the 'ignorant and expensive alternative of war or peace' would be rejected. Europe needed to 'bring its full weight to bear at the international level and within the United Nations in order to balance the hegemonic unilateralism of the United States.' Any future design of world order could not be accepted without the participation of the EU. In a 'complex global society' it is not only military power, but also the 'soft power' associated with negotiations, economic advantages and institutionalized relationships that count.

For Habermas, 'European identity' reflects the historical traditions and elements of the political culture of Western Europe.[3] European societies and states, having been taught bitter lessons by the experiences of class struggle, imperialist war and colonial exploitation in the 20th century, have come to support the construction of 'Europe', i.e. 'government beyond the nation state', and to embrace the social security and solidarity of the welfare state. The experience of war, of totalitarianism and especially of the Holocaust, according to Habermas, has strengthened the moral basis of politics in Europe (e.g. with respect to the death penalty), and has proved the value of an approach to international politics that tries to prevent war by supranational forms of cooperation.

Europeans, according to the Manifesto, have learnt to respect differences; they have a feeling for the dialectics of enlightenment, modernity and technological progress. In European societies the relationship between religion and the state is different from that in the United States: 'We could hardly imagine a president opening his daily work with a public prayer and referring to divine missions while announcing political decisions with serious consequences.' And in Europe, there exists 'trust upon the civilizing potential of state intervention' which corrects deficiencies of the market and enables solidarity and equality. This is a legacy of the struggles and the power of the working-class movement – as well as of Christian social traditions – in 20th century Europe. So, Europeans still prefer the ethics of 'more social justice' against the individualistic ethics of competition that accept extreme social inequality.

As Habermas put it elsewhere, these elements of a 'European (postnational) identity' should enable the EU 'to confront the USA with an alternative (universalistic) vision and concept of world order'[4] which has emancipated itself from eurocentrism and nourishes the Kantian vision of global domestic politics regulated by law and by stable (and powerful) international institutions ('global governance'). Obviously, Habermas is concerned with outlining the basic elements of a counter-hegemonic project which – represented by an EU which has acquired more 'qualities of a state' (including military forces) – might be able to balance US unilateralism and world dominance. In the Manifesto's words, this would counter the 'hegemonic vision, which not only rhetorically but also practically determines the present government of the United States and which is in sharp contrast to the liberal principles of a new world order which were proclaimed (in 1991) by the father of the present president.'

II

What are we to make of the European 'counter-hegemonic project' that Habermas's Manifesto represents? At most it might be said this is a project in the making, a 'still fragile and not very strong EU-centered West European game of balancing against US hegemonic power politics' that Gowan has called 'subversive bandwagoning'.[5] To be more than this, such a project surely requires considerable financial investment in the coordination and modernization of European military forces, which would have the paradoxical effect of draining resources away from the welfare state, and thus undermine Europe's alleged distinctiveness. Yet, for the kind of Europe Habermas has in mind, military power is not the decisive factor in defining the characteristics of counter-hegemony, but rather the concept of 'good governance', which focuses on human rights and 'on rule-based treaty regimes on a global scale instead of power politics and stresses the peaceful resolution of conflicts.'[6]

When Habermas wrote his Manifesto for the renaissance of Europe as a reaction to the Iraq-War he was convinced that this was a good historical moment for concentrating these elements of a European identity into a political force supporting the international politics of the governments of Germany, France and Belgium within the EU. To overcome the problems faced by an unfinished European project still weakened by inner contradictions and national interests, Habermas advanced the concept of 'intensified cooperation' among the countries that make up 'core Europe'.[7] As the Manifesto puts it: 'If Europe is not to fall apart the core-European countries have to apply the mechanism of "intensified cooperation"… in a 'Europe of different speeds' they must take the initiative for a Common Foreign,

Security and Defense Policy.' This avant garde of 'core Europe' – built around the French-German-axis and the Benelux-countries – should not separate itself from the rest of the EU but act like a locomotive eventually pulling the others behind them.

Germany always had to fight to introduce this procedure into the Treaty; resistance came from France and Britain as well as from the smaller states – which all share the suspicion that Germany might use this opportunity to impose its national politics and interests (especially in the economic and monetary field) upon the EU as a whole by strengthening a 'two class' Community divided between Germany and its allies on the one side, and the weaker countries of the periphery on the other. In May 2000 Joschka Fischer, Germany's Foreign Secretary, set out the terms for the renewal of the project of 'core Europe' in a lecture at Berlin's Humboldt University. He argued that the coming enlargement of the EU from fifteen to twenty-five or even thirty member states underlined the necessity of institutional reform to enable Europe to act in world politics, and that the new constitution had to allow intensified cooperation of some members in certain policy-fields. In this way a 'centre of gravity' in the EU would be formed which could function as a locomotive for the 'completion of political integration'.[8]

The relationship between Habermas and Fischer dates back to the time when Habermas was teaching at Frankfurt University and Fischer was operating from Frankfurt first as a Green Party member of the state parliament of Hessen, and then as a minister in the government of Hessen, before becoming leader of the Greens in the Bundestag in Bonn. In 1999 Habermas had supported the position of the German government – and especially the position of Fischer as Foreign Minister – in the Yugoslav War. He justified the attack on Yugoslavia by NATO (and Germany's participation in this) with the argument that the use of military force was a necessary element in policing universal human rights and legal conventions, in this case preventing genocide in Kosovo. However clear it became how easily this idealistic cosmopolitism could be abused for the uses of American and European power politics, Habermas has never revised this position. But in 2003, against the background of the decision of the German and French governments not to join George W. Bush's coalition for the attack against Iraq, and in a climate of widespread criticism and protest against US-politics all over Europe and the world, Habermas again backed the German government (and Fischer, of course). His Manifesto elaborated Germany's position against the US war policy vis-à-vis Iraq into a concept of potential European counter-hegemony against a new US imperialism.

Unfortunately, the project of 'European identity' and 'counter-hegemony' against the USA is far from being able to balance US power in world politics and in international institutions. It might best be characterized as a 'Third Way' project for international politics dominated by social democratic and liberal governments in the EU supported by smaller states (e.g., the Benelux countries) that could never profit from globalization by enlarging their military power. Obviously such a project is viewed by 'policy elites in Washington … with real hostility,'[9] and this fed the polemics across the Atlantic that intensified during the run up to the Iraq war. Yet, this is not a strategy to strengthen an alternative to American imperialism or to the neoliberal capitalist globalization it oversees.

Habermas's Manifesto obscures a rather crucial dimension in its representation of Europe. Since the beginning of European integration the Western European bourgeoisie has always had two parallel aims: to profit from being a junior partner (what Brzezinski went so far as to call a 'vassal') of the USA, but at the same time to construct a strong European competitor of the American economy and state. The objective of Jacques Delors' project for the Single Market and Monetary Union was to strengthen the competitiveness of European capitalism in respect to American capitalism. The introduction of the common currency was inevitably accompanied by the question, as Gilpin put it, of 'whether or not the euro will replace the dollar as the world's principal currency, what the consequences for the United States would be if it did, and how the euro would affect the functioning and management of the international monetary and economic system.'[10] At the same time the enlargement of the EU to Eastern Europe – though raising a lot of difficult problems – has been successfully pushed forward by the motive to improve the competitive position of 'Eurocapitalism' within the world market.[11]

As Robert Kagan has said: 'By binding together into a single political and economic unit – the historical accomplishment of Maastricht in 1992 – many hoped to recapture Europe's old greatness in a new political form. "Europe" would be the next superpower, not only economically and politically but also militarily. It would handle crisis on the European continent, such as the ethnic conflicts in the Balkans, and it would re-emerge as a global player of the first rank.'[12] Yet during the '90s, as Kagan himself concludes, Europe actually failed to intervene as a unique actor in international politics and crisis management. This was evident in relation to the war on Yugoslavia, but it was true in much else as well, especially in the international economic sphere.

Indeed, since the first steps to Monetary Union at the end of the 70s, and the new dynamics of European integration launched by the Single Market project after 1985, the EU has been dominated by the politics of neoliberalism. The most important 'new constitutionalism' in Europe in this sense has been the one that Stephen Gill over a decade ago identified as associated with applying the ideology that national governments have no choice but to adapt to the constraints of transnational markets and competition, to dismantle the welfare state, deregulate labour markets, privatize public goods and owner-ship and weaken trade unions.[13] This has become the dominant tendency in European politics in the '90s. Though Jacques Delors promised to strengthen the 'social dimension' of the EU, the results were very modest. Trade unions enjoy enlarged participation rights in European policy networks, yet social legislation at the EU level has not made real progress. Unions rather confront a paradox: their co-optation into the neoliberal projects of the EU (Single Market, Monetary Union, European Financial Market, Common Market for Services, Eastern Enlargement etc.) has not contributed to overcome the crises of the trade union movement in Europe. It rather weakens their capac-ities to fight neoliberalism 'at home'.[14]

Habermas does not even mention these dominant tendencies which are steadily destroying the European welfare states and transforming them into 'workfare' regimes.[15] Thus, his Manifesto's appeal to 'European identity' was less convincing than the earlier public letter of criticism organized by the late Pierre Bourdieu against the neoliberal politics of the EU and its member states.[16]

The dominance of neoliberalism is precisely the mechanism through which the EU is integrated in and subordinated to the American Empire. Though in the past few years social protests (including general strikes and mass demonstrations organized by European trade unions in cooperation with the anti-globalization movement) have become much stronger, they have not had any considerable influence upon European politics, and portend nothing like the 'fundamental change in the domestic balance of social forces' that would be required to bring about a 'disarticulation' of European states and/or the EU from the American empire.[17] Transatlantic relations thus remain based upon a complex system of common and competing interests. European states and the leading fractions of European transnational corpo-rations and financial institutions have an interest in creating a strong European economy on the basis of the euro as the new common currency and the construction of a European financial market. But at the same time they have remained bound into the 'Dollar-Wall Street Regime',[18] and have accepted the leading role of the American state in reconstructing the capi-talist world order after the end of the Cold War.

Insofar as intra-imperialist rivalries can still be said to exist, they are much weaker than they were in the period between 1914 and 1945, and are not really characteristic of the 'new imperialism' of our time. Of course, nobody can exactly foresee the full political and economic consequences of the disaster Iraq has become for the USA and its allies. And the American economy still is burdened by many risks. If world politics and the world economy become increasingly turbulent, the concept of 'European counter-hegemony' might acquire more importance, used to strengthen the position of EU against the USA and to build alliances (e.g. with Russia and China or with Middle East countries) in the United Nations and other international organizations. Still, the majority of European economic and policy elites favour the strategy of partnership with the USA. They merely criticize the politics of the present neoconservative American government and hope for a political change in the USA that will tilt the balance towards multilateralism based upon the recognition of international law.

III

Habermas's Manifesto was criticized on many sides. To some it was simply a document of 'European anti-Americanism'; others blamed Habermas for being too close to the German government and especially its Foreign Secretary, Fischer. As the governments of the new members of the EU in Eastern Europe (already members of NATO) supported George W. Bush and Donald Rumsfeld, and so strengthened the position of Tony Blair, José Maria Aznar and Silvio Berlusconi, it was quite obvious that the Franco-German-Belgian-coalition was in a minority position and far too weak to be a serious 'core' or 'centre of gravity' within the newly expanded EU. Some critics argued that Habermas and his friends had forgotten to include any intellectuals from Eastern Europe and the Anglo-Saxon world. Richard Rorty, on the other hand, wrote an article praising the Habermas initiative as a relief for American intellectuals protesting against neoconservative politics. Yet, more telling was the fact that on the whole Habermas was far more confronted with the argument that his appeal contributed to the split of Europe rather than to 'Europeanize' its intellectuals.[19]

Such criticism might explain why the Manifesto did not gather massive support and its prominent subscribers remained politically and intellectually isolated. More important, however, was the process which finally decided the fate of the Franco-German initiative which had proposed to lead the EU into opposition against the US policy on Iraq and, at the same time, to realize projects of political integration. This, as Habermas's Manifesto remarked, might indeed have improved the EU's 'qualities of a state' under the leadership of the Franco-German alliance. The Bush administration, of course, tried to break up this strategy, well aware that its allies in Europe are not only governments that are closely bound to the US by security interests (as in Eastern Europe) or by ideological motives, but also those economic and political forces that prefer transatlantic partnership led by the USA instead of inter-imperialist rivalry or any counter-hegemony defined in terms of the welfare state. In Germany, for instance, the Christian Democratic Party (but also some dissidents within the Social Democratic Party) attacked Chancellor Schröder for 'anti-Americanism' and for following an extremely dangerous 'German way' in international politics. Though the majority of people all over Europe were clearly against the war, many among the political and economic elites warned against putting the Atlantic partnership at risk.[20] Since Schröder likes to present himself as an ally of modern German capitalist management (especially in the automobile industry), he must have been quite sensitive to pressures from the management of German corporations and banks engaged in the American markets not to go too far. And indeed, by the spring of 2004, the German Chancellor was being warmly received in the White House: Bush and Schröder emerged with a joint statement stressing common interests and positions in the transatlantic partnership. At the same time, Foreign Secretary Joschka Fischer now proposed a new direction for Germany's vis-à-vis Europe: he said goodbye to the project of 'core Europe' pushing forward political integration, and spoke in terms of 'strategic Europe in continental dimensions' (including Turkey), a concept based primarily on the big Common Market.[21] A year after the issuing of Habermas's Manifesto, it was all but forgotten.

Obviously, these changes were produced by painful facts. On the one hand, the disaster of the American occupation of Iraq in the context of a presidential electoral campaign has made the Bush administration more willing to look for compromise with the European states outside the 'Coalition'. On the other hand, the Franco-German-Benelux Alliance did not succeed – a majority of EU-members (as well as of new members) rejected the claim for leadership by those states associated with 'core Europe'. The minority position of these states, moreover, was not only confined to the Iraq war but expanded to a series of central issues of integration policy – especially the European Constitution which was accepted by the Convention and the Council but then rejected by the governments of Spain and Poland (both firmly on the side of the USA in the Iraq question). Consequently, in the second half of 2003 the EU approached paralysis and crises. The resolution of this crisis in the spring of 2004 took the form, not of the victory of the Franco-German-Benelux Alliance (whose meetings in Brussels were ridiculed as 'chocolate summits'), but the renunciation of the project of 'core Europe' itself.[22]

This failure does not mean that the project of a 'European counter-hegemony' against American imperialism does not exist any longer. It is still a project of those in Europe who aim to strengthen the EU – politically, economically and ideologically – as a global political actor capable of balancing US imperialism and unilateralism. But however much this project might be justified in terms of 'soft power' and 'good governance' based upon international law, human rights, transnational civil society and democracy (while also serving to stave off any suspicions that it might be seen as a project for a new 'Euroimperialism'), it is clear that such a project connected to the claim of leadership by the Franco-German alliance has no chance. Within global capitalism, the American state is strong enough to rely upon the mechanisms of 'disciplinary neoliberalism' and to activate its political and social allies to oppose such a project of 'European counter-hegemony'.

Perhaps the main lesson that may be learned from Habermas's failed Manifesto is that the field of international politics, dominated as it is by competing interests among states within the EU, let alone with the American state, is not the appropriate place for rallying critical intellectuals against American imperialism. At the moment progressive movements inside and outside the EU are not able to change the basic relations of forces dominated by global capital and neoliberalism. They need, however, to be addressed as potential actors for the construction of a counter-hegemony which is not based upon the competition between two neoliberal variants of capitalism but upon the programme of a real alternative to American and European-led global capitalism, i.e. a new socialist project.

NOTES

1   Jacques Derrida und Jürgen Habermas, 'Unsere Erneuerung. Nach dem Krieg: Die Wiedergeburt Europas', (After the War: The Renaissance of Europe), *Frankfurter Allgemeine Zeitung*, May 31, 2003, pp. 33/34. Unless otherwise indicated all the following quotes are from this text.

2   Zbigniew Brzezinski, *The Grand Chessboard: American Primacy and Its Geostrategic Imperatives*, New York: Basic Books, 1997.

3   Cf. Jürgen Habermas, *Die postnationale Konstellation*, Frankfurt/Main 1998. In 2001 Habermas had supported the project of a European Constitution launched by the Summit of Laeken. He spoke of 'the necessity of a European civil society, the construction of a political public in Europe and of the creation of a political culture which is shared by all citizens of the EU' (Jürgen Habermas, 'Warum braucht Europa eine Verfassung?', *Die Zeit*, 27/2001.

4   Jürgen Habermas, 'Europäische Identität und universalistisches Handeln', *Blätter für deutsche und internationale Politik*, 7/2003, pp. 801-6.

5   Peter Gowan, 'America and the World in the 21st Century: Possible Variants of Change', Paper presented to a Conference of the Korean Political Science Association in Seoul, October, 2002, p. 305.

6   Peter Gowan, 'America and the World', p. 305.

7   This has been a central element of German European policy since the Maastricht Summit in 1991, when the government of Britain refused to join the Economic and Monetary Union and rejected the 'Social Charter', which

was accepted by the other members but only added to the Maastricht Treaty as a 'Social Protocol'. Since the foundation of the European Community in the '50s unanimous voting has been the basic principle of decision making within the Council; this rule has always strengthened the smaller countries and imposes strategies of negotiations open for compromises ('package deals'). The Single Market programme of the 1980s weakened this principle in favour of majority votes. The enlargement of the Union from twelve member states in 1991 to twenty-five in 2004 proceeded on the basis of the 'two speed Europe' introduced in the Amsterdam Treaty (1997) as the 'procedure of intensified cooperation', and was further strengthened by the treaty finally signed at Nizza in 2001 (the chaos of the Nizza summit and the protest of the Spanish and Polish governments against the draft of the European Constitution in 2003 was produced by conflict over the question how to define the majority). The draft of the new European Constitution institutionalizes 'intensified cooperation' in Chapter III/Article 3.The procedure allows those 'member states that intend to intensify their cooperation' (for instance in the field of monetary policy or in the field of Foreign and Security Policy) to advance, while those who don't want to join or who are not yet able to join can wait and join later. Yet the rules of the Treaty are very narrow and stress the exceptional character of this mechanism.

8   Joschka Fischer, 'Vom Staatenbund zur Föderation – Gedanken über die Finalität der Integration', *Integration*, 3/2000, pp. 149-56. Note that Fischer stressed he was speaking in his private capacity.

9   Peter Gowan, 'America and the World', p. 306.

10   Robert Gilpin, *Global Political Economy*, Princeton and London: Princeton University Press 2001, p. 255.

11   'The closest thing to an equal that the United States faces at the beginning of the 21st century is the European Union (EU). Although the American economy is four times larger than that of Germany, the largest European country, the economy of the EU is roughly equal to that of the United States; its population is considerably larger, as is its share in world exports. These proportions will increase if, as planned, the EU gradually expands to include the states of Central Europe over the next decades. Europe spends about two-thirds of what the United States does on defense, has more men under arms, and includes two countries that possess nuclear arsenals ...', Joseph Nye, *The Paradox of American Power*, Oxford: Oxford University Press, 2002, pp. 29-30.

12   Robert Kagan, *Paradise and Power: America and Europe in the New World Order*, London: Atlantic Books 2003, p. 20.

13   Hans-Jürgen Bieling und Frank Deppe, 'Die neue europäische Ökonomie und die Transformation von Staatlichkeit', in Markus Jachtenfuchs und Beate Kohler-Koch (Hrsg.), *Europäische Integration*, 2. Auflage, Opladen: Leske & Budrich, 2003, pp. 513-40. For Gill's concept of 'new constitutionalism' see his 'The Emerging World Order and European Change', *Socialist Register 1992*, London: Merlin Press, 1992.

14   Frank Deppe, 'Die Gewerkschaften und der "Eurokapitalismus"', in Martin

Beckmann, Hans-Jürgen Bieling und Frank Deppe, eds., 'Eurokapitalismus' und globale politische Ökonomie, Hamburg: VSA-Verlag, 2003, pp. 169-95.

15   See Robert Jessop, 'Globalization and the Nation State', in S. Aronowitz and P. Bratsis, eds., Paradigm Lost: State Theory Reconsidered, Minneapolis: University of Minnesota Press, 2002, esp. pp. 202ff.

16   Pierre Bourdieu et al., 'Les perspectives de la protestation. La résistance sociale outre-rhin, foyer d'une autre Europe', Paris: Editions Syllepse, 1998.

17   Leo Panitch and Sam Gindin, 'Global Capitalism and American Empire', Socialist Register 2004, London: Merlin Press, 2003, p. 33.

18   The term is Peter Gowan's, from his The Global Gamble, London: Verso, 1999.

19   Richard Rorty, 'Demütigung und Solidarität', Süddeutsche Zeitung (München), May 31, 2003.

20   Notably, the policies of Alan Greenspan and the Federal Reserve to drive down the exchange value of the US dollar which severely hits German export industries and functions as one of the brakes on economic recovery in Germany, were not denounced even though these amounted to an act of 'financial warfare' much more effective than the polemics of Donald Rumsfeld.

21   'Fischer nimmt Abschied von Kerneuropa-Idee, Financial Times Deutschland, February 28, 2004.

22   In March 2004 this alliance was strengthened by the victory of the Spanish Socialists under Zapatero in the general elections which threw José Maria Aznar, the best friend of George W. Bush besides Tony Blair, out of office. The terrorist attack in Madrid shortly before the elections and the crude manipulation of information by the conservative government (implying ETA responsibility) might have influenced voting behaviour. Yet, the decisive fact was that from the beginning of the Iraq war a huge majority of the Spanish population was against the war and especially against the participation of Spanish troops. So, this was not a 'victory of terrorism', but a victory of the anti-war movement. Zapatero declared immediately the retreat of troops from Iraq as well as a closer relationship of Spain with France and Germany within the EU. At the moment (May 2004) it is far too early to evaluate the consequences of this change of the relation of forces within the EU. If the Italians would throw Silvio Berlusconi out of office and replace him by Romano Prodi, the current president of the European Commission, then the debate around a European 'counter-hegemony' might be continued on the basis of a different setting of the relation of political forces within the EU, with the initiative now emerging from beyond the states of 'core Europe'.

BUSH AND BLAIR: IRAQ AND THE UK'S AMERICAN VICEROY

Tony Benn

IN CONVERSATION WITH Colin Leys

CL: In September 2002, when the US invasion of Iraq was already impending, you went to Baghdad and talked with Saddam Hussein. What perspective does this give you on what has since transpired?

TB: I first went to see Saddam in 1990 and had three hours with him. I went with only one objective, to get the hostages returned. Ted Heath went with the same aim. In the end they were all returned.[1] One of the things that came out then was his sense of utter betrayal. He said that April Glaspie, the American ambassador in Baghdad, had said to him in the summer of 1990, 'If you go into Kuwait we will regard it as an Arab question.'[2] He felt utterly betrayed by the Americans. After all, Rumsfeld had just been there a few years earlier, selling him chemical weapons (that was confirmed by Tariq Aziz when I saw him again last year). I said, 'Well, you'll have to withdraw from Kuwait'; and he said, 'Even if I do so the Americans will destroy me, because I'm too strong' – and in a sense he was right about that.

Then in September 2002 it was obvious war was coming again, so I wrote and said, could I do an interview with Saddam? I paid my own fare, and my hotel bill – it was a lot of money but I didn't want to be beholden to anyone. Before I went I sent a message to Number 10, saying, 'I'm going, and is there anything you would like me to do?' Number 10 then issued a statement denying they knew I was going. And coming back I rang Number 10 from Amman and said, 'I'm coming back, would you like to see me?' I never heard a word. They were not interested.

It was a full interview. I asked him: 'Do you have weapons of mass destruction?', and he said no. 'Do you have links with Al-Qaida?' and he said no. Then I asked him about the UN and a few other questions of that kind. I also had long talks with other people, including Al-Saadi, the chemist who once headed Iraq's advanced weapons programs, and who was in charge of dealing with Blix. He told me the whole story that has now come out. He said, 'We tried a nuclear programme and we dropped it', and so on with other weapons of mass destruction. I was really persuaded that that was true, so I said, 'Why don't you let the inspectors in?' He said the reason was very simple: 'the Americans would not suspend the no-fly zone, and they could be bombing us when the inspectors are there, and we're not having responsibility for that.' But at a very late stage I rather think Saddam did offer to let the Americans come in, before the war; it's never been publicized, but from bits of information I picked up later I think that around that time Saddam did offer to let the Americans in, to prove there were no weapons of mass destruction. But of course by then Bush was determined to go to war.

That's the background. And the arguments used to justify the war – that Iraq had weapons of mass destruction, that it had links with Al-Qaida, that the coalition would bring democracy – every statement made has turned out to be a complete lie. What it is about is very clear: the American need for oil – every empire needs resources, but America is utterly dependent on oil. And remember, Iraq was one of the Arab states that didn't even recognize the existence of the state of Israel, and Wolfowitz and Perle and Cheney and the neoconservatives in general saw the interest of Israel as being the important one; there is a link between the Palestinian and the Iraq issue.

CL: Let's talk about the situation now. The Americans are trying to install a puppet government, and will try to ensure that another puppet government emerges from any elections that are held. They are also trying to create a puppet army that will take care of internal control, backed up by US forces in their new bases in Iraq, which will also control the wider region. The question is, can this work? Will most Iraqis eventually accept this, or will they continue to sympathize with, and in enough cases give practical support to, the resistance? How far will the new phenomenon of suicide bombing, by people trained in a fundamentalist version of Islam, perhaps largely non-Iraqis, alienate the majority who have grown up in a formally secular society? Will alienation from violence, and weariness from insecurity, make people inclined to support an American-backed puppet regime against the bombers?

TB: I can't speculate about the future but let's look at the past. Genghis Khan went into Iraq in 1258 and killed a million Iraqis. He took the books from the library, the oldest library in the world, and threw them in the Tigris. When I was there they told me the Tigris then was black with the ink from the books, and red with the blood of the Iraqis who defended the country. And Britain liberated Iraq from the Turks in the first war. Six hundred thousand British troops were sent into Iraq; forty thousand of them died in the next ten years, before Iraq became so-called independent, under a king imposed by Britain. So from an Iraqi point of view, this is an old problem. I think they see Bush as Genghis Khan. And what Bush has done has united the Shiites and the Sunnis – they both want him out. That's quite an achievement. And the transfer of power is completely fraudulent. The new Iraqi government won't really control Iraq.

There are twelve American bases in Iraq. Whatever happens, these will be maintained. I don't think Bush is interested in any of the things he says he is interested in, in peace and justice for Iraq; what he is interested in is the continued flow of oil. It will be rather different from the British empire, where there was an element of, I won't say consent, but bitter acceptance of it all. Quite a small military presence held India down, using the Rajahs and Maharajas to govern on our behalf. I suppose they hope that Allawi, a CIA man, will be able to do the same in Iraq.[3] I don't know if he can. But my feeling is that so long as Bush has got his bases, he doesn't particularly care. Look at Afghanistan, it's a good case in point. Poppy production has gone up – it's just market forces operating there. The Americans and their allies only control Kabul; the rest is just back to the warlords, and you never hear about that any more. I presume that the Americans think they can protect the pipeline through Afghanistan from the Caspian, which is what the whole thing was about anyway, and I imagine that Bush thinks in the same way about Iraq.

Will this project survive? Speculation is very difficult, but Arab pride in maintaining themselves against American power is very, very strong. I personally don't see much moral difference between a Stealth Bomber and a suicide bomber. They both kill innocent people for political purposes. It is a fact that the suicide bombers kill people. But how many people have been killed by the Americans and the British in Iraq? What the world is now coming to realize is that you can have Stealth Bombers, or Star Wars, but it doesn't protect you – 9/11 proved that.

CL: But if Bush's interest is largely in controlling oil supplies, can a regime without any internal legitimacy, resting chiefly on permanently-occupied American bases, ensure that Iraqi oil does flow reliably to the west? If Allawi can't form a stable government, with a degree of acceptance, however grudging, you think the Americans won't really care? They will rely on force and money to make the oil flow, and not be concerned about anything else? I'm inclined to agree about their attitude, but I'm doubtful if it is possible to make oil supplies – as opposed to opium supplies, which provide farmers with their livelihoods – reliable under such conditions.

TB: Iraq's pipelines, all pipelines, are very vulnerable. If you are in a country you haven't really conquered and held down, that is still in a state of resistance, the capacity to disrupt the oil supply is infinite. And if Iraqi oil supplies stopped, and the US went in again with full force and restored the conquest, it still wouldn't guarantee the oil supply. Though I don't have a lot of contacts now, the Iraqis I know think that violence will intensify and that free elections will be impossible in the instability caused by that. So I think the American project won't work. Of course the sheer capacity of their military forces to maintain bases is unquestionable. But let's recall that in 1839 the British Governor General of India sent an army into Afghanistan to deal with trouble there. Kabul was easily captured. Eighteen mnonths later the army was forced to leave and out of 16,000 troops and civilians barely a hundred made it back to India. That is one of the weaknesses of the Bush and Blair way of thinking – it is just utterly bereft of any historical perspective.

CL: Let's turn to Britain's role in this. Blair's support has obviously been invaluable to Bush, but the result is that his position is rather like that of Gorbachev, who is lauded in the West but regarded in Russia with something like contempt; Blair is lauded in Washington but increasingly distrusted and disliked in the UK. The question is, how much does this matter? A key problem for the new American empire will be that governments in the advanced capitalist countries will lose legitimacy when they are carrying out American policies that are unpopular with their own electorates – rather like the way the western Communist Parties were discredited by having to support all the twists and turns of Soviet foreign policy enforced on them by the Comintern. Blair wants Iraq to be forgotten, and the Conservatives, who support Bush and the war, fully agree. They both insist that what people are really interested in are domestic issues – immigration, security, health, education, taxes. The question is, will they succeed? Assuming British troops are withdrawn by the end of 2005, as we are being told they will be, do you think people will eventually just accept what has happened?

TB: I do think that without Blair, Bush would have found it much harder to go to war. Memories of Vietnam were at the back of people's minds. He was able to talk about the 'coalition of the willing', a new version of 'the free world' or 'the international community' – whatever words you use to describe something other than the UN. I think Blair's motivation was twofold. First of all, the positive: now we haven't got an empire, if you piggy-back on Bush's military force you become an empire again, and 'Bush-and-Blair', 'Bush-and-Blair', are spoken about in the world as if Blair was

Vice-President of the United States. Secondly, the price we would have paid
for standing up against the United States would have been terrifying. It
wouldn't just have been making it difficult to sell French wine or having
Americans calling French fries 'freedom fries'. It would have meant taking
away our nuclear weapons and generally punishing us. So what you realize
is that even if you wanted simple things like jobs, trade union rights, no
means test for pensioners, no student loans, no privatization and no war –
even if you wanted those things, for the US you'd be a 'rogue state'.

But Blair has paid a very heavy price in Britain. The price he's paid is easy
to describe: people don't believe a word he says about anything. In the end,
in a democracy, there has to be some basic understanding that what you are
told by the government is true; and if you think that it's not true, and it's all
dictated elsewhere for other purposes, it has a fundamental effect on the
confidence people have, not just in this government but in politicians altogether, as the European elections have shown – there was a great cynical,
protest vote, that's potentially very dangerous.

The impact on British politics is very profound. You've got a whole group
of people who are against Blair on this: the Left, the Greens, and there's also
the pro-European Conservatives – Ted Heath is passionately opposed to this
war, as he was against the Gulf War, and the Kosovo war, because he sees it
as a threat by America to dominate the world without Europe as a counterbalance – and two million people came out against it last year, and anti-war
meetings are going on all over the place. You've got a very strong combination of forces against it. So I think it will damage Blair, and Britain's so-called
special relationship with the US, fundamentally. In September 2002, Blair was
asked on television if the 'special relationship' meant that Britain was prepared
to fight American wars, to 'pay the blood price'. His reply was that yes, it does:
'At moments of crisis', he said, the US 'need to know "Are you prepared to
commit? Are you prepared to be there when the shooting starts?"' So what has
happened has reopened the whole issue of the special relationship.

People are beginning to realize that we are a colony of the United States.
I've written about that many times and been rebuked for it, but talk about
a puppet government in Iraq – what about the puppet government in
Britain? The Americans have God knows how many bases here. They've got
Star Wars based here. We are exchanging our intelligence with them. We
don't have our own nuclear weapons – the Americans lend them to us, and
we can't use them independently; the Americans control their use. We are
a puppet state. And people are now openly feeling and saying that we didn't
elect Blair to be Vice-President of the United States. We elected a Labour
government to govern Britain on our behalf, not on Bush's behalf. The fact
is that we now have to think about a liberation movement in Britain.

CL: In one of your *Morning Star* articles last year you described Blair as a 'Viceroy' of the American empire. What do you think being a semi-colony of the US, ruled by a local Viceroy, implies for British politics? There are popular movements in Britain opposed to American control, and a number of people even in mainstream politics who think in multilateral terms, who still have a commitment to a rule-regulated world order. But thinking about what is still the only major political party with left traditions, the Labour Party, it's been captured by the so-called modernizers around Blair who accept the 'special relationship'. They've re-written the party constitution so that it's very difficult for policy to be changed and they're supported by a media system that's partly owned by supporters of the neoconservative agenda, while other elements, especially the BBC, have been browbeaten and bullied, and are vulnerable to the same forces that Blair represents. New parties are effectively barred by the first-past-the-post electoral system – and anyway you've always advocated working within the Labour Party. But it's hard to see how a left, anti-imperialist majority can advance within the Labour Party within the sort of time scale I'm concerned with, which is the next five to ten years.

TB: It is so important to understand the way progress occurs. It begins with pressure outside the system, and then the pressure gets so strong that inside the system they have to say to themselves, what are we going to do to defuse this? And if they think the only way to retain control is to concede, they will concede – unlike the French ruling class, the British ruling class don't go to the guillotine rather than give up, they always withdraw. They withdraw, they appear to concede. They decapitate the leadership of the opposition by putting them in the House of Lords, by honouring them, and then with their support they come back again. If you understand that, you know what you've got to do: you go on and on and on pressing. And if you go on and on pressing even the spin-doctors get the message and say, Prime Minister, you can't go on like this. That's where the time scale is so important. You don't get immediate results. You didn't on the suffragettes, you didn't on the Charter issues, you didn't on the welfare state, you didn't on trade union rights, you didn't on apartheid – you didn't on anything.

There is a sort of left pessimism which says it is all hopeless, all you can do is demonstrate. I'm the President of the Stop the War Coalition, they honoured me with that. But it hasn't got a policy on anything else, it's just about the war. And you can't win public support on the basis of just being against the war, you've got to be for things. In New York there was this chant I heard: 'Money for health and not for war', 'Money for jobs and not for war', 'Money for homes and not for war'. That's the beginnings of a policy, at any rate. Confidence is what it's all about. We are winning by the usual slow process: to begin with, your argument's ignored, then you're mad, then you're dangerous; then there's a pause; and then you can't find anyone at the top who doesn't claim to have thought of it in the first place. That's how progress is made.

So for me, the Labour Party is stage one in winning the battle for public opinion. I'm not defending the Labour Party, although I've been a member of it all my life. I simply say, without them, what's the instrument? Where do you get progress – not just on the war but on all the other things that have to be dealt with. We've got many, too many, different socialist parties in Britain, and not enough socialists. My argument is a straightforward one: if you can't win the Labour Party you can't win Britain. And it's Britain we have to win back. I don't mean anything like armed struggle. I mean that you have to ask yourself what would an independent British state, pursuing an independent foreign policy, be like? It would be a non-nuclear state, putting all its effort into trying to make the UN work – because that's the only long-term hope.

CL: In an article you wrote last year you sketched what a reformed United Nations would look like, with members of the General Assembly directly elected, in numbers proportional to populations, and a Security Council elected by the Assembly, with representation from all regions, and the World Bank and the IMF and the WTO and multinational corporations subject to UN control. You wrote that these were 'dreams at present', but that without a vision of this kind the global anti-capitalist, anti-war movement can't move forward: there has to be a goal. So this is a question about the coherence of that goal: how would a reformed UN be able to impose sanctions on these other bodies and companies?

TB: The WTO or the IMF impose their conditionalities, and force countries to give corporations access to billions of dollars' worth of public service spending, by economic pressure. You have to ask, what is the counter pressure? You can't deal with the IMF except on a global scale. The General Assembly, by a majority of nations, is on the side of the poor and not the rich. A majority for change there puts the Americans in the position of not just repudiating the Security Council and the Charter but also the General Assembly, the whole idea of internationalism. And then the question is, would the American public accept that? I don't think they would.

One of the interesting things is how imperialism ends. How did it end in Britain? An important element was that there was an alliance between the progressive forces in Britain and the anti-colonial movement. If you talked to the leaders of the old anti-colonial movement, like Gandhi and Nehru, they did recognize that the alliance with the progressive forces in Britain was an element in changing British opinion about the desirability of trying to maintain an empire when you couldn't afford it. All empires come and go, and if the American empire declines it will be because the American people see that it's not in their interests to try to run the world – the cost is enormous, the casualties are enormous. This why I keep arguing that the left in the world has got to keep in touch with the left in the United States, because they're the only ones who can bring about a regime change in Washington.

CL: I want to share your inveterate optimism, but I would like to probe it a little bit. When the UN was formed it was the product of over forty years of mayhem in Europe – people had gone through hell – and so the relatively advanced European capitalist countries put their weight behind the project. But can we imagine a reconstructed, democratic, egalitarian world order today, if the so-called North hasn't undergone a period of suffering? Since Somalia the US has been determined to minimize its own casualties, and while hundreds of Americans have lost their lives, or been maimed for life, in Afghanistan and Iraq, they have mostly been professional foot soldiers, so-called grunts, from poor backgrounds, and moreover their deaths and injuries have been largely kept from public view. Most ordinary people in the North as a whole really feel no pain so far, not even economic pain. It is not clear to me that anyone in the North is hurting enough to make the sacrifices needed to create a new world order of the kind we are talking about. What drives the ecological movement, and to some extent also the anti-corporate movement that is linked to it, is an awareness that neoliberal global capitalism can't go on, i.e. anxiety about what will happen. But can you win mass support for a transformation of the global order, relying only on anxiety?

TB: The entire human race is related, if you think about it – we have common ancestors – and we are like survivors in a lifeboat, with one loaf of bread. There are only three ways of distributing the loaf – you sell it, so the rich get all of it; you fight for it, so the strong get all of it; or you share it, so everybody gets a bit. That is the choice for the human race. That point is gradually reaching everyone through the environmental movement. And if that is the case, are we going to have wars with China, to see they don't get oil? With India, to see they don't get oil? With Brazil? Of course we're not. The whole balance of the world is against that. And then the crisis of the UN is going to come back in a big way.

Even if they don't make the same dangerous mistakes they have in Iraq, can they really occupy every country that's got oil? Of course they can't. If you put that argument people understand it. Nobody wants to pay more for petrol, nobody wants rationing. But when you come to it, reality is the argument that counts. People understand it. Leave aside left morality or left analysis; really you can't hold people down, and that has been the lesson of history. So it's a very long-term ground for optimism, but I think it's an easy argument to make. You don't have to have read Marx and Lenin to make it. People understand it. And the internet has transformed things. The amount of information available to all thoughtful people, all the organizers, is now such that they all know what's going on.

CL: I agree of course that the internet has transformed activism, but it hasn't transformed the mainstream media. The mainstream media get all this information, and stock it, but most of them only use it when the owners, or editors, decide it is convenient and safe to use it. Most people are not active, and only read or hear what the mainstream media publish.

TB: The mainstream media are the modern church. The most powerful religion in the world at the moment is not Christianity or Buddhism. Money is the great religion; people worship money. The business news is given every hour, what's happened to the FTSE, what's happened to the Dow Jones averages; at least in the American media, it's a constant hymn to capitalism. It's no accident that Henry VIII nationalized the Church of England, because he wanted a priest in every pulpit every Sunday, saying 'God wants you to do what the King wants you to do.' And the Tories nationalized the BBC because they wanted a pundit on every channel telling you the government was right. I thought the BBC was ghastly during the Iraq war, but even just allowing a different view to be aired brought them down. I was doing a regular broadcast with William Hague and they took me off because on one broadcast I attacked Hutton and said it was a rotten report. They didn't use it, and dropped me from the programme.

But it's very difficult for the media to deny what people know. They know they can't get a pension because the money is going to kill pensioners in Iraq. They know they can't get education because the money is being used to bomb students in Iraq. It's such an easy argument to put. I go round the country doing meetings. On Tuesday night I was in Manchester. One thousand seven hundred people turned up at a theatre and sat for twenty minutes and an hour and a half of discussion. I don't know what their politics were, but by God there is an audience now, which there never was before, in the early days of New Labour, when politics were 'dead', and people were apathetic. Now there's this great audience to hear positive, hopeful things. People are angry that no one listens. They don't believe what they're told. And anger and mistrust are not the same as apathy. There's a force developing. It hasn't yet got into the parliamentary system, but it will have to.

NOTES

1   Several hundred western foreigners, including 82 Britons, were taken hostage by Iraq when it invaded Kuwait in August 1990. The former Conservative Prime Minister Edward Heath went on a similar mission to Benn's. The British hostages were released in December 1990.

2   For a transcript of the meeting between Glaspie and Saddam, confirming Saddam's claim, see http://www.whatreallyhappened.com/ARTICLE5/april.html.

3   Iyad Allawi, appointed executive prime minister in the interim government before the June 30, 2004 'transfer of sovereignty', was well known 'as the darling of the State Department and the Central Intelligence Agency as well as the British MI6', according to one of the most knowledgeable western journalists covering Iraq. 'Alawi's Iraqi National Accord (INA) was as prolific in supplying false information on Iraq's weapons of mass destruction as its rival Ahmad Chalabi's Iraqi National Congress. The INA was the source of the sensational claim that Iraq was capable of firing its weapons of mass destruction within 45 minutes of a Saddam order to do so. During the bargaining at the Security Council over the new interim administration's rights to its own security forces and its relationship with the US-led Multi-National Forces (MNF), the French insisted on an Iraqi veto over any large scale MNF offensives. By failing to support the French demand, Alawi proved his pro-American bona fides to top U.S. officials.' Dilip Hiro, 'Tipping Point in Iraq', www.TomDispatch.com, June 23, 2004.

Socialist Register – Published Annually Since 1964

Leo Panitch and Colin Leys – Editors
2004: THE NEW IMPERIAL CHALLENGE

"As Rosa Luxemburg observed, it is 'often hard to determine, within the tangle of violence and contests for power, the stern laws of economic process.' This is what Panitch, Gindin, Harvey, Gowan, and their colleagues on the Marxist left are trying to do …. For this, whatevever our other differences, the rest of us owe them much gratitude" George Scialabba, *Dissent*, Spring 2004

What does imperialism mean in the new century?
Do we need new concepts to understand it?
Who benefits, who suffers? Where? Why?

Contents: Leo Panitch & Sam Gindin: Global Capitalism and American Empire; Aijaz Ahmad: Imperialism of Our Time; David Harvey: The 'New' Imperialism - Accumulation by Dispossession; Greg Albo: The Old and New Economics of Imperialism; Noam Chomsky: Truths and Myths about the Invasion of Iraq; Amy Bartholomew & Jennifer Breakspear: Human Rights as Swords of Empire; Paul Rogers: The US Military Posture - 'A Uniquely Benign Imperialism'?; Michael T. Klare: Blood for Oil - The Bush-Cheney Energy Strategy; John Bellamy Foster & Brett Clark: Ecological Imperialism - The Curse of Capitalism; Tina Wallace: NGO Dilemmas - Trojan Horses for Global Neoliberalism?; John Saul: Globalization, Imperialism, Development - False Binaries and Radical Resolutions; Emad Aysha: The Limits and Contradictions of 'Americanization'; Bob Sutcliffe: Crossing Borders in the New Imperialism.

290 pp. 234 x 156 mm.

0850365341 hbk £30.00   085036535X pbk £14.95

Leo Panitch and Colin Leys – Editors
2003: FIGHTING IDENTITIES – Race, Religion And Ethno-Nationalism

"these contributions... show a left able to avoid both economic reductionism and post-modern identity-fetishism in confronting and understanding a world of mounting anxiety, instability and violence." Stephen Marks, *Tribune*.

Contents: Peter Gowan: The American Campaign for Global Sovereignty; Aziz Al-Azmeh: Postmodern Obscurantism and 'the Muslim Question'; Avishai Ehrlich: Palestine, Global Politics and Israeli Judaism; Susan Woodward: The Political Economy of Ethno-Nationalism in Yugoslavia; Georgi Derluguian: How Soviet Bureaucracy Produced Nationalism and what came of it in Azerbaijan; Pratyush Chandra: Linguistic-Communal Politics and Class Conflict in India; Mahmood Mamdani: Making Sense of Political Violence in Postcolonial Africa; Hugh Roberts: The Algerian

Catastrophe: Lessons for the Left; Stephen Castles: The International Politics of Forced Migration; Hans-Georg Betz: Xenophobia, Identity Politics and Exclusionary Populism in Western Europe; Jörg Flecker: The European Right and Working Life- From ordinary miseries to political disasters; Huw Beynon & Lou Kushnick: Cool Britannia or Cruel Britannia? Racism and New Labour; Bill Fletcher Jr. & Fernando Gapasin: The Politics of Labour and Race in the USA; Amory Starr: Is the North American Anti-Globalization Movement Racist? Critical reflections; Stephanie Ross: Is This What Democracy Looks Like? -The politics of the anti-globalization movement in North America; Sergio Baierle: The Porto Alegre Thermidor: Brazil's 'Participatory Budget' at the crossroads; Nancy Leys Stepan: Science and Race: Before and after the Genome Project; John S. Saul: Identifying Class, Classifying Difference

396 pp, 234 x 156 mm.

0 85036 507 4 hbk £29.95   0 85036 508 2 pbk £16.95

Canada: Fernwood Publishing; USA: Monthly Review Press; UK and Rest of World: Merlin Press

Leo Panitch and Colin Leys – Editors
2002: A WORLD OF CONTRADICTIONS

Timely and critical analysis of what big businesses and their governments want, and of the problems they create.

Contents: Naomi Klein: Farewell To 'The End Of History': Organization And Vision In Anti-Corporate Movements; André Drainville: Québec City 2001 and The Making Of Transnational Subjects; Gérard Duménil & Dominique Lévy: The Nature and Contradictions of Neoliberalism; Elmar Altvater: The Growth Obsession; David Harvey The Art Of Rent: Globalization, Monopoly and The Commodification of Culture; Graham Murdock & Peter Golding: Digital Possibilities, Market Realities: The Contradictions of Communications Convergence; Reg Whitaker: The Dark Side of Life: Globalization and International Crime; Guglielmo Carchedi: Imperialism, Dollarization and The Euro; Susanne Soederberg: The New International Financial Architecture: Imposed Leadership and 'Emerging Markets'; Paul Cammack: Making Poverty Work; Marta Russell & Ravi Malhotra: Capitalism and Disability; Michael Kidron: The Injured Self; David Miller: Media Power and Class Power: Overplaying Ideology; Pablo Gonzalez Casanova: Negotiated Contradictions; Ellen Wood: Contradictions: Only in Capitalism?

293 pp, 234 x 156 mm.

0 85036 502 3 hbk £30.00   0 85036 501 5 pbk £16.95

Canada: Fernwood Publishing; USA: Monthly Review Press; UK and Rest of World: Merlin Press

Previous volumes:

Leo Panitch and Colin Leys – Editors
2001: WORKING CLASSES, GLOBAL REALITIES

Socialist Register 2001 examines the concept and the reality of class as it effects workers at the beginning of the 21st Century.

"an excellent collection". Bill Fletcher, *Against The Current*

Contents: Leo Panitch & Colin Leys with Greg Albo & David Coates: Preface; Ursula Huws: The Making of a Cybertariat? Virtual Work in a Real World ; Henry Bernstein: 'The Peasantry' in Global Capitalism: Who, Where and Why?; Beverly J. Silver and Giovanni Arrighi: Workers North and South; Andrew Ross: No-Collar Labour in America's 'New Economy'; Barbara Harriss-White & Nandini Gooptu: Mapping India's World of Unorganized Labour; Patrick Bond, Darlene Miller & Greg Ruiters: The Southern African Working Class: Production, Reproduction and Politics; Steve Jefferys: Western European Trade Unionism at 2000; David Mandel: 'Why is there no revolt?' The Russian Working Class and Labour Movement; Haideh Moghissi & Saeed Rahnema: The Working Class and the Islamic State in Iran ; Huw Beynon & Jorge Ramalho: Democracy and the Organization of Class Struggle in Brazil; Gerard Greenfield: Organizing, Protest and Working Class Self-Activity: Reflections on East Asia; Rohini Hensman: Organizing Against the Odds: Women in India's Informal Sector; Eric Mann: 'A race struggle, a class struggle, a women's struggle all at once': Organizing on the Buses of L.A.; Justin Paulson: Peasant Struggles and International Solidarity: the Case of Chiapas; Judith Adler Hellman: Virtual Chiapas: A Reply to Paulson ; Peter Kwong: The Politics of Labour Migration: Chinese Workers in New York; Brigitte Young: The 'Mistress' and the Maid' in the Globalized Economy; Rosemary Warskett: Feminism's Challenge to Unions in the North: Possibilities and Contradictions; Sam Gindin: Turning Points and Starting Points: Brenner, Left Turbulence and Class Politics; Leo Panitch: Reflections on Strategy for Labour.

403 pp. 232 x 155 mm.

0 85036 491 4 hbk £30.00   **0 85036 490 6 pbk £16.95**

Canada: Fernwood Publishing; USA: Monthly Review Press; UK and Rest of World: Merlin Press

Leo Panitch and Colin Leys – Editors
2000: NECESSARY AND UNNECESSARY UTOPIAS

What is Utopia? An economy that provides everyone's needs? A society which empowers all people? A healthy, peaceful and supportive environment ? Better worlds are both necessary and possible. "This excursion to utopia is full of surprise, inspiration and challenge". Peter Waterman

Contents: Preface; Transcending Pessimism: Rekindling Socialist Imagination: Leo Panitch & Sam Gindin; Minimum Utopia: Ten Theses: Norman Geras; Utopia and its Opposites: Terry Eagleton; On the Necessity of Conceiving the Utopian in a Feminist Fashion: Frigga Haug; Socialized Markets; not Market Socialism: Diane Elson; The Chimera of the Third

Way: Alan Zuege; Other Pleasures: The Attractions of Post-consumerism: Kate Soper; Utopian Families: Johanna Brenner; Outbreaks of Democracy: Ricardo Blaug; Real and Virtual Chiapas: Magic Realism and the Left: Judith Adler Hellman; The Centrality of Agriculture: History; Ecology And Feasible Socialism: Colin Duncan; Democratise or Perish: The Health Sciences as a Path for Social Change: Julian Tudor Hart; The Dystopia of our Times: Genetic Technology and Other Afflictions: Varda Burstyn; Warrior Nightmares: Reactionary Populism at the Millennium: Carl Boggs; The Real Meaning of the War Over Kosovo: Peter Gowan.

301 pp. 232 x 155 mm.

0 85036 488 4 hbk £30.00   **0 85036 487 6 pbk £14.95**

Canada: Fernwood Publishing; USA: Monthly Review Press; UK and Rest of World: Merlin Press

Leo Panitch and Colin Leys – Editors
1999: GLOBAL CAPITALISM VS. DEMOCRACY

The essays here not only examine the contradictions of both neo-liberalism and 'progressive competitiveness', but demonstrate that no democracy worth the name can any longer be conceived except in terms of a fundamental break with it.

Contents: Preface; Taking Globalisation Seriously: Hugo Radice; Material World: The Myth of the Weightless Economy: Ursula Huws; Globalisation and the Executive Committee: Reflections on the Contemporary Capitalist State: Konstantinos Tsoukalas; Contradictions of Shareholder Capitalism: Downsizing Jobs; Enlisting Savings; Destabilizing Families: Wally Seccombe; Labour Power and International Competitiveness: A Critique of Ruling Orthodoxies: David Coates; Between the Devil and the Deep Blue Sea: The German Model Under the Pressure of Globalisation: Birgit Mahnkopf; East Asia's Tumbling Dominoes: Financial Crises and the Myth of the Regional Model: Mitchell Bernard; State Decay and Democratic Decadence in Latin America: Atilio Boron; Comrades and Investors: The Uncertain Transition in Cuba: Haroldo Dilla; Unstable Futures: Controlling and Creating Risks in International Money: Adam Tickell; Globalisation; Class and the Question of Democracy: Joachim Hirsch; The Challenge for the Left: Reclaiming the State: Boris Kagarlitsky; The Public Sphere and the Media: Market Supremacy versus Democracy: Colin Leys; The Tale that Never Ends: Sheila Rowbotham

364pp. 232 x 155 mm.

0 85036 481 7 hbk £30.00   **0 85036 480 9 pbk £14.95**

Canada: Fernwood Publishing; USA: Monthly Review Press; UK and Rest of World: Merlin Press

Recent Books from the Merlin Press of interest to readers of Socialist Register

THE GLOBALIZATION DECADE
A Critical Reader
A Socialist Register Anthology

Edited by Leo Panitch, Colin Leys, Alan Zuege & Martijn Konings

Over the past decade the contributors to Socialist Register have been widely recognised as providing the most distinctive investigations on the left today of the contradictions of globalisation, the internationalisation of the state, progressive competitiveness, the new imperialism and popular global mobilisations against it.

This anthology provides:
The most searching analyses of the political, economic and cultural contradictions of globalisation available - essential reading for students in troubled times.
The best set of readings on the role of states - and especially the American state - in making globalisation happen, and on the problems they now confront in trying to keep it going.

Contents: Leo Panitch: Globalization And The State; Manfred Bienefeld: Capitalism And The Nation State In The Dog Days Of The Twentieth Century;
Jim Crotty & Gerald Epstein: In Defence Of Capital Controls;
Greg Albo: A World Market Of Opportunities? Capitalist Obstacles & Left Economic Policy;
Hugo Radice: Taking Globalization Seriously; Constantine Tsoukalas: Globalization And The Executive Committee: The Contemporary Capitalist State;
Wally Seccombe: Contradictions Of Shareholder Capitalism: Downsizing Jobs, Enlisting Savings, Destabilizing Families;
Ursula Huws: Material World: The Myth Of The Weightless Economy;
Gerard Dumenil & Dominique Levy: The Nature And Contradictions Of Neoliberalism;
Elmar Altvater: The Growth Obsession
A Guide to Additional Readings

2004 325 pp. 234 x 156mm.   0 85036 516 3 pbk £16.95
Rights: EU and Rest of World - Merlin Press Canada - Fernwood Publishing

David Coates – Editor
PAVING THE THIRD WAY: The Critique of Parliamentary Socialism
A Socialist Register Anthology

The parliamentary road to socialism has held the attention and loyalty of much of the Left in the UK for more than a century. But has the strategy worked, and could it yet work? Writings on Parliamentary Socialism inspired by Ralph Miliband provide an important answer to these questions, and in the process throw new light on the history of the British Labour Party.
In this book David Coates brings together key original texts, adding critical commentary, annotation and some of his own writings, to contributions by Ralph Miliband, John Saville, Leo Panitch, Colin Leys, and Hilary Wainwright. Given the centrality of the Third Way

to social democratic politics globally, this collection will be of interest to students and practitioners of left-wing politics in all advanced capitalist economies.

Contents: Acknowledgements; Introduction; Part 1: LABOURISM AND ITS LIMITS; Ralph Miliband: Introduction; Ralph Miliband: The Climax of Labourism; Ralph Miliband: The Sickness of Labourism; John Saville: Labourism and the Labour Government; Ralph Miliband: Postscript; Leo Panitch: Conclusion; David Coates: The failure of the socialist promise; PART 2: FROM OLD LABOUR TO NEW LABOUR; Leo Panitch Socialists and the Labour Party: A reappraisal; 9.Ralph Miliband Socialist Advance in Britain; Leo Panitch: Socialist Renewal and the Labour Party; Colin Leys: The British Labour Party's transition from socialism to capitalism; David Coates: Labour Governments: Old Constraints and New; Parameters; PART 3: MOVING ON; Hilary Wainwright: Once More Moving On; Hilary Wainwright: Building New Parties for a Different Kind of Socialism: a Response; 15. David Coates and Leo Panitch: The Continuing Relevance of the Milibandian Perspective.

2003 234x156mm   270pp   0 85036 512 0 pbk £16.95
Canada: Fernwood Publishing; UK and Rest of World: Merlin Press

Ralph Miliband
MARXISM AND POLITICS

What is class conflict? How do ruling classes and the state reproduce capitalism? What is the role of the Party? and what are the differences between reform and revolution? This is a readable and engaging survey: mainly of key Marxist texts – Marx, Engels and Lenin- and of Marxist political experience. Miliband believes in a socialism which defend freedoms already won: and to make possible their extension and enlargement by the removal of class boundaries.

Reviews of the previous edition: "This is probably the best introduction to Marx's Politics currently available and is as non-sectarian as the subject allows." Teaching Politics
" A job excellently done…" New Society. "the best primer on Marxism and politics ever written and Miliband's best book."
Leo Panitch: Professor of Politics, York University, Toronto

Contents: Introduction: Class and Class Conflict: The Defence of the old Order 1: The Defence of the old Order 2: Class and Party: Reform and Revolution: Bibliography: Index.

2003 220x157mm   viii+ 200pp   0 85036 531 7 pbk £10.95
Canada: Fernwood Publishing; USA: Monthly Review Press; UK and Rest of World: Merlin Press

Michael Newman
RALPH MILIBAND AND THE POLITICS OF THE NEW LEFT

Based on exclusive access to Miliband's extensive personal papers and supplemented by interviews, this book analyses the ideas and contribution of a key figure in the British and international Left from the Second World War until the collapse of communism. Miliband's life and work form the central focus, but the book also provides an interpretative history of the evolution, debates and dilemmas of socialists throughout the period, and of the problems they faced both at work defending academic freedom and in society at large.

"comprehensive: scholarly: sensitive and readable: ..one of the kindest men and the best minds in our generation" from the Foreword by Tony Benn:
"admirably clear in its construction and scrupulously researched..."
"Miliband's own interventions in his time live on: in his books and essays: but his personal writings, amply extracted here, give a vivid sense of the man behind them-making this a good book to have." New Left Review:
"not just a biography of one of the great socialist minds of the 20th century, it is the history of an entire period of Leftist activity, buffeted as it was by WWII: Vietnam and the decline of the Communist bloc........ a full and incisive a biography as he could have wished" Red Pepper

Contents: Introduction; Socialism and Identity (1924-1946); Apprenticeship (1946-56); The New Left and Parliamentary Socialism (1956-1962); The Sixties (1962-69); Free Speech and Academic Freedom; The State in Capitalist Society and the Debate with Poulantzas; Marxism and Politics (1970-77); An Uphill Struggle (1977-91); In Pursuit of Socialism; Conclusion: Ralph Miliband Today; Notes on Sources & Bibliography; Index.

2002 234x156mm   384pp. 8 pages of photos   **0 85036 513 9 pbk £18.95**
Canada: Fernwood Publishing; USA: Monthly Review Press; UK and Rest of World: Merlin Press

Ursula Huws
THE MAKING OF A CYBERTARIAT: Virtual Work in a Real World
with a foreword by Colin Leys

A new global labour force is being created working in call centres, homes and electronic sweatshops. New technologies are also transforming daily life. This book presents a coherent conceptual framework within which these developments can be understood. This book explains the impact of technology on the workplace, and relating its arguments and analyses to the work-situations of real people, showing how larger trends influence daily activities and shape the possibilities for collective action. It portrays working conditions experienced by both men and women, but focuses especially on the double impact on women, as workers and as consumers.

Contents: Foreword by Colin Leys, Introduction, Chapter One — New Technology and Domestic Labor Chapter Two — Domestic Technology: Liberation or Enslavement? Chapter Three — Chips on the Cheap: How South East Asian Women Pay the Price, Chapter Four — Terminal Isolation: The Atomization of Work and Leisure in the Wired Society, Chapter Five — The Global Office: Information technology and the Relocation of White Collar Work, Chapter Six — Challenging Commodification: Producing What's Useful Outside the Factory, Chapter Seven — Women, Health, and Work, Chapter Eight — Telework: Projections, Chapter Nine — Material World: The Myth of the Weightless Economy, Chapter Ten — The Making of a Cybertariat: Virtual Work in a Real World, Notes, Index.

2003 213x135 mm: 208pp.   **0 85036 537 6 pbk £13.95**
UK: Merlin Press; Canada: Fernwood Publishing; USA: Monthly Review Press

In case of difficulty obtaining Merlin Press titles outside the UK, please contact the following:

Australia:
Merlin Press Agent and stockholder:
Eleanor Brash: PO Box 586, Artamon: NSW 2064 Email: ebe@enternet.com.au

Canada:
Co-Publisher and stockholder:
Fernwood Books, 8422 St. Margaret's Bay Rd, Site 2a, Box 5, Black Point, Nova Scotia, B0J 1B0
Tel: +1 902 857 1388: Fax: +1 902 422 3179 Email: errol@fernwoodbooks.ca

South Africa:
Merlin Press Agent:
Blue Weaver Marketing
PO Box 30370, Tokai, Cape Town 7966, South Africa
Tel. and Fax: +27 21 701 7302 Email: blueweav@mweb.co.za

USA:
Merlin Press Agent and stockholder: Independent Publishers Group, 814 North Franklin Street, Chicago, IL 60610.
Tel: +1 312 337 0747 Fax: +1 312 337 5985 frontdesk@ipgbook.com

Publisher: Monthly Review Press:
Monthly Review Press, 122 West 27th Street, New York, NY 10001
Tel: +1 212 691 2555 promo@monthlyreview.org